HENRY
ADAMS

HENRY ADAMS

A Biography

Elizabeth Stevenson

WITH A NEW INTRODUCTION BY THE AUTHOR

TRANSACTION PUBLISHERS
NEW BRUNSWICK (U.S.A.) AND LONDON (U.K.)

Library of Congress Catalog Number: 96-30672
ISBN: 1-56000-919-5
Printed in the United States of America

Library of Congress Cataloging-in-Publication Data

Stevenson, Elizabeth, 1919–
    Henry Adams : a biography / Elizabeth Stevenson ; with a new
introduction by the author.
        p.   cm.
    Includes bibliographical references and index.
    ISBN 1-56000-919-5 (paper : alk. paper)
    1. Adams, Henry, 1838–1918.   2. Historians—United States—
Biography.   I. Title.
E175.5.A2S74 1996
973'.0702—dc20
    [B]

For my Mother
Bernice Upshaw Stevenson

Ring within ring he uncovered his pain:
found light in darkness, then darkness again:
world whorled in world the whorl of his thought,
shape under series the godhead he sought:

Conrad Aiken
on Henry Adams
in *The Kid*

Contents

Henry Adams

Introduction to the Transaction Edition

Another Look at Henry Adams, Forty Years Later

HENRY ADAMS seems to have a claim on us, as a person and as a thinker who wrote in an incisive and provocative way. He lived a long life across an eventful period, and he never ceased to react to events and trends. He was *in* time, but never really *of* it. The seemingly successful politicians and entrepreneurs of the time, the late nineteenth century and the early twentieth century, overshadowed the lives of Adams and his circle of friends in the arts, the professions, the world of perception, thought, and creation. Adams was a curious, contradictory person, a stimulating skeptic but also an imaginative lover of color, style, beauty. He was sardonic about having fallen away from the Adams family tradition of an active role in public life, but he relished his good and privileged spot from which he observed the spectacle.

He created portraits of medieval periods of unity, of militant St. Michael on his Mount, of the compassionate Virgin in her window in a cathedral, showing that it had been humanly possible in western civilization to achieve a kind of unity of effort and belief. In his own time he deplored what looked like a kind of disintegration under forces not controllable, leading very possibly to dire destruction, to a state of society that he called multiplicity.

It is this older, prophetic Adams upon whom historic imagination has seized, but there were other previous Adamses: the unformed child, youthful assistant to his father, the developing human consciousness, the curious journalist, the reforming article writer, the novelist, historian, traveler, letter writer, tragic widowed husband, friend of artists and thinkers from whom he took much and to whom he gave much, and at last the recluse who was contradictorily the warmhearted fosterer of the young.

Yes, Henry Adams haunts this writer who first tried to tell his story forty years ago. I have learned more about Henry Adams since, and would write about him today in a slightly different way, but I find that I stand by him still. Or rather, I find him to be a figure still looking over my shoulder at what is happening today.

E.S.

DECATUR, GEORGIA
August 1996

9

Preface

But what we want is a *school*. We want a national set of young men like ourselves or better, to start new influences not only in politics, but in literature, in law, in society, and throughout the whole social organism of the country—a national school of our own generation.

> —Henry Adams, in a letter to his brother
> Charles Adams, November 21, 1862

During these twenty years he had done as much work, in quantity, as his neighbors wanted; more than they would ever stop to look at, and more than his share. Merely in print, he thought altogether ridiculous the number of volumes he counted on the shelves of public libraries. He had no notion whether they served a useful purpose; he had worked in the dark; but so had most of his friends, even the artists, none of whom held any lofty opinion of their success in raising the standards of society, or felt profound respect for the methods or manners of their time, at home or abroad, but all of whom had tried, in a way, to hold the standard up.

> —Henry Adams, in his *Education,* first
> privately printed in 1907

How CHART the course between the young man's words calling for a transformed society and the old man's words looking back upon his life lived out and wondering if it had been worth while? This is the task attempted. I had thought, reading and re-reading Adams, that today we might attempt to see if the life did not indeed matter greatly. The book was conceived in that conviction.

In his own time he seemed peripheral, outside the doing and thinking that were making over a continent. Today we can see that his thought, which to his contemporaries seemed to have such slight connection with themselves, had strong subterranean connections with unseen forces which have since come to the surface and matter greatly today. He was a seismograph recording earthquakes of the future. We are engulfed in them now, having traveled far along the road he foresaw. We can read him with more appreciation than his own generation could.

To read him is to read the life as well as the works. Therefore I have tried to place the fallible man in a recollection of his real background, and I have tried to clothe his ideas in their local circumstances. He walked into blind alleys as well as brilliant avenues of thought. He was occasionally dominated and led wrong by emotion as well as led right.

But the flaw makes for drama and the fallible for tragedy. This life, lived out against America's brutal adolescence, has the quality of tragic drama. I have tried to suggest the drama contained in the facts, the opinions, and the consequences which can be recovered. Adams was a complex and often contradictory soul. He puzzled himself as well as his friends. Some of the contradictions must stand. Some areas must remain dark. But the life as a whole is one that makes lighter rather than darker both his own time and ours.

The proud young Adams filled with impatient ambition and calling for a "school" never found his school, and would never have approved or joined one if he had found it. Yet he found and kept a number of friends in a group of men who did valuable and even brilliant work in the arts, the sciences, and in public affairs. Their lives' work cut across the grain of their time. It was not flavored by the majority mind. Their work was individual, their product the whole person's doing and making.

What they did—in geology or statesmanship or glassmaking or building or reforming—came to seem, like Henry Adams's history and biographies, somewhat lost in the great mass of popular work done all around them. Yet the ragged array that they made, pushing out in various directions, mostly against rather than with the current of their society, accomplished something. It was a considerable assault upon the natural materialism of a nation's growing pains.

Therefore, Hay and King, Richardson, La Farge, Saint-Gaudens, Agassiz, Pumpelly, Schurz, William and Henry James, George Cabot Lodge, Charles and Brooks Adams, these men, and others, belong to Henry Adams's America. They and others of whom the world never heard created a nourishing universe in which Adams lived congenially and breathed easily. Such non-public men as James Lowndes, William Hallett Phillips, and others had as much to do with the ordering of his ideas as those who for one reason or another lived in the public eye.

Perhaps of even more importance in creating the atmosphere of his private world were the women, most of them shadowy figures seen only obliquely through the chance words of the more carefully recorded men. Adams had a singular capacity for genuine friendship with women. He found them easier in conversation, more accessible in sharing feelings as well as thoughts that the men—husbands, lovers, brothers, fathers—living in a much more competitive atmosphere which often stripped them of shadings, subtleties, and leisure. Such names, some of them only names to us, as Louisa Adams, Emily Beale, Rebecca Gilman Rae, Clara Hay, Anna Lodge, Elizabeth and Martha Cameron, Edith Wharton, Margaret Chanler, and Maggie Wade, too, belong in his story. One name particularly, that of his wife, Marian Hooper Adams, belongs to the core of his story. She shared his best moments, and some of his worst. Her memory haunted him, after she was gone, all the long-lasting remainder of his life.

Adams's friends who were women, in the United States, in England and France, and a few in the islands of the Pacific, stood to him for a whole complex of living vitality which the more active striving men of his society seemed almost to have forsworn. His long life was one consistent drama, a long-drawn-out transfer of his loyalty from the inherited traditional values of the rational and the cerebral to the virtues of the feelings, the senses, and of act itself.

In trying to get back into the center of Adams's field of vision, I have tried not to use a false galvanization, tried not to make up connections, or force a liveliness where I could not find it. Yet words put down long ago are even today not entirely dead. Malice helps as well as admiration in restoring the quick of life. A phrase or a sentence can knock a hole through time.

One begins to re-see Henry Adams. His goal was power, or rather the control of power. This is a strange aim to discover in a man who lived so quietly. But he was a descendant of a line of practical public men. It was part of his inheritance to think that man to live well should live well in relation to his surrounding social organism. Unlike the great individualists of his time, he could not conceive of man alone but thought always in terms of man living among his fellow men, and somehow regulating or failing to regulate the energies of society.

His greatest unhappiness came from a disappointment of this conception; his most fruitful insights, from seeing this idea in various aspects. Adams found the social organism to be made up of warring elements. He expanded his studies to show the natural world beyond man to be similarly composed. The forcefulness of his writing lies in his great concern, his great passion, for the right ordering of this conflict.

Adams's gift and his flaw was pride. His saving was the transcendence of that personal pride into humanity's. His thought is most valuable as a leaven. Deposited among the over-complacent truths of the democratic society, it preserves and transforms them into a better kind of bread.

E.S.

ATLANTA, GEORGIA
August 31, 1955

14

Acknowledgments

I SHOULD like to express my thanks to the Trustees of the John Simon Guggenheim Memorial Foundation for giving me a year of the time I spent at work on the book. I particularly thank the Secretary-General, Mr. Henry Allen Moe, for his friendly encouragement as well as for his efficient helpfulness.

The quotation from *The Kid,* published by Duell, Sloan and Pearce, Inc., New York City, in 1947, is used through the kind permission of the author, Mr. Conrad Aiken. For this gift my thanks are due and gratefully given.

For permission to read and to quote from Henry Adams's unpublished letters held in the Houghton Library, Harvard University, I am most grateful to Mrs. Robert Homans. I am grateful too to the Librarian of the Houghton Library, Mr. William A. Jackson, and to his staff for their kind assistance.

I should like to thank Mrs. Frank E. Harris, Superintendent of the Adams National Historic Site, Quincy, Massachusetts, for a long afternoon of talk about Henry and Brooks Adams and for reminiscences of her years as secretary to Brooks Adams.

My most grateful thanks are due to and tendered Mrs. N. E. Byers, Librarian of Agnes Scott College, and to Miss Lillian Newman of the staff of the College Library, for their several years' help in ordering necessary rare, obscure, and out-of-print books for my use through the Inter-Library Loan Service.

To the staffs of the following libraries I offer my admiration and thanks for help given: the Atlanta Public Library, the Boston Public Library, the Butler Library of Columbia University, the Library of Congress—both Reading Room and Prints and Photographs Division—the Massachusetts Historical Society Library, the New England Deposit Library, the New York Public Library, the Widener Library, Harvard University.

Most of all, I wish to thank my mother, Bernice Upshaw Stevenson, for her long-enduring encouragement, understanding, and stimulation, and for her unrecompensable labor in completing the typescript of the book.

In a sense, every place one has seen, every person one has

known enters in some degree into any work of the mind. Friends, teachers, books, delights of the mind in the arts of singing, dancing, acting—all in some degree, remote or near, enter into the work. The book is an indirect thank you to them all.

Chapter 1

Starting Place

THERE WAS a child once who sat upon a kitchen floor and stared at sunlight filtering through a window and making that floor warm with the color yellow.[1] The house was a New England house, and the surrounding world—of family, emotions, ideas, the very air—was a New England world. It was a New England of a secure time long before the Civil War. Exactly, it was the year 1841. The child lived to be an old man who pondered his past and identified this earliest memory.

He was born on February 16, 1838. His family name was Adams, his own, Henry Brooks. He was the fourth child of Charles Francis Adams and Abigail Brooks Adams. We can look ahead to the end and see him come full circle to color once more after veering away from it through the rationality of line and the logic of determinism. He came back at the end to staring once more at pure color, finding it as important then, in certain church windows, as it was on the kitchen floor of a New England house on Boston Bay.

Color the child loved, and color meant summer and Quincy. It was a small place then, a town down the South Shore a little way from Boston, but a separate place, not a suburb. Here, every summer, Charles Francis Adams brought his family to live near his father, the former President, John Quincy Adams, who was Representative to Congress from the Plymouth District of Massachusetts during the growing up of his grandchildren.

Henry's own family—father, mother, and children—lived in what they thought of as the "house on the hill." The fierce-seeming, bald-headed grandfather and his exotic, sweet-tempered wife, Louisa, lived in the house they thought of as the "real" house, the "old house," the "house down the hill." [2]

"Summer was drunken," [3] Henry said lovingly, looking back to those seasons. Summer was freedom, and the center of that grateful summer freedom was the Old House, an unpretentious, clapboarded dwelling house, gaining an addition in width nearly every generation, or pushing out behind in the direction of the sloping orchard. This growing house, topped by its chimneys, sunk in the shade of its elms and silver-green beeches, marked the center of existence for all the generations of the family.

The center of this center was John Quincy Adams, an old man remembered by the grandchildren as seated in the study forever writing, or as strolling, stick in hand, down some rutted country road nearby, his head bent in thought. His study was a room with window seats where Henry could sit and read as the old man worked. The grandfather was both important and familiar.

The old man's tenderness to privileged children could gather into decisiveness. He could take by the hand one child, unwilling one day to go to school, and lead him, in understanding silence, out of the house, down the street, and into the school: demonstration rather than expostulation. Henry Adams remembered that act, and the superiority of act to word, all the rest of his life.

The grandfather's larger activities were only guessed at by the grandchildren. He was a daily, taken-for-granted figure while the enthrallment of Quincy was the world outdoors: the sea down below the town, the hills and woods and streams back of and above the town, the village center with its meetinghouse and tavern where stagecoaches on the way to Plymouth stopped to pick up or set down passengers, and where the Quincy topers sat and judged their neighbors' doings.[4]

It was a town settled in comfort, offering to remembrance the greatest possible contrast to the New England and America which were to surround and swallow it. People worked in Quincy, but not in a competitive way. It was a shoemaking town, but there was no factory as yet.[5] Each shoemaker had a small annex attached to his house. There he did his work, with family help, and the summer sound of shoes being made was a lazy sound, as natural as the insect noises of the fields not very far away.

If Quincy was summer, then Boston was winter. Just as the grandfather dominated the summer scene, so Henry's father dominated the winter scene in Boston. Boston, as memory was to reconstruct it, meant constriction and constraint, dull hours in the house on Mount Vernon Street, or dull hours at school, in David B. Tower's private school in the basement of the Park Street Church, or in Mr. Dixwell's private Latin school, which seemed a time of competent routine rather than stimulation.

Very probably Henry, looking back, exaggerated the dullness of his Boston childhood. But his principal memory was no doubt true: that there was in those days, in the forties and fifties of the nineteenth century, an unnecessary stoppage put upon spontaneity and play. Too often children were treated as small adults. The fault was not Charles Francis Adams's alone, although his temperament added weight to the heaviness of his own household; it was the fault of the generation.

"In my boyhood," said Charles, Henry's next oldest brother, "nothing whatever was done to amuse children." [6] The youngest brother, Brooks, reacting in his memories of that time against Charles's strictures, conveys the idea that their father was a man of passionate feelings, but of passions strongly controlled.

Certainly it was control that was advocated for the younger generation. Perhaps this movement of will in Charles Francis was a distaste for the excesses of feeling that his father and grandfather had often betrayed. Yet it was their emotional excesses which had made them lovable. Charles Francis had brought the roughness of love and hate under control and wished his children not to be betrayed by the family tendency toward strong passions. It was his success that betrayed him. He had no endearing faults. His very virtues were ice-bound. There was something pitiful in his inarticulateness. His second son, Charles Francis, came almost to hate him, and expressed his crudity of reaction publicly in his own memoirs. The youngest son, Brooks, in reaction, was sharply defensive of his father, defensive in a manner that showed he felt some need for the attitude. Only Henry, late in life, seemed to have arrived at a balanced admiration, yet it was an admiration expressed in terms of justice rather than love.

Charles Francis was a good and just father, but not an easy one. His family of opinionated, sensitive, and self-conscious children could not confide in him. They were thrown upon one another in their inexperience, and upon their mother. She was a woman of a positive character, dominating, not always tactful, but sympathetic, and interested—entertained by her children. Henry's easygoing letters to her in his first youthful absence from home at the age of twenty show that he relied upon her quick understanding and upon her sympathy. She seems to have submerged her separate interests in her family's and to have lived altogether for her husband and her rather difficult children.

The children of the family turned to one another in their growing pains. They wrestled with one another, occasionally physically, but more often with all the expanding mental powers of which they were capable. They were strong and bright. Louisa, the oldest, was the leader; John, the second child, was the gayest mannered, the quickest to make friends; Charles had a sort of bulldog tenacity and frankness; Henry was smaller, quieter, with a quick sense of humor. To these older ones, Mary and Brooks were as yet negligible, children to dominate and patronize. Arthur the last child, died at five.

If the father was not much good for children as such, he was rather exciting for children turned into premature politicians. And this they were. Political theory and action blotted out interest in anything else. Where other generations of New England children might have been morbid over religion or precocious in literary expression, this one, or the Adams part of it, concentrated its young mind on desperate hopes concerning a national cause.

Henry said of himself that he was "a ten-year-old priest and politician." [7] Sitting in a corner listening to his elders, he could hear experts expound political theory and practice. Or leaving the hill he lived on and going down into the crowded lower squares of the city, he could see practical demonstrations of what was talked of at home: mob action flaring up with an irregular regularity during these years.

His father represented good society in political radicalism. He and his friends—Dana, Palfrey, Sumner, and a few others—worked quietly, good-manneredly for an end condemned by their next-door neighbors. Other little boys' fathers were for Daniel Webster and harmony. Henry's father and grandfather embarrassed these gentry. They pointed out keenly the real split that existed between the two sections: the unblinkable fact of slavery. The fact that Henry's family discussed slavery at all, instead of leaving it alone as good taste demanded, isolated it to a real extent. Good men of North and South were anxious for compromise.

Sharing the Adams family's isolation in politics was their remote and nobly talking friend Charles Sumner. He was a bleakly upright person, without warmth, not dealing in humor, or even recognizing it, but all the same, exhilarating and refreshing in his candor and courage. His political heroism affected Henry's imagination. He was the boy's first hero.

For Henry, as for his brothers and sisters, the fight that filtered into his mind was simplified and no doubt distorted. But, little as he might understand its complexity, he could grasp the emotion of his famous grandfather's fight. He might even have recognized the family's household mood in his grandfather's diary of a time before he himself was born.

As early as 1820, John Quincy Adams wrote in connection with the struggle in Congress over Missouri's entry into the Union, and the question of its being slave or free: "I take it for granted that the present question is a mere preamble—a title page to a great tragic volume. . . . The President thinks this question will be winked away by a compromise. But so do not I. Much am I mistaken if it is not destined to survive his political and individual life and mine." [8]

Monroe was the President mentioned. He himself was to be the next President, from 1824 to 1828. Then, beaten painfully by Jackson, he was to be sent home, whipped, as it seemed, ill and in debt, with the old house at Quincy mortgaged.

But John Quincy made a surprising return to politics. Against the advice of his own son Charles Francis, he ran for office as congressional Representative from the Plymouth District, and was elected. Once in, he found his true place. The unhappy constraint of the Presidency was gone. He could hit as hard as he wished, and did so with a zest unknown to him before.

But John Quincy Adams had the hard lot of the forerunner. His was almost the first respectable voice to cry out against slavery. He fought against great odds enumerated with whimsical bitterness in the following passage from the diary:

One hundred members of the House represent slaves; four-fifths of whom would crucify me if their votes could erect the cross; forty members, representatives of the free, in the league of slavery and mock Democracy, would break me on the wheel, if their votes or wishes could turn it round; and four-fifths of the other hundred and twenty are either so cold or so lukewarm that they are ready to desert me at the very first scintillation of indiscretion on my part. The only formidable danger with which I am beset is that of my own temper. . . .[9]

Such strenuousness could have its rewards in a thankfulness as extreme as the fearfulness. When Henry was six, he might have had some inkling of the stir made in the family by the repeal of the hated Gag Rule, a rule of procedure which had been in force in Congress since May 26, 1836, and which had, from that date until its repeal in 1844, tabled every bill, every petition, even every mention of slavery, and prevented its discussion. Repealed at last, principally through his own efforts, John Quincy rejoiced in his depths. In prostrations of thankfulness he wrote at that time, "Blessed, forever blessed, be the name of God!" [10]

This high temperature of feeling must to some extent have burned through to the child's consciousness. There was not a time in his backward-glancing memory when members of his own immediate family had not been involved in political struggles of first importance. The national self was a second skin for an Adams; what wounded the nation wounded him.

By the time Henry was seven, not only his grandfather, but his father, too, was taking an active part in the national issue of slavery and free soil. Charles Francis had already, in Henry's younger days, given his father support in the legislature of Massachusetts. Now, in 1845, he and a few other gentlemen of Boston purchased and began to publish a political newspaper, the *Boston Whig*. In it, Charles Francis, supplementing the fight John Quincy was carrying on in Washington, gave a voice to the anti-slave Whigs of New England and tried to wean them away from Webster.

The year 1845 was also the year in which Charles Sumner, impressive in the clear, honest beauty of his look and manner, discovered his voice. When in November he addressed an audience of anti-slave Whigs, in Faneuil Hall, to protest the entrance of the new state of Texas into the Union as a slave state, he amazed his audience and himself. From this time forward, Sumner lived in public. He was the prophet of the movement while Henry's father, with his unquestioned integrity, was its skillful, practical persuader.

The Whig party soon crumbled in a political heat it could not stand. Then Charles Francis Adams, Charles Sumner, Richard Henry Dana, and a few others in Massachusetts instigated a new party, one to be called the Free-Soil party. Its reason for being was to work for the prevention or extermination of slavery in every piece of territory controlled by Federal rather than state law. During the first year of the party's life, these men bravely named a slate of candidates for the national election: Martin Van Buren for President, Charles Francis Adams for Vice President. They lost, but the effort was not a waste. They kept their issue before the public; they made the Democrats uncomfortable; they prepared the way for a new, stronger party not yet born.

That Henry's father should flout financial and commercial Boston, should go against the advice of his influential father-in-law, Peter Chardon Brooks, was remarkable in him. Family tradition was behind him, but he had also the encumbrance of money, which John and John Quincy Adams had never had. From the time of his marriage to Abigail Brooks, the daughter of the wealthiest man of his generation in Boston, Charles Francis was thus burdened and thus helped. Choosing to follow his own family tradition rather than class tradition proved him to have some of that family's iron in him. His very mildness made him more formidable.

His father died in 1848, struck down, as he might have wished, in the heat of battle, under the Capitol roof. He died there two days later. Peter Brooks died the next year. Thus, with father and father-in-law gone, Charles Francis Adams saw the way cleared for him, both politically and financially. He was the heir of a political tradition and the heir of a share of the Brooks money. Family energy could now be concentrated and centered entirely on politics, no matter what the outcome might be.

In former decades some of that energy might have gone into other vital interests, religion being the principal passion alternating with politics in earlier generations. Perhaps the cushioning effect of money had something to do with a falling off of a living interest in matters of faith. John and John Quincy Adams had all their lives been buffeted adventurously from faith to doubt and back to faith again. Perhaps the tenterhooks of poverty aided them by telling them that if man could be materially insecure, he could be spiritually insecure, too.

Now, for the first time, the head of the family was financially secure. Charles Francis Adams believed, but he did not examine the grounds of his belief. He exacted from his children the performance of certain acts—the going to church, the learning of hymns, the saying of prayers—but he did not talk to them about the joys of belief or the pains of unbelief. He did not have the temperament for it. When the father's controlling hand was lifted from the lives of his children, they fell away from these duties, and fell away with relief. The subsequent strenuous beliefs and disbeliefs of Brooks and Henry Adams built themselves up out of negation. Their wrestlings and doubtings and acceptances were a kind of reversion, in strange forms, to the religious temperament of earlier generations.

But in Charles Francis's time, politics was a kind of religion. And Charles Francis's father, John Quincy, was a true martyr of this faith. Living as he did, dying as he did, he gave a fervent tone to politics, a heat that burned out lesser faiths. Charles Francis's children, brought up correctly but coldly in the old New England faith, were swept with ardor into the newer New England faith, one that ended only in the fire of war.

When, in 1850, two years after his father's death, Charles Francis Adams went to Washington to pay a visit to his widowed mother, Louisa Johnson Adams, who continued to live in the Capital after her husband's death, he went out of New

England and into the upper South as a person of considerable importance. He took with him his fourth child, Henry, a boy of twelve, who kept eyes and ears open to every new sight and sound.

Early in the morning of his first day in Washington. Henry went out to see the town.[11] He walked out from his grandmother's house to inspect the queer-looking, unfinished white shaft to be named for the Founding Father. He sniffed the strange morning air—a mixture of rich mud and flowers. He gaped at the dusty, broken streets, the scattered buildings. He was scandalized by the raggedness of the yards, the pigs in the streets, the President's horse grazing on the White House lawn. The child had come out of an accepted, unquestioned New England—neat, well acting, right-thinking—and been plunged too quickly into its opposite—this careless city of the South—not to feel a mental shock.

The climax of his surprise came at Mount Vernon when he realized that Washington, the Founding Father, had been a Southerner, too, and a slaveowning one. How could slavery, "the sum of all wickedness," [12] as he had been accustomed to think, produce a George Washington and a Mount Vernon, beautiful at the end of a rutted country road? [13] The place was even a little like the Old House at Quincy. He felt at home in it. Yet all around him and his upright father—conducting his small son's tour in perfect good faith—was the howling wilderness of slavery. These Southerners, living off slavery, were being punished by its appurtenances: bad roads, slatternly towns, and lazy ways. He was dismayed to find that he liked the South, disarrangement and all. Something in it touched a nerve that had never been touched in the purer air of Boston (where later he would remember that he had never, even as a child, felt at home, never planned what street he would live on). The attraction of the disreputable South was as yet an undecipherable puzzle.

Charles Francis Adams removed Henry shortly from this puzzlement of the South, and took the boy home to New England. Here the father occupied a new place of importance. He was now chief of the Adams clan in Quincy and Boston and, as sign and symbol of the fact, moved the family down the hill to live properly in the Old House. His was the third generation, his children's, the fourth, to make the rather neglected old house their home. Brooks money began to refurbish it. The house was soon to be enlarged, more pretentious stables were to be built, the grounds to be better groomed and, later, red plush furniture to be brought home from England to crowd the seventeenth and eighteenth century chests and tables into halls and out of the parlors.

The removal from one house to another was an act to serve notice: the new generation of the Adams family was ready to do battle. All of Charles Francis's cool and capable energies were required. Henry's adolescence was a time of deepening passions for respectable and conscientious radicals. It was true that New England now swayed toward them; they were not so alone as they had been; Sumner was becoming a general hero, not just Henry's; but also, step by step, whatever legal gains they had made in Washington were being lost. The aroused Southerners, who saw their entire way of life threatened, were afraid, and began to entrench their control of the national government by stringent and extreme laws in support of slavery.

In 1850, the year of Henry's childhood visit to Washington, Henry Clay's great compromise bill was passed. It galled more than it helped, for its outstanding result was to make it easier for Southerners to fetch back to the South fugitive slaves who had taken refuge in the North. They had them now simply for the asking, and under escort of Federal troops. Formerly indifferent Bostonians were stung awake when they saw particular human beings moved out of their city under armed guard and sent back to slavery. It was at last necessary, even for the formerly indifferent, to take sides.

In 1851, when Henry was thirteen, Charles Sumner was elected to the United States Senate, but only after a long-drawn-out and bitter fight in the Massachusetts state legislature. Boys, who were otherwise Henry's friends, wore black armbands the day Sumner won. To show where he stood, Henry wore a white armband.

It was in these impressionable years that Henry heard preached among his father's friends the duty of disobeying the Constitution if conscience over-ruled it. All New England was in flux. It was heated and bent by emotion to become a tool for change.

In these white-hot years the scholar Norton could write to his friend Clough in England that a Boston which could let the slave Anthony Burns be sent back to slavery resembled more a tyranny than its proper self.[14]

This very sight made Henry Adams, who never forgot the day Anthony Burns was returned to slavery, feel a kind of frenzy. He, like the mob of which he was a part, wanted to work mischief. His own friends, who were in the militia, against their will, enforced the hated law.

This scene was the high point of his adolescent political awakening. It occurred in the spring of 1854, when he was sixteen, and marked a kind of climax. But his emotional climate changed very quickly; in the fall of the year he went across the Charles and dropped completely out of the wrought-up Boston state of mind. For in that season he began to live as, and become in himself, a student at Harvard College.

Chapter 2

Negative Happiness

LIFE UNDER the slender elms of the Harvard Yard buffered
the passions that raged across the river in Boston. Politics, except the college variety, seemed no longer important. Henry
Adams of Harvard had new ideas, new emotions, and several
new prejudices. He could no longer pay proper attention to
the daily papers or to the tone of home conversations during
those week ends he spent in the Adams house on Mount Vernon Street.

At home, politics seemed to grind hungrily upon itself, like
sliding gears. The other side seemed to be having it all its own
way. Buchanan was in the White House; the Supreme Court
belonged to the South; Charles Sumner was beaten at his desk
in the Senate Chamber, and congratulations were offered to
his attacker. There seemed now to be no cure for the situation. So—let it go, let it fade, let the new world of school fill
all one's being. Test it, and try it, to see what it can give.

In the shut-in world of the school, it was easy to do so. For
the first time in his life, Henry Adams was living in an environment which was not family, not reform, not politics. He was
free for the first time from several powerful pressures which
he had not recognized till their force let up. He did not know
that he was coming under the force of other pressures.

This is a photograph of Henry Adams as an undergraduate:
strong, black brows; serious dark eyes; sensitive mouth; a good
growth of dark hair, well brushed to one side; a large, even
fantastic, dark bow tie; white shirt front; white handkerchief in
dark coat pocket. The young man peering out of this picture
is pliable, his qualities not yet set.

The school was small as yet.[1] There were only approximately four hundred students and an average of fifteen teachers. The teachers held themselves aloof from the students; the
students looked on the teachers as natural enemies. The relationship between the two groups was unfortunate. The intellectual atmosphere of the classrooms of this period was not stimulating. Harvard was at possibly its lowest ebb in the late
1850's. Its formal program influenced Henry Adams almost
not at all. An exception to this rule—a James Russell Lowell

or a Louis Agassiz—was remembered all one's life. But it is important to realize that Harvard for young Henry Adams was not the formal regime of classes, not the discipline of the administration, which was legalistic, unfair, and generally scorned; but the friendship of his contemporaries, and a negative freedom to indulge vanities and youthful ambitions. It did not take much time for a bright boy to rid himself of homework. What took up his time, his thought, and his energies was almost exclusively extracurricular.

The scene of this easygoing life (in which going to classes was a minor kind of nuisance) was fairly primitive. The dormitory rooms were cold and often dirty. Baths at home in Boston were events to be noted down in one's diary. Water was carried upstairs to the dormitory rooms from pumps in the Yard. Sperm-oil lamps lighted the Yard through Henry Adams's freshman year.

Everything was personal and social—an opposite kind of emphasis from the transcended puritanism of home, where everything was public, passionate, and sacrificial. At Harvard young Adams switched abruptly to a new tempo. Here, in this small community, a brake was put upon untempered enthusiasm. The tone was of a not too eager enjoyment, an easygoing leisure which favored the growth of private indulgences. The place gave scope to idleness and curiosity. It gave one time to find out something about human nature, including one's own.

There was time to talk, to play billiards or whist; to go swimming, boating, or walking; to ride into town on the horse-cars and eat a good dinner at Parker's, to go dancing with the girls of Cambridge, or, in winter, to go skating on the Fresh Pond. Nothing was organized. Sports were a purely personal and voluntary kind of recreation. Reading could be done as one wished, little, none, or a great deal—according to one's own taste. The only bar was eccentricity. There, the tyranny of the mass mind intervened. Nothing could have been more severe than the boys' own judgment of one another. No one was very anxious to stand out from the good-tempered mob. Life was framed and formed by the limitations of young men who were half clownish boys, half self-conscious gentlemen.

The differentness of tone from home was at first a benefit to Henry Adams. He needed the relaxation, the toning down of the over-tense thought of the Adams house. But in the long run Harvard Yard had probably much less to do with forming him than the house in Boston.

The first good of the place for him was in friendships. With

28

a large and demanding family encasing him in his early years, he had hardly before ventured outside it except in response to the flattering attentions of his father's friends—men of a generation or two older than himself. It was important to find that he could make friends and like or dislike on easy, equal terms with his contemporaries.

His new friends were for the most part from New England. He knew them and their background by heart. But there were a few others, of slightly different cast of character, who were from the South. Because they were different, they had a disproportionately large effect on him. Henry found the Southern temperament disturbing. Its propensity to act without thought was outrageous to someone reared in the household of Charles Francis Adams. One time, soon after he went to Harvard, one of the Southerners, May of Virginia, thinking he had been insulted, began looking for his gun for the purpose of shooting the insulter. He was soothed only with some difficulty.[2]

Action from feelings, from intuition, from the body—how approve it when one had been taught all one's life that action came properly from the mind, from thought, from consideration? Yet the naturalness and spontaneity of the Southern boys appealed to him. He admired particularly the Lee boy, William Henry Fitzhugh Lee, whom Adams and his classmates called Rooney Lee.

By midwinter of his sophomore year, Henry Adams was settled in a relation of easy give-and-take with a group of intimates. These friends included several of the Southerners as well as Boston and New England boys.

One of young Adams's intimates, Nicholas Anderson, from Kentucky, kept a diary. He recorded on February 29, 1856, something of the self-satisfaction which this small group felt with itself: "On my return last night I was invited by Lee to join a new table . . . one of the nicest little assemblies in the city, consisting of the following men—Crowninshield, Lee, Bradlee, Elliott, Hunnewell, Adams, May, and Anderson."[3] Having found one another comfortable, good props to one another's self-esteem, the little assembly let the rest of the school "go hang."

Benjamin Crowninshield, another member of the little assembly, kept a journal as assiduously as Anderson. He wrote with juvenile relish of a typical social occasion: "Today we had a little 'spat' between Joe Bradlee and Henry Adams. Joe threw some bread at Henry, who was late at dinner. Henry threw a rice croquette at Joe and it bid fair to be a fight, but ended in words like many a storm."[4]

At another time Ben Crowninshield remembered to set down the fact that he had had a satisfactory game of billiards with the boy from Louisiana, Henry Hobson Richardson. The slim, graceful Richardson soon became a regular member of the little assembly. He had an easy attractiveness, an open charm, a quality that Charles Adams later characterized as Creole (although his heritage was English, altogether—his maternal grandfather having been Joseph Priestley). Richardson—Fez, they called him—played the flute, was very good at chess, brilliant at math. He stuttered badly when excited.

Of all the small, self-pleased assembly, Richardson was the only one, with the possible exception of Anderson, who would mean much to Adams later in life. During these years of spats and brandy suppers, of scanted classes and serious games of billiards and whist, Adams and Richardson probably guessed little of the closer friendship to come. Richardson's ambitions were formed earlier than Adams's. He knew before he left Harvard that he was going to try to be an architect. He was mature in other ways too. He had fallen in love with a young woman of Boston, but was troubled by the fact that he could not marry her till he could make a living at his chosen work. Southern openness could hide much. Adams probably saw only the lighter side of Fez Richardson, and the manners of the little assembly encouraged triviality of tone rather than the revelation of painful interests.

Alexander Agassiz, too, was to be an important person in Adams's life. Yet Alex Agassiz of Harvard was only a distant figure of Henry's horizon. He was the son of the great Louis Agassiz; he liked to row on the Charles with Ben Crowninshield and the tutor Charles Eliot. But he was older, out of the range of the childish interests of the little assembly. He had come to America a half grown boy, broken in to hardships and sorrow before he was out of his teens. By the time young Adams was a freshman at Harvard, Alex was a remote senior. By the time Henry was a sophomore, Alex had graduated and gone to work teaching in his brilliant stepmother's school for girls—teaching, keeping books, earning his way before he had had a chance yet at his own chosen work—research science. He was formed in character while Henry and his friends yet loafed.

In the meantime, as the lazy years passed, young Henry Adams had as good a time as possible. The resources for riotous living were not great, but in a mild sort of way the little assembly spent a great deal of time eating, drinking, and arguing—all with the utmost innocence and naïveté.

Only one teacher mattered. This was Alex's father—Louis Agassiz. His was the only course which used up as much of Henry's energy as debates, play acting, or ice skating. All the rest of Henry Adams's life he was to find a part of himself held by interests first stimulated by the great Swiss popularizer of the geological sciences. The kind of zest Louis Agassiz aroused was the best kind of education. It was a part of a general awakening of enthusiasms. Adams at Harvard did not so much learn facts, as attitudes. Some were prejudices of place and time, no doubt, but on the whole the new attitudes were broadening.

He read hungrily; he talked a great deal, rather loftily and with strong opinion; he debated; he wrote for the *Harvard Magazine,* a student magazine founded recently in 1854. His writing, if not brilliant, was at least straightforward. He tried, occasionally, to do good with the self-respect and good conscience taught at home. He wanted, once, to abolish the fraternities, and unite them and their libraries all in one. This new arrangement would be sensible and useful. He failed. But he did set to and catalogue and clean up—with Anderson's help —all the books in the Hasty Pudding Club.[5]

Acting, rather than writing or reforming, seems to have been Adams's most conspicuous school role. In his junior year he performed creditably the female part in the farce *Lend Me Five Shillings,*[6] by John Maddison Morton. He had a success in his senior year as the "argument-loving Sir Robert" in George Colman's *The Poor Gentleman.* It was thought the part suited him. He was Captain Absolute in Sheridan's *The Rivals.*[7]

Also in his senior year he delivered an oration at the Hasty Pudding Club on the subject "The Fool's Cap and Bells." [8] The club members celebrated afterward at what they called a "French supper" in Boston. "Finally it degenerated," his classmate Ben Crowninshield wrote in his diary with some satisfaction, "with a few exceptions into a general and exceedingly jolly and fiendishly noisy drunk. A next door neighbor complained and we had the pleasure of a call from 3 watchmen." [9] There is no reason to think the speaker of the evening was a sober exception.

At the end of his senior year, Adams was elected Class Orator, for the approaching Class Day celebration, an occasion much more important to the students than graduation itself. To be elected Class Day Orator was a kind of peak of school existence.

Class Day came, and Henry Adams delivered his oration in

the Unitarian Church of Cambridge; another classmate, Noble, spoke the class poem—"Both good, the latter splendid," wrote Ben Crowninshield with partial enthusiasm.[10] The meeting adjourned to the college, and the students entertained their families, friends, and fellow students in final spreads. They had an outdoor dance; they marched round the grounds and cheered the buildings, "getting the flowers round the tree"— the Class Day tree which lived till 1911. Then there was a pause. School was over.

Henry Adams was ready to leave Harvard. He had grown up to it, got out of it what he could, and had at last begun to feel an impatience with it and its limitations. The place had given him a small world of casual friendships and almost aimless but absorbing occupations, very different from the single-minded purpose of home. Harvard had kept him from a narrowness which might have been the result of the exclusive domination of family politics.

He had tried hard during four years to make himself over in the Harvard image. With his innate actor's skill he had almost convinced himself that the school self was the real self. But he had gone too far, pressed the note too hard, pushed through the image and found out its thinness. One can see him doing this in a piece, "My Old Room," which he wrote for the *Harvard Magazine.*[11] "Many a time when in the bright frosty forenoons the sun has cheerfully shone into my room, and the fire blazed warmly in the grate, I have asked myself whether life here is not as full of enjoyment as life can be, and whether negative happiness, the absence of all real discomfort, is not, after all, the best that is granted to men."

He had asked the question—there was the rub. Negative happiness seemed a small kind of climax. The curious super-calm of "My Old Room" give away the feeling of boredom. Surely there were other ways of living and feeling and thinking than the way of negative happiness.

Chapter 3

Maiden Voyage

IN THE YEAR 1858, in the month of September, Henry Adams, twenty years old, went on board the steamer *Persia* in New York harbor. He was on the way to Europe as one of a group of recent Harvard graduates. They were going abroad before settling down to what seemed a sure fate, an undisturbed, well regulated life of marriage and work in an unchanging New England.

The America of their parents—not theirs as yet, for they had not yet asserted themselves as citizens, hardly as persons —seemed to have taken a shape it might hold for decades: that of a deeply troubled, deeply split nation, controlled inexorably by its Southern half. The South, having won the Presidency two years before, seemed destined to hold that control and continue to direct the energies of the government to the ends of its own landholding, slaveowning, agricultural community, whose way of life was beyond the imagination of the Boston boys.

Adams, a slight young man with dark hair and eyes, could not have attracted much notice from onlookers. Among the boys assembled on deck, eager to get away from a preordained existence, he must have looked what he was superficially: quiet-mannered, Harvard-educated, Boston-bred. He and the others, trying to be at ease and unexcited, caused perhaps a few smiles at their expense.

These young men had had exaggeration bred out of them. They would have been embarrassed at an excess of admiration, yet they would have granted a certain prestige to Henry Brooks Adams. Among them, their college perspective unshaken, he was looked up to with a certain regard, as a busy writer for the *Harvard Magazine*, as a clever actor in the farces of the Hasty Pudding Club, and as their Class Day Orator of the recent hot day in June when they saluted the buildings and said goodbye to the school.

The Atlantic, upon which the *Persia* soon made its way, lost no time in making at least one of its passengers seasick. Adams recorded the facts decades later. And he was somewhat seasick for other reasons. Below the surface of his good fortune and good manners, there was a turmoil, too, in his emotional being. He felt the need of seeming secure in his self-regard, and for protection assumed such a manner. But he carried doubts and fears with him.

His going from home was more a flight than a reasoned expedition. He had assumed a reason where he had none, for the benefit of his family, and told them confidently that he was going abroad to study law and languages so that he would be better able, upon returning home, to take his proper place as an energetic and forceful member of society. But his emotions and thoughts, jostling each other as the waves of the Atlantic jostled the ship, were more muddled than his words had been. They were only a very vague forward-thrusting of himself into the future.

He puzzled himself as he had puzzled his parents, who sent him not exactly with a blessing but with tolerant good wishes for his pains. They, Abigail and Charles Francis, had made his self-exile undramatic by their compliance. At the last moment they had most kindly walked with him to the railroad station in Quincy to say goodbye.

But their good will was uncomprehending. Henry's older brother, Charles, was to say of their father that ". . . his theory was that the proper thing for every young man was to get to work as soon as could scrabble through college, begin to make a living, marry, and become, as he would express it, 'a useful member of society.' " [1] Henry had a dim apprehension of disapproval and resented it, in spite of the fact that he could not make his going reasonable to himself.

As he went out from under his parents' roof, as he went out of New England, and out of America altogether, he had a sense of reprieve. This journey was to be a holding off of the future till he could choose it for himself. The person who had come into the world as Henry Brooks Adams on February 16, 1838, in the city of Boston, was setting out to assert his oneness: to say I am I.

The *Persia* landed at Liverpool on October 10th. Almost a month of sightseeing followed, through England, the Netherlands, Belgium, and the German states. The size and darkness of London, already concentrated and clenched upon itself in a way no city of the United States was, frightened Henry. It foreboded something he did not want to know. Pictures in the churches of Antwerp warmed him and confused him. Such richness was beyond him. He had not come to Europe to look at sights, he thought. He had almost roughly to shake off the company of the other boys to get about his business. For he must do something, be something, in order to justify his stay and satisfy his family in Quincy, whom he pictured at home awaiting word of his progress.

By early November Henry had found a room for himself in a dull and inexpensive section of Berlin. He paid, first, $16.50 a month; then $10.00, for a second room to which he moved for economy.[2] He was a half-hour's walk from the university and he intended to go daily on foot. He was touchy about criticism from home on the spending of money. He pointedly informed them there of his economies.

The other boys had scattered across Europe, or were living in other parts of the city. He was at last face to face with his independence. He found it a painful independence during the first few months of solitude. His manner, when he wrote home, was a mixture of cocky superiority and desperate lostness.

"I have never felt quite so glad of being out of Boston," Henry wrote to Charles in December. "There was in it a sort of contented despair, an unfathomable depth of quiet misery that gave me a placid feeling of thankfulness at being where I am. If Boston hadn't been to me what you describe it [Charles too had been, and continued to be, unhappy at home], if I hadn't felt society to be a bore even while I was yet on the threshold; if I had found one single young woman who had salt enough in her to keep her from stagnation; I believe I never should have thought of leaving home." [3] All of which revealed rather more misery in Henry than in Boston.

He over-stated his present good fortune, indicating that he would soon make German friends, would soon begin to attend classes at the university, would soon be at home there and probably wearing one of their ridiculous student caps.

But Henry's situation worsened, whatever he wrote home to the contrary. He tried the university and found, as he should have known, that a month or two of private tutoring in German was not enough to prepare him to follow law lectures, some of them in Latin. He dropped out as soon as he started. He had nothing to entertain him except his own unhappy company, the monotony of his small room, and a diet of beer, sausage, and sauerkraut.

His plan of life, outlined in large terms, was only a whistling in the dark: "Two years in Europe; two years studying law in Boston; and then I propose to emigrate and practice at Saint Louis." [4]

Only by writing grandiose letters could Henry get away from his immediate problem: bad meals, an impervious language, and the failure to qualify as a student. And when such a letter had been written, he was thrown back upon himself. When he first came to Berlin, he had had his sister Louisa's company. Now she was gone, and sheer physical loneliness began to ache in him.

One day he saw a familiar face. It was Charles Sumner, a Boston apparition in a passing cab. The sight of his bleak honest face was beautiful to Henry. He ran after him to offer him the homage that his recent fate seemed to deserve: his beating at the hands of the Representative from South Carolina and his present situation, a wandering from one health resort to another in the attempt to regain his broken health. Sumner enjoyed devotion and was pleased with the attention.

When he was gone, Henry kicking out against the wintry bleakness of the city, wrote to him in an unconscious attempt to use Sumner to get himself out of his situation. "Why not give up at once the prospect of returning this winter to America and go away? . . ." "I am myself rather disgusted with politics. . . . If you will go and travel in Siberia, I will leave German, Law, Latin, and all, to go with you, and take care of you." [5]

We can assume that Sumner was astonished. We know that he refused. When Henry mentioned to Charles that he had corresponded with Charles Sumner, he camouflaged the tone of that desperate exchange, indicating that he had sensibly advised Mr. Sumner how to go about his business.

Henry's imagination had run away with him. He had been brought up short and was now thrown back upon his Adams practicality and ingenuity, qualities operating in him between attacks of extravagance and gallantry.

An older American studying music in Berlin (Robert Apthorp) suggested one of the state-operated public schools as a good place to learn German. Without asking anyone else, Henry applied to enter such a school. In January he began a new kind of life. He was, at least, no longer bored. What he suffered was acute, but it was not negative.

Going into this boys' school marked his coming of age, the first act of his life which was his own deliberate choice. For the first time he concentrated his whole being in one act. And for the first time he wrote a creditable account of a firsthand experience.

What we know of this episode comes from a two-part sketch he wrote shortly after the trial was over. The articles were not published. Henry became dissatisfied with them, stuffed them in the bottom of his trunk, and carried them home, unshared. They were lost to sight for years and printed only in 1947 as curiosities in the *American Historical Review*. Yet they read rapidly and amusingly and contain much revelation of the state of mind of the young man who sat down with little boys to learn their language.

The director of the Friedrich-Wilhelm Werdersches Gymnasium politely introduced him to his class on his first day. They were forty-four boys averaging fourteen years of age, but ranging from ten to nineteen. They were the children of the hard-pressed petty bourgeoisie—bakers, plumbers, and shopkeepers.

The twenty-year-old American received special privileges: he was not obliged to recite. But he did attend classes regularly. The masters treated him considerately, and he found himself attaining his first object of learning German. But he found something more interesting than German to hold him to the daily going and coming. He found his imagination pricked by the children's over-concentrated, unspontaneous lives. He found himself, in spite of some distaste, trying to get inside their dirty skins.

"A room neither high nor large. Air which it would be a compliment to call vile. One small blackboard in the corner. Nothing on the walls but coats and caps. Instead of separate desks and seats, only nine rows of benches and just room enough to allow for writing on the narrow board that served for desks. . . . general neglect and dirt pervaded the room." [6] Thus his first impressions of the boys' prison.

He found that he could not be impersonal. The human situation of the children became his primary interest. "The boys were shockingly pale and, if possible, yet more shockingly dirty. About some of them was a heavy, stupid, leaden look which was bad enough. Others were pale and puffy. One or two of the smallest, too, had in contrast, bright cheeks and flashing eyes, and if we had been in America, I should have expected within the year the departure of another fiery little soul. . . ." [7]

He felt pity and was uncomfortable. He tried to get air into the room and had a long, fruitless struggle with the masters on the subject of open windows. Whenever the teacher left the room, Henry would shove them up. Whenever the teacher came back, down they would come tight closed, and the atmosphere, physical and emotional, would smolder.

A sense of humor rescued him and kept him at the problem of the boys' shirts. He tried to work out mathematically how long each one wore his. He found the general practice to be a clean shirt on Monday morning, that same shirt growing grayer during the week. He wondered, but did not quite dare ask, if the shirt were worn to bed at night.

Yet he found that he admired these boys, different as they were from any he had known at home. In spite of bad food, no play, continual spying on by the teachers, and bullying by older boys, they were quick and attentive. They learned. They mastered more facts than Henry could fancy any child taking in.

He found that this repulsively earnest, single-minded system worked. He had thought his own desultory days at the Boston Latin School unhappy. Now he could only thank God (as he wrote) that he had not been educated in one of these progressive German schools which were considered the best and most efficient in the world.

The paradox of the perfection of this instrument of education and its day-to-day dreariness caught his acute attention. "A perfect system is a very curious and admirable thing, but it's not always a very pleasant thing," he wrote.[8] "From what I have seen, I admire its perfection very much, but infinitely prefer the less perfect and more free and human education which we know, or used to know at home."[9]

He saw the boys stuffed full of facts, never served brutally, but all the time thoroughly watched and completely caught in an airtight, deadly system. "You must see at once how this continual watchfulness, this forcing of the memory, this combination of a whole school into one class, must hammer ideas into the head of the stupidest. . . . The great fault that I found with them was just the principle on which they depend. They cramp the individual horribly. . . . The fact that human nature varies, that one sort of development suits one mind and a wholly different one suits another; the fact in short, which I believe is in all the world only in America practically carried out, that each individual ought to walk the path for which God has best fitted him, and not that which man's regulations have planned out for him; this was wholly ignored." [10]

He rejected the system, but he could not reject the children. He tried hard, in spite of the barrier of the language, in spite of their initial distrust of him, in spite of his own shyness, to reach them. He tried naïvely to make them fight fair, to hit only with their fists, and to hit only those their own size. He failed, except in protecting some of the smaller ones, but during his time with them he could not prevent one of the boys having his arm twisted and broken by an older bully.

The underfed children began to trust him. They ceased

lifting up their thin arms as if to ward off blows whenever he approached. But, "It needed week after week of continual effort on my part to convince them that I would not hurt them." [11] Having succeeded, he was literally run over by the boys: "They insisted on riding on my back, and sometimes two or three would get on together; they would climb all over me, sit on my shoulders, play with my watch, and worst of all, make me eat some of their breakfast of black bread, which they themselves put into my mouth. . . . To the very end many of the younger were not yet quite decided whether to believe or not my accounts of my three squaws and six papooses in the wigwam at home." [12]

Henry Adams's own teaching of many years later would bear the remote consequences of this experience. He was never an easy teacher, but he was considerate of his students' opinions, and as a basis of the teacher-student relationship insisted first of all that they have opinions.

The piece he wrote, and then buried in his trunk unread, concludes with a passage showing the beginning of an ability to make connections and hint at the larger relationships. There was, he seemed to say, a darker order lying below that of the school system. "Directly under the walls of the school ran one of those black, unhealthy arms of the Spree, such as in Berlin are always turning up in the most unexpected places; coming from under houses and disappearing beneath what seems to be perfectly solid streets, so that they seem to be a type of the state of society of the city, where the dark currents are forced out of sight into darker corners, and one only sees what is really round him when he leaves the thoroughfares and burrows through out-of-the-way places; gets, so to speak, the backyard view of human nature." [13]

This, at the age of twenty, was his first effort to get the gist of one particular matter. It is characteristic, that he expressed the emotional significance of the experience in a figure of speech.

Adams not only attended classes diligently, he went to the central education office and asked questions about the history and structure of the public-school system. Then he sat up nights to put his impressions into words. The school experience, and the writing about it, was an emotional and mental effort of the first order—the first he had demanded of himself.

He stuck to his place in the class from January till April 1st. By then he was tired of the school and ready to get out of it. The teachers had got wind of his going over their heads, and misinterpreted his motives. They began to fear him and make his situation uncomfortable. He was tired of the unhealthy atmosphere and the steady grind he was sharing with the boys. In April he burst his bonds and escaped. He abandoned any pretense of scientific self-improvement and set off from Berlin with the congenial Apthorp family and two New England boys, Ben Crowninshield and Jim Higginson, upon a walk across the German landscape. He had no intention of stopping at a set time or of learning anything at all from the experience.

"I tell you what, young man," he wrote to Charles just before walking out of the city, "Boston's a little place, but damn me if it isn't preferable to this cursed hole. . . . I've eaten German dishes till I'm nearly run to pieces. I've lived in this air till I'm all used up. I've studied the damned language till I'm utterly lost in it." [14]

Henry and Jim and Ben outwalked the Apthorps and soon left them behind, but collected another young New Englander upon the way, John Bancroft. The four young men then wandered gipsylike through Wittenberg, Dessau, Weimar, Eisenach, Georgenthal, Königsee. They walked through a forest and up a hill or two; they got tired and rode mules or farm wagons, or even trains; they stopped at draughty inns and drank too much of Ben's homemade punch. All of it pleased Henry, jaded and tired of being dutiful.

By April 22nd he was settled again, boarding with a family in Dresden, in a very different situation and a new frame of mind. The next months saw him deliberately unlearning all that he had learned of living in Berlin. There he had clenched the will hard. Here he learned to relax it. Any serious study of law or Latin or German was a mere form, a turning over of a few pages per day. "I feel precious little like working hard here, I can tell you," he wrote home. "With the exception of a few pages of Roman law every day, I don't do much labor, unless you call long walks on fine afternoons and talking nonsense with the Fräulens labor." [15]

He took a zestful interest in his Dresden family's social life. He presented all the daughters with bouquets upon the occasion of their brother, the lieutenant's, marrying. He escorted them to the church and attended them to the reception.

"The servant opened the folding door and I was horrified at seeing before me an army of white dresses and sternly fixed countenances arranged in order, and all staring, gravely, as if it were a funeral, at me as if I was the coffin. With that grace and suavity of manner for which I am famous, I marched up and stormed the phalanx by a series of bows." [16] He had a good time. "It is true I found myself alone among the female portion; all the males standing in a corner and talking together." [17]

Henry needed company; he found it in Dresden. His friends of Harvard, Anderson and Crowninshield, were in the city. Henry and Ben Crowninshield fell into the habit of taking easy walks to see the sights. They looked at churches and churchyards; they drank beer at convenient cafés, looked at the passers-by, listened to music of all kinds of concerts, looked at miles of pictures in the various museums, and walked out onto the dusty roads of the country and admired the landscape.

Henry could well claim that this life was "regal." His senses had been for a long time underfed; now he was grazing them on whatever he could see, hear, smell, touch. He was the young American in Europe about whom Henry James would soon be writing his earliest stories and novels.

Whenever he and Ben went, whether to a graveyard near the town or on a river expedition up the Elbe, it was Henry's sensibilities and susceptibilities which were attacked. It had been the agreeable Fräuleins of his Dresden family who had especially pleased him. On a riverboat one particular young woman, a pretty Russo-Swede, made him quite dizzy for the space of the afternoon. Coming to him out of the unknown, just as soon to go, she enchanted him. The delightful working order of his senses pleased him. "She was clever, highly cultivated and interesting. Had just come from Italy and was strong Italian. Spoke pretty English. Was a little taller than I in figure; slim; light eyes; distingué. We talked of traveling, of poetry, of art, of Italy, and of many other things." [18] He was pleased with himself for having been pleased with her. He felt alive that afternoon as he had never felt in Berlin.

Summer came on, and he and Ben left Dresden to peregrinate over Germany. He was in an ecstasy over the otherness of Nürnberg and "passed the day in a couple of great churches, lying on the altar steps and looking at the glorious stained glass windows five hundred years old, magnificent colors and quaint Biblical stories." [19]

In the late summer the two boys joined Adams's sister, Louisa, and her husband, Charles Kuhn, and saw the Swiss mountains in congeniel company. Henry had time for a first quick look at Italy with his sister, but rejoined Ben to escort him back to school in Berlin. He could no longer endure Berlin himself. He went back to Dresden and settled down for several more months of valuable idleness.

41

He boarded with another family, this second season in Dresden. The head of the house was an educated man, Heinrich Reichenbach, a botanist and geologist, the keeper of the royal natural history collection of Dresden. The brother of the family, Theodor, became Henry's friend, and was as interested as he in old coins. The daughter, the Fräulein Augusta, was simply the most serious threat to his susceptibilities yet encountered in Germany.

He wrote to his mother about the girl in a letter that shows the easy relationship he had with Abigail Adams at that time: "As for the Fräulein, ain't she a one-er, that's all. She reminds me all the time of Nelly Lowe; in fact I call her "Miss Nelly" now. She's a will of her own and gives me the most immense delight. A perfect little Tartar, and smooth as a cat." [20] Later, to his brother, he soothed what family alarm he might have created, saying with puzzled regret that he was not quite in love: "The daughter, the Fräulein Augusta, is a brick. She might be dangerous if—well, if it only weren't that to me she isn't. I don't know why. One can't explain these things." [21]

Meanwhile he proclaimed himself settled for the winter and disturbingly calm about wasting his time. "Three mornings in the week at nine o'clock I go down and take riding lessons; three others my fencing master comes and teaches me how to use a rapier." [22] Thus nonchalantly he outlined to Quincy his tolerably regular routine.

Evidently there was some protest from home, but from his new calm he explained to them what he was gaining. "I acknowledge therefore as broadly as you wish, that so far as my plan, went, I have failed and done little or nothing. At the same time, I feel for myself convinced that this last year has been no failure, but on the contrary worth to me a great deal; how much depends on the use I make of it; but the worth is there. You say you think I'm a humbug.[23] . . . [And he went on bravely.] So far as education goes, I consider these two years as the most valuable of my life." [24]

At the same time, he began to have a suspicion of an ambition. He felt now that he might, after all, write. But he was cautious in his statement of the ambition to Charles. "Amusing, witty, clever I am not, and to affect the style would disgust me and bore you. If I write at all in my life out of the professional line, it will probably be when I have something to say, and when I feel that my subject has got me as well as I the subject." [25] Delicately, precisely, in these words, he outlined exactly the course his career as a writer would take. He had gained some insight in Dresden.

Another spring came, and Henry grew restless. He set off on his travels, Louisa and Rome his goal, but with time, along the way, to stop to enjoy various German, Austrian, and North Italian towns. As he went, he wrote up his impressions of the sights, the citizens, the soldiers, the confusions in this region just being embroiled in a war. He had the satisfaction of traveling as a paid correspondent of a newspaper, the *Boston Courier*. Charles, acting as his agent, had placed his travel letters with that newspaper.

Affecting a dilettantish air, proper for the recent Harvard graduate, he informed the subscribers of the *Courier* of the manner in which he spent his last night in Dresden, listening "to two pieces of music so tremendously classic that it is as good as high-treason to say that the first one exhausted me so much that I could hardly enjoy the second." [26]

In Venice fastidious detachment—somewhat assumed one can suppose for the sake of the article—grew upon him. "It was delicious to glide along the water, and to bask in the sun; and the islands and lagoons looked so charmingly that it seemed almost a crime to go back to the six-feet broad, and very unpleasantly smelling alleys of the city." [27] A far cry from strenuous New England, or strenuous Berlin. One can see Henry bent over his reporter's job, writing thus with a delighted air, thinking how very changed he was since that grim day in November when he first settled down to Europe.

He saw the King in Florence, at the races, and found that "il nostro Re"—who was soon to be King of a newly united Italy—looked like a very "vulgar and coarse fancy man, prize fighter, or jockey." [28] In Rome he saw the Pope, and being in a crowd the Holy Father blessed he felt that he might be somewhat the better for it. Real enthusiasm broke through here: "This is the life in Rome. I am helpless against the charm of it." [29]

For the traveler who had spent his first European winter in Berlin and found an improvement in Dresden, Rome was overwhelmingly better than either. Here was the good of Dresden—leisure, art, good company—magnified a thousand times. Rome, soon to fall under conquering armies and suffer a change, was in that May of 1860 what it had been through stagnating centuries, not modern, not rational, lazily indifferent to everything Berlin or Boston might care for. Its soul, wrote Henry Adams, was medieval. For the first time he began to praise that quality, although he hardly knew what he meant.

He felt at home. ". . . we Romans make excursions out to

Tusculum and Tivoli, or rambling about the catacombs, or lounging and smoking cigarettes in artists' studios." [30] This was the Rome of William Wetmore Story, the Rome of the youthful fervent Browning and his delicate wife. It was the city Henry James was to capture in *Roderick Hudson,* a novel whose hero resembled but surpassed the actual American artists, the Story and Wildes, whom Adams came to know that spring of 1860.

A month later the young reporter of the *Courier* had real news to report to his readers. Garibaldi had just taken Palermo and was there yet. United States Government dispatches were to be sent to the American consul in that city, and to the American naval officer of the ship *Iroquois,* in Palermo harbor. By hook or crook, Henry Brooks Adams secured the authorization to carry these dispatches to their destination. He set off from Naples on the steamer *Capri* to see a dictator face to face.

Besides a retelling of the course of Garibaldi's progress through Sicily, done with considerable narrative ability, Henry's two Sicilian sketches, [31] published in the *Courier* on July 10 and 13, 1860, reveal a great deal about the state of his knowledge and emotions in 1860, and show him in the act of living up to what he knew to be history. The best part today, at this distance from the events, if his firsthand impression of the city.

The ship, towing supplies from Naples to Palermo, had carried him into a harbor booming with big-gun salutes. When the guns, at a distance, sounded like fighting, he wondered momentarily what it would be like to be shot. But Garibaldi was in control. The port was in wild confusion, but the war was over.

The next morning Henry found Henry H. Barstow, the consul, and the captain of the *Iroquois,* and delivered his papers to them. He was free then to see Palermo and make what he could of the city and its situation, not yet recovered from battle and delivery by Garibaldi.

It was only as an afterthought that he considered how strange his well dressed civilian and unarmed self must have appeared wandering through the alleys and along the avenues of the demoralized city. "I never dreamed of going armed, and was all alone, and looked I suppose a good deal as if I had just stepped out of the Strand in London, so far as dress went, but no one spoke to me or interfered with me in any way." [32]

He began to respect the personal force of Garibaldi who

could hold together such a band of pirates and brigands as grinned at him from every corner. He walked the streets through "crowds of desperately patriotic Sicilians," [33] saw the General's headquarters, the Senatorial Palace, from the outside, ate ice cream on a street corner and, dreadfully tired, went down to the port again, to his hotel.

He ate a noonday dinner among a troop of reporters and an aide-de-camp of Garibaldi. There were, among the company, the correspondent of the London *Times,* the correspondent of the *London Illustrated News,* and, pleased with himself, the correspondent of the *Boston Courier.*

Late that afternoon a group of five newspapermen, including Adams, was conducted to the Senatorial Palace to meet the General. "Garibaldi had apparently just finished his dinner, and was sitting at a corner window talking with four or five visitors, gentlemen and ladies of Palermo. He rose as we came in, and came forward, shaking hands with each of the party as we were introduced." [34]

The *Courier's* correspondent missed little. "He had his plain red shirt on, precisely like a fireman, and no mark of authority. . . . I was seated next him, and as the head of our party remarked that I had come all the way from Naples in order to see him, he turned round and took my hand, thanking me as if I had done him a favor. This is the way he draws people." [35]

Among Garibaldi's intimates was a priest with a striking appearance. "I have met him several times, rushing about the streets with a great black cross in his hands. He has a strange, restless face, all passion and impulse. The others were Garibaldi's famous captains—a fine set of heads, full of energy and action. Here I was at last, face to face with one of the great events of our day." [36]

This display of force and energy was to work away in the young man's mind at a furious rate of agitated thought. His mind was set racing by the sight of the unnecessary destruction in the Royal Palace which he and some new friends, English and American naval officers, visited and, in their turn, looted.

"We had the run of the whole place," he reported, not entirely pleased with his own behavior, "except state rooms, and of course made any amount of noise, and satisfied our curiosity, by going everywhere and examining everything. . . The rooms were full of boxes, beds, scraps of uniforms and soldiers' accoutrements, fragments of manuscripts, books about religion and war, indiscriminate dirt and fleas. . . .

Still, plunder is plunder, or 'loot,' as the Englishmen call it, and the party loaded itself with old wooden epaulets, braid, books, handcuffs, and so on, as mementoes. In the stables, we found an army of hungry rats and a dead horse. In the guard-house a wretched man who was to be shot within twelve hours for an attempt at assassination. . . . When we came out again on the square we had a grand flea-hunt, for the beasts were all over us by dozens. . . . Loaded with plunder we marched back again, the grinning red-shirts presenting arms to us everywhere." [37]

He felt uneasy about a too easy acceptance of the triumph of one side. To ease his conscience, he secured permission to visit the prisoners, the royal troops, to find out what he could of them. He brought with him from Naples a letter to an officer held there, a member of the Swiss Legion. This he delivered. Then he proceeded to interview, to investigate, and to take notes.

He was impressed, and his feelings wrought up, by the excitement of Palermo. But he was dubious about the good of the movement. It seemed somewhat like a poor satire on American institutions. "Europeans," he wrote, "are fond of calling him [Garibaldi] the Washington of Italy, principally because they know nothing about Washington. Catch Washington invading a foreign kingdom on his own hook, in a fireman's shirt!" [38]

Henry went on board the *Capri* again on the 10th of June to return to Naples. Sleeping on the deck among hundreds of soldiers, his hands encased in gloves to keep off fleas, he had much to think about. He saw, for one thing, that government, even government in Massachusetts, was not to be taken for granted; that brutal and personal forces could move masses of men in a forcible manner; that representative government, such as Papa stood for at home, might not, after all, be immortal.

By midsummer Henry was out of Italy, in Paris, enjoying himself there in pure frivolities, suspecting that he ought not to like it so well but, like his great-grandmother, finding that he very soon got used to those portions of Parisian life which shocked him in the beginning. Unshocked, jolly, and thoroughly at home, in Paris too was his college friend Henry Hobson Richardson, who fitted into the students' and artists' world like a native. He had money from Louisiana and lived largely—working hard, playing hard. He was studying for the entrance examination into the Beaux Arts, knowing that his being a foreign student might make it harder for him. We do not know if the two Henrys met. We only know that they could have done so.

Home affairs began to pull on Henry Adams. To go from southern Italy into France was almost to start home, and he felt nearer to those matters that engrossed his family. Even before he left Dresden in the spring, he had begun to notice intimations of trouble from the United States.

Since he had been in Europe, his father had been elected to Congress. Charles Francis Adams was marked for attention there, for he was one of a small group of Northern men who held a central position. They were attempting to prevent secession and the remote possibility of war by granting as much as one could with honor to the South. Their particular aim was to hold on to the border states. They held an uncomfortable position at best.

"Papa may not be much encouraged by knowing that his son ever so far off and without much acquaintance with the matter, thinks as he does, and enters with all his heart into his view of what are his duties," he wrote to his mother in March. "We young ones don't count much now, but it may at least please papa to know that those who are nearest and dearest to him, go heart and soul after him in this path." [39]

The fall elections were near. It was of the utmost importance to the new Republican party that it name a good man for President. Charles Francis Adams was for Seward, a sound Eastern man, the former Governor of New York. But whoever was named, the fortunes of the Adams family would be bound with his. Henry decided to go home. He could be back in Quincy in time to vote.

His father, of whom he was very proud in spite of intra-family differences, might need one son at hand. Not sure that he would enjoy living in Washington, but willing to try the experiment, he offered himself to his parents as a kind of prop. No doubt he over-estimated their age and helplessness and over-stated his own use, but the offer was generous. "So if papa and you," he wrote to his mother, "approve this course and it's found easy to carry out, you can have at least one of your sons always with you." [40]

He came home, and was in Quincy by October. Berlin and Dresden were far behind him, as were Rome, Sicily, and Paris. He found himself confronted with the name Abraham Lincoln, and cast his first vote for that name.

Chapter 4

The Winter Before the War

CONGRESS MET in gloomy strife on December 3, 1860. It was to have the distinction of being the one Congress to adjourn for a civil war. Congressman Charles Francis Adams and his family settled for the winter session in Washington in a rented house on I Street overlooking Pennsylvania Avenue.

The change from Boston to the lively apprehension of Washington suited Henry Adams. He was out of New England and the law office which he had tried uncertainly and without enthusiasm during the fall; he was living in the center of things; he was at work. To be busy to the point of exhaustion, up to his eyes in public and private scenes of importance, seeing and even sharing in what looked to him to be real control of affairs, not knowing whether he was happy or not—paradoxically: this was true happiness for him.

Henry's father was an important man at this moment, and his father's secretary saw at close view how things went on in Washington. Young Adams was daily at the Capitol, looking down on its angry scene where members strapped on revolvers and bowie knives before debate. [1] He went in and out of committee rooms and reported at home that papa was a very Jove in committee. He heard news and gossip from Congressmen, newspapermen such as Raymond of the *New York Times,* whom he met at this time, and other young secretaries like himself, who thought themsleves the keenest men in the city. [2]

Every night, when official work was done, he sat down exultingly to pen and paper to write down what he had seen, felt, and thought. He was composing anonymous political letters as the *Boston Advertiser's* "own correspondent." He had a great quantity of energy to keep him going, and the writing of the newspaper letters was an exhilaration, not a duty. To his joy some of them were quoted or reprinted in the *New York Times* of his new friend Henry J. Raymond.

The fact that the times were out of joint failed to depress him. He wavered, of course, as Congress wavered. as society wavered, and as newspaper readers wavered, up and down, from hope to despair and back again to hope, but he was doing so much, working so hard, and so sure in his conviction that what he did mattered, that his mood was mostly joy: joy at being where he was, doing what he was doing. Partly it was the hardheartedness of youth.

Ruffians and brutes he named the opposing Southerners; heroes, his father and his father's friends. The South had no pathos as yet. That quality would come only after defeat. At this moment, just before the war, the Southerners had been in control of national politics for fifty years. They had been arrogant and superior. Now they would reap a fierce return for their scorn.

From the public scenes in the Capitol building young Adams could return each evening to private scenes in his father's house: scenes taking place nightly, played by the leading men of their own side, men who enjoyed the good port wine and cigars and talk in Representative Adams's dining room. The heathen might rage, both of the North and the South, but the young secretary was sure in his mind that what really mattered went on in his father's house.

In the early days of the winter Charles Sumner came to them and ate with them. But his lofty striking of attitudes began to irritate Congressman Adams, who felt the present need for caution in order to save what one could for the North, if the South should be so foolish as to fight. Sumner in turn was disappointed in Adams for certain public compromises he had made on the floor of the House. Soon there was an open break, and Senator Sumner came no more to dine. This matter hurt Henry. He considered it a defection in his hero, an almost fatal lack of understanding. He never forgot it, never got over it.

What Henry grasped was the necessity of the time for the practical manager and maneuverer. William H. Seward, he saw, was the sort of man needed, a man of a different type from Sumner, a type all his own, combining integrity with outward indigestible traits of eccentricity. He had execrable manners; he coughed and belched and told dreadful stories; he dressed like a tramp and had the effrontery to hold forth in their dining room on the subject of clothes. He made Henry laugh till he choked. Even Charles Francis mellowed and laughed too.

These two men thought that at this moment they might hold the key to blocking the South's pretensions. Adams and Seward, one in the House, one in the Senate, stood for a cautious, careful, watchful policy, one that would avoid an open break with the South, that would put the secessionists in as black a light as possible, that would hold hard onto the border states, surrounding the newly seceded ones with a strong containing wall of loyal states, and in the end, if possible, win back the South by political rather than military means.

Seward had earlier proclaimed an "irresistible conflict," yet at this hour he and Adams behaved as if there would be none, trying to make their hope come true. Henry, being young and incautious, believed, probably more strongly than his father or Seward, that their means could succeed.

Meanwhile, young Secretary Adams could sit in on the evening conferences, keenly alive to the crossfire of interest and conflict, admiring Seward of the outrageous manners, studying him for his abilities, taking note of the exercise of political power. On December 9th he wrote to Boston to his brother Charles: "I sat and watched the old fellow with his big nose and his wire hair and grizzly eyebrows and miserable dress, and listened to him rolling out his grand, broad ideas that would inspire a cow with statesmanship if she understood our language. There's no shake in him. He talks square up to the mark and something beyond it." [3]

Seward could be kind to Henry's generation. "Yesterday," wrote Henry to Charles, "we had the funniest little party. Seward once invited us all down to dinner, but we insisted that not more than one of our younger set should go at a time with the parent birds. So finding that he couldn't manage it any other way, he invited us four children to dine with him yesterday: Loo, Mary, Brooks and I. Loo had to leave her bed to do it, as she was just under one of her headaches, but do it we did in grand style. The Governor was grand. No one but his secretary, Mr. Harrington, was at table with us, but he had up some Moselle wine that Baron Gerolt had sent him and we managed to be pretty jolly. He is now, as perhaps you do not know, virtual ruler of this country." [4]

It required youth to maintain cheerfulness in this city which changed shakily and crazily from day to day. Each day another Southern member of Congress resigned, made a speech, and went home. One of them was L. Q. C. Lamar, the studious Congressman from Oxford, Mississippi, one day to come back after the war, to serve again in Congress, and to be a friend of Henry Adams.

Henry's mother was distressed that her friends could no longer receive her, or she, them. She broke down and cried for them. Henry could not walk out of their house without seeing government clerks wearing badges of disunion and boasting openly of what part they should play when Washington was theirs.

It was known in the city that John B. Floyd, the Secretary of War, instead of preparing the government for war, was busily shipping arms and munitions to the Federal arsenals in Southern secessionist territory. "The President" (Buchanan), wrote Henry to Charles, "divides his time between crying and praying; the Cabinet has resigned or else is occupied in committing treason. Some of them have done both. The people of Washington are firmly convinced that there is to be an attack on Washington by the Southerners or else a slave insurrection, and in either case or in any contingency they feel sure of being ruined and murdered." [5]

But, interestingly enough, in spite of secession actually under way, in spite of waverings of his cheerfulness, with the advantage of youth and curiosity and free entry into public and private gatherings, he enjoyed himself. By February he had put behind him two months of newspaper writing. On February 4th, Hale, his editor, arrived from Boston to take over the job. Hale had annoyed Henry by cutting out gossip and opinion and, as he said, juicy bits, leaving his letters arid and sketchy. Henry confessed himself satisfied that the job was over. He announced to Charles that he would now be able to do something better: write a full-length article and call it "The Great Secession Winter of 1860-61." [6]

He would go to parties, too. Henry would have had Charles think that he was not astonished at the peculiar sights of social Washington, but in truth he panted after all novelties and curiosities, whether political or social. He had a thirst for crowds and noise and the clash of personalities, whether on the floor of Congress or the polished parquet of a ballroom.

He enjoyed, most of all, a youthfully intolerant scorn and sense of superiority. One night in February, free of his newspaper work, finished for that day with being secretary, he went to a party given by Senator and Mrs. Douglas of Illinois. [7] There was a great crush there. Trying to get through the crowd, going from one room to another, he almost got into a fight, he said, with several men and women, so much more like a battle than a party was the scene. The champagne was awful, though one should not complain about one's host's wine. But then one's host was a brute. His wife was handsome, but dull, poor girl. And the admired of the undiscriminating mob were those ancient, prehistoric heroes Tyler and Crittenden. Thus wrote Henry to Charles.

Lunches, dinners, receptions, balls and new acquaintances

occupied more and more of the secretary's time. Charles came down from Boston for a while, and went with Henry one day in February across the river to dine at the Lees'.

The visit can be reconstructed from Charles's memoirs:[8] the two young men seen ascending the hill through the deep shade to the house on the hilltop; their reception at the door by their host, young William Henry Fitzhugh Lee, who had been with them at Harvard; their welcome by his sister Agnes; their sitting down to eat with a whole tableful of "future generals and colonels who would soon be fighting each other"— friendship unspoiled, war not really smelled as yet, the fact of friendship and good spirits still possible.

Long after the war, Henry would look back to that day, seeing their world, even then, unknown to them all, trembling on the edge of destruction. He would use it as a backdrop for a good scene in his novel of Washington, *Democracy*.

When Henry and Charles Adams ate dinner at Arlington, war was not yet sure. Uneasiness, uncertainty tormented them all, but peace seemed as possible—with the political downfall of the secessionists and the collapse of their movement—as the actual crackle of gunfire. It was thought that the arrival of the new President, Lincoln of Illinois, might make a difference in the air of Washington and sway the mood definitely one way or another. The President's coming made no noticeable difference, for before his inauguration he was very quiet. But the arrival with him of John Hay, of Warsaw, Illinois, made a great difference for Henry Adams.

In John Hay, Henry found a friend. They had only a brief time to learn to know each other, to feel out awkwardnesses and congenialities, but the shortness of this first acquaintanceship had little to do with its solidity and duration. Henry was to remember, and to develop a theory from the experience, that their friendship was born, not made.

It is not surprising that they liked each other. They had much in common, and their characters differed enough to prevent flatness in their relationship. They were almost the same age—Henry just twenty-three, John Hay, soon to be. They met in a city in crisis where friendship took the place of security. They were both secretaries to men of importance; the two young men were intelligently devoted to their jobs, thinking that what they did mattered; and they shared, besides, the relief of a sense of humor, its flavor being exaggerated and irreverent laughter.

Both Hay and Adams were interested in writing—Adams as a newspaper correspondent; Hay, as a poet. Both had studied law—Henry for a short time only; Hay, long enough to be admitted to the bar. Both boys—for they behaved much of the time as boys—had had satisfactory, even flattering, college careers.

John Hay was a Westerner. But he had come east from Warsaw, Illinois, to go to college at Brown University in Providence, in September, 1855, an unsophisticated, snub-nosed boy, with a long, full shock of hair, cut straight across his forehead. In college his good humor and general brightness and quickness made him a favorite. He adapted his Illinois dress and haircut to Eastern standards and became passionately fond of what he thought of as the superior knowledge and good manners of Providence.

He helped edit the school paper; he wrote verse with long-winded celerity; he was praised and spoiled by a literary circle of poetesses who surrounded him with a hot-house encouragement. One of these was Mrs. Sarah Helen Whitman, who did not forget her encounter with Edgar Allan Poe of a decade before, and one was a younger woman, Miss Nora Perry, who was Hay's special encourager after he finished college and went home to what he thought of as exile in the West.

In Warsaw he felt out of sort and out of place. Grand in its physical setting, high above the Mississippi River, with much wild and uncultivated land still surrounding it—for him it was isolation. His interests were not shared by his near-pioneer neighbors.

On the banks of the Mississippi he found that

> . . . the heart hangs lone like a desolate lyre
> That moans forever its wildered wail
> And pours the voice of its vague desire
> On the heedless ear of the mocking gale.[9]

He would have been astounded if he could have known that within a few years his best verse would be raw with Western slang and hearty with Western feeling. But even then, fresh from the impressiveness of the East, he had within him a sub-strata of adaptability in his self-pity. He had a real interest in Western politics, just waiting to be waked up. He came of an anti-slave family, half of it derived from New England. It was the politics of anti-slavery, of the new Republican party, that roused him. In Springfield, where he studied law, he became friends with John Nicolay who was a friend of Abraham Lincoln, the lawyer who had outtalked Douglas in debate and just missed beating him for the Senate.

Nicolay helped Lincoln in the summer of 1860 in the presidential campaign, and Hay helped Nicolay. Thayer, in his life of John Hay, tells how Nicolay, burdened with more work than he could handle alone, suggested to Lincoln that they should take Hay along with them to Washington. He quotes Lincoln as saying, "We can't take all Illinois with us down to Washington," but adding, after a pause, "Well, let Hay come." [10]

On February 11, 1861, at the age of twenty-two, John Hay set off for Washington in the wake of John Nicolay and Abraham Lincoln. After a roundabout route the presidential party arrived on February 23rd. John Hay and Henry Adams met almost immediately and, having met, began a dialogue that never bored them, and that would last them the rest of their lives.

What Hay had tasted of tentative disappointment in Illinois blew away in the strenuous air of the Capital. The President's second secretary soon began to keep a diary so that all the newness might not be lost. He was to record not only the expected daytime adventures of a secretary, the sights seen, the people met, the appointments made; but the nighttime experiences as well, the visits of a gaunt President in a nightshirt, come to wake up his young secretary to talk and to share his insomnia. His duties were to include hearing Shakespeare read, or going to the theater where he and the Old Tycoon, as he said, both made eyes at certain young ladies.[11]

Like his friend from Boston, Hay was interested in the people of the Washington scene. One of the first to catch his attention by a certain dramatic flair in his aspect and manner was Carl Schurz, the German emigrant revolutionist, who had come into the city with a pair of ready pistols packed in his bag, the very ones he had used in Berlin not so many years before to effect the rescue of a fellow conspirator from prison. Schurz was already a fiery American, with only a few years' residence in Wisconsin behind him. In the recent campaign he had spoken for Lincoln, particularly among the Germans of the Midwest. Now he wanted to do something more than go to Spain as United States Minister, a job which at this moment seemed tame and superfluous.

The man was gangling and awkward until he talked; then he was warmth, eloquence, persuasiveness itself. He played the piano very well, for he had had a thorough musical education in Germany. Now, fervently one afternoon, the emigrant democrat sat down to play for the President.[12]

A caller who got no farther than the secretaries' antechamber was a fellow Westerner, W. D. Howells, of Ohio, who had written the Republican campaign biography of Lincoln. Nicolay and Hay sympathized with him for his background and for his tentative literary ambitions; they spoke for him, and got him his consulate in Venice.

Howells was to remember "the sobered dignity of the one, and the humorous gayety of the other, and how we had some young men's joking and laughing together, in the anteroom where they received me, with the great soul entering upon its travail beyond the closed door." [13]

Into the confusion of the city where Lincoln, Schurz, Howells, Nicolay, Hay, and Adams, each in his place, was trying to fit into a new arrangement of living another caller came. He passed quickly through the secretarial antechamber and out again in some disgust. This was the professional soldier William Tecumseh Sherman, who had been living in the South, as head of the state military academy of Louisiana. He had sensed there that war was coming, had resigned his job and come here, to offer his services and advice.

He had gone to the Senate to talk to his brother, John Sherman, and the two of them had gone to see the President. Here is the way Sherman, many years later, in his *Memoirs,* recalled the meeting. His brother had introduced him to Lincoln, saying, "Mr. President, this is my brother, Colonel Sherman, who is just up from Louisiana; he may give you some information you want. 'Ah!' said Mr. Lincoln, 'how are they getting along down there?' I said, 'They are getting along swimmingly—they are preparing for war.' 'Oh, well!' said he, 'I guess we'll manage to keep house.' I was silenced, said no more to him, and we soon left. I was sadly disappointed, and remember that I broke out on John, d—ning the politicians generally, saying, 'You have got things in a hell of a fix, and you may get them out as you best can,' adding that the country was sleeping on a volcano that might burst forth at any minute, but that I was going to St. Louis to take care of my family, and would have no more to do with it." [14]

Before the month was over, William Tecumseh Sherman was named head of the Fifth Street Railroad in St. Louis, presumably for life,[15] but when war broke out in April he came back East to get into it. But his premature disappointment with Lincoln was typical rather than exceptional in the waiting period before the fighting broke out. Lincoln was an unknown quantity, and rather scorned than respected.

This was a time of aching indecision. A futile peace conference met. In Alabama a new nation was born, and Davis, looking a long way in front of him down the straight street leading from the capitol in Montgomery, was sworn in as the Confederacy's first president.

In spite of chaos, a kind of routine was kept. The winter session of Congress neared its end. On March 13th the Adamses left town to return to Boston; Henry had to say goodbye to John Hay among his other new friends. The national mood was one of distraction and futility. But the Adams family's own sense of marking time ended abruptly with the arrival, one morning, of a fateful telegram from President Lincoln appointing Mr. Adams as Minister to Britain.

Henry's brother, Charles, tells in his memoirs how on March 19th this news affected them. It "fell on our breakfast table like a veritable bombshell, scattering confusion and dismay. . . . My mother at once fell into tears and deep agitation; foreseeing all sorts of evil consequences, and absolutely refusing to be comforted; while my father looked dismayed. . . . It is droll to look back on; very characteristic and Bostonese." [16]

Henry had been wondering whether he himself should go into the Army, if fighting broke out. His father's new job cut short these musings. He was required; he was to continue to be his father's secretary in England.

In the meantime the Adamses were not quite geared to the desperation of the times. They stayed on in Boston for John Adams's marriage. They were yet in the United States in April when Fort Sumter was fired on; they were yet there when Virginia seceded. Charles Francis Adams knew that he and Seward had lost their gamble to keep Virginia with the North. And Henry, whatever he thought or desired, in regard to going into the Army, could now no longer choose.

Only on May 1st did Charles Francis Adams and his family set off. The secession winter was over; its emotions were done with. Henry's record of those days, his "Great Secession Winter of 1860-61," was passed on to Charles to sell or shelve as he wished; Charles did not think it worth publishing, and it was printed in 1910 only as a curiosity. Yet it holds much of the quick of that time.

On May 1st Henry Adams left America for the second time. The impatient young man would have been appalled to know that he would remain abroad for seven years and two months before turning home once more.

Chapter 5

Outpost

THE ADAMS family arrived in England on May 13, 1861, and bad news met them the day they landed. The Queen's government had issued a Proclamation of Neutrality and in effect recognized the South's belligerency before the representative of the North could arrive at Court to state his case. It looked as if Minister Charles Francis Adams would have an uneasy, and perhaps short, tour of duty. There was no way of knowing at this time if Britain would remain neutral. It was a possibility that she would join the war on the side of the South.

Henry's family in London included his father and mother, his sister Mary, and his young brother Brooks. They found no natural and easy place there when they first arrived. In the first year of their stay, it looked as if they never would attain such a place. Henry was twenty-three at the beginning of this desperate time. He was of an age and a temperament to find his family's situation more dire than it actually was. He was a long time gaining his equilibrium. He was far from physical war, and never lost some sense of guilt over that fact. He knew, intellectually, that the work he was doing in the London Legation was of greater importance than anything he could have done in America, and it was work of a more difficult kind; yet he had a private and ineradicable conviction that he had evaded responsibility and danger. Even in the busiest times of the London "War," he felt that he was imprisoned in some sort of vacuum far away from the places where the important things were happening. The news of battles in America, coming in delayed messages from across the Atlantic, added a sort of agony to his position.

Henry's father had the advantage of a natural self-restraint and self-respect. He kept his cool eye on the business at hand and kept his small staff busy. Henry found plenty of work to do in the Legation Office. This office, for all the size of the Portland Place house, was lodged in the crowded basement. Here began the North's slow work of building a relationship with a great power disposed to be unfriendly. In the basement were Charles L. Wilson, the Secretary, and Benjamin Moran, the Assistant Secretary, of the Legation. Henry was the only other clerical help. These three were the whole staff. Although Henry received no salary from the State Department, and worked also as his father's private secretary, he necessarily performed many official duties of the London Legation.

Wilson, Moran, and Henry Adams—under the direction of the Minister—did all the work of the American Legation in London during what were probably the most difficult years any American diplomatic post endured in that city. Wilson seems to have been a negligible person who was eventually eased out. Moran, the Assistant, who had held his job long before the arrival of the Adamses, did the largest share of the unavoidable and important routine work of the office. He was a capable, but not a likable, man. He regarded Mr. Adams, Mrs. Adams, and the younger members of the family, with a critical eye. He confided his bitter, underdog thoughts nightly to a diary, which sheds some amusing, if biased, light upon the daily life of the Legation. Moran feared for his job. He thought that the Minister, as an ambitious father, was planning to push young Henry into his place. He was astounded when later, Wilson being out, the opportunity for this event came, and Henry declined. In the meantime he studied Henry with a mixture of jealousy and reluctant admiration. Moran was a natural snob, and he half envied Henry the airs he could rather easily assume at the big, inhuman parties where the small fry of the diplomatic world stood about uneasily, and were disregarded. There is probably much truth in Moran's spiteful description of Henry at one of the early agonizing parties "pretending that he disliked it yet asking to be presented to everybody of note." [1] He commented on Henry's manners rather carefully one day, noting, "As Henry Adams says after you bowed to the hostess, made some original remarks to her about the weather, and looked at the family pictures, the stock of amusements is exhausted; unless you find some barbarians present with refinement enough, or if you please sufficient confidence in you to present you to a chatty young lady, who will talk, it is a waste of time to remain." [2]

Henry soon saw the spite behind the little sarcasms that Moran affected. He drew back instantly into his shell and put on rather more superiority than he felt. This inflamed Moran all the more, and their personal relations became difficult. Moran treated Henry as an immature boy; Henry tried, less effectively, to ignore Moran.

Whatever the personal differences among the three men in the basement, they all worked, with all their might. There were hours of routine copying, reading, and filing. There were whole mornings and afternoons spent listening to the complaints, the fears, the unsolicited advice of visiting Americans. Charles Francis Adams tightened requirements on visas for Americans going home and required an oath of allegiance from each one. Henry became adept at detecting perjury.

In spite of racking anxiety, the members of the Legation had to continue to act as guides for tourists or as escorts for Union mothers and daughters being presented to Queen Victoria. Going to Court was for them all something of a comic excitement. They dressed up immensely for these occasions. The Minister wore a blue naval coat with much gold embroidery and white vest and knee breeches, black shoes with gold buckles, and carried an eagle-headed sword. The dress for the Secretaries, including Henry, was only slightly less resplendent. Moran commented, on the first occasion of their getting themselves dressed for Court: "The whole Legation looked well in this costume. . . . Mr. Adams, altho' a small man, made an excellent appearance, and Mr. Wilson and Mr. H. B. Adams looked exceedingly well." [3]

In spite of a back-breaking routine of Legation work, Henry determined to do something on his own. He hit upon journalism as his way of striking a blow in the war. He had planned, even before leaving Washington, to do something of the sort. He now arranged, through his brother Charles, still fidgeting in Boston as to whether to go to war or not, to send a series of articles to the *New York Times*. He knew the editor, Henry J. Raymond, from his newspaper days in Washington. He intended to furnish Raymond with a sort of gossip column of opinion about the war, the temper of the British, and other lighter matters. His purpose was to inform the American public of the attitude of the British, and perhaps help stave off actual conflict between the two countries. The articles were to be unsigned.

He thought that he might perform a helpful act which would also be an independent act. He was careful not to tell his father what he was doing. He intended consciously, to relieve his father of responsibility for his opinions. Unconsciously, perhaps, he was making a move toward independence of family. He saw that he was tied by the war to a subordinate family role in London just at a time when he was anxious to be independent. He rebelled against this circumstance. He wanted, desperately, to be more than the son of the Minister.

He wrote three articles in May. The first appeared on June

3rd in the *Times* as *From our own Correspondent,* the second, on June 7th, as *Important from England.* They received good space. Adams could feel that he was doing something. He wrote three articles in June, three in July, and continued at this rate for several months. All were published.

His articles ran along easily upon indifferent or light matters—Derby Day, the English hedges, the sights of Rotten Row—in order to catch the eye of the casual reader. Then followed the theme: that forbearance and moderation toward Britain were necessary; let England roar a little; she would calm down, and no harm would be done. Meanwhile, his own nerves were scraped by British arrogance. There was a strike among the masons at this time. Henry was hotly for them and wrote angrily, in a private letter: "Knowing how hardly the lower classes are situated here and how common it is for capitalists to grind them down, one's first sensation is of sympathy for them, and good will toward them. Moreover the object of the present strike does not seem to be extraordinary, nor the action violent or illegal. They are merely doing what they are perfectly justifiable in trying for." [4]

During the summer of 1861, Henry's work on his articles had given him something to think about. He had gained confidence in himself and in the Union. But on August 5th the Legation heard the news of the defeat at Bull Run and his good mood was gone. He wrote to Charles to get him a commission and he would come home. [5] Charles refused. They raged at each other in one letter after another. Henry hesitated. He could have resigned against his father's wishes and gone home to fight. But he stayed, and the Legation became even more desperately busy than it had been before. It was obvious that he was needed where he was.

Events seemed to have decided for him. In writing to Charles, Henry tried to be matter-of-fact about his staying. "Work has increased to such an extent . . . that I am absolutely necessary here. . . . So you need not at present feel any alarm about my blundering home, as you call it, for I promise you fair warning so that you may be down at the wharf to receive me with the towns-people." [6] He sent Charles some money to help outfit him for the war, for Charles had at last decided to go.

Meanwhile, Henry had got into trouble through his writing. He had gone to Manchester for a few days to study the cotton shortage there, and had written an account of his observations. This article was more ambitious than the ones he had been doing for the *Times.* Charles placed it with the *Boston Cour-*

ier, and it was published on the front page on December 6th under the heading *A Visit to Manchester, Extracts from a Private Diary.* Disregarding Charles's instructions to keep it anonymous, the editor identified Henry Adams, the American Minister's son, as the author.

All this happened at a time when British feelings were highly exasperated against America. An American naval vessel, the *San Jacinto,* had stopped a British ship, the *Trent,* on November 8th and by threat of force removed the two Confederate agents Mason and Slidell, who were on their way to England. Exasperated feelings demanded a scapegoat, and Henry was it. His readable article had been reprinted in the Manchester papers on January 4th and 8th and then in extracts in the London *Times* on January 9th. The *Times* commented on January 10th with an editorial at the expense of this young American who had dared to laugh at certain British manners. Here was the opportunity the newspaper world and the public needed just then for ridiculing an American, who was, by a wonderful chance, the son of the American Minister.

The main import of the piece was disregarded. Certain lighter passages, written in a casual, first-person style, were seized upon and held up for scorn. In them Henry had commented upon the dreariness of the London social world and praised Manchester's more bourgeois and saner social life as friendlier and easier. "Manchester society seems to be much more like what one finds in American cities than like that of London. In Manchester, I am told, it is still the fashion for the hosts to see that the guests enjoy themselves." [7]

Certain incautious words he had dropped about the particulars of London parties—the inadequacy of the food, which usually consisted of hard seedcakes and thimblefuls of ice cream—were repeated to the point of nausea. Stripped of context, they sounded quite foolish. Henry heard repetitions of the famous seedcake passage even in the basement office of the Legation. He probably failed to see that Moran's teasings carried some unwilling admiration.

On the night of the excitement, Moran wrote in his diary: "We have had a little fun at his expense and have told him that it is not every boy of 25 who can in six months' residence here extort a leader from *The Times.*" [8] (Moran had put Henry's age at twenty-five; he was actually twenty-three.)

But Henry was hurt out of all proportion to the occasion. It marred his adaptation to the English scene; it kept him, for a long time after this, from even trying. He knew that he

61

could do no more journalism (his contributions to the New York *Times* might similarly be exposed), and he knew that he had hurt his father. For the newspapers had hit the American Minister through his son. What was hardest to bear, his father said not a word to his son. Henry could not even apologize.

Thus in early winter of 1861, Henry was at a low pitch. On December 28th he wrote to Charles: "For my own part I am tired of this life. Every attempt I have made to be of use has failed more or less completely." [9]

There was actual, as well as temperamental, reason for depression. Henry's level-headed father thought in December that he might be asked to leave within a month. But Henry's despair was compounded of personal, as well as national, feelings. He had made as little headway in his social, as in his journalistic, efforts. He had wanted to conquer the great world of society and had come off bruised in that war too. He had believed that there might be greatness behind the bigness. When he found stiffness, dullness, empty formality much more prevalent than brightness and wit, he was youthfully disgusted. He wrapped himself more tightly in his false cloak of superiority. He was lonely, caught in a kind of paralysis of effort. He continued to go to the parties. He saw much of the life of the times come and go at his father's. But he himself seemed outside the liveliness.

With journalism gone, and social life more painful than pleasurable, Henry was stung back into his crab's shell of solitude. But he gained something in his loneliness. He began to think, and found that he could use his mind hard without getting tired; that he could exercise it and it would not fag. He found his mental powers developing at an extraordinary pace.

If he could no longer write for pay or for patriotism, he could write for himself. Luckily he found a subject that carried him through months of disinterested difficult labor. He remembered, by chance, a few words dropped one day by John Gorham Palfrey, at home in Boston, on the subject of the veracity of the Pocahontas story. He had not paid attention at the time, but the germ of the idea had stayed with him, and now it haunted him.

What if he should find out the truth of the old story? What was there to the old legend about the Indian girl's saving the Captain from death? How much of a liar was old John Smith? What other sources, than his dubious word, were there? Had not Pocahontas come to England? Would there not be other accounts of her here in England?

By March 20th of the next year, 1862, almost a year from the time he had first landed in England, he wrote to the New England historian:

I am "fou" of the Pocahontas matter. . . . I hardly know whether I ought not to be ashamed of myself for devoting myself to a literary toy like this, in these times, when I ought to be helping or trying to help the great cause. But my pen is forced to keep away from political matters, unless I want to bring the English press down on my head again, and in society I am a failure. So perhaps the thing is excusable, especially as it is in some sort a flank, or rather a rear attack, on the Virginia aristocracy, who will be utterly gravelled by it if it is successful. I can imagine to myself the shade of John Randolph turn green at that quaint picture which Strachey gives of Pocahontas "clothed in virgin purity" and "wanton" at that, turning somersets with all the little ragamuffins and "decayed serving men's" sons of Jamestown.[10]

His method was strict and simple But it was to have a cumulative effectiveness. He planned to demonstrate, in the Captain's own words, how Smith's story grew and grew through the years. He would place excerpts from his first account, *A True Relation,* written in 1608, side by side with the second account, the *Generall Historie,* written in 1624. The dramatic rescue was not mentioned in the first account; it had appeared only in the second, after the other principal actor in it—Pocahontas—had died. Adams planned to reinforce his point by quoting other firsthand accounts recently rediscovered in England. The evidence that Smith lied, or at least enlarged, would then be clearly established for the first time.

But Adams, in the completed article, was to do more than tear down. From each source—Smith, Wingfield, and Hamor—he selected and ordered descriptions and reactions, and by arranging and contrasting, made stand, clear and whole, a complete characterization of Captain John Smith. As he worked to clear away the literary underbrush, Adams developed a sort of fondness for the braggart, and a tenderness, too, for the "wanton" Pocahontas.

This was Henry Adams's first attempt at writing history. It was a small-scale work, but it was a first-rate job. In doing it, he learned how to work with documents, how to discriminate and to select among a large collection of facts, how to build the narrative into a dramatic whole, how to maintain a particular tone. When the piece was finally finished after the war (he could not complete it in 1862—he could only peck away at it in his spare time), it was to be a competent and entertaining piece of work. It was to have both the evidence of scholarship and the evidence of something above and beyond scholarship—a light, keen air of discernment and enjoyment. It was Adams's first mature piece of historical writing. It can be read with as much pleasure today as when it was first set down.

With this pressure upon him—pressure of the war outside, pressure of thought inside—Adams matured rapidly. He was lonely in 1862 and 1863, but his life had, through his own efforts, become interesting. His whole being was pricked to effort. He broke out in all directions at once. He became interested in drawings and in contemporary verse. He studied geology and biology. He read American history, finding it now personal to himself.

And as he found ways to use his mind, he began to climb tentatively out of one despair after another, each time achieving a slightly more stable adjustment. He began again to be personally ambitious; his ambitions now were complex and private; they had little to do with diplomacy or society, but were concerned with the subterranean life of thought.

It was to his brother Charles, now a soldier in Virginia, that he wrote such thoughts as were sharable. Charles too was changing. His life was an intensified practicality concerned with survival for himself, his men, and his horses. His war became Henry's war. Charles wrote to London whenever he could. He wanted his family to see his careless efficiency, his new un-Bostonian free-and-easiness.

It is not surprising that Henry felt occasionally put down by the news from Virginia. "Meanwhile it worries me all the time to be leading this thoroughly useless life abroad while you are acting such grand parts at home." [11] Yet for the Londoners, and particularly for Henry, the war opened new vistas. One of these was the new role that science would have in the world of the future.

The mood he felt was an enthusiasm qualified by an intellectual shudder. On April 11, 1862, Henry discoursed to his brother on the outdating of the British warships—a fact discovered as soon as the news of the *Merrimac* had become public:

Only a fortnight ago they discovered that their whole wooden navy was useless. . . . I don't think as yet they have dared to look their position in the face. People begin to talk vaguely about the end of the war and eternal peace, just as though human nature was changed by the fact that Great Britain's sea-power is knocked in the head. But for my private part, I think I see a thing or two. . . . Our good country the United States is left to a career that is positively unlimited except by the powers of the imagination. And for England there is still greatness and safety, if she will draw her colonies around her, and turn her hegemony into a Confederation of British nations.

You may think all this nonsense, but I tell you these are great times. Man has mounted science, and is now run away with. I firmly believe that before many centuries more, science will be the master of man. The engines he will have invented will be beyond his strength to control. Some day science may have the existence of mankind in its power, and the human race commit suicide by blowing up the world. Not only shall we be able to cruize in space, but I see no reason why some future generation wouldn't give it another rotary motion so that every zone would receive in turn its due portion of heat and light. . . .[12]

These were brave thoughts, but toward the close of the same letter he could betray his heart: "The 24th did well at Newbern. I wish to God I had been with it." [13]

He continued to stretch out feelers of exploration. He read at a greate rate. On January 9, 1863, he wrote to Charles, "I am deep in international law and political economy, dodging from one to the other." [14] On February 20th he stated: "My promised land of occupation, however; my burial place of ambition and always, is geology and science. I wish I could send you Sir Charles Lyell's new book on the *Antiquity of Man*." [15] Spring came. He studied De Tocqueville and John Stuart Mill. "I have learned to think De Tocqueville my model, and I study his life and works as the Gospel of my private religion. The great principle of democracy is still capable of rewarding a conscientious servant. And I doubt me much whether the advance of years will increase my toleration of its faults. Hence, I think I see in the distance a vague and unsteady light in the direction which I needs must gravitate, so soon as the present disturbing influences are removed." [16]

As the months went on, the shell around him began to crumble. The dun fabric of his life began to take on a kind of color. He began to discover that after all there were acts he could perform, not only for his father and his country, but for himself.

First of all it became apparent that he was not useless in the more important work of the Legation. The Minister used him in work requiring judgment and initiative. He sent him to Paris to observe Louis Napoleon's maneuverings in regard to the war. He sent him to Denmark with diplomatic gifts for the King.

In London, Henry began to look about him more objectively than he had done before. It was as if he had just begun to see the great city's show for the first time. He saw London and the whole of Britain stirred to the depths by Lincoln's Emancipation Proclamation. He attended various workers' meetings as unofficial representative of America and was impressed by the validity of the emotion they expressed. "The old revolutionary leaven is working steadily." [17]

He had the wit to see a connection between the successes of the Union—including the Proclamation—and the working of this revolutionary leaven in London. His father was in a position where a delicate touch might move much. "We have strength enough already to shake the very crown on the Queen's head if we are compelled to employ it all," [18] he wrote to Charles. "The conduct of the affairs of that great republic which though wounded itself almost desperately, can yet threaten to tear down the rulers of the civilised world, by merely assuming her place at the head of the march of democracy, is something to look upon. I wonder whether we shall be forced to call upon the brothers of the great fraternity to come in all lands to the assistance and protection of its head. These are lively times, oh, Hannibal." [19]

What was important to Henry Adams in these days was his coming to see that what his father did really mattered. He saw Charles Francis Adams, the American Minister to the Court of St. James's—one particular person—exerting an observable influence on the course of history. It was a sight that stirred his imagination.

In winning his diplomatic battle with Lord John Russell and stopping the Laird rams from delivery to the Confederacy, Charles Francis Adams was established in the Kingdom as a personage. The British admired him as an excellent and honest opponent. He became popular.

Charles Francis's son partook in his diplomatic victory. This was also the season when Vicksburg fell and when the fateful battle of Gettysburg was fought. Henry's imagination was inflamed and exalted. He realized that at home a new nation was coming into being.

He wrote home to the brother at war: "It's a pity that we're civilized. What a grand thing Homer would have made of it. . . . There's a magnificence about the pertinacity of the struggle, lasting so many days, and closing, so far as we know on the eve of our single national anniversary, with the whole nation bending over it, that makes even these English cubs silent." [20] So he wrote on July 17th, on the news just received about the fighting in Pennsylvania.

And he went on: "Dreadful I suppose it is, and God knows I feel anxious and miserable enough at times, but I doubt whether any of us will ever be able to live contented again in times of peace and laziness. Our generation has been stirred up from its lowest layers and there is that in its history which will stamp every member of it until we are all in our graves. We cannot be commonplace." [21] Thus, danger brought exaltation. And as this crisis passed, and the North moved a little closer to winning, Henry Adams entered a new phase of his life in London.

Chapter 6

A London Bachelor

IN AUGUST, 1863, Henry Adams, aged twenty-five, and his brother Brooks, aged fifteen, took a vacation from the house in Portland Place. They went away from the family, the city, and the war, and turned their noses toward the edges of civilization. This holiday to Scotland marked the end of one part of Henry's life in England, the beginning of another, better part.

The weather was bad. Transportation was poor. Brooks got sick. There were long stretches of boredom. Yet it was a real holiday, a real change. For Henry the trip came to be associated in his mind with a relaxation of the tension in which he had lived for two years. The war at home was not quite so hopeless. His own war in London was not so desperate. His personal situation was beginning to have some compensations. In the western isles of Scotland he shrugged his shoulders, heaved a sigh of relief, and turned a corner into a new emotional climate.

One of his letters to the soldier-brother Charles fixes almost to the hour the change he underwent. Crossing the arm of the sea to the Isle of Skye, stretched out for three hours upon the seat of the boat, watching the forbidding mountains of that remote island grow larger, he let go of something which had tied him in complex knots for many months.

Civil wars, disgust and egotism, social fuss and worry, responsibility and worry, were as far at least as the moon. They left me free on the Sound of Sleat.[1]

When he came home to London, he found that he was now better able to cope with the city and its complex life. He had caught a sort of idea of its greatness by this time, and he enjoyed being a part of it, even if a small, comparatively idle, and unimportant part. Adams's conception of himself, at whatever age, determined his behavior. Now he conceived his part as that of a London gentleman. He could survive in London. He had found his mode. He was a London bachelor, who took part in all the frenzy, but who was not fooled by it.

A person, or rather a personage, who helped Henry Adams to become a London gentleman was Richard Monckton Milnes. He had been drawn to the American Legation by sympathy with the Union cause. He was a friend of Henry's father first, then, his. A dandy, a versifier, a liberal, an authority on Keats, a friend of America, a man of keen mind posing as a dawdler, he lent the younger Adams some of his own audacity and courage in society. He fed him, talked to him, showed him off, in other words, threw him, good-humoredly, into the social frying pan. He was responsible for young Adams meeting Swinburne, among others, and probably watched Henry's astonishment with some sardonic amusement of his own.[2]

Henry found another friend casually, upon a doorstep. This was Charles Milnes Gaskell, a distant relative of the great Monckton Milnes, a young man of his own age, with no distance of position or experience between them. The two young men met one morning when they came together at Sir Henry Holland's door for breakfast.[3] Gaskell was just finishing at Cambridge. He knew Adams's cousin, William Everett, who was studying there. Henry called on the two of them: his difficult New England cousin, and his easy new English friend. They made him free of their college world. In London he and Gaskell were soon inseparable. They were friends the rest of their lives.

At home at No. 5 Mansfield Street, Portland Place, in the large black city of London, Henry Adams was securely anchored by the war, unknowing of his future, and puzzled by it. He was caught, he knew, in a kind of trap, but it was a trap whose limits he now began to explore more happily. From the middle part of the year 1863 until his departure from London in 1868, he would sway many times from depression to exhilaration and back again, but he would not go so far from stability as he had in the first years of the war.

He wrote large, lonely thoughts to Charles, telling him in October, 1863: "The truth is, everything in this universe has its regular waves and tides. Electricity, sound, the wind, and I believe every part of organic nature will be brought some day within this law. But my philosophy teaches me, and I firmly believe it, that the laws which govern animated beings will be ultimately found to be at bottom the same with those which rule inanimate nature, and, as I entertain a profound conviction of the littleness of our kind, and of the curious enormity of creation, I am quite ready to receive with pleasure any basis for a systematic conception of it all." [4] But the end of the letter was, as often happened, a heartfelt cry, quite out of keeping with his foregoing self-possession: "I am becoming superstitious. I believe Nick Anderson's killed. Write me that he's not yet gone under, and I will say defiance to the vague breath of similar chimaeras. . . ." [5]

He wrote disquieting thoughts to Charles during the long lonely midnight hours in the Legation, but his daily existence was less chilly. He was still very shy of women, and was capable of an almost adolescent silliness about them in his letters to his English friend Charles Gaskell. But with some friends of his own sex he was at ease. Eating, drinking, riding, and talking now formed a considerable portion of his day. The war was less acute. He had more time to amuse himself. He got away oftener from the manual labor of the Legation office.

He had come to appreciate his own good seat in society. He could be one of a group that heard Browning tell what he thought of eternity. He could read a copy of the new anthology *The Golden Treasury,* fresh from the hand of its editor, his friend Francis Palgrave. He would pass the book on to Charles to carry across Virginia in his saddlebag.

He tried to subside from an eagerness which could disappoint, into a tolerant and equable habit of observation and participation. With Charles Gaskell and other friends—Ralph Palmer, Robert Cunliffe, Francis Palgrave, and others—he could chance attendance at the big parties, or skip them, without feeling utterly downed. He and his friends made their own parties and constituted their own resources. Since they were, none of them, of an age or a position to make history, or to block it, they contented themselves with witty comment on those who did.

Henry might wonder about his American friends. What command did young Lee hold now in the desperate South? Where was Nick Anderson? How did John Hay like his job with the President? Yet everyday life bound him to London and London's horizon. The world he had shared with those others seemed far away and irrecoverable.

The thought of Henry Richardson, and the occasional sight of him in Paris, reminded him very little of their old secure world at school. For Richardson's situation was as changed as his own, and far more insecure. Richardson had lost touch with his family and friends in the besieged South, yet he had determined, with the artist's one-track mind, to hang on to his work in Paris. He barely lived, and was, more than once, half hungry. He studied and worked day and night merely to exist.

70

Yet when Henry saw him, he was the same large-natured, humorous Richardson. His gaiety hid a force and a purpose that no circumstance could baffle.

Far too, from Henry, far from their former shared environment, was his brother Charles, facing unimaginable sights, leading an unimaginable life as a cavalry officer. He, too, belonged to a world of change rather than to one of stability. Like Henry, he was cut off, irrevocably, from his pre-war life.

Henry had never lost a sense of guilt for being where he was rather than where Charles was. He had, at intervals, a sense of nightmare, of awakening with a kind of shudder to the triviality of his life. At such moments he regarded the London bachelor's life with great distaste. While Charles fought in Virginia, while Sherman grew great in Georgia, he, Henry Adams, went on a picnic in Shropshire. Thus must have run his thought, with some tinge of bitterness.

Yet the picnic in Shropshire was important. It had some intrinsic value. For at Wenlock Abbey in Shropshire, Henry Adams, a foolish and proud young man, caught a glimpse of the intoxication of history, of the allurement of science, and saw himself in a relationship of some importance to those studies.

Henry called his stay with the Gaskells a picnic because they thought of their stay there in that manner, themselves. Their home was in Yorkshire. The Abbey in Shropshire was an expensive toy, not yet completely repaired or fitted out for living. Yet the chilly grandeur of the place enlisted Adams's sympathy. He liked it better for not being bourgeois and comfortable.

Such a curious edifice I never saw, and the winds of Heaven permeated freely the roof, not to speak of the leaden windows. We three, Mrs. Gaskell, Gaskell and I, dined in a room where the Abbot or the Prior used to feast his guests; a hall on whose timber roof and great oak rafters, the wood fire threw a red shadow forty feet above our heads. I slept in a room whose walls were all stone, three feet thick, with barred, square Gothic windows and diamond panes; and at my head a small oak door opened upon a winding staircase in the wall, long since closed up at the bottom, and whose purpose is lost. . . . In the evening we sat in the dusk in the Abbot's own room of state, and there I held forth in grand after-dinner eloquence, all my social, religious and philosophical theories, even in the very holy-of-holies of what was once the heart of a religious community.[6]

Here he lost his shyness and shared his ideas, whether they were nonsense or not. He badly needed an audience, and the

Gaskells made a good one. He not only found good listeners and told them what he thought and dreamed, but he found a new relish for the ordinary good things of life. He awoke to the sensuous joys of good wine, good food, and unspoiled country scenery.

It was by such sudden leaps that Henry Adams found himself. A picnic in Shropshire, a boat-crossing in Scotland: they helped him to discover himself. No time could be too short, no place too unimportant for such a transformation.

Wenlock would gather significance as the years went by. The place, the people, and the countryside were to become a reference peg from which to hang, in later writings, several of his major preoccupations. The name Wenlock would support several pages of speculation upon his discovery of geology, evolution, and the relativity of truth. Not much of this development of thought belonged to the early mute seeing of the place, but the beginning was there. It was a starting place; as Berlin had been; and Dresden; and Washington.

Curious and difficult was this time of his life. He was dragged back and forth from pleasure to pain, from importance to abasement. Other people's doings were obviously important; his were not. Yet in himself he believed in these incommunicable trifles of emotion about subjects as remote as the moon from war and British neutrality and Southern privateersmen. This bemuddling of his interests could not but make him feel some guilt.

Just such a mixture of enjoyment and guilty exasperation did he feel in the early months of 1865. He had been pressed into service as tour conductor for his mother, sister, and brother, who needed a vacation from London. Henry found himself acting in this particular humiliating capacity just at the time when, in America, the Confederacy was breaking up and many men over there were dying either to accomplish the breakup or to prevent it.

Adams managed his tour efficiently, but contemptuously. He hated himself whenever he discovered that he was having fun. Events in America were so much more important than his courier's job. He wrote to Charles Gaskell from Sorrento on March 3, 1865:

My dear Gask:—Since I last saw you, I have made a ponderous march across Europe. It took precisely four weeks to reach this place, never sleeping more than three nights, in the same house. I took a vettura at Nice and we did the Cornice, coming down to Spezia in that way. Our whole journey was a success, but that part of it was a triumph, and I consider myself to have earned the laurels of high Generalship in my skilful direction of this arduous campaign in mid-winter.[7]

While he traveled, Richmond fell, Lee surrendered, and Lincoln was killed. In a mood of self-abasement, Henry wrote to Charles from Florence on May 10th: "I can't help a feeling of amusement at looking back on my letters and thinking how curiously inapt they must have been to the state of things about you. Victories and assassinations, joys, triumphs, sorrows and gloom; all at fever point, with you; while I prate about art and draw letters from the sunniest and most placid of subjects. I have already buried Mr. Lincoln under the ruins of the Capitol, along with Caesar. . . ."[8]

The distance separating the Legation from America seemed all at once to widen. The death of Lincoln meant the end of something for them too. Just what, they could not yet tell. The Adamses, in London, began to try to feel out the character of the Johnson Administration.

Kept still in London—his father was being held to his post by the new President—Henry was restless. He wrote to Charles on July 14, 1865: "Politics seem queerly confused in America. Sumner, Dana and the rest are in an amusing provincial hurry to get into operation. Why so fast? We have done with slavery. Free opinion, education and law have now entrance into the south. Why assume that they are powerless, and precipitate hopeless confusion? Let us give time; it doesn't matter how long."[9]

Change, coming faster than one could calculate, seemed rushing at them all. Yet, personally, Henry felt that he stagnated. The quiet seemed shameful. It was like being left behind while all one's contemporaries whirled ahead in a rush.

Henry Adams's oldest brother, John Quincy, was already coping with the difficulties of reconstruction. At home in Massachusetts, where he had remained to look after the family's financial affairs, John Quincy was achieving notoriety. He had taken the unpopular side in New England and was advocating moderation in reconstruction. He opposed the now dominant fanaticism of the Republican party. He was also one of the first to scent the corruption that had come with victory, and to speak out against it.

Significantly, Henry thought his brother John the most to be admired of his family just then. He was at least doing something. What if he himself were ever so preciously *being?* Henry did not admire mental action. The perfectly palpable, crude, and open political act was to him, then and always, the highest kind of action.

In June, 1865, another doer, young John Hay, appeared briefly in London. He was on the way to Paris to serve as Secretary of the Legation. He brought with him a fresh sense of what Lincoln's death meant. But Hay was resilient. He was ready for a change, and had even asked for a foreign appointment before Lincoln's death. He had not had the years of Legation work which Henry had had to numb him. He was elated by the prospect of new sights, and expectant of fun.

Thurlow Weed would write of him shortly: "Hay is a bright, gifted young man, with agreeable manners and refined tastes. I don't believe he has been spoiled, though he has been much exposed." [10]

Henry Adams's soldier-contemporaries were finished with their war, too. Charles Adams was at Quincy wondering what to do with himself. Nicholas Anderson was safe and planning to be married. Rooney Lee had survived. Wilkinson and Robertson James, the soldier-sons of Henry James, Sr., were at home in Cambridge. They, like Major Henry Higginson and his wife, Ida, planned to return to the South. They meant to try farming with Negro wage labor. Both the James brothers and Major and Mrs. Higginson were to fail. They did not understand how complete a breakdown had come about in the South. And ruined Southerners were not sympathetic. They were in no mood to distinguish behind high-minded and low-minded carpetbaggers.

Ida Higginson's brother, Alexander Agassiz, was in Cambridge, tending his father's natural-history museum while Louis Agassiz and a team of young Americans collected specimens from the Amazon. Among the young men was William James, hoping that the experience would help him make up his mind as to a career. He too was undecided what to do.

Alex Agassiz, lacking the theatrical flare of his father, worked quietly at home. He did not care greatly for being a museum keeper, and worked, privately, on several research problems. It was at this time that he published his first results: *Acalephae* and *Embryology of the Starfish*. Thus began, modestly, a great career.

The fourth of the James brothers, Henry, Jr., was still at Cambridge, living at home, trying to write, but, like William, restless, undecided, unsettled. He spent vacations at Newport talking art with the young painter, John La Farge, who had had, before the war, the envied advantage of a season in Paris.

Already gone abroad was another young American, Augustus Saint-Gaudens, the immigrant shoemaker's son, gone on a pittance to satisfy a curiosity as to whether he could make himself into a sculptor. He was just ending an adolescence of work as apprentice to a cameo cutter in New York City, work to which he had been apprenticed, In European fashion, when he was a tense, white-faced boy of thirteen. All the years between he had bent his back in this hard labor and missed his growing up. But he had discovered the Cooper Union and studied in its free classes at night during those years in which the Union soldiers had marched down Broadway on the way to the war.

With the war over, Henry Richardson returned to the United States. He did not go South, where there was no work and no hope, but returned to the North, where his fiancée was, and where there was some hope for architecture. He had been well trained in France, and had had even the beginnings of a successful career there. But he came back to tie himself to the alien half of his own country.

He married and lived precariously without work for many months. At last he was given a church to build, a Unitarian church in Springfield, Massachusetts. He welcomed this first commission with tears of relief and an exclamation: "That is all I wanted—*a chance.*" [11]

These names—Hay, Agassiz, James, La Farge, Saint-Gaudens, Richardson—were in the shadows as yet. But they were to come into the light. And these men and their works were to be entangled with Henry Adams's future emotions, thoughts, and acts. They were to be crucial elements in his life and in his understanding of the life of his country. These men were to be—and Henry Adams was to be one of them— a kind of yeast in the national existence during the years between the Civil War and the First World War.

The great American war had changed much. The ferment of post-war life changed much more. Even in the comparatively small world of the American arts, there was a new, clean slate for a beginning over again. Young William Dean Howells brought the freshness of Ohio to Boston when he came there to be assistant editor of the *Atlantic Monthly*. The Anglo-Irish newspaper correspondent Godkin struck a new note in his weekly the *Nation*. Word of the magazine reached Henry Adams in London. He asked Charles to send him a subscription.

Other shiftings were downward. After an almost forgotten fame, Herman Melville published no more novels. Whitman, crammed with war, drifted away from activity into disregard.

Nothing of this time was settled or certain. The arts were the least element in the national life.

It was the westward movement that was swaying American minds and pocketbooks. Clarence King came into Washington and, in spite of youth and an unknown name, charmed appropriations and position out of Senators and generals. When he had got what he wanted, he went West again and began the ten-year-job of the Fortieth Parallel Survey. Thus, before Henry Adams came home to the new America, this friend of the future was already engaged in mapping and surveying it.

It would be untrue to say that Henry Adams in London was conscious of all the various examples of movement and change in which his generation was already engaged in America. Most of it he did not know at all. Yet it is perfectly true to say that in the later London years he was conscious of change on the other side of the ocean.

He had grown into the life of the city of London. He was almost at home there. Yet, however agreeable the diversions and the studies of the city were, he felt that his life there moved in a circle. Word from the other side of the Atlantic told of life streaming off in a kind of staggering line straight ahead into the unknown. He was impatient of the known good of London, impatient to try the unknown good of his own country. It was no wonder that every visitor from home was welcomed greedily and was subjected to a searching questioning as to what had happened to the United States in the last few years.

Two such visitors were Dr. Robert William Hooper and his daughter, Marian. They sat down to dinner at the Legation, among other guests, on Derby Day, May 16, 1866.[12] Presumably, Henry Adams and Marian Hooper met on this day for the first time. Henry might have recalled her brother, Edward, who was at Harvard part of his time there; his friends Henry Richardson and Benjamin Crowninshield had known him.

We have no recorded word from either Henry or Marian Hooper as to the importance of this first meeting. They had Boston Bay in common—the Bay, the city, and all the unconscious assumptions of New England. The geography of growing up was a common one. The Agassiz family might have made another link; Marian had attended Mrs. Agassiz' school for girls in Cambridge while her brother went to Harvard.

We have no way of knowing how crucial this meeting was, but it is possible to picture them as they were when they confronted each other across the Legation table. Henry was twenty-eight. The London years had matured him; his forehead was higher, the hair still dark and generous, worn long and swept back behind the ears; he had the mustache of buccaneer, bold eyebrows, eyes deep in their sockets and piercing; nose eagle-like; the mouth well cut and incisive.

Marian Hooper was twenty-three, slender, dark, not strikingly handsome. Her mother died when she was five; she was accustomed to ordering her own life; she adored the one parent she had left, and was agreeably imperious in her relationship with him. Dr. Hooper, possessed of enough money to live without practicing, had given up active medicine, and cultivated the gentlemanly arts. He had designed this holiday in Europe for his daughter's pleasure. Pleasure, for the doctor and his daughter, was always to mean, not excess, but a luxury of discrimination.

Boston, Marblehead, Beverly, and Cambridge had molded and perhaps limited Marian Hooper. She was always to regard people and things outside certain bounds as alien. But within her limitations she was flexible and brave. Her keynote was a pathos of eagerness and sensitivity in the midst of provincial limitedness.

Captain Wendell Holmes was her friend, as were William and Henry James, Thomas Sergeant Perry and his sister Margaret, John La Farge, whom Margaret Perry married, and Minny Temple, the exquisite young cousin of the Jameses.

Henry James, a few years later, would link together Clover (Marian) Hooper and Minny Temple with a few revealing words. In a movement of distaste at what he then conceived as British stiffness and the British woman's dowdiness, he was to write: "I revolt from their dreary, deathly want of—what shall I call it? Clover Hooper has it—intellectual grace—Minny Temple has it—moral spontaneity." [13]

When she came into the Legation, Clover, or Marian, Hooper brought an innocent zest with her, and an untried youthfulness. Perhaps she told them, that night at the dinner table, of her strenuous enjoyment of the Grand Review of the armies which she had seen in Washington just after the end of the war. In the white heat of that occasion, she had written to a friend, "For one week I have had my eyes wide open and my ears and my mouth, and my pulse and heart going like race horses." [14] At any rate, the Legation liked the Hoopers and asked them back for the Fourth of July. Soon, however, they continued on their travels, touring France, Switzerland, and Italy. Adams did not see her again for some time.

While Henry Adams scrutinized Americans from across the ocean, and tried to deduce America from them, he reacted violently to the political news. "At this distance I am very open to deception, but it does seem to me as though everything in America had turned a back somersault. I find the pure northern Congress, just such a one as we prayed for twenty years ago, violating the rights of minorities more persistently than the worst pro-slavery Congress ever could do. . . . I find all our old friends in Massachusetts, those who suffered so bitterly as a minority, utterly savage, intolerant and intolerable towards minorities now that they have themselves become a majority." [15]

America had moved beyond his ken. The Londoners were reduced to watching and waiting. Henry Adams turned again to writing. He had now the time as well as the inclination. He looked up what he had written on John Smith and began wrestling with it once more. Another American, Charles Deane, had recently brought out a new edition of Smith's first narrative. Adams had been in touch with Deane through Palfrey, and knew that Deane deserved much credit for the proper unearthing of the Smith facts. He saw that his own manuscript should be recast in the form of a review of Deane.

"Mr. Deane has left nothing for me to do, so far as I can see. I may certainly review his book and make, I am almost sure, an interesting magazine article out of it," he wrote to Palfrey.[16] Continuing in this letter of July 5, 1866: "I am absolutely ignorant who edits, and what is edited. If, however, you know any of those wonderful beings who read M.S.S. and can get him to promise me room for any particular number of his honored but heavy publication, I will be sure to be ready. The thing would want about thirty-five pages of the *North American*." [17]

Palfrey secured Adams's publication in the *North American*. Adams, in the triumph of having an editor's attention (Charles Eliot Norton's), sent two articles rather than one. The second was his *British Finance in 1816*. Both were published; *Smith* in the January, 1867, number, and *British Finance* in the April number. The success of the first article both in the United States and in England, where Henry Adams's friend Francis Palgrave read it and marked his copy furiously with underlinings and exclamations points, encouraged Adams in the year 1867 into a fury of writing.

For the sake of further sales, he shifted his emphasis to finance. There was, at this time, a great floundering among politicians, generals, financial advisers, bankers, and borrowers over the difficulties caused by wartime inflation. The great question of the hour was whether the Government should redeem the greenbacks issued during the war. Adams treated the problem by reference in his second financial article, *Bank of England Restrictions of 1797–1821.*

His moral for contemporary America was not to despair. Britain had at least resumed specie payment in a similar crisis without ill effect. But Adams arranged the evidence to show that since other than financial matters entered into national depression or prosperity, the situation would have righted itself anyway, whether specie payment was resumed or not. This viewpoint, aimed implicitly at the American situation, did not exactly support the sound-money position, but it did not oppose it either.

The article was all dry gristle, made up facts, discriminations, sequences, without any allurement of surface charm. It was good writing of a kind, but without overtones. It lacked the particular good of *John Smith*—a multiplication of reference and a richness of association.

In the spring of his last year abroad, Adams found another subject. This was geology, his gateway to science. Sir Charles Lyell had brought out his tenth and importantly revised edition of his *Principles of Geology*. Adams took it upon himself to review the book, not completing the job until he returned to the United States. In going over the older man's slow, honest, and conservative acceptances and rejections of evolution, Adams reviewed his own reactions to the subject. Set to thinking on fossils and stratifications in the lazy days at Wenlock, he now read the contemporary master, and tried within himself to solidify his groping thoughts.

In the review he underlined areas of cleavage between Lyell and Darwin and Louis Agassiz. He underscored particularly Lyell's wrestling with Agassiz's glacial theories which seemed to have unsettled, or shaken, the idea of an altogether gradual and uniform development of the earth's crust, and the species living upon that precarious crust.

Young Adams warmly supported Lyell's late acceptance of Darwin's ideas. He put himself on record as a promoter of those notions which "many excellent men consider revolting." [18]

Occasionally in the review there occurs a flash of Adams's own characteristic later style. "Sir Charles wanders among the monotonous and flowerless forests of coal-measures without saddening our spirits, and describes the enormous reptiles of the lias in language as calm and little sensational as though ichthyosauri were still gambolling in shoals along the banks of the Thames." [19] And this: "We find in so old a deposit as the oolite the delicate stamp of the dragonfly undisturbed, though mountains have been raised near it, and every form of animal and vegetable life has been repeatedly changed since its entombment, while from the miocene strata we are shown so strangely evanescent a memorial as the tender pattern of a butterfly's wing on which are still to be traced colors that may well be twenty million years old." [20]

Henry Adams wanted, in his capacity as reviewer, to state an adherence, to say that he, too, was of the new age.

The review of Lyell's book was the last piece of writing Adams began in Europe. From the early part of 1868 he knew that his time there was limited. He went about saying goodbye to places he had come to love.

At last, in July, 1868, the Adams family packed their belongings, closed the door of the house in London, and turned homeward. The seven years of exile, now ended, had been important for the fourth child of the family. He was no longer a child, or a boy. He was going home to America a little out of step with his native land, yet within himself more of a person, more concentrated in his gifts and his faults, anxious to do and be.

He had broadened his interests through study and writing so that his intellect had become firm and flexible and capable of expressing emotion and thought. He had exercised a talent for writing and made it into a skill. His personal barometer, after much seasick wavering, had steadied. Yet several of the darker elements of his character had been defined and individualized. Immobility had confirmed a minor strain of morbidity; doubt, constriction and bafflement had inflicted permanent wounds. Isolation and inaction had made him, at times, doubt the efficacy of any action. A newly acquired fatalism (to which he almost gaily pledged himself) had helped to sooth personal frustrations. But this was a tentative pessimism. It would require tragedy, and not just the pinpricks of disappointment, to sweep him over into an emotional, as well as intellectual, acceptance of necessity.

Public affairs were still his window to the world. Through watching his father's success in England, he had had reinforced in the depths of his being his inherited Adams idea that a good man could do much good, or at least exert force. Such a belief, in spite of a superficial and rational pessimism, would lead him to a continuity of effort—in journalism, reform, and education—through several decades of busy and ambitious living.

Going home to America in the summer of 1868, he was fortunate in all his outward circumstances. He half believed that he himself was going to be an exception to the working out of his great principle of determinism. Pride and activity were his medicines, and it was toward prideful and youthful activity that he was going.

Chapter 7

Washington Reporter

IN THE FALL of 1868 a new actor came on the scene in Washington. The capital was still dusty, still provincial. Yet it was a true city—small enough to be a stage for those who would be actors, attentive enough to enjoy a well played role. The newcomer was not to be a major figure on this stage, but he would find here a satisfying small part among newspapermen, reformers, assistant secretaries, special commissioners, and unrepentant politicians.

This was Henry Adams, home from London, particularly at home in Washington. He had tried New England once more, pretending to study law in Boston, dallying in Newport, nervously putting his feet into the current of the newspaper world of New York, and not quite liking the tempo or the temperature of these places. He was glad, after three months of tentativeness, to say goodbye to the North and emigrate southward once more.

He came into the city with William M. Evarts, who had picked up the lonely young man on a street in New York and asked him to come to his house in Washington until he could find a place of his own. Adams enjoyed Evart's humor, as he had in London when Evarts had visited the Legation as a special agent of the President. And the Attorney General's house was a good place from which to view the city after being gone from it almost eight years. Evarts took Adams to see President Johnson. The visit did not spoil Adams's eccentric view of the strength in that small, harassed man.

Other men of the older, heroic generation of the war were still—in this limbo between Johnson and Grant—in prominent places. But Adams found that a great distance in age and viewpoint had come between him and them. Charles Sumner was yet the great man of the Senate and could still smile on Henry in spite of the break that had come between him and the Adamses. Seward was still Secretary of State, but he no longer talked as he once did. Adams went to call on Salmon P. Chase. He learned to respect Hamilton Fish. But he turned more and more to the younger, impatient men of the town. He had outgrown his adolescent worship of older men. He wanted to do something with his own hands, joining in the effort with others of his own age, men who shared the same jokes and who looked at things with a certain impudence.

Another young New Englander, Moorfield Storey, who had come down from Boston to be Sumner's secretary, wrote home about a new friend.

"I have met recently Henry Adams, Charles Francis's son, who is here for the winter to study literature, and I find him very agreeable," Storey wrote to Miss Helen Appleton on January 3, 1869. "I dined with him last Monday at Mr. Sumner's, and after dinner had quite a chat with him, I arguing that the politics of the country, and its life generally, were purer and better than they were eighty years ago, and he the reverse." [1]

Later, in a fragment of autobiography, Storey described his first sight of Adams—"a strange young man . . . who was monopolizing the conversation, as it seemed to me, and laying down the law with a certain assumption. I took quite a prejudice against him during this brief acquaintance, but the next day I met him in the street and he was so charming and his voice so pleasant that my prejudice vanished, and we formed a friendship which was lasting." [2] The two young men shared their social, as well as political, pleasures. They were to suffer the reputation, and not deny it very heartily, of being two of the three best dancers of the Capital. The waltzing was concurrent with the arguing.

One must picture Henry Adams at this time as an opinionated young man, full of enjoyment as well as fight. With such friends as Moorfield Storey and Sam Hoar, the son of Judge Ebenezer Hoar, of Massachusetts, he formed a kind of front. The whole tribe of irreverent newspapermen was on their side, Too: such men as Henry Watterson, Charles Nordhoff, Murat Halsted.

Henry and his young friends found leadership in two able men of Johnson's administration: Hugh McCulloch, the Secretary of the Treasury, and David A. Wells, Special Commissioner of Revenue. McCulloch and Wells were intelligent and bright, willing to give a lead. They saw the need for sensible, scientific management in a government that was bursting its buttons in size and complexity now that the war was over and post-war problems were clamoring for attention. They needed support in the newspapers and magazines. Adams, for one, decided to help them.

As long as Johnson was President, one's aim was simple— to clean up confusion, waste, and stupidity. But as soon as

Grant was inaugurated, difficulties in the face of reform multiplied enormously. The new regime—from the day of the appointment of Grant's first Cabinet—seemed a gigantic laugh at their sensible aims. Adams's friends fought on, rather lightheartedly, even under Grant. They had a great deal of fun making plans, pulling off small coups, making pinprick raids against the entrenched enemy. There were some good men in the middle of the new corruption. They appealed to these men, and sometimes got their ear. They did not lose their fight all at once.

Adams found it easy to slip into place among the reformers. He spoke later of his mood, of his "rage for reform." [3] His own name meant something in Washington. His father's prestige was high. John Quincy, his brother, in Boston, was becoming a power in the Democratic party of Massachusetts. Charles was beginning to write a series of jolting criticisms of the railroads. Henry's own articles were being read and admired.

The political and newspaper world was the background. But the core of his life was a private place. For him, a sensuous appreciation of a landscape or a private reflection upon his own mood was to matter as much as a public act. To know him at any stage in his life, one must know him as a feeling human being, not just a rationalizing one.

What surprised him in Washington was the sympathy he felt for the place itself. The city pleased him in its physical appearance. He found rooms of his own far out toward Georgetown where he could sit at his window and see a wide sweep of the river and much of the city. He possessed it with his eyes and laid hold of it with his emotions. "From the window of my room I can as I sit see for miles down the Potomac, and I know of no other capital in the world which stands on so wide and splendid a river." [4]

What he was discovering was a personal landscape, one that would matter to an intense degree for the rest of his life. Whatever time he could spare from writing, he spent in exploring the city and its surroundings. The luxuriant flowering of the Southern forests and fields appealed to him strongly. The woods of Maryland and Virginia came into the city itself. The forest life, of trees and shrubs and flowers, was a refreshment from the urban occupations of his rational self.

Within the city he had an easygoing, if busy, life. Washington was still a "happy village." It was a place for personal dealings, where one person did not seem so unimportant, as perhaps he had in London. Friends and enemies met daily.

Feuds were carried on face to face. Friends rubbed the rough corners off each other in daily contact. There was always time to talk.

Adams had two assumptions about Washington. One was that the life of the government was diseased. The other was that he himself, in his proper person, had to do something about it. The something he had to do turned out to be the writing of articles. He found that the start he had made in London gave him the necessary momentum to carry on in Washington. He seemed to have the ear of the *North American*. Its editors took whatever he offered them, and it was not difficult to find other outlets.

By the spring of 1869—his first spring as an independent journalist in the Capital—he had placed two articles. One of these, "American Finance: 1865–1869," appeared in the April issue of the *Edinburgh Review*. American writers in 1869 found that they gained more attention at home by appearing in English magazines.

Adam's *Edinburgh* article reviewed the intelligent and unappreciated teamwork of McCulloch and Wells in a survey of their official reports for their years in office. And while he ostensibly discussed the issues of those reports—currency, taxes, greenbacks, the tariff—Adams sketched in a more personal picture of the post-war society as he had seen it. Its efficient machinery was a corrupt Congress working hand-in-glove with a corrupt business system.

One passage said: "Nor was it only in the national service that venality showed itself superior to Government and more powerful than law. The great corporations whose wealth and power were now extending beyond limits consistent with the public interest, found no difficulty in buying whatever legislation they wanted from State Legislatures. . . ." [5]

He found that a new result of the high tariffs was "to increase the wealth of individuals and corporations at a more rapid rate than the wealth of the public at large. Capital accumulates rapidly, but it accumulates in fewer hands, and the range of separation between the wealthy and the poor becomes continuously wider. Mr. Wells, in his last report, has collected a great amount of evidence to prove that the burden has in fact fallen upon wages. . . ." [6]

In other words, Henry Adams was showing where he himself stood upon the new capitalism. He was expressing also an assumption for a certain role for government that unfortunately seemed to be disappearing: government as an arbitrator with real power, a force above any one class or group in society, regulating the competing powers of the various groups, for the common good. This was orthodox Adams thought, in a straight descent from John Adams and John Quincy Adams, but more apt than ever, it seemed, in 1869.

His second article, "The Session," appeared in the April *North American Review.* It was the first of a series he hoped to do, in which a discussion of the past session of Congress would be an occasion for writing about the main topics of the day from the Independent viewpoint.

By the time he saw this article in print, he had come to think of himself as something called an Independent. And the Independents, a group of ardent, intelligent, conscientious critics—both within and without the Grant regime—had come to think of themselves as a defined element. Henry Adams was one of them, busily going to meetings which were as yet private and unofficial. He thought his articles might help the movement and composed them partly for the pressure they might exert.

The tone of this first "Session" was youthful plain speaking. "So far as we understand the object of creating governments, it is that they may do the work of governing; and we should like to know for what earthly purpose Presidents and Congressmen are elected, except to perform this duty, and to see at their peril that no corruption follows." [7] One should imagine the context of circumstances—pressure coming from outside governing circles, principally from business. He wanted government not to tyrannize, but at least to govern, to exert itself, and to take its proper arbitrating position between capital and the people.

As earnest as he was, he stood aside in his own mind and smiled at himself and his reforming friends. "If you could see the gravity with which I attend private meetings of discussion which are to settle the coming policy, you would roar with delight. What a humbug one is," he wrote to Gaskell in England. [8]

In spite of the skills and energies of the Independents, the tide was set against them. Their country was entering its longest, most expensive period of laissez faire. Most of Adams's fellow reformers shared with their nominal enemies—the corruptors—a belief that government should govern little. They held out only for minor repairs. Adams, beginning here, came to see the difficulties as structural and fundamental. He would be more and more lonely in his conviction.

He grew tired of talking and writing as spring came on. He got out of the city, off the pavements, and into the woods where dogwood and redbud dropped their last blossoms. "Washington is almost empty," he wrote to his brother Charles, "and the country perfectly lovely. All the trees are in leaf, even the oaks. Such a place for wild flowers I never saw. I pass my days in the woods." [9]

Summer came with a rush, and it was very hot in the city. He went home to Quincy to spend three quiet months of study and writing.

At the beginning of the summer he invited a few Independents up to Quincy for a strategy talk—among them former Revenue Commissioner Wells and young James A. Garfield, who was beginning to show ability in Congress. He thought, too, of including James G. Blaine; perhaps he might become one of them. (Strange conjunction that just failed of coming off. Blaine was as yet untainted.) "Garfield will talk about a railway schedule with you," he wrote ahead to Charles, who was to be there too, "for his census—which is a bore. So get ready to help him for he may help you some day. We may never come up, but he probably will swim pretty strong." [10]

Henry and Charles Adams prided themselves on their political practicality and hoped that they were not squeamish. The Adams family tradition was one of the possible, workable act, not that of a theory operating in a void. The Adams course had been rich in adjustments and compromises. Henry and Charles were playing an old game.

The visitors came and went, leaving them quiet again. For many days writing was Henry's daily occupation. He stuck to his desk and scarcely went out of the house. By the end of a rather lonely summer, he had done another article, "bitter, rather slashing," [11] as he characterized it. Again the *North American* accepted. The fall issue would carry his "Civil Service Reform." Adams, freed from the pressure of words to be put in order, sat under the elms of the old house and read Gibbon.

His civil service article, which he thought of as his "Session" II, was a description of the heartbreak in Washington at the time of the inauguration of a new President. He had just seen Grant come into office and had at his fingertips examples of the crush of greeds, despairs, ambitions, fears which flared up in the Capitol at such a time. He thought the detailed description and the naming of names, the stating of cases, was the best propaganda for the cause.

The summer's job done, he returned to Washington for another winter as a Washington reporter. "I am lonely as a cat here," he wrote to Gaskell, but also, "I am writing, writing, writing." [12]

This was to be the season he discovered the crooks of business, as the year before, he had discovered the crooks of government. His brother Charles was writing at that time one article after another on railroad corruption ("Chapter of Erie," "Railway problem in 1869," "The Government and the Railway Corporations," and "An Erie Raid"—all in the *North American Review* between July, 1869, and April, 1871). Charles invited Henry to go with him to New York to brave the Erie stronghold, Jay Gould's and Jim Fisk's headquarters in the gaudy Pike's Opera House. There they talked to Fisk himself, and Henry gained an unforgettable impression of the man.

In September, before Henry returned to Washington, there occurred the Wall Street crisis of "Black Friday," the spectacular stock-market crash resulting from Gould's almost successful attempt to corner the gold market. Henry made this particular tangle his own assignment. The track of corruption led from New York to Washington and even into the White House, for Grant's brother-in-law, Corbin, had acted there as Gould's eyes and ears. The filling in of gaps and the tracing of devious relationships were to occupy him all during the coming winter. He attended Congressional investigations and carried on his own private one. It was a thorough education in the new corruption.

Meanwhile he passed the winter of 1869-1870 much as he had passed the previous one. He spent some good part of his time dancing, talking, exploring the environs of Rock Creek. But he was hooked on the interest of the political scene. He liked to imagine himself getting to be an intriguer. "I am only a very small fly on the wheel," he said rather proudly to Gaskell. "But it amuses me as a play would, and so, though I have no power whatever and am held up solely by social position and a sharp tongue, yet I float—till later advices." [13] This was a kind of enjoyment. He was not dull in Washington.

Yet he grew tired of all the dirtiness in which he meddled. Even in mid-winter he began to look forward to a summer vacation in Europe, far away from all American forms of corruption. He wanted to slough off all responsibilities, put his conscience to sleep, and rest his sense of duty. "I shall experience three months of civilisation again," he wrote to his English friend, on March 28th, "and wash the dirty linen of my mind." [14]

By spring he had accumulated a backlog of three articles.

In April the *North American Review* carried one of these, an article of which he was only half author, his collaborator being his friend General Francis A. Walker, who had gathered statistics and made notes. Adams had done the polishing. Their piece, "The Legal-Tender Act," traced the origin of the money bill which had created the inflationary greenbacks of the Civil War. They found the bill inexcusable in 1862, and unnecessary now.

Henry had finished also his third "Session" for the *North American*. And he carried to Europe with him his "New York Gold Conspiracy." He was sore about it, for the *Edinburgh Review* had just turned it down as controversial and troublesome. The *Quarterly,* in England, would refuse him, too, during the summer. It would be accepted at last by a third English magazine, the *Westminster,* whose editor did not notify him, but let him wait to see it in print in October.

Before his departure Adams was distractedly busy. He rather emphasized the distinguished nature of his activity to his English friend Charles Gaskell. He told him that he had been offered the editorship of the *North American,*[15] that he had refused, but that he might become its political editor, and that he had had a regular convention, recently, of important newspaper editors in his room.[16]

But he could, as he wrote, look up from his letter paper and see his steamship ticket lying on his desk. He savored his coming freedom and irresponsibility. He wanted to look at old houses, old churches, old tombs, and sit down with Gaskell for intimate and irreverent conversation. "We will rail in set terms at everyone we choose." [17]

By April 29th he was writing Gaskell a series of requests. He wanted a new suit made by a tailor in Jermyn Street; he wanted a horse for riding in the park; he wanted one or two memberships in clubs. "I want to meet everybody, talk with everybody, and know everybody. I propose to be as tender as an angel to all the young women. I propose—God have mercy on my soul—to talk with all the rising young men. And I propose that you shall carry me about everywhere and do the same things, else how can we laugh at them together!" [18]

Adams arrived in London in May in a mood for relaxation and fun. He had no article to write, no tilting or sparring to carry on with difficult political or economic gangsters. He wanted to blink at the bad and see only the amusing surface of European society. He deliberately refused to find anything reformable in it. He resigned his indignation at the dock and was determined to be frivolous. To himself, and to others, he seemed most fortunate.

At this high pitch of youthful satisfaction he stumbled into the first tragedy of his life. He received news from Italy that his sister, Louisa Kuhn, had bruised her foot in a carriage accident and was ill. Since he was the only one of her immediate family abroad, it would be best if he came at once to Lucca, where she had been put to bed.

A bright moment of the summer was to have been his seeing Louisa again. She was yet the most attractive woman he knew. He had not forgotten her kindness to him in his first lonely days in Berlin in 1858, nor the happy casualness with which she had introduced him to Switzerland and Italy, nor their happy-go-lucky carriage expedition in and out of the Austrian and Italian military lines in 1859, whisked through on the strength of her beauty and her wit. She was the kind of person with whom it was impossible to associate mortality.

He came to Lucca and found that she was desperately ill with tetanus. It was like passing out of light into darkness. Louisa had been grasped by the terrible disease for a week when Henry arrived on July 1st. She was to struggle with it under his eyes for thirteen more days before she died. He spent fifteen hours of each of those days with her. He forced his reluctant will to share her experience, and if he spoke of her struggle, in a letter to Gaskell, with some sang-froid, it was the self possession of the afflicted. What he tried to convey was the perfectly conscious, humorous courage of his sister, who was enduring the unendurable.

Such a struggle for life is almost worth seeing. She never loses courage nor head. She knows what is the matter with her, and her own danger, but in the middle of her most awful convulsions, so long as she can articulate at all, she gives her own orders and comes out with sallies of fun and humorous comments which set us all laughing in spite of our terror at the most awful crises. Of course her talking is only a growl between her teeth and even this often quite inarticulate, but we have learned to understand it pretty well, and habit has made even so horrible a disease as this, so familiar that we stroke and joke it.[19]

But she died; the courage and the gaiety did not stop the dying.

Her husband, her brother, and her friends had to go on living. Adams took charge of his shaken brother-in-law and helped him get ready to return to America. Then, getting away himself, he took refuge with Gaskell at Wenlock. The

90

Franco-Prussian War, breaking out at this time, seemed another personal outrage.

Even as he moved about, made arrangements, met trains, wrote letters, saw people off at docks, a great part of him was numb. This death was too much for his equilibrium. He tried hard to quench the display of feeling. He lived. He breathed. He performed the functions of efficient travel. But the event itself vibrated in his flesh and along his nerves.

He could not bring himself to a reconcilement. Justification in any terms—religious or merely rational—seemed monstrous to him. He found that he had no consolation from the remembered fragments of a childhood faith. That too crumbled and lay about as dust in his mind. He could not come to grips with his emotions or his thoughts. Just now he was incoherent and speechless with feeling. He could only wonder, as he traveled across Europe, how the hot sunshine, the soft southern air, the bright sky could stay the same. He resented the brilliance of the natural world.

Chapter 8

Professor Adams

EMOTION HAD jarred Henry Adams off his balance when he came home to tell his family the story of Louisa's death. There he found them united in urging him to accept an offer of a job teaching history at Harvard. He had first refused the offer when President Eliot had written to him during his sister's sickness. At home, he could find no reasonable excuse. His family thought the offer proper and his acceptance proper. They wanted him to settle down in New England and make a life there. Successful as he had at last been in Washington— and the capital now knew him as a dangerous critic—yet he had not made a living being a reporter. Added to the outside pressure, there was in him a real curiosity stirring as to what he could make of being a teacher. He went to Cambridge to talk to Eliot and was further persuaded by a promise of freedom. He would be able to go about his new job as he liked.

Adams had no preconceptions and a taste for experiment. This, Eliot saw in him. Adams was just the kind of unformed, unprejudiced instructor he wanted to help him remake the College into a University. He had just hired William James for the same reason. Yet it was largely chance that brought him and young Adams together at this time.

Eliot was a young man himself, sure of his aims, undoubtful, yet broad, humane, impatient for change. He was strong for science, and for freedom within diversity. He barely knew Adams as a student. He himself was at that time an unhappy and unprepossessing tutor. Yet Adams's having gone to Germany after graduation impressed him. Anything smacking of German education pleased him. It was not a small thing, either, that Henry Adams's father was serving Eliot well on the Harvard Board of Overseers. What might, with another college president, have been a drawback—Adams's political journalizing—only endeared him to Eliot in 1870. Eliot too was "independent." Everything, from the most trivial social tie to the most pertinent intellectual reason combined to make Eliot choose Adams in spite of Adams's relative youth and inexperience and apparently flippant attitude.

Adams could think of no very good reason for refusing

Eliot's good offer except a dislike for Boston winters and an affection for the woods of the District of Columbia. Therefore, in October, 1870, he found himself yawning at a faculty meeting, a bona fide assistant professor of history, smiling to himself whenever anyone addressed him by his title.

He felt himself an alien. "I am writing this at a faculty meeting," he wrote to Henry L. Higginson on October 24th, "and there is not a student here who would feel less at home in the company than I do."[1] But he was content to be a foreign body. "I don't believe in the system in which I am made a part"—he was thinking of his own student days— "and thoroughly dislike and despise the ruling theories of education in the university. So I have undertaken to carry on my department on my own bottom, without reference to the Faculty or anyone, and unless I am interfered with, which is improbable unless I make great blunders, I shall quietly substitute my own notions for those of the College, and teach in my own way. There will be some lively history taught, I can tell you."[2] These words Adams wrote to Charles Gaskell, with whom he had renewed and deepened his friendship during the past difficult summer.

Wenlock, where Gaskell had taken him in after Louisa's death, was a lucky instance for him. He could improvise an entire chapter of everyday medieval life out of the recollection of its appearance. He fed his students a rich dose of abbey life constructed almost entirely out of his imagination of Wenlock in its original state.

His first necessity was to find his own way. He and his students hunted together in the medieval wilderness which was his first area of study. Learning—with Professor Adams egging them on—became for his students a kind of game. Adams worked at this play of the mind with heat and concentration, and with an excitement at the odds against him: pitting his little knowledge against much ignorance in himself, his students, and the College.

He taught at first an average of nine hours a week. His courses during the school year of 1870-1871 were History I, a general history of Europe from the year 987, and History II, Medieval History, probably split into two sections. Thirteen juniors faced him in History I, and forty-five seniors and forty-two juniors in History II.[3]

The new professor made an approximate $4.00 per day from his teaching. He lived alone in two rooms to the left of the front door of Wadsworth Hall, as it was then known, just off the corner of Harvard Square. His brother Brooks was upstairs, a law student. Brooks was twenty-two in 1870; Henry, thirty-two; they were beginning to be friends as well as brothers. They found several other friends among instructors and graduate students to dine with them at a Cambridge boardinghouse.

Brooks Adams said later of his brother at this stage of his life: "No man could have been more petted than he at Cambridge. I know, for I lived with him."[4] Henry lived simply, but it was a rich kind of simplicity. He had no entangling personal relationships. He could see his family, or neglect them, as he wished. He could please himself, and did so. He lived comfortably and took care to furnish his rooms attractively. After the first wrench of coming to New England to live, he began to enjoy himself. He found that learning to teach was a kind of fun he could relish. His selfishness was prodigal, eager, and hopeful.

He carried home armloads of books each night in the attempt to keep somewhat ahead of his class in facts as well as in improvisation. Not knowing all about his subject was stimulating. "There is a pleasing excitement in having to lecture tomorrow on a period of history which I have not even heard of till today. I like to read three or four volumes of an evening, and to leave as many more unread, which are absolutely essential to the least knowledge of the subject."[5] Thus he wrote to Charles Gaskell, apologizing for the picture he gave of his hard work.

He was his own best student. He learned very quickly, and as the years went by he gained a solid foundation on which to base his lectures. Yet at the end of his teaching career what he gave his students was what he gave them at the beginning. It was something essentially personal and intangible. He had a daily way of stimulating, exciting, enhancing the mental life of the student. No student ever forgot him or could quite spell out what Professor Adams had given him. He remembered only that in that class he had had a desire to learn and had achieved at least a momentary imagination of an epoch.

While Adams was learning to be a teacher, he was also learning to be an editor. When he came to Harvard to be Professor Adams, he came also to be Editor Adams, of the *North American Review*. His friend Ephraim Whitman Gurney had persuaded him to take the editorial job, as he had helped Eliot to persuade Adams to teach. Gurney had been editor, but as head of the History Department and as the newly appointed Dean of the College (the first of that title), he was too busy in other matters to continue to run the *North American.* He shifted this burden to Adams's younger shoulders.

Adams intended first of all to make the *North American* an outlet for the Independent movement. He did not want to drop his connection with the movement when he left Washington to go to Boston and the magazine seemed to be his chance to keep in touch. But first he discovered the desperate importance of advertisements. The magazine was about to fail, and a certain number of pages of advertisements meant the difference between publishing the next issue and not. Fortunately, Adams could be editor without a salary. This helped the magazine, but it crowded out his friend Thomas Sergeant Perry, who had been helping to edit the magazine in the interim. He had hoped for the job Adams got.

Adams's own financial situation had changed for the better. As evidence we have his oblique word to Gaskell on September 29th that on coming home from Europe he had found that "One of my aunts with whom I was very intimate here, had suddenly died in the interval. I found myself growing in consequence. . . . What with one thing and another my income is about doubled."[6]

Being financially independent as well as mentally so, the new editor could afford to be ambitious. He proposed first to make the magazine count for the Independents. While he was away in Europe, his "Session" III had appeared and given him a shove into prominence. The Democratic party pirated the article and used it for campaign material. A Republican Senator, Howe of Wisconsin, had denounced him in Congress, and trying to belittle the bumptious young man, labeled him a "begonia."[7]

An additional boost to his reputation with the Independents was the appearance of his article "The New York Gold Conspiracy" in the fall issue of the English magazine the *Westminster Review.* It was being widely read on both sides of the Atlantic just as he was sitting down to his first faculty meetings and his first editorial conferences. It won him friends and enemies, praise and blame, and even one or two threats of physical violence. As a newcomer on the campus, he would be pointed out, not so much as one of the Adamses, but as the man who had written the notorious piece about Jay Gould and Jim Fisk.

The "Gold Conspiracy" was Adams's most complex piece of writing since "John Smith." It exhibited qualities differentiating it from pure journalism, although it was a good job of reporting. It predicted the qualities of his historical writing: a rich, dense texture, a quiet use of irony, and a pointing up of the salient qualities of a whole society by the use of discriminating detail. The piece is readable today for the picture-making of the author. Gould and Fisk live in it yet —Gould secret and cool and quiet, spinning webs like a spider, and Fisk, butcher-like, gross and cheerful.

Not only through writing, but in his own person, Adams planned to exert direct pressure on events. The previous autumn in Washington, on November 8, 1869, he had written a letter to J. D. Cox, Grant's conscientious Secretary of the Interior: "Give the country a lead! We are wallowing in the mire for want of a leader. If the Administration will only frame a sound policy of reform, we shall all gravitate towards it like iron filings to a magnet."[8]

That chance was gone. Grant had let Cox go, or rather made it impossible for him to stay. Cox had resigned on October 5, 1870. Now he too was an Independent. Professor Adams and Editor Adams asked leadership of Cox once more. On October 31, 1870, he wrote to Cox, "All we poor privates ask is a leader, but our leaders all run away."[9] Adams was asking for an article, incidentally, but in reality suggesting much more. "With your aid and Wells's, which is promised, I believe I can secure my success and assist the reform movement."[10]

He was thereafter in constant correspondence with Cox— trying to help connect the scattered parts of the sporadic movement into one whole—writing him on November 17th that he had maneuvered an absence from the classroom. "I go to New York next Tuesday to meet our friends in council. Horace White, Grosvenor, Schurz, Wells, and others, are to be there. My lambs here must go without their shepherd, and my lectures must be intermitted for a few days. I am pleased with my lambs, and they seem to like me; at least I heard no complaint. But the devil is strong in me, and my rage for reform is leading me into an open war with the whole system of teaching. Rebellion is in the blood, somehow or other. I can't get on without a fight."[11]

He reported from this meeting to Cox on November 28th:

We proposed the appointment of a central committee with a view to calling a convention in the summer in case Congress should fail to act. Here a serious difficulty arose in the selection of the Committee. I was soon satisfied that there was great danger of

96

our committing a serious blunder without sufficient preparation, and when it was clear that your name must be put on the list, without consulting you, I turned round and with Nordhoff and my brother, resisted the movement to the utmost. After a long struggle we carried our point and adjourned without naming the Committee. As it now stands, we are to wait the doings of Congress, holding our Convention as a threat over the party. Next spring, if a Convention seems desirable [a convention of Independents], we shall issue a call signed as generally as possible, and on this it will be necessary for us to have your declared support.[12]

There was no convention of Independent Republicans until May, 1872, but in the meantime they simmered. The passage quoted is an illustration of the atmosphere in which he and the others worked. They were hopeful, pugnacious, proud. They schemed, as well as proclaimed. Adams longed to bring Evarts into the movement but found him reluctant: "He seems to be too careful of his own reputation." [13]

Edwin L. Godkin, of the *Nation,* noticed the Adamses (Henry and his brother Charles) at the New York reform meetings of the winter of 1870-1871. He wrote to his wife on December 22nd: "Went in the evening in torrents of rain to the meeting of revenue reformers. There were about forty present. It was very successful, and I was amused by the growing deference with which my opinions are treated. The two Adamses were there. All our people are in high spirits. The Lord is delivering the politicians into our hands." [14] He continued, next day: "Did chores till half-past 12. Then had lunch with the Adamses, and went about with Henry arranging with the booksellers to push the *North American Review.*" [15]

The Adamses, Godkin, Schurz, and the others of their fluctuating circle were sanguine. They were buoyant in their rather opportunistic actions. Adams was one of them in seizing upon any convenient reform by the handle nearest to him, working for it in his magazine, and considering such scattered effort as justified.

Any dent which they could make in the pompous, heavily garrisoned fortress of the entrenched Republican Administration they thought justified. If the position gave at any point, it might crumble all round. Their basic assumption, which they probably never put into words, was that the machinery of the government was sound—it needed only to be cleared of the corrupt incumbents and administered cleanly. Adams himself had doubts which cut deeper, but for the time he shelved them.

He was filled with a strong amusement. He liked his life. Although his manner was puckish, he acted to bring about real change. In teaching, he wanted to stimulate his students into the action of thought; in editing, he wanted to move opinion into action itself.

Although a certain effervescence induced by untested reform was the key to this period, yet teaching and editing brought Adams other interests. The subject matter of his teaching, into which he plunged gaily and recklessly, was to affect the direction of his thought. His taste for research and scholarly analysis was reinforced.

As editor, he was not altogether the reformer. The *North American Review* had a reputation for scholarship in many fields. Its policy was to secure an expert on a subject and allow him thirty or forty pages to develop his thought. Since the magazine did not depend upon a large popular audience, it could afford to publish long articles whose authors did not try to be easily amusing. Adams entered into these interests and broadened himself doing so. He put out feelers in directions which certain of his political friends might have thought futile or precious.

The October, 1870, issue was not his own, but the January, 1871, issue was. For the Independents it had Charles Adams's "The Government and the Railroad Corporations" and J. D. Cox's "The Civil Service Reform." But it ranged widely, for it also contained William Elder on "Aborigines of Nova Scotia," Russell Sturgis, Jr., on "Modern Architecture," James Russell Lowell on "Pope," John A. Church on "Mining Schools in the United States," and H. W. Hemans on "Prussia and Germany."

Adams's interests were catholic. He secured Lowell's quiet, humorous essays, and in the first year he asked Charles Eliot Norton for something on Italy and Samuel J. Tilden for something on Tammany. He came to know and eat at the same boardinghouse table with Chauncey Wright, the reserved mathematical genius of Cambridge, and elicited from him a series of essays for the layman.

Adams was busier than he had ever been before. He wrote to Gaskell ruefully that he had had to give up the pretense of not working. He had little time for a personal life. "Here in Cambridge there is but one house at which I am intimate; that of Professor Gurney, Dean of the Faculty, and my predecessor of the *North American;* he married a clever Bostonian of about my own age, and his house is an oasis in this wilderness." [16]

Gurney's wife was the former Ellen Hooper. Her younger unmarried sister was Marian Hooper, whom Henry Adams had met at the dinner table of the Legation in London several years before. The acquaintance was renewed. But he said no word of her as yet in the long letters he wrote to his English friend. The only deepening cadence of his private life which he allowed to get into these letters was an admittance that he was lonely.

By June he was giving exams—"My rule in making them up is to ask questions which I can't myself answer" [17]—and planning a summer trip to the Rockies. "One of my friends who is engaged on a government survey [Samuel Franklin Emmons] in the West has asked me to go with his party on an expedition. . . . We carry our camp with us and geologise, shoot, fish, or march, as occasion requires. I shall not be back within reach of mankind before the 1st of September, and my next letter to you may perhaps be written from a country wilder than anything in Siberia." [18]

Estes Park might have been in Siberia, so far was it from the enclosed and little world of the East. To get into the park at all, one must climb up to it from the brown plains through one canyon or another where bare rock walls glittered above swift streams. The park was a natural meadowland, cupped high in the front range of the Rockies, where beaver streams wandered crazily. Framing this floor in an aloof dignity stood the great snow peaks. The air was so pure as to hurt the lungs. Nights were cold, and the grass stiff with frost in the mornings. But the days were warm, and the sun struck through the air with a fiery vigor never known to Adams before.

One morning he left the camp of the geologists on the side of Longs Peak and went down into the park to fish. He fished all day without much luck, and sunset caught him alone and uncertain of his trail. He let his mule find the only cabin in the park. One of the three men who came out to meet him there was Clarence King. [19]

He found the head of the survey a young man of ability and charm, carrying his talents easily. He had done the things which Adams had not done—crossed the Continent as a pioneer, worked in the Nevada silver mines, climbed the Sierra peaks, and, in the matter of the survey, bent the Government to his will.

In 1867, when Adams was still a London bachelor, Clarence King, at the age of twenty-five, had come into a tough, confused Washington and, knowing exactly what he wanted, secured money and authority from Congress, the President, and the Army, and fitted out the great geological expedition which he had first imagined at the age of twenty-one when he crossed the plains and the mountains on horseback and on foot.

King's Fortieth Parallel Survey was, as Adams came to see, the greatest civil adventure yet backed by a government, the first modern piece of legislation passed by the American Congress. Adams would become its unpaid publicist in the *North American Review,* trying to impress his readers' minds with its importance. The survey was a comprehensive, systematic, and enlightened study of the untouched land one hundred miles to the north and to the south of the Rockies, through the tangle of the mountains in Colorado, Utah, and Nevada, all the way to the border of California where the survey adjoined land already explored by Whitney and Brewer in the Sierra expeditions of the late 1860's. King had taken part in those earlier California studies.

He had been the first man to climb many of the highest peaks of the California region, including the one he had named Whitney for his chief. He had found the first glaciers to be discovered within the borders of the United States— on Mount Shasta—and he had speculated in pioneer fashion about the glacial scouring of the Sierra valleys. He had helped survey the boundaries of the territory which was to become Yosemite Park. He had been captured by Indians; he had killed grizzly bears; he would, next year, lay bare the largest swindle of the West—the great diamond swindle of Wyoming. In other words, he had led, and was leading, a very different kind of life from that of his new friend, the Harvard teacher of history, and yet they were very easily good friends, and they never ceased to be so.

A part of their congeniality was emotional, a part, intellectual. Adams was quick to grasp the large importance of what King and his cool young men were doing in the wilderness. King's expedition in the middle Rockies and Powell's, farther south, on the Green and Colorado rivers, were mapping and surveying a continent and all its resources, doing their job, in the middle of Indians, and out of reach of help, with the calm, unexploitative competence of the scientist. This was a promise, it seemed to Adams, of a possible policy of enlightened land use. He saw what King was doing fitted with the policy of the Independents, who, above all, wanted government to be rational, beneficent, and scientific. What might it not mean for the future? In the summer of 1871 neither America's future, nor Henry Adams's, nor Clarence King's, was in any way determined. There was a delightful unpredictability about tomorrow.

King and his young men, accustomed to living in the rough wilderness of the Rockies, yet civilized and erudite in their talk, were somewhat past the halfway mark in their work. King was already planning the many-volumed *Report* of the expedition which would be a synthesis of all their discovering, compiling, exploring, and measuring. He would have admitted, with a smile, that it was going to be a classic.

King's smile was something to remember. He was to be a man universally recollected for his charm. Adams would write, much later, after how great a change in his own, in King's, in his country's fortunes: "Every one who met him thirty years ago remembers how he bubbled with life and energy, and how his talk rippled with humor and thought quite new to our rather academic life in the East." [20]

King was twenty-nine when Adams met him in Estes Park, at a peak of a life that promised much—in many fields. He was known to Eastern editors. Howells of the *Atlantic Monthly* had, in March of that year, published a scientific article by him: "Active Glaciers Within the United States," and while King entertained Adams in Colorado the *Atlantic* began also to bring out his sketches of California mountain climbs and California mountain people. *Mountaineering in the Sierra Nevada* would make King known to many thousands of people who had only the vaguest notion of him as a scientist. He was to be briefly famous as a teller of stories. Yet just now, as a scientist, he was preparing to bring his survey to a triumphant conclusion.

He might do anything, be anyone. And he had, in addition, the gayest, easiest manners that Adams had ever run across. Beneath his Westernness there remained much of the granitic New Englander. King was a Connecticut man, from New Haven, a graduate of Yale and of its new Sheffield Scientific School. He and Adams had a common ground. They could understand each other's motives.

King was at this time, before he began to put on weight, a slight man with blond, close-cropped hair and beard. He had blue eyes and, as all his friends remembered, an alert, energetic awareness. He was a man of thought, but not obviously so. He had all the equipment of the scholar, but not the manner of one. The physical adventurousness in which he had soaked himself for the last decade must have struck Adams with something like envy. King seemed more complete as a human being for this easy balancing of the physical with the mental.

Adams was with King for the rest of the summer in his peregrinations up and down mountains and canyons. In a remote West, innocent yet of a standardized or romanticized version of itself, before Custer, before the Cowboy, without a roof over the head to keep off the bright sun, they talked on and on—fluently, excitedly, humorously. "We had ideals then, ambitions, and a few passions. . . . They were as fresh and exciting as the air of the Rocky Mountains, and the smell of the camp fires in which we talked till the night grew tired of us." [21]

King's professional keenness intensified Adams's interest in geology. King's line of thought fell in with his own previous agreements and disagreements with Darwin and Lyell. King's men, moving among the catastrophic peaks of the Rockies, were somewhat scornful of the then current dogma of an absolute uniform and harmonious development of the earth's crust. They swung Adams more completely into that camp of thought which believed that somehow, at some times, geological development moved faster than at others.

If there was not much akin in their everyday pursuits—Adams working in the raw material of his students' and subscribers' minds, and King in the raw material of an unexplored wilderness—yet there was much common ground between them in the way their minds worked, the way their wit played over the mind's matter, the way they had of looking at the future.

We can assume that they had a common friend, too, in John Hay, who was at this time in New York City, writing editorials for the *Tribune,* under the editorial leadership of Whitelaw Reid. Adams had not seen enough of Hay since their winter meeting in Washington—the great secession winter of 1860–1861. Hay had come through London in the years of the Legation battle, not once, but several times. But after Adams came home from London, they had not crossed paths very often. But King, the previous winter, had fallen in with Hay and Hay's friends of the newspaper and magazine world of New York.

Hay was just then beginning to pour out, as if from a pent-up stream bed, his slangy Western verse. "Little Breeches" had appeared over his initials in the *Tribune* of the preceding December 2nd, and "Jim Bludso" on January 5th. Everyone was quoting one or another of their stanzas. People who did not know Hay knew his lines:

One wife in Natchez-under-the-Hill
And another one here, in Pike;
A keerless man in his talk was Jim,
And an awkward hand in a row,
But he never flunked, and he never lied,—
I reckon he never knowed how. [22]

Hay's verse, retelling Midwestern frontier anecdotes in dialect, was crude, sentimental, concerned with good-natured, God-fearing folks of rough and uncouth manners. It was fresh; it was anti-literary; it made a great impression. There was kinship between it and King's own stories of the California poor whites of the played-out mining towns and forest trials, just now beginning to appear in the *Atlantic*. And there was a family likeness between Hay's and King's work and Bret Harte's, Joaquin Miller's, and Samuel Clemens's— all of them bursting out just now with a fresh Western brogue—giving the New England magazines something new to publish.

Whatever King talked about—rocks or the new literature— he made more alive by the movement of his mind. His witty, paradoxical, glancing talk was almost the best part of him. Even in repose, he was alert. He seemed to have a kind of animal aliveness. Adams began, that summer, a lifelong study of one of his favorite topics—Clarence King. The man had opened a new window to the universe. He took the new view home with him to Cambridge in the fall.

There he was soon busy again, but more the master of his dual jobs than he had been the year before. He had time this year for at least two extracurricular interests. One was a public interest, with a personal coloration. The Independents at last gathered themselves together and became a party. They called a convention for May, 1872. They talked of nominating Henry Adams's father for President.

His second interest was personal altogether. His loneliness was broken into and abated. He found himself with an unsubduing interest in a particular young woman. His daily living was flavored with the irrelevancy of happiness.

He wrote little, this year, but the hurried book reviews for the back pages of the magazine. But he had the satisfaction in the fall of seeing a book published with his name as author, second to his brother Charles's. Their collection of articles on railroads and speculation came out as *Chapters of Erie*.

And in January, Adams as editor let Adams as writer

appear in the *North American*. "Harvard College, 1786-1787," was a period piece derived from his grandfather's college diaries. It emphasized the faraway quaintness of the school of that time, but also demonstrated (for President Eliot and his new ways) that the old ways were not so good, that the teaching was poor, that work and play then were both juvenile, and said, by implication, that the new regime was desirable.

In his own classes Adams demonstrated his beliefs. He found that if he treated a student as adult and equal—and not as a tiresome and overgrown child—he could pile work on him till he groaned and yet gain an eager asking for more. Fire could be struck from a mind that was stimulated rather than browbeaten.

He organized debates, discussions, arguments. He incited differences in preference to agreements. He did away with textbooks, requiring his students to dig their information out of the sources. He prodded their intellects until they hurt. And he never pretended to be anything but a student himself.

The new Liberal Republican party met in convention in Cincinnati on May 1, 1872. Carl Schurz called them to order. "This is a moving day," he began, and they all felt it to be true. [23] Charles and Henry Adams sat below him in the hall, realizing that their articles had had something to do with the fact of the convention. Henry had written and talked and schemed and gone to numberless private meetings—all of which culminated here. The Adamses, Godkin, and many others had welded their Eastern movement onto the stronger Western one stemming from Missouri. The previous fall Schurz, in Missouri, had broken with the state Republican machine and issued a call for an Independent convention. Here, then, they all sat, glowing with untried hope and unpunctured pride.

It should have been a great occasion. Its distinguished participants wondered for the rest of their lives how it degenerated into farce. All the able reformers, good newspapermen, and notable satesmen who were dissatisfied with Grant were there. The absent figure of Charles Francis Adams (who had gone abroad for the preliminaries of the *Alabama* claims arbitration) seemed at the beginning to dominate the meeting. Henry Watterson, the charming, featherbrained newspaperman of Louisville saw them with irreverent eyes: "A livelier and more variegated omnium-gatherum was never assembled. . . . There were long-haired and spectacled doctrinaires from New England, spliced by short-haired and stumpy emissaries from New York—mostly friends of Horace Greeley as it turned out." [24] Watterson was skeptical. He had come as a Southerner to see what good the South could get out of the meeting.

Depending on the point of view, the Cincinnati gathering might have seemed an assembly of serious-minded notables, a conclave of cranks, or a flock of geese to be plucked. The reformers had called them together. Unfortunately, it was the professionals who took over the meeting and adroitly managed it. For they had scented success in its over-auspicious beginning. It smelled too much of a general public reaction, and was therefore dangerous.

First of all, they put Schurz out of the fight by honoring him with the permanent chairmanship and getting him off the floor where he could have carried on a formidable fight. Then B. Gratz Brown came in late from Missouri, hurt because Schurz had canvassed there for votes for Adams and not for him. Brown seized upon a moment of hesitation among the delegates to join with Whitelaw Reid's backstage promotion of his superior on the *New York Tribune,* Horace Greeley. The convention was brought to nominate Greeley, a figure of comic pathos, instead of one of the two men who might have pushed Grant seriously for votes: Lyman Trumbull or Charles Francis Adams.

All the Independents' aims—except a better feeling between the North and the South—seemed to have been pushed aside with decided cynicism in Greeley's nomination. Schurz quailed, and had to be pushed hard to make a few half-hearted speeches for Greeley, and not the glowing ones he could have made for Adams. Poor Greeley died just after the election which put Grant in the White House for a second term.

But even in anticlimax the Independents' convention had its impalpable gains. It frightened the regulars. It furnished artillery for the Democrats who, two years later, won a good majority in both houses of Congress. The Independents wilted, but did not die. They revived a few years later as Mugwumps. Henry Adams was disappointed, but rather glad for his father whom he saw escaping an exhausting and dubious race. He continued his own individual fight in the act of composing each issue of his magazine and in teaching a few young men to think.

In his private existence he was engaged in an absorbing complication which crowded out other interests. His friend Gaskell might have guessed as early as the previous fall that something new and important was taking place in the life of his friend. He received a letter from Adams dated October 2nd saying, "My own purpose still holds of going over next June" (when his family would be abroad), "but I have so many projects in my head and am so much bothered by their interference with each other that I daren't count on anything. Just now the great burden on my mind is the necessity of taking a house and setting up an establishment of my own. My present style of life is too barbarous to endure." [25]

If Gaskell had had detective inclinations, he might have pounced on an aside in a letter of January 22nd: "Not that I find society unpleasant here. The women especially are bright, pretty, and terribly well-bred." [26] On February 8th Adams was telling Gaskell of a "larky" luncheon he had just given in his college rooms, "at which I had the principal beauty of the season and three other buds, with my sister to preside. . . . They made an uproarious noise and have destroyed forever my character for dignity in the College." [27]

Adams was engaged to be married within two or three weeks after this party. He wrote to Gaskell, on March 26th, about the fact:

Having now had a month to quiet down, I start on another letter to tell you all I did not tell you before. Imprimis and to begin with, the young woman calls herself Marian Hooper and belongs to a sort of clan, as all Bostonians do. Through her mother, who is not living, she is half Sturgis, and Russell Sturgis of the Barings is a fourth cousin or thereabouts. Socially the match is supposed to be quite unexceptionable. One of my congratulatory letters further describes my "fiancée" to me as "a charming blue." She is certainly not handsome; nor would she be quite called plain, I think. She is twenty-eight years old. She knows her own mind uncommon well. She does not talk *very* American. Her manners are quiet. She reads German—also Latin—also, I fear, a little Greek, but very little. She talks garrulously, but on the whole pretty sensibly. She is very open to instruction. *We* shall improve her. She dresses badly. She decidedly has humor and will appreciate *our* wit. She has enough money to be quite independent. She rules me as only American women rule men, and I cower before her. Lord! how she would lash me if she read the above description of her! . . . I must stop to make love.[28]

Adams had gone more and more often to the Gurney's house and found there sensitive understanding and encouragement. In Gurney himself, a scholar and gifted administrator, he found friendship. In Gurney's wife, Ellen, whom Henry James was to call "exquisite," he found the woman's friendship he had missed since Louisa died. He must too have renewed acquaintance with Ellen's brother, Edward Hooper, who had been a younger student at Harvard during his undergraduate days. Hooper had spent some time during the war as a kind of civilian missionary to the freed slaves at Hilton Head, South Carolina. Since then he had studied law. Within a few years he would become Treasurer of Harvard.

Last of all, in the younger sister, Marian, he found a person he could love. We know from her early letters that she was impetuous, generous, and swiftly, intuitively sympathetic. Three years earlier she had stumbled upon the fact that a teacher whom she had known at Mrs. Agassiz's school was ill and in want. Very persuasively and gently she gave her money for a year abroad and made little of doing it. "I am not making any sacrifice," she wrote to this older friend, Miss Catherine L. Howard, "nor entailing any degree of self-denial on myself. I am ashamed to get the credit of it. I often think, with a prophetic shudder, of the old man who, when he was dying, devoutly said, 'Thank God, I have never denied myself anything.' Now if you will give in simply and go away and get strong, it will be a pleasure to me that you will have to share the responsibility of, if it comes under the head of self-indulgence." [29]

The children of Dr. Robert William Hooper—Ellen, Edward, and Marian—were left early without a mother. Ellen Sturgis Hooper died when Marian was only five. She wrote verse, of which, a few lines may illustrate something of the mixture and conflict in her children:

> *I slept, and dreamed that life was beauty;*
> *I woke and found that life was duty,*
> *Was thy dream then a shadowy lie?*
> *Toil on, and heart, unceasingly;*
> *And thou shalt find thy dream to be*
> *A truth and noonday light to thee.* [30]

From their mother, Marian, as well as her sister and brother, seemed to have inherited an extraordinary sensitiveness or susceptibility. The father who reared them was evi-

107

dently of tougher, sturdier material, although his means allowed him to be something of a dilettante. The three children, in the midst of refinement and ease, were fed a strict moral fare of New England duty. The combination of dutifulness and extra susceptibility seemed to put a heavier burden on them than was desirable.

Marian Hooper was not characteristically silent, nor melancholy, when Adams came to know her. Rather, her charm seemed to be a particular vivacity of mood. But a certain fragility was hidden in this liveliness. Adams was full of her in his letters to England. He must constantly explain her, picture her, define her to his friend. "My young female has a very active and quick mind and has run over many things, but she really knows nothing well, and laughs at the idea of being thought a blue. She commissions me to tell you that she would add a few lines to this letter, but unfortunately she is unable to spell. I think you will like her, not for beauty, for she is certainly not beautiful, and her features are much too prominent; but for intelligence and sympathy, which are what hold me." [31]

On the 23rd of June Adams wrote to Gaskell from Dr. Hooper's cottage at Beverly Farms: "When you know my young woman, you will understand why the world thinks we must be allowed to do what we think best. [He had been speaking of the kind of quiet, unpretentious wedding he and Marian planned to have.] From having no mother to take responsibility off her shoulders, she has grown up to look after herself and has a certain vein of personality which approaches eccentricity. This is very attractive to me, but then I am absurdly in love, and I won't guaranty your liking it." [32] He admitted that the world might think it peculiar for him to settle down where he was, in the Hooper cottage, for a month before his marriage, but he cared little, and Marian, sharing his companionship for these weeks, cared nothing what the world might think. They were both used to their own way and would have it, and Dr. Hooper, as Henry explained, was tolerant as well as very much "a slave to his two daughters." [33]

Marian Hooper and Henry Adams were married at her father's house, in the presence of their brothers and sisters, and her father (Henry's parents were in Europe) on June 27, 1872. They spent a few days at Cotuit in the house lent by one of Marian's uncles and sailed for England on the *Siberia* on July 9th. They would not return home until September, 1873.

Adams had broken off all his occupations with a kind of leisurely and high-handed pride. He had a year's leave from Harvard, and he had severed his connection with the *North American,* perhaps permanently. He and Marian had before them a year and a half of isolation from familiar persons and places. This going away was a deliberate emphasis in their lives. They would be slightly different people when they came home again to New England.

Chapter 9

Mr. and Mrs. Adams

ONCE MORE, in July, 1872, Henry Adams crossed the Atlantic. This time he took with him a wife whom he wanted to introduce to what he knew of Europe. Their passage on the steamer *Siberia* was cold and rough. It was an unpleasant trip, and even the wit of their fellow passengers—Lowell, Parkman, and John Holmes, who were among the easiest of their Boston contemporaries—was dimmed in the wet, dull passage of an unkind ocean. Mr. and Mrs. Adams, attempting to amuse themselves, wrote Marian's father a day-by-day account of their rueful journey.

Henry wrote, on July 12th, in their joint communiqué: "Long fight with seasickness. Clover quite upset. Wishes she had staid at home. Much sleep. An hour or two walk on bridge. Wretchedness aggravated by the idea of a week more of it. Can't read. Homesick for Cotuit. For Beverly." [1]

Marian wrote, on July 13th: "Cold and fog. Deck too exposed. H. and I lie and gaze at each other. Wonder if life has anything in store for us. Swallow beef tea. Think it may have. Struggle on deck at two; fog lifts. Mr. Holmes has at last knocked under; Mr. Parkman confesses he has been happier; Mr. Lowell quotes Shelley and revels in pig's cheek and cabbage followed by spiced tripe." [2]

The weather improved, the voyage ended, and they got off the ship at Liverpool. Next day they went to look at medieval Chester, and the next day, went on to Wenlock Abbey where Charles Milnes Gaskell, Henry's devoted friend of the war days, was their host.

The land-locked calm of Wenlock and the beauty of the Shropshire countryside was a blessing to them after the bad luck of their crossing. Here began for Henry a backward dive into associations: his first acquaintance with the Abbey, his digging for antiquities with Gaskell, his visiting neighboring farms and houses with his friend, and his own first tentative, daring meditations upon geology and evolution. Marian wrote home long descriptions of the place. Her interest in the deep past, which surrounded her, showed an apt ear for good tutoring. She told her father that "Henry's and my

110

rooms . . . are in the old Norman wing,—eight hundred years old,—with long narrow lancet windows, old carved furniture, and modern luxury combined in a delightful way. We breakfast in an oak-panelled chapel with a stone altar at one end in a mullioned window recess. I feel as if I were a 15th-century dame and newspapers, reform, and bustle were nowhere." [3]

From Wenlock they went to London. Here Marian met several of Henry's friends of his bachelor days—Ralph Palmer, Francis Doyle, and Francis Palgrave. Palgrave brought them a mass of curious and rare drawings picked from recent auctions and tempted them with a Nebuchadnezzar of Blake, which at that time they could not quite persuade themselves to buy. They looked for bargains in water colors, as well as in drawings, and scoured London shops for Danish ware and for Morris and Rossetti wallpapers.

Marian was caught up in Henry's interests; he in hers. They lived and breathed history, house furnishings, and art. Reform, politics, New England, and the Adams and Hooper families were forgotten for a time. Henry, as historian and book collector, found his way smooth. His English friends were good to him and his wife. Yet a notion of prejudice, a trace of a passion, came between him and his surroundings. There remained in him a relic of the resentment he had felt in the war days when it had not been so easy to make friends. Marian, in her loyalty to her husband, and in a really all-sufficient New England pride, was pointedly American in society. She made jokes with Henry's monarchical friends about their absurd and out-dated customs. She was, she said, for plainness and the republic. Was not their generation—that of the American Civil War—the very last to feel the full force of the orginal American touchiness about being a newer, rawer, less powerful, less rich society?

They did not stay long in England. They crossed the Channel and went on to Antwerp, the Hague, and Amsterdam, and then to Germany, where Henry had had two years of late adolescent pain. He was engaged in showing his wife these traces of his past, and also, with a detective zeal, in hunting down the books and the men of his trade. Marian wrote to her father that at Bonn "Henry saw Professor von Sybel and found him kind and communicative; but as for buying books there, it was about as easy as in Beverly. They had never heard of any book Henry asked for." [4]

History and tourism pulled them in a rush from one city

to another: Bonn, Cologne, Bingen, Heidelberg, Baden-Baden, and Basel.

They stopped for ten days in Geneva to join the elder Adamses in celebrating the coming happy conclusion to the *Alabama* negotiations. Charles Francis Adams, more than any other person, had coolly and keenly compelled Britain to the payment of reparations for the damages inflicted on Northern ships by the Southern privateers outfitted in England. He had reached his happiest moment, and capped the achievement of his war service with a more difficult triumph. Henceforth he would be shoved aside, would lose his usefulness, and find all his abilities congealing within him. None of them, in Geneva, could foresee this treacherous turn of luck, and they danced on the bubble of Mr. Adams's greatest moment.

But the crush of parties and crowds and continual movement began to suffocate Marian. "I think a dinner of thirty is rather a bore. Last night a dance at the Evartses' which Henry had to go to, but I had a headache and cold and so went to bed." [5] (Henry Adams's mentor, William M. Evarts, was one of the American counsels in the negotiations at Geneva.)

Carrying a growing library of history books, the young Adamses moved again across Germany. At Nuremberg, Marian wrote, "We take a bit of bread and then sight-see for a couple of hours, and then a noon breakfast when the heat is too much, then a late sortie." [6] They stopped at Dresden, where Henry had been happy long ago; then at Berlin, where he had been unhappy; there George Bancroft, who was the American Minister at the time, invited them to a dinner to meet a group of historians: Pertz, Mommsen, Grimm, and Curtius. Mrs. Adams felt she was somewhat lost in the midst of so much argumentation in German.

Next they turned southward and moved in zigzags down the Italian peninsula. They tried to enjoy Como in a rising flood, but gave up and fled to Venice. Venice was moody in the rain. Villa-living in Florence, as practiced by their friends, the Bootts, seemed too much like camping out. At the dead end of the summer, they reached Brindisi and sailed from that old Roman port for an even older land. Egypt was to be the happy climax of all their travels.

In Alexandria they went aboard a rented houseboat, the *Isis,* and began, in considerable luxury, the long sail and pull up the Nile into the warm, dry air of the uplands of North Africa. Slowly they climbed the river, reading, taking pictures with their newly purchased camera, walking at sunset along the riverbanks, staring at such great lost monuments as Abu-Simbel, picknicking with other houseboaters who had anchored near them, going on parties with these new friends to look at what ruins or villages they came upon in the limited variety of the river. It was a great wash of leisure, a sudden access of blank time after the hurry and motion of Europe.

And what should have been a great happiness became a near tragedy. Henry could amuse himself with his books and could even, on the spot, improvise a new theory of ancient Egyptian law. But his wife did not have her husband's interest in objective facts and theories, and suffered now from that fact in the isolation of their Nile journey. Her wedding trip was a first uprooting from an unusually intimate and closely knit and partly orphaned family.

She became distrustful of self, painfully irresolute and cast down. She found herself lacking in enthusiasm, unable even to write interesting letters, or to take in what she experienced on this slow voyage carrying them farther and farther away from everything she had known. Her mood became one of slow, dull care. She could not, all at once, tear out the roots of an old dependency. "I miss you and want to see you, though Henry is so utterly devoted and tender that I am sure you would wonder at my ever feeling a yearning for the old diggings, which I often do." [7] The farther they went into Africa, the direr grew her feeling of isolation. She lost her usual gay effrontery and bright self-possession. She fell into an apathy and into a mood of abnormal self-abasement.

The following excerpts from her letters to her father—torn out of context, for example—illustrate the downward spiral of her emotions.

Travelling would be quite perfect if only one could go home at night. [8]

Do enclose a bright red maple leaf so that I may feel that I have had a glimpse of autumn. [9]

I'll try to make up my shortcomings when I come home, and you must keep my place open and let me come into it again. Henry will be very busy and hard-worked and I shall come to you for advice and get very dependent on you. [10]

Have tried to write in the past ten days, but gave it up in despair. You know how feeble my powers of writing are at best, and for a long time past I have found it impossible to get my ideas straightened out at all. [11]

I must confess I hate the process of seeing things which I am hopelessly ignorant of, and am disgusted at my want of curiosity. [12]

I never seem to get impressions that are worth anything, and feel as if I were blind and deaf and dumb too.[13]

How true it is that the mind sees what it has means of seeing. I get so little.[14]

Perhaps hindsight over-emphasizes the sway of feeling from one pitch to another. There is no witness except her own words in her letters. It is necessary to read Marian Adams's story here with caution and delicacy and without forcing a theory. Yet it does seem that her misery was unnatural and exaggerated. One can only guess that her husband was anxious. Yet he was not looking for symptoms. And very probably he buried his fears and almost forgot them when their cause, his wife's depression, disappeared.

Marian's emotions gradually righted themselves. In the last part of their journey she took a more normal interest in her surroundings. When the small boat turned northward and sailed smoothly downriver, she was almost happy. By the time they had left the *Isis* and gone on board a comfortable French liner which was to take them from Egypt to Italy, all that had confused and depressed her seemed to be far gone in a dead past. She wrote tremulously then to her father: "Here we are out of sight of land, with Egypt and Africa like a far-off dream. It is pleasant to move north with birds and flowers and soft winds." [15]

Her vivacity of reaction returned and she chattered in her letters of a duke who was shabby, of two "lovely" monkeys, of the friendly captain, of the good food, and of the necessity of staying up to see Italy. Perched on a trunk she saw the welcome coast and "the sun rise between the two summits of Vesuvius." She wrote from Naples that she was no longer homesick. And Amalfi was a climax. [16]

Henry and I made an expedition to a natural arch on the Amalfi side of the bay and found it enchanting. We went on ponies, the path lying between stone walls covered with ferns and violets, with oranges and lemons hanging over our heads. Old women with distaffs in their hands, like Michael Angelo's Parcae, smiled and kissed their hands to us and looked as if they would not cut the thread of our lives as their cruel grandmama might. Small children and dogs turned and ran as if we were ogres. We picked huge bunches of wild flowers and were glad we had not died when we were babies.[17]

As they traveled from Naples to Rome, to Florence, to Paris, and to London, Marian's reactions regained all their brightness and quickness. She was keen and critical and impudent—a sure sign of enjoyment with her. In London, Charles Gaskell lent them his house and they set up house-keeping in it. From spring to midsummer they remained in London, and Mrs. Adams thoroughly enjoyed the advantage that her husband's previous residence gave them in society. They were busy from morning to night in an intense partici-pation in the "season," and in their own invented discrimi-nations in finding and buying pictures, glass, china, and rugs to take home with them.

When they came home at the end of the summer to Marian's beloved Beverly Farms, they had a sense of well-being and content—in each other and in the role they had discovered and created for themselves in relation to the world outside. Henry spoke his happiness crookedly in a letter he sent back to Gaskell:

Here we are again, bobbing up on this side the ocean, like a couple of enthusiastic soap bubbles, and telling interested groups of friends how we saw the anthropophagi and men whose heads did grow upon their shoulders. The first sense of relief at getting home is prodigious. To be quite sure that the ocean is behind us; to look out over it when one gets up in the morning, and to damn its eyes, with a sweet sense of security, at least for some years, against its insults, is one of the most rapturous pleasures my existence has ever known. Life seems all a garden of flowers— mixed with cabbages—when the ocean is behind one. . . .

My own work will begin in about six weeks, and I am likely this year to have my hands full. But as I am now pretty solidly fixed in my seat, I don't feel very much worried about success.[18]

Chapter 10

Marlborough Street

THE FALL of 1873 was a season of eagerness for Adams. The *North American Review* was soon to be his again, and in the classroom a number of history students would be facing him once more, asking something of him. He was expectant of himself, full to bursting with a fury of ideas. He needed, and was glad of, the pressure of work—poundage put upon his ideas—to convert them into lectures, articles, reviews, letters, and more notions than he had ever thought to entertain at one time.

From Marian Adams at this time there is silence. She was near her family and wrote few letters. We can conjecture happiness for her in the security of Boston and Beverly Farms and in a settled routine in her own house. She had called herself a "tabby cat" [1] on her travels and had longed for a private fireplace. Now she had one, in a tall narrow house in a row of close-set houses near the corner of Marlborough and Clarendon streets.

Professor and Mrs. Adams, at 91 Marlborough Street, almost beyond the radius of Beacon Hill, comfortably removed from a too close containment by the College at Cambridge, a part of the activity of the new Back Bay area, were hospitable and attractive. There was soon much traffic through their door by students who were glad of a chance to argue with their professor. Adams and his wife listened to them, fed them, stimulated them.

One of his students noticed a resemblance between his new teacher and the pictures of that teacher's grandfather, John Quincy Adams. The student, J. Laurence Laughlin, later wrote down his impressions of the physical appearance and personal tone of this teacher whom he was to know as a friend, too. "Henry was small, short, bald, with a pointed clipped beard, a striking brow, but he was not as stout as his grandfather. There was in both the same air of self-contained strength. In the younger the pugnacity was genial. His nature was positive, not negative. His smile had in it fellowship, welcome, and heartiness; the laugh was infectious, preceded by a sibilant intake of his breath, with a gay twinkle of humor in his eyes and in the wrinkles at their corners. It might often be ironical, of course, but always good-humored. He might show anger, but never lost his temper. His manner was animated and brusque, but kindly. Although short in stature and unconventional in manner, he never lacked dignity." [2] Such in appearance and manner was Henry Adams as teacher and journalist in Boston and, shortly, as historian and observer in Washington. So he would remain through the 1870's and early 1880's. It was only in the fatal year 1885 that he would change and become something and someone different.

Adams in 1873 was sure of himself and of his own ideas, but the times were not. This was a year of unrest. On September 18th Jay Cooke and Company failed. A depression set in that stretched a grayness across the decade. Adams, once more walking the paths of the Harvard Yard, was not in the least cloistered by his interests. He stretched his mind to the utmost to encompass what went on in the world outside as well as what stirred inside. In the *North American* he dealt with the rough-and-tumble of contemporary American affairs. In his classes he dealt with another world—the medieval one—but he saw it as tumultuous, too, uncertain, and violent.

During the school year of 1873-1874 he taught History II, a General History of Europe from the Tenth to the Sixteenth Centuries; History III, Medieval Institutions ("only for candidates for honors"); and History IV, a History of England to the Seventeenth Century (constitutional and legal). The following year, (1874–1875), he would continue to teach History III and IV, drop History II, and add History V, the Colonial History of America to 1789. He would take on, also, a seminar in Anglo-Saxon law for Ph.D. candidates. His classes for the year 1875–1876 would be: History III, Medieval Institutions; IV, History of England to the Seventeenth Century; V, Colonial History of America to 1789; and a graduate course in Early English Institutions. During his last year of teaching he continued classes in the familiar courses History III and IV, dropped the course in American colonial history, offered instead History VI, History of the United States from 1789–1840, and gave, again, a graduate course in Medieval Institutions. [3]

In 1873 Adams had behind him two preliminary years of teaching. He began now to attain his scope as a teacher, concentrating first upon a great area of medieval history, considering most closely the growth of law and civilization in the Germanic and Anglo-Saxon peoples. He carried his own interests, and those of his students, gradually nearer to the modern world, and in his last two years was personally immersed in American, rather than European, history.

His teacher's manners were memorable. He refused to sit quietly in his professor's seat, but cracked the passivity of his role and that of his students. He thought a stirring-up a certain good. He set his students one against another in debate, asked impossible questions, sent them to looking for source material, and disclaimed final authority for himself.

He demanded, almost with a threat of bodily violence, study space in the library, and got it, as well as reserve shelves—an innovation. He frightened away, deliberately, all but the bravest students. These half killed themselves trying to learn an impossible range of fact and theory. He taught one lesson in every lesson: that a way of learning was more important than an accumulation of dead facts. He fascinated his savage remnant, not only by the ideas he threw at them, but by the swagger of his person. His students—not more than three hundred in all—were to remember and transmit, some of them as teachers, something of his influence. Comments from several of them testify to the impression he made on them.

Henry Cabot Lodge said: ". . . in all my four years I never really studied anything, never had my mind roused to any exertion or to anything resembling active thought until in my senior year I stumbled into the course in medieval history given by Henry Adams. . . . Mr. Adams roused the spirit of inquiry and controversy in me, and I was fascinated by the stormy careers of the great German emperors, by the virtues, the abilities, the dark crimes of the popes, and by the tremendous conflicts between church and empire." [4]

Lindsay Swift said: "The course was held in Harvard Hall, up one flight I think. The room was crowded, Mr. Adams sitting on a rather low platform with a small table at his right. . . . There was no closing of the eyes in slumber when Henry Adams was in command. All was wholly unacademic; no formality, no rigidity, no professorial pose, but you may be sure that there was never a suspicion of student roguishness or bad manners. We faced a well-disposed gentleman some twenty years older [not quite that much older, but perhaps he seemed so] than ourselves, whose every feature, every line of his body, his clothes, his bearing, his speech were well bred to a degree. . . . He would make us laugh until we ached, but it was the laughter of a club and not a pothouse. . . . 'One fact or a thousand—that makes no difference,' he said on one occasion. Now and then he would walk up and down before his chair, always with his hands in his pockets, speaking with entire informality, as if talking to himself." [5]

J. Laurence Laughlin said: "In the classroom Adams was original, unexpected and even explosive. . . . When asked what exactly 'transubstantiation' was, he exploded with: 'Good Heavens! how should I know! Look it up.' He was the first man in college to awake in me a real interest in learning. . . . He conveyed to one unconsciously the true concept of education as the power to think in a subject. . . . It was a virile education that he meted out to his students in our day." [6]

Henry Osborn Taylor said: "For facts as such I have a profound contempt,' he said one day in his classroom. . . . He was the first teacher of history at Harvard to discard the textbook, and put his students to work for themselves." [7]

Professor Adams was also Editor Adams once again. He took back the *North American* from Thomas Sergeant Perry in January. Perry, a friend of Marian's, and of the Jameses, had put out five issues of the magazine during Adams's absence. Perry could not afford to work without a salary (as Adams could), but he did continue to contribute reviews, and in his year in control had secured an important new signature for them, that of his friend Henry James, Jr. Adams, with the magazine in his hands again, asked his former student Henry Cabot Lodge to be his assistant on the magazine. He, like Adams, could afford to take the job without pay, and felt the honor acutely. "I know the exact spot on the road where he made the announcement to me," he was to remember.[8] Lodge was enrolled as a law student, had recently married, and would become a father for the first time in this same year of his going to work with Adams. There was a large element of hero worship in his attitude to Adams. There would continue to be something of this between them all their lives. Lodge continued as a law student to study under Adams as well as to work with him. He took his graduate course in Anglo-Saxon law this same year. Adams wanted Lodge to be a teacher, and within a few years, by negotiations behind his back, had secured him a teaching job in his own department.

As an editor, Adams was a hard taskmaster. He demanded from his assistants and his contributors more than could reasonably be expected, and stimulated the more than reasonable response. To Lodge the hardboiled Adams stressed short

119

sentences, the knocking out of superfluous words, the study of Swift, and constant rewriting. He shoved upon the grateful Lodge all the drudgery of the magazine, and let him learn by doing, reserving for himself an absolute veto and all the pleasures of high-level decision on policy matters.

The editor himself wrote little except a number of the unsigned reviews in the back pages. He put his initials, H. A., under them only when what he had written might offend a friend or an enemy. He missed the experience of writing, but divined his role as an editor: to get hold of the best men, and to get the best out of them.

Under Adams the *North American* assumed an angelic reader, capable of going wherever its writers wanted, willing to put up with shoals of statistics, pages of analysis, paragraphs of thought, Adams's writers were mostly specialists, and he gave them their head. Yet the *North American* remained a journal of criticism, as Adams had planned when he took hold. "In order to break entirely from old connections I have become editor of the *North American Review,* and propose to make it a regular organ of our opinions," he had written in 1870 to David A. Wells, his friend and ally in reform.[9] During the second term of Grant, the *Review* remained a critical paper, flinging out at respectability examples of the dirt in which respectability was dabbling.

But this was not all. The magazine, and Adams, broadened. It took on in depression years the job of pointing out American opportunities: in public life, in the sciences, in philosophy, in history, and in literature. The magazine's main lack was a variety of mood, which might have been supplied by the inclusion of fiction and the lighter belles-lettres; its vice was a certain indigestibility and heaviness.

Yet Adams secured a variety of compelling interests, and his own touch in the reviews was light, direct, positive, yet discriminating, presenting an available, educative intelligence. The *North American* under Adams assumed that the framework—in the political, economic, and academic worlds—was worth keeping; it wanted simply to make things go; to smooth the works. Government should be scientific; so should universities; so should the currency policy. Stupidity was the enemy even more than corruption. Such was the tone of the unconsciously rationalistic viewpoint that the magazine and its editor assumed.

Even before he came home, Adams had set his tone and his goal in an unsigned review he had written for the July, 1873, number. Speaking confidently and prophetically of the recently dead Henry Thomas Buckle, he said: "Buckle's History of Philosophy, unfinished as it is, certainly marks an epoch in historical literature. It was the first attempt, on a considerable scale, to apply to the concrete treatment of historical phenomena the laws that govern these phenomena, and by this means to bring history into the category of the exact sciences." [10]

It is only the present-day reader, looking over his shoulder, who can see the movement of his mind. This phrase and similar ones scattered through the pages of his reviews showed which way he was going. When in April, 1874, he covered a French translation of a rather special German book by the historian Sohm, he praised that writer for "establishing the exact basis of history." [11] The exact basis of history in America was just what had not, so far, been established. Adams was going to try to do what had not been done.

He himself reviewed all the major historical works as they appeared in print, and rescued something of this disregarded and specialized literature of research from oblivion. He enjoyed explaining and popularizing obscure but solid works which might not otherwise have an audience.

Ancient law was an obsession. Whatever appeared on the law and social organization of early peoples became his special province. How did the early American Indians manage such things, he asked one expert, Lewis H. Morgan? He had him answering, shortly, in a series of erudite and entertaining articles. Adams wanted to push back history into times that had been thought to be pre-history. The historical study of early law was his tool.

Yet ancient law, the editor's hobby, was only one thread of interest in the *North American*. One can get some idea of the range of its interests by running lightly over some of its contributors and their topics for the editorial years 1874 and 1875.

In April, 1874, the first issue for which Adams was wholly responsible after his return, Francis Parkman's "The Ancien Régime in Canada, 1663–1763," appeared as Article I. Article IV was the puff by Henry James, Jr., for the relatively unknown Ivan Turgenev: "We know of several excellent critics who to the question, Who is the first novelist of the day? would reply, without hesitation, Iwan Turgeniew." [12] O. W. Holmes, Jr., reviewed the twelfth edition of Kent's *Commentaries on American Law.*

In July, 1874, at the age of twenty-six, Brooks Adams made one of his earliest impatient pronouncements: "Viewed as a consolidated empire, the United States offers peculiar advantages to the adventurer. The ordinary State is not too large to be controlled by a few audacious, unprincipled men, backed by the wealth and weight of the general government. Once secured, it affords him a firm foothold in Washington." [13]

The astronomer Simon Newcomb, one of the great American workers in exact science of that time, had his say in October, 1874, writing on "Exact Science in America." In the same issue Henry James wrote on Gautier.

In January, 1875, Adams gave space to a broadly gauged article by W. B. Hazen, "The Great Middle Region of the United States and Its Limited Space of Arable Land." Article IV was "The Wage-Fund Theory" by Francis A. Walker, Adams's friend of the reform days in Washington, here stepping on orthodox toes and opening his honorable career as an economist of broad humanity. Article V was "The Reign of the Ring," by Charles F. Wingate, the second of a series on the breaking up of the Tweed interest in New York. Howells's new novel, *A Foregone Conclusion,* was noticed.

If Henry Adams occasionally took the time to look up from his work, which grew surprisingly, and involved him in political entanglements as well as in all the legitimate routines of teacher and editor, he might have surprised himself into recognizing that he was happy. He had found a center to the whirlwind of activity in which he tilted. "I can't pay much, as you know, but glory shall be our main reward," he wrote to David A. Wells after matter-of-factly instructing him in the same letter, "I want to have the Massachusetts tax-system ripped up without mercy." [14] To Wells also (April, 1875) he wrote, "Marriage makes a man quiet." [15] It was always in an aside that the happiness showed through. Discussing teaching methods with Sir Henry Maine, after telling him that he had "taken a class through your *Ancient Law,* encouraging them to dispute, and overthrow if they could, every individual proposition in it;" he said too, more personally: "My own life is of the calmest kind. My wife and I jog on as peacefully in this remote corner of the Arctic Circle as though we had half a century behind us." [16]

The reader of his magazine in April, 1875, could take his choice between "Comtism" by Gryzanowski or "Spenser" by Lowell. Or he could read Charles Adams's optimistic treatment of the Midwest's rural uprising, the Granger Movement: "The good will survive, while the evil will pass away," he wrote, considering the farmers' anger against the railroads as well justified in principle, if not in particular act.[17]

In July, 1875, J. D. Whitney wrote about "Geographical and Geological Surveys," taking the opportunity to praise, among others, Clarence King, and his measuring and assessing a broad slice of the new land where settlers were now moving in to live and work. There was in this issue another Tweed Ring episode by Wingate. And Adams, in an unsigned but recognizable review, praised Green's *Short History of the English People* for its "learning, its style, its imagination, and, almost above all, its sound common-sense." [18]

The issue of October, 1875, had an article on "American State Universities" by Charles Kendall Adams, who praised those brash and prosperous new schools for their necessary and stimulating competition for the older private institutions of learning—such as Harvard, for instance. There was a major review of General Sherman's intelligent *Memoirs* as well as a sympathetic coverage of Francis A. Walker's *Statistical Atlas of the United States,* a book which was a by-product of his work as director of the census. His work represented a new kind of intelligence at work in the government, the kind the *North American* was advocating.

A fixed station, settled purposes, and the movement of time had marked Adams. A photograph of 1875 shows the thoughtful head as palpably older. The head dome was balder, the lower face covered by a pointed beard and decorated by a full mustache. The fashion of whiskers gave him, as it did all his generation of friends, a premature look of gravity. He was dressed, in the picture, somewhat stiffly, the high collar, the dark full tie, the tightly buttoned vest, the heavy expensive suiting seeming to encase him in a kind of armor of class and station. Yet the deep-set eyes looked out nervously, restlessly, impatiently, not altogether belonging to the look of settled and completed status.

He was in the habit of comically deploring himself. "The only truth that I can think of is that I am no better than a procrastinating cuss and since being married I do less than ever before. Here is another winter gone [the date was May 24, 1875, and he was writing to Charles Gaskell in England] and I am again nursing nasturtiums and feeding mosquitoes. I am going on to thirty-eight years old, the yawning gulf of middle age. Another, the fifth year of professordom is expiring this week. I am balder, duller, more pedantic, and more lazy than ever." [19]

And he was perfectly delighted with himself. It was summer, and he and Marian were building a summer house in the woods above the ocean at Beverly Farms—in the shade of a wavering curtain of mosquitoes, as put it.[20] If he felt impatience and disgust with the stupidity of human nature, it was an intellectual disgust; his emotional resiliency was unimpaired. The only cloud upon him was a shadow of boredom. He had begun to see into Boston and to think he saw through it, as he had done before in 1858, in 1860, and in 1868. He felt its limitations as strictures upon himself. He looked outward from Boston, beyond the end of Marlborough Street, beyond the Back Bay, beyond Beverly Farms. He noticed too, in Boston, what the Bostonians were often blind to: eruptions of genius which were alien to or original to the city taking place within its boundaries.

His friend Henry Hobson Richardson was one such eruption of singular genius. The architect had already completed two modest churches in Massachusetts towns outside Boston and had put up the new Boston and Albany railway station in Springfield. In Boston he had finished the Brattle Square Church with its angelic banding of the tall square tower and was now beginning to lay the strong foundation blocks of Trinity Church upon the thousands of pilings set down in the miry ground of the new Back Bay land.

Commissioned to do the work in 1872, Richardson had moved permanently to Brookline in 1874 to live near his great cathedral. Adams would find it easy, from his near corner on Marlborough Street, to walk to the church site and watch the building, year by year, grow upward. He must often have stopped to speak to Richardson, large, generous, humorous, and unhurried in the middle of confusion; he must often have walked round its queer, triangular plot which offered an original problem to the builder; and he must often have tried out on his curious eyes it rich color scheme of honey tans and bourbon browns, so different from the older, chaster meetinghouses of the city.

This was the beginning of Richardson's ascendancy. A boy of the obscure streets of Boston, who would one day build greatly himself, recollected that he saw one day a man—who must, from the context, have been Richardson—"a large man of dignified bearing, with beard, top hat, frock coat, come out of a near-by building, enter his carriage and signal the coachman to drive on." [21]

The boy, who was Louis Sullivan, struck by this person's authority and grandeur, had questioned a workman about him and was astounded and delighted to learn that he was an "archeetec," and that an "archeetec" did not mean owner of a building, but builder of a building, and that every building had one. "Louis," who wrote this of himself, "was incredulous, but if it were true it was glorious news." He asked the workman how such a man worked and heard: " 'Why, he made it out of his head; and he had books besides.' " "The 'books besides' repelled Louis: anybody could do that; but the 'made it out of his head' fascinated him. . . . Then and there Louis made up his mind to become an architect and make beautiful buildings 'out of his head.' " [22]

So he did, and a clear line of inner relationships runs from Richardson's work to Louis Sullivan's and to Sullivan's apprentice Frank Lloyd Wright. Despite all difference of temperament and the difference in choice of material, there is a unity of integrity shared among these builders. In both Sullivan's and Wright's recollections, there is a sense of gratitude to the first: the mighty and imperious, the utterly natural and childishly joyful Richardson.

Richardson, delightedly showing off his church, bent Adams's mind toward color and shape and style. The architect at this time very probably introduced Adams to John La Farge (if he had not already become acquainted with him through Marian or through William and Henry James, or T. S. Perry), and to young Augustus Saint-Gaudens. La Farge was directing the interior decoration of the church, and Saint-Gaudens was helping with the giant murals which time would so cruelly obscure to a mere shadowing of warm color.

These artists' tasks, and all the complicated but delicately differentiated work being done by so many different hands under the one guiding thought, impressed Adams immensely. He stored away the scene—of blocks being piled upward one upon the other, and of the interior, bare, dusty, and cold, scaffoldings swung from its height of ceiling—and was to recollect and recreate the scene with all its reverberant emotion in his novel *Esther*.

Inside the church—for services were held at an early date in a completed chapel—there was another source of Adams's shaping: the dazzling power exhibited by his cousin Phillips Brooks in his great sermons to Boston. Although the church was Episcopal, its minister addressed himself, almost nonsectarianly, to the entire city, and Boston responded with a greater and greater enthusiasm until Brooks became a public figure.

The very fact of his undoubted moral superiority helped to focus their own religious problem for Professor Adams and his wife. The traditional answers in religion put pressures upon them and aroused dissatisfactions in them that seemed unanswerable. They were together straying farther and farther into overt skepticism. Phillips Brooks was sincere and good. He had reached a peaceful self-assurance in matters which only brought them trouble and unease. Adams would be saying shortly of the heroine of his first novel: "She herself had not entered a church for years: she said it gave her unchristian feelings." [23]

While one friend—a Richardson—inclined Adams to art, two others of these years—an Agassiz and a Pumpelly—inclined him toward science. Innate qualities of his nature were being powerfully reinforced by his openness and willingness to learn. He was sensitive to influences and leadings; the findings and soundings of others were valuable to him. With these two friends of science it was literally a matter of explorations. With Alexander Agassiz it was the ocean bottoms; with Pumpelly it was the far-off spaces of the American and Asiatic continents.

Alexander Agassiz was already a lonely man in the middle 1870's. He had lost his wife in 1873 and been left alone with three young boys within a few days of the time his father died. He had made fortunes for friends, relatives and, almost indifferently, for himself, by his development of the Calumet and Hecla copper mines in Michigan.

Death and loneliness had strengthened and concentrated his abilities, and left him sadly without distraction. He had time and he had money; so he went about his business of oceanography which very few knew of or, if they knew, comprehended. In 1875 he sounded the coastal waters off South America and explored Lake Titicaca, and wondered, humanely, how the deprived workmen of that region could live.

Agassiz belonged to the Harvard community, and returned to it between trips. He found there perhaps the most intelligent understanding of his undertakings in his stepmother, Elizabeth Cary Agassiz. They were both deprived and they turned to each other, inventing a new kind of friendship. She cared for his three boys, and he furnished her with the deeply relished intellectual atmosphere to which she had been accustomed as Louis Agassiz' wife and assistant. The hidden drama of a neighbor's life must very early have brushed Adams's consciousness, for he meditated long on Agassiz.

Pumpelly, who explored and sounded land, instead of water, was an entirely different kind of person. Born in New York State of comfortably and artistically minded Presbyterians, he had prepared at New Haven for Yale but, with characteristic independence, gone to Europe instead, and worked and studied in Germany, attending the Royal Mining Academy at Freiberg in Saxony.

But one year older than Adams, he had, before they met in the 1870's, led a violently adventurous outdoor life, somewhat in the manner of Clarence King. He had spent the first year of the Civil War in the Southwest, as an engineer attached to the Santa Rita gold mines; had got out of that wild territory just ahead of an Apache uprising and gone farther west; from California he had gone to Japan to be engineer adviser to the Japanese Government; from Japan he had gone to China; and from China, in 1863, he came home overland across Siberia to Europe and America.

In 1865 he had found his country changed, a place where speculation muddled all mining ventures and where all the businesses in which he might engage, from gold and silver to oil, were afflicted with a gigantic lack of fastidiousness. But Pumpelly had a jaunty adaptability, and always landed on his feet. He took part, as adviser and guide, in many exploitations after the Civil War without seeming to be touched by their darker side. He came breezily in and out of the Eastern cities, bringing the breath of large open spaces with him. At Harvard he held, rather loosely, a professorship of mining, but seldom taught, being more often away from the school on other ventures. He made sudden exits to look at mineral properties in the Lake Superior regions, to plan a canal across the Keweenaw Point of upper Michigan, or to inspect the Hoosac Tunnel.

In New York and Boston he became popular and famous. His book *Across America and Asia* was widely read. He was a personable man, dressed with a sort of careless elegance, and of a tall, commanding appearance, with the trademark of a flowing red-gold beard. His friendship with Henry and Marian Adams, although more evident in their letters of the next decade, had its beginnings in these years when he came occasionally to Harvard to dazzle the settled inhabitants. He spent the fall of 1875 and the winter of 1876 in Cambridge, for instance, writing a geology textbook for Harvard, and using a spare room in Agassiz' Museum as his workshop.

In trying to trace the fertilization and cross-fertilization of the mind of the Professor of History, it is evident that the combined friendship of Agassiz and Pumpelly was powerful, as was that of Pumpelly and King. There was a further tangling of the skein in the fact that Pumpelly knew John La Farge and valued him. They had met in New York, and Pumpelly, in his large, free way, had shown the artist his collection of loose jewelry, ceramics, and tools from the East and had persuaded La Farge to write the chapter in his book on Oriental art.

As for Clarence King and John Hay, whose joint friendship would one day mean very much to Adams, these were not years of intimate association. Geography interfered. King was mostly in the West, and Hay was either in New York working for the *Tribune* or in Cleveland assisting a wealthy father-in-law in business, or trying to find the spare time to set down the first words of his share of the biography of Lincoln which he and John Nicolay had planned long before.

In these final years in Boston, when Adams hungrily reached out after other modes of doing and being, the teacher of history and the editor of the small, influential magazine was accomplishing a great deal in these fields which he knew now were not to hold him. The years 1875, 1876, and 1877 saw several culminations of furious concentration.

The first issue of the *North American* of 1876 was, as he said lightly, his monument. It celebrated America's centennial year and contained six broadly gauged and deeply meditated articles on religion, politics, abstract science, economic science, law, and education between 1776 and 1876. Its authors included W. G. Sumner, Simon Newcomb, and Daniel Coit Gilman. It was a conscious, well organized survey of the entire field of knowledge in America in the hundred years since its founding.

In June, 1876, Adams saw his first graduate students in History take their degrees. He financed the publication of their theses in a book, *Essays in Anglo-Saxon Law*. The published essays include H. C. Lodge's "The Anglo-Saxon Land Law," Ernest Young's, "The Anglo-Saxon Family Law," and J. Laurence Laughlin's "The Anglo-Saxon Legal Procedure." His own fifty-four-page study, "The Anglo-Saxon Courts of Law," headed the collection. He believed in the good of his students' work and spoke his pride in a letter: "They have shown qualities which I believe to be of the first order. It is true that the highest quality of the mind—imagination—is utterly wanting in our American character. . . . Setting this aside, I believe that my scholars will compare favorably with any others, English, German, French, or Italian. I look with more hope on the future of the world as I see how good our material is." [24]

A footnote to his Germanic studies was a lecture he gave in December, 1876, at the Lowell Institute on the "Primitive Rights of Women." His talk, reprinted in his *Historical Essays,* reveals the Adams temper of 1876: that of conscious modernity and progress, of impatient rationality, and impatience with the enforced uniformity of the Middle Ages. He thought the medieval treatment of women a lower step in human affairs than that of the ancient Greeks, or even of the Icelandic or Germanic tribesmen; he retold, very entertainingly and with racy colloquialism, certain Icelandic folk tales illustrating the jaunty independence of their women.

Eighteen seventy-six was a political year, and political interests broke into academic and editorial interests, or rather redirected them. Adams was conscious of the fact that he had a considerable, if undetermined, influence in his hands, and with some enjoyment prepared to use it. His general purpose was to defeat Grantism; his particular purpose, to defeat Blaine, in his chances for the Republican nomination. If the Republican choice would not do, then he and the other Independents could throw their weight to the Democrats. His own father would be nominated in the fall for Governor of Massachusetts on the Democratic ticket. Henry himself became once more an active and amused member of the loose group of public and private men, economists, teachers, newspaper writers, who called themselves Independent or Liberal Republicans, and who had worked together in 1872. Carl Schurz was, more or less, their public head.

With Lodge as his lieutenant, Adams wrote letters, attended meetings, considered and abandoned a scheme to buy a newspaper and get Schurz to edit it for them, and continuously searched Republican ranks for a suitable candidate.

"My scheme is to organize a party of the centre and to support the party which accepts our influence most completely," he wrote to Gaskell as early as May, 1875.[25] "Although we have unquestionably the power to say that any given man shall not be President," he wrote to the same correspondent, almost a year later, on February 9, 1876, "we are not able to say that any given man shall be President. Our first scheme was to force my father on the parties. This is now abandoned, and we have descended to the more modest plan of pushing one of the regular candidates, or splitting the parties by taking one of their leaders." [26]

A few days later, on February 17th, he was writing to Lodge: "Our object is clear enough. We want to break down party organizations which are the source of all our worst corruption. Does Mr. Bristow recognize this necessity? If not, can he be brought to do so?" [27] Benjamin H. Bristow was Grant's honest Secretary of the Treasury, who had disclosed the Whiskey Ring scandal. He was at the moment the Independents' choice.

On February 20th Adams wrote to Lodge, in a conspiratorial manner: "But the time of action is now at hand and I may have to take your place here in our organisation till you return. So continue to write every day if you can. In case you want to telegraph, you will have to use some caution in mentioning names. Schurz and Bristow had better figure as Smith and Brown. I have done nothing about the *Post*, but am willing to put $5,000 into it if Bristow is our candidate." [28]

The Independents—Henry Adams among them—met in New York on May 16th and 17th and endorsed a ringing speech by Schurz:

> We shall support no candidate, who, in public position, ever countenanced corrupt practices or combinations, or impeded their exposure and punishment, or opposed necessary measures of reform. . . .
> We shall support no candidate, however conspicuous his position or brilliant his ability, in whom the pulses of the party manager have shown themselves predominant over those of the reformer.
> We shall support no candidate who, however favorably judged by his nearest friends, is not publicly known to possess those qualities of mind and character which the stern task of genuine reform requires.[29]

This statement was supposed to ward off the evil of Blaine or of Conkling or the assumed mediocrity of a Hayes. But the regular parties held their conventions; the Republicans, influenced to a certain extent by the Independents, named Hayes rather than the more obnoxious and more popular of their candidates; the Democrats named Tilden, an intellectual and rigorously honest, as well as successful, reform governor of New York. The Independents failed to hold together as a group. Schurz satisfied himself of Hayes's liberalism on certain points and announced Hayes as his man. Many others— and Adams was one—threw their support to the Democratic candidate.

Adams told his rueful story to his English friend Gaskell on June 14th: "We organized our party, and as usual have been beaten. After our utmost efforts we have only succeeded in barring the road to our opponents and forcing them to nominate as candidate for the Presidency one Hayes of Ohio, a third rate nonentity, whose only recommendation is that he is obnoxious to no one. I hope to enjoy the satisfaction of voting against him." [30]

He wrote to David A. Wells, on July 15th: "I can't quite follow our friend Schurz back into the Republican fold, but I am glad he is so likely to be powerful there. I shall vote for Mr. Tilden. Indeed after chattering for years about voting for the best man without regard to party, I cannot well do otherwise."[31]

Adams decided to throw the support of his magazine openly behind Tilden. He and his brother Charles together concocted a political manifesto, "The Independents in the Political Canvass," and Adams placed it in the fall issue of his quarterly. He was content to vote for Tilden, to speak for him in his magazine, and on this issue, to split with his publishers. For he had found the limits of his freedom as editor. He placed the article in the fall issue, and the publishers disclaimed him publicly in an insertion in the magazine.

Adams might have patched up his difficulties with the publishers, but deliberately chose not to do so. He used this disagreement as an opportunity to resign. He had, in recent months, felt confined in Boston, and all at once wanted to get out. He quit his editorial job, abruptly, in October when his manifesto was safely published. And he came to the conclusion, at very nearly the same time, to make this his final year of teaching at Harvard.

There is the appearance of a sudden painful break here, but the appearance is deceptive. It was simply that a long slow accumulation of superior interests had washed out those of teaching and editing. Adams had exclaimed earlier in the year in a letter to Lodge: "Anything which takes a man morally out of Beacon Street, Nahant, and Beverly Farms, Harvard College and the Boston press, must be in itself a good. . . . I yearn, at every instant, to get out of Massachusetts and come in contact with the wider life I have always found so much more to my taste." [32]

(Henry James had one time gazed down the length of Marlborough Street and exclaimed pensively: "Do you feel that Marlborough Street—is precisely—*passionate?*" [33] Adams had some such movement of the mind when he rejected Marlborough Street and Boston.)

Whenever anything shoved him from his perch, it was natural for him to turn southward and go to Washington. Once again, in the fall of 1877, he followed this pull and came to rest at last, permanently, near the Dome, the Monument, and the River. His occupations would be two: to write history (which he could not do while teaching it) and to observe history. Perhaps in that close observation he would at last be able to put his finger on history's living pulse and, in comprehending, lay hold upon it.

Disappointment in the field of political action had not dulled his interest in the subject. But now the principal satisfaction he required was an intellectual one; that he should satisfy himself in his mind as to the reasons for these happenings. He required of himself, as a historian, that he connect his present with the past. He had by luck recently received into his hands, and had been asked to edit, two sets of manuscripts—those of New England Federalism of the time of its near treason and those of Albert Gallatin, Thomas Jefferson's Secretary of the Treasury. The opportunity was irresistible. By leaving Boston and going to Washington, where he could watch the making of history, as well as write about it, he could deliberately create the occasion for a gathering together of all his energies.

Chapter 11

Lafayette Square

THE TIME of his life when Henry Adams, in the company of his wife, lived quietly by Lafayette Square was one in which his interests and abilities steadied and intensified. It is hard to see in him the desperate youth of Berlin or the unsure one of London. He had both achievement and happiness. He did work he enjoyed, and the amount of it was remarkable. Yet, to an outside, he seemed to have an uncluttered, leisurely existence.

Henry and Marian Adams were to see during these years, November, 1877, to December, 1885, four Presidents living in the large white house across the square: Hayes, Garfield, Arthur, and Cleveland. Adams was to see his country changing, and in spite of a darkening intellectual scheme he enjoyed, rather than fretted at, the political spectacle. He lived securely behind his domestic ramparts. Adams thought his way of life a success, and said so several times. He did not see, until it was too late, that there were dangerous cracks in the structure of his happiness. He was to say then, in a state of agony over loss, that he had had, at least, the happiness of those years.

The Adamses became residents of Washington in the fall of 1877. The Hayes-Tilden dispute of the past year was a dead issue. Almost a new time seemed beginning. There was a respectable solidity to life under Rutherford B. Hayes. This President, against whose accession Adams had been so bitter, was modest, quiet, and able, in office. Adams soon came to respect and like Hayes. He saw the Administration as a time of necessary quietness and steadiness and small innovation, if not of brilliancy.

As the Adamses settled themselves in a rented house on H Street (No. 1501), Henry found himself working in his new environment in a mood of tranquil energy. He wrote to Charles Gaskell, on November 25:

We have made a great leap in the world; cut loose at once from all that has occupied us since our return from Europe, and caught new ties and occupations here. The fact is I gravitate to a capital by a primary law of nature. This is the only place in America where society amuses me, or where life offers variety. Here, too, I can fancy that we are of use in the world, for we distinctly occupy niches which ought to be filled.[1]

Although their house seemed at first too large for them, yet in the city itself they felt at home. Knowing the proper people in the proper places helped Adams in his historical research. And, as he was outside politics, no one was afraid of him, or jealous. He liked the small, yet complete social world of the Capital under the trees. He predicted something more for it than pleasantness. "One of these days this will be a very great city if nothing happens to it. Even now it is a beautiful one, and its situation is superb." [2] Adams was as confident of its future as he was of the nation's. "As I belong to the class of people who have great faith in this country and who believe that in another century it will be saying in its turn the last word of civilisation, I enjoy the expectation of the coming day, and try to imagine myself, with my fellow *gelehrte* here, the first faint rays of that great light which is to dazzle and set the world on fire hereafter." [3]

By November, 1877, Adams had finished the editing of one set of papers he had brought with him from Boston. He set down a title—*Documents Relating to New England Federalism, 1800–1815*—and on November 29th signed his Preface. In that Preface he wrote in part:

This volume has no controversial purpose. Under the ashes of half a century the fires of personal and party passion still glow in these pages; but only curious students of history care any longer to stir them. For such as these this volume is printed. . . .

So far as the editor is concerned, his object has been, not to join in an argument, but to stimulate, if possible, a new generation in our universities and elsewhere, by giving them a new interest in their work and new material to digest.[4]

The volume contained letters and other papers of the time of President Jefferson's embargo on commercial shipping and President Madison's war, when New England threatened to leave the Union. It had, also, a section dealing with the aftermath of this old bitterness which plagued John Quincy Adams a generation later. In contradiction to his declaration of coolness, there was a warmth of interest in his pages, in the Preface, concerning his grandfather. He told here the story of President Adams's loneliness and his identification of that loneliness with a chance phrase in an aria sung in an opera popular in his time. Blondel's song to the abandoned King

Richard rang in the abandoned President's ears: " 'O Richard! O mon roi! L'univers t'abandonne.' " [5]

The *Documents* hardly cold, Adams plunged with full vigor into a more ambitious job which was yet another pre-study for his *History*. This work was the editing of the copious papers of Albert Gallatin (put into his hands shortly before by Gallatin's son in New York City). He had determined to use the papers to write a first-rate life of Gallatin. Albert Gallatin's life stretched significantly across the tract of time he intended to measure in his *History*.

He secured permission to search the files of the State Department and the National Archives for additional material. He began to select, and to have copied, a growing set of documents on which he could base a truthful life and an authoritative history. (He made friends with the State Department's Librarian, T. F. Dwight, and had the use of a desk in the State Department.)

He worked very quickly at a large, complex job. By January 6th of the new year, 1878, he could tell Henry Cabot Lodge: "Gallatin goes bravely on. I have just finished the whiskey rebellion." [6] By April he thought he would complete the work in one more year. He took his materials to Beverly Farms for a summer stint.

Gallatin could not alone hold him. Gallatin, the conscientious man, suggested Burr, the unconscientious one. Adams amused himself simultaneously with these opposites. He threw together the materials for a life of Aaron Burr at the same time he worked on Gallatin. And, such was the press of available energy, he began considering the possibility of writing a novel about Washington: the city and the society. Gathering materials for it would be a part of his play.

It was in "play" that Washington surpassed Boston. For all of life outside his writing was a kind of play of human forces. Human nature was here frank, exposed, and unfailingly amusing. Therefore easy talk and laughter, chaff and satire, the comings and goings, the rubbing shoulders with all kinds of men and women were as important as, perhaps more so than, research. Marian could write acutely that they learned much more out of books than in them. Talk was more important than act, and there was endless time for talk.

One night the President stopped in at Carl Schurz's house and found Schurz, his Secretary of the Interior, L. Q. C. Lamar, the Senator from Mississippi, E. L. Godkin of the *Nation,* and Henry Adams sitting about idly talking and smoking. Hayes found them dull, and went away to say so.

Adams's reaction to the report of the President's reaction, " 'What dull owls we were,' " has in it a contented egotism: "There was much truth in his observation, which does credit to his penetrative faculties. I am often struck with the same fact." [7] But he seemed to be saying, too, to his Beverly Farms correspondent, that to be dull in Washington, and in such good company, was for him better than to be bright elsewhere.

But there was much brightness in their situation. Clarence King came to town to live. They hoped he might stay a while. A group of scientists, with King and John Wesley Powell at their head, with the assistance of Representative Abram S. Hewitt, had propagandized for the merging of all the scattered government geological surveys into one. They at last got their bill passed. King did not particularly want the Washington job, but Powell had made too many enemies to take it at this time. He and others persuaded King to be the first head of the United States Geological Survey. But King was a restless man and would not be held long in the city. He was pursuing a number of rainbows at the bottom of a number of mining pits, forever hopeful, forever disappointed. He was a tiny animated piece of the national exploitative urge; he was a scientific genius as well. He thought he needed to be rich. He spent years hunting wealth and wasting much of the time he should have devoted to scientific research.

King was to be handy to the Adamses, at this time, for only two years. At the end of that time, with his organization set up and broad principles set forth, he named his successor, Powell, who well deserved the job, and slipped neatly out from under his Washington responsibilities. Yet while he stayed, King dazzled. It was in 1878 that Volume I of his Survey Report came out: his *Systematic Geology*. In this preliminary description of the segment of the American continent which he had surveyed, he united two methods: those of the scientist and the artist.

John Hay came into Washington again. He received. late in 1878, an appointment as Assistant Secretary of State under William M. Evarts. He had previously served the State Department after the Civil War in three foreign countries. He had failed then to get the promotion he wanted and had quit the government for newspaper work. Then he had wholeheartedly fallen in love, married Clara Stone of Cleveland, and gone to live in that city. He had worked since that time as a sort of factotum for Mrs. Hay's father, the wealthy Amasa L. Stone, who was a railroad builder and had been an early supporter of Abraham Lincoln. In his private time, Hay worked away at the research and compilation and the early writing of his part of the great biography of Lincoln which he and John Nicolay had projected as long ago as the war days.

Yet Cleveland was not altogether good for Hay. He needed the bondage of public office. Cleveland gave him wealth and leizure; gracefully and good-naturedly he accepted both. Yet the city encased him in a kind of stuffy, comfortable insulation in which it was fatally easy to take on the dogmas of the rich men who were his neighbors and friends on Euclid Avenue. Washington shook him loose from a pleasant prison. It gave him his own kind of work to do. It gave him Clarence King and Henry Adams to talk to.

It was in this prosperous period for them all that Clarence King, John Hay, and Henry Adams formed their triumvirate. They had had scattered meetings and interrupted associations before. Now they could try each other steadily and find that they suited each other well and durably. Something of common humor, something of common aspiration, something of lucky likability in temperament welded them at last into close friendship.

The two women—candid, sweet-tempered Clara Hay and bright, sharp Marian Adams—were the leaven of the group. Clarence King was a lonely man for all his gaiety. He was particularly grateful for the kindness of the two women, and graceful in accepting it. He sent flowers on suitable or unsuitable occasions. He came when he wanted and did not even ask if he might.

"The universe hitherto has existed in order to produce a dozen people to amuse the five of hearts. Among us, we know all mankind. We or our friends have canvassed creation, and there are but a dozen or two companions in it." [8] So Adams would write to Hay on October 8, 1882. He wrote extravagantly, but the satisfaction about the companionship of the "hearts" was sincere.

One time Henry Adams composed in fun a little prayer that John Hay should deliver over his—Adams's—grave, if he should precede his friend graveward: "Fellows, this departed heart first discovered the true meaning of sac and soc; he liked sack and claret; he invented Jefferson, Gallatin and Burr; he laughed at King's puns and Hay's jokes; also at Emily Beale's; and any man who could do all that, deserves all he will get when he gets there." [9]

Emily Beale was Marian Adams's particular consolation

for dullness. She lived with her father, General Beale, across the corner of the square, and could be counted on to say the unexpected, the outrageous, or even the censorable thing upon any dying or dull occasion. She was to figure as Henry's Victoria Dare in *Democracy*. His "little Daredevil" probably libels Miss Beale, but the original, however much she protested, during those months when discussions raged about the possible author of the book, never minded too much. She never knew, when she talked about the wicked book with Mrs. Adams, or guessed with her at its supposed author, that it was Mr. Adams who had written it. Only the "hearts" and William Godkin and Henry Holt knew.

According to Holt's recollection, Adams brought the novel to him to be published in the late spring of 1879.[10] Adams had finished his *Gallatin* and delivered it to another publisher, Lippincott, who would shortly bring it out in four ponderous volumes: three, of papers; one, of Adams's *Life*. Now, cramming his novel into Holt's hand, and making him swear secrecy, Adams had a sense of completion.

He was ready for a trip which he and Marian had been planning for over a year; a trip which was to take them abroad for many months; a trip which would let him concentrate upon the foreign documentation of his *History*. He and his wife were setting off on a sort of American conquest of Europe. He intended to ransack the archives of three countries—Britain, France, and Spain—and lay hands on those papers which would help him document his story of the crystallization of the American character.

On May 28th they set off, crossing the Atlantic on the *Gallia*. They were to be gone from home for a year and a half on a long and fortunate trip. They would like Europe as they never had before. History was their excuse, and Henry would work conscientiously. But they let themselves wander off on several personal by-paths.

Non-historical travel took them in the late summer of 1879 as far north as the English lakes and as far south in the early winter as the Arabic city of Tetuán in North Africa. Delays kept Adams away from his work for months at a time. In these intervals husband and wife rummaged about Europe with a real-unhurried enjoyment. They indulged their taste for collecting, for partying, and for traveling. When they returned from southern Europe to London after a winter in France and Spain, they set up housekeeping for several months at 22 Queen's Gate, London. They saw old friends, and made some new ones.

138

They fell in with Henry James in London. He would come to see them, stand on their hearthrug and warm his back at their fireplace, talking to Marian Adams familiarly as if they were all still in Cambridge.[11] James was at a happy moment in his career. He was just between *Daisy Miller* and *The Portrait of a Lady.* He had tasted popularity. He knew now what he could do and that it was good. He had also found a home in England. He would never be more fortunate.

When the Adamses went to Paris in search of illusive papers, James went too, to share their company. He was their companion in Paris for meals, for the circus, for a café-chantant, or for the theater.[12] With his innocent unshockability, he squired Marian to several varieties of drama which, in Boston or Beverly Farms, she could not even have imagined. "Very indecent and charmingly acted," was one, she wrote to Dr. Hooper. "If *huissiers* had come in and borne actors and audience to the nearest station house, I should have conceded that they had a strong case." [13]

Marian went to see a languid Mr. Worth to order a new gown. "He was standing pensively by the window in a long puce-coloured dressing gown with two exquisite black spaniels—twins—sitting on two green velvet chairs. This is what he wants me to have: the main dress gold color, the velvet only to lay the lace on and at the bottom in front. I have become bored with the idea of getting any new gowns, but Henry says, 'People who study Greek must take pains with their dress.' " [14]

Mrs. Adams studied Greek, but was most unscholarly; she had an exquisite taste for life, but it was for life, for books, for people, in good-tasting mouthfuls; she never had, nor ever desired, to discipline herself for the long dry spell the scholar must endure. She was, like her father, something of an anachronism—a puritan of dilettantish tastes.

Henry Holt ran across the Adamses at this time. He remembered in Paris how he would meet them by engagement at the Venus of Milo in the Louvre, and how they would "go off for lunch together." [15] He remembered them as good company and caught a characteristically New England remark from Adams, one day, about lunch: "Adams remarked that a lunch should have two characteristics—that it should be (I think) digestible and (I know) economical which latter surprised me a bit from a rich man." [16]

He noted too that Adams spoke with an "Anglicized" pronunciation, saying "Sir Frahncis" with a broadened *a.*[17] Marian could have assured Holt, and asuredly would have, if she had known his criticism, that no American heart beat righter than Henry's, however his tongue strayed into foreign ways.

Their pronounced American-ness in Europe, a part they played consciously and righteously when they went abroad, was noticed. William James had written home, according to his sister, Alice, probably at the time of the Adamses' earlier trip: "You never saw such a pair of patriots as Lowell and Henry Adams and his little cockatrice of a wife—I use this term most affectionately for she is delightful." [18] "Delightful" but also a little frightening. One comes upon this tone toward Mrs. Adams more than once. She recognized the quality in herself, speaking of it as "the *picador,* which is latent in me." [19]

One must picture them in Europe as cocky, independent, a little standoffish, as they went about and partook superiorly of European culture. They never quite learned, as Henry James did, to let go and drift, and emerge from the drift unscathed and refreshed. They were always a little mistrustful, especially of the more attractive aspects of these alien ways. One is irresistibly reminded of the earlier New Englanders abroad, of Abigail Adams, in a state of shocked delight at her first view of the ballet in Paris.

Only in Spain did they forget American pride entirely. That country was so utterly different as not to compete at all. They had their happiest time in southern Spain, getting away from archives and foggy winter weather. In Granada they enjoyed the spontaneous hospitality of Don Leopoldo Equilaz, whom they met quite by accident, but who thawed their reserve, and was soon reading them Arabic inscriptions, taking them into old courtyards, and arranging a happy journey by muleback into Arabic Africa. [20]

At last Adams got to his papers: first in Madrid, by a casual and friendly sort of personal bribery; then in Paris; last on London, where a number of the rules had to be broken or bent. [21] He worked, then, with an intense sort of concentration, early and late. He read and took notes in various government record offices from morning till night, and continued reading and studying in his hotel, from dinner till bedtime. A large part of his work was selective; he left behind. in the three cities, instructions for copyists to set to work. He would receive these documents in large bundles after he got home.

By throwing himself into the one object with all his being, he was disciplining himself as he never had before, and he found himself equal to the work. The trip was succeeding, not only in the collecting of materials, but in giving him perspective. America of the time of Jefferson, looked at from this side of the Atlantic, was bright, distinct, and complete, a landscape viewed through the wrong end of binoculars. He knew that he would at last sit down one day and write the first sentence of Adams's *History*.

When Henry and Marian Adams returned to Washington in the late autumn of 1880, they came home as natives of the place. They lived first for a few weeks at Wormley's Hotel while an old house leased from William Wilson Corcoran was redone for them. They had rented it for six years, and Corcoran had agreed to remodel it for their needs. They got behind him and behaved, during the early winter, in Marian's words to her father, like the "two driving New Englanders" they were, goading the contractor into finishing with his paints and plumbing.[22] Henry Adams became a happy householder. No delay or inconvenience fazed him. On an icy morning, when all of Washington's pipes had burst, he could be seen on his rooftop, sweeping out his frozen gutters.[23]

This house, No. 1607 H Street, where they could look out at the changing seasons in Lafayette Square, was to be a comfortable and well used home for the time left to them to be together. The "old barn," as they called it, was to be the scene of the remembered gaieties of the Adams marriage— not the beautiful and original house Richardson was later to build for them. For Marian was to be dead before they could move into it. But time, although it was running short for them, seemed long. There did not seem to be any countable end to the contented routine into which they now settled, happily and willfully. "I look forward placidly to recurring winters and summers in Washington and Beverly, until a cheery tomb shall provide us with a permanent abode for all seasons," Adams had written the preceding summer, in a letter to Henry Cabot Lodge from London.[24]

They found their new house roomy and easy to live in. They had stables and a garden in the back, and flowerboxes and a dog run in the front. They had their drawings and water colors on the walls, their books in new bookcases made for them by a Washington cabinetmaker. They expected to get the most out of their good seat for the social and political spectacle. "The town is filling fast and we expect an interesting winter," wrote Marian to Dr. Hooper, on November 21st.[25] "Sunday we had a quiet, pleasant dinner with the Beales and an hour in the evening with the Bancroft Davises. Wednesday, dined with the Schurzes, he playing deliciously to us after dinner. Last evening, dined with the John Hays, only Schurz and his daughter—it was lively and amusing." [26]

They were never as energetic and cheerful and busy as in this winter of 1880–1881. Mr. Schurz brought his Report for Marian to read. He was concluding his term as Secretary of the Interior. Aristarchi Bey, the Turkish Minister, brought the Japanese Minister and his wife to dine. Abram Hewitt brought Mrs. Adams some tea; General Miles gave her a pair of white Sioux moccasins. All this in one week in early December. It was no wonder that Mrs. Adams was a little spoiled, a little delicate and fastidious.

Being bystanders at the capital's circus was honest fun. The spectacle teased Henry's historian's curiosity as much as it satisfied his and his wife's honest human interest in gossip. Marian's letters to her father, who she says was very like herself, were inspired gossip: gossip which had a real sensitivity to tones of character; gossip which caught the very tone of the time.

Yet their quiet life, lived to themselves, when they deliberately cut off all the distractions of the human scene, was as important to them as the amusing things their neighbors said or did. They had to manage their social life, or it would have managed them. Henry had to give hours to his work. This he did unobtrusively, writing, reading, note-taking all through the hours of the morning and early afternoon. Then he was ready to be idle.

Marian kept his door. She amused herself for hours, dividing a morning between reading Greek and trimming a hat. Perhaps she planned a new flower bed or supervised the cooking of special dishes in which she became adept: soft-shell crabs, terrapin, chestnut-stuffed turkey. She copied these recipes copiously for her father and sent him samples as well as instructions for the cooking.

Every fall and every spring, and in winter, when the weather allowed, the Adamses rode their horses—Prince was Henry's, Daisy was Marian's—out into the nearby spaciousness of trees. Henry had loved the landscape of the District from the time he had been a bachelor in Washington in 1868. Now he introduced his wife to it.

They went to considerable trouble each year to ship their horses and light carriage by sea from Washington to Beverly, and from Beverly to Washington. It was only one aspect of their life which sufficient money made possible. Marian, perhaps, never realized how many of their pleasurable discriminations were bound up with money. Yet they never thought of themselves as wealthy. They looked with disfavor on all the showier forms of display. The strange blooms of the new industrialism did not appeal to them.

Henry might keep "his nose to the grindstone" all the dark winter long, but when a good day came in January they got out to take advantage of it. "Yesterday," Marian wrote to her father on the 23rd, "I goaded Henry into a ride, the thermometer saying 40°—and such a ride! The horses not sharpened, and the roads proved solid ice under the mud. The beasties balanced themselves on their tails, and when Georgetown Cemetery was reached, it seemed wiser and more economical to dismount and save future transport, but curiosity led us on to see if we could get home. We slid gaily down a long hill and crawled over horsecar tracks, frozen and penitent, to our stable." [27]

Fall and spring were the good seasons for riding. During the long-drawn-out weeks preceding winter or summer, Marian and Henry took longer and longer rides of exploration. They got hold of some Army maps of the Civil War and looked for military tracks and traces. They hunted for the earliest flowers and the latest fall leaves. They came home late to dinner and neglected their neighbors.

When the weather outdoors was bad, they sat inside and toasted themselves by their fireplace. Their dogs were as important to their indoor life as their horses were to their outdoor life. Marquis, Possum, and Boojum, the three Skye terriers, were personages in the city. Without compunction, Marian called in a doctor, a friend who was an oculist, to treat Boojum, when he had eye trouble. John Hay and Clarence King gravely diagnosed the case. "Cataract," said Hay; "tom-cataract" quipped King.[28] The doctor agreed with King.

Henry Adams examined his dogs' traits as curiously, as profoundly, and as amusedly as a child. There is a photograph of him sitting upon the front steps of No. 1607, his dog's head in his hand, gazing into his face as if for some word. Although Adams had an intense life of the mind, he was not the kind of thinker who could wander through a house, a city, abstracted from its common life. The life of an animal—or of a man—might strike him with as real an interest as the conquest of a theory.

Henry and Marian Adams kept a space in their lives cleared for themselves alone. They were comfortably settled in a city and a society which they considered entertaining and worth cultivating. They did not hold themselves aloof.

If they wished, they went out, and they often wished it. If they preferred, as they more often did, they held a kind of informal court at home, and had whom they would come to them there. This way of living caused them to make some invidious distinctions, but it was, at least, a conscious effort at an art living in the midst of a racketing abundance of life.

Only in analysis could one separate their interests. In their days and nights in Washington, history, politics, gossip, friendship, enmity, boredom, interest, all chased each other round their busy clock. Yet one can guess at their typical day or week. One finds it candidly set down in Mrs. Adams's letters to her father, to whom she wrote a kind of report each Sunday. All of their life is not in these letters—not their most private or inner life, not their life of thought—but the true color and movement of their social life most certainly is.

Reading these letters, one sees and hears the life of the early 1880's buzzing once again around Lafayette Square. In the background is the noise of the coming and going of Presidents. Hayes was out in 1880, and Garfield was in. Then Garfield was shot, dying all through the summer of 1881. Arthur then came in and did not do perhaps as badly as had been expected. Then, in 1884, Cleveland came in, with Henry Adams's blessing for having beaten Blaine.

Diplomats came and went. The best of these for the Adamses was the Turkish Aristarchi Bey, who became their good friend. Senators, Representatives, Cabinet members, newspapermen, the scientists of the Smithsonian, and of the various government surveys, came and went. Henry and Marian knew the interesting ones.

Their closest friends were not sedentary. They were always coming into town from far-off places, or very suddenly going off again. King was with them—for two years the reluctant head of the Geological Survey—then went off to Mexico with Alex Agassiz, and then to Europe, to stay away till 1884. Hay was in Washington as Assistant Secretary under Hayes, then in New York during the summer of 1881 to manage the *Tribune* in Reid's temporary absence, then once again in Cleveland. Alexander Agassiz was, each summer, dredging some stretch of ocean that had not been explored before, but he came into town between expeditions. From 1881 to 1883 Raphael Pumpelly was in the Rocky Mountain northwest, exploring the resources of the Montana country through which the Northern Pacific was building its route. Henry Richardson was building a series of railway stations in Massachusetts, and in 1882 went to Europe for a vacation trip with the minister of Trinity, Phillips Brooks. After his return he received a commission to build a house for Nicholas Anderson in Washington and was soon bustling in and out of the Capital with news of architectural work in Albany, Pittsburgh, and Chicago.

Washington at this time was essentially a small town. When the Adamses first moved into No. 1607, the President's wife, across the Square, sent them some cut flowers to adorn the new house.[29] A day or two later Mr. and Mrs. Adams paid a call on Mr. and Mrs. Hayes. They "sat in big Hadley rocking chairs in front of a wood fire" in the White House, and Marian reported subsequently that "It looked almost pleasant in that upholstered barrack. I stoutly defended Henry James and Daisy Miller to stout Mrs. Smith of Chicago, and protested that the latter was charming and the author adored her." [30]

Almost as soon as they were at home, Carl Schurz and General Francis A. Walker called. Both were full of Indian affairs. Schurz, in his term as Secretary of the Interior, had made the first attempt to treat the Indian problem with intelligence and compassion, and he had, of course, got into trouble as a result. General Walker brought them word of the wanderer Clarence King: "Ill, shaken with fever, and heavily out of pocket" stranded somewhere in Mexico, as Marian retold her father. "We hope daily to see him here, but he is so reckless of life and strength that his friends feel uneasy about him." [31]

Mrs. Adams found a new friend at a reception. She was the new Mrs. Cameron, the wife of the boss of Pennsylvania, Senator "Don." "She is very young, pretty, and, I fear, bored, and her middle-aged Senator is fighting a boss fight in Harrisburg; so she came on Friday, wailed about Harrisburg, and was quite frank in her remarks about men and things. Poor 'Don' will think she's fallen among thieves when he comes back." [32]

A Sunday *Boston Herald* of this time could gossip about Mrs. Adams, calling her a "hostess of liberal proclivities." [33] But being an Independent did not much limit Mr. and Mrs. Adams in picking their friends whom they chose for wit or beauty or honesty, but not too often for political complexion. Only a very few were beyond the pale. One of these was their personal devil, James G. Blaine. They never called on the Blaines; never spoke, if they could help it; and Henry was to be put to it to finish his research in the State Department before Blaine, under Garfield, came in as the new Secretary.

He would not set foot in the Department until after Garfield's murder, when Blaine was gone from there. Then Adams went back happily to his State Department desk hunting more papers.

They carried on friendship amidst dangerous waters. The Blaines were friends of the Camerons and the Beales, while John Hay and Clarence King could not see why it was wrong to support the man from Maine. But the undercurrents gave an added excitement to their coming and going. By the time the winter snows had weighted the trees in the square, their social life had taken on a fierce velocity. For self-protection they would occasionally rebel—not enough to cut out fun, but enough for a little relief. "This coming week is pretty full," wrote Marian on February 6th: "a dinner at L. P. Morton's Wednesday, at the Bancrofts' Thursday, at the Schurzes' Saturday, besides evening toots if one is energetic. Lunches I despise and lie myself out of. Fine sleighing, brilliant sun, clear, cold. History goes on quietly. We barricade our doors till near sunset and are envied by our harnessed friends." [34]

There was a quiet satisfaction in Marian Adams's tone. She enjoyed the fact that they managed so well. Her good and easy position in Washington which, painlessly, with any exceptions she desired to make, allowed her to go as she pleased, was valuable to her. She liked too to have the reputation of saying what she pleased, when she pleased. She liked to be satiric, and was sorry only when her victim missed the point.

She was bored at dinner one night when her near neighbor at the table was L. P. Morton, banker, Congressman, and future Vice President. "He is a lightweight and very ordinary; if he can be a successful public man, none need despair. He asked my political opinions. I told him I was a boss-Stalwart, believed in the machine, and the chaff spread; but he was too dull to catch chaff." [35]

At last, after much expectation, King, who was never dull, who never missed chaff, came into town. "Mr. King turned up on Sunday," was Marian's tale in a February letter, "after a fearful fourteen hundred miles on mule-back from Mexico; drowned in a flood and lost all his money and papers; is very well and jolly." [36] A recollection of wit and good feeling is hard to conjure back. But something of the flavor of Clarence King's personality lingers in the few phrases that one friend or another set down as his.

Marian Adams wrote her father that "Mr. King, speaking

of the banking firm of Morton & Bliss, says with a happy turn: 'If ignorance is Bliss, what the devil is Morton?' " [37] King loved his friends, but respected them not to their face. He teased Adams with his personal explanation of the climate of Boston: "Boston was 1,387,453 years under the ice; and then the Adamses came." [38]

One friend of King—William Crary Brownell—remembered King saying, "A painter should always paint in his third manner." [39] Another—John Hay—recorded how King outwitted Ruskin, whom he met when he went abroad for the first time. "Ruskin took him to his heart, entertained him at Coniston, and offered him his choice of his two greatest water-colors by Turner. 'One good Turner,' said King, 'deserves another,' and took both." [40]

Another friend, who was associated with him on the Fortieth Parallel Survey—James D. Hague—told a story of King at home on a train: "A nervous old lady once found him much too obliging when, having entered a crowded railway car, she was about to take the only available vacant seat alongside King, but, having suddenly spied his gun standing in the corner, she walked the whole length of the car . . . and returned again to King's place, saying severely, 'Young man, is that gun loaded?' to which King instantly replied . . . 'No, ma'am, but I can load it for you in a minute.' " [41]

The easy way King had of coming into their house and making himself at home is illustrated in a letter Marian Adams was trying to write on Sunday, February 27, 1881: "Mr. King has just come in and though I've entreated him to take a book till I've finished this letter he will keep babbling." [42]

Sorrow touched them in the middle of laughter. Marian's sister-in-law died in Cambridge, leaving five little girls for her brother Edward Hooper to care for alone. Marian did not go to Boston at this time. Henry refused to let her go.[43] Perhaps he feared the effect of the tragedy on her oversensitive nerves. They seldom parted. Only once—in April, 1883—did Marian go off on a holiday alone when she accepted an invitation to pay a four-day visit to a friend, Anne Palmer, in New York. Otherwise Henry was always with her.

With a new President in the White House in 1881, there were new people to be met and assessed. Spring found Marian weighing Garfield's Cabinet quite professionally. "The only members whom we know are Wayne MacVeagh and Lincoln [Robert Todd Lincoln], whom we met only at Mrs. Hayes's dinner. The former is a square out-and-out Independent, clever, lively, a great talker and laugher. We have seen him from time to time unmuzzled; how he will appear as an official I am curious to see." [44]

Wayne MacVeagh was married to Mrs. Don Cameron's sister. The two husbands were enemies in politics, both in Pennsylvania and in Washington. Yet they managed to stay personal friends, and both families were friends of the Adamses. Their difficult but sustained relationship was typical of many which could only be maintained by good nature and good humor.

Life was quite like walking a tightrope. Was not John Hay an admirer of Blaine? This was a fact incredible to the imagination, but a fact none the less. Marian said bluntly of him, "He is a stout Stalwart and shuts his eyes and opens his mouth." [45] Yet she and Henry loved John Hay, and he them. He and King, who agreed with Hay on the crucial Blaine issue, entertained the Adamses royally in New York City when, in the late spring of 1881, after a splendid year on the tightrope, they were passing through on the way to Beverly Farms.

Their quiet summers were a necessary contrast to their winters of social brightness. They had friends to visit them at Beverly. Once both Clarence King and James Lowndes (the original of Carrington in *Democracy*) were sick in bed at their house, and were tended by them. But generally they were without much company in summer. They saw few people except their seaside neighbors. They had time for enjoying the ocean and the pine woods and the New England air.

But they were always glad in the fall to go back. "Found the house in perfect order, fires burning, dogs in ecstasy, roses in boom in garden, maples red and yellow in front and behind, Margery gave us a very nice dinner and, in short, all our plans were carried out." [46] Thus wrote Marian to her father of their homecoming. The busy season—their second in No. 1607—began immediately. "Yesterday P. M." wrote Marian, in the same letter, "Mrs. Senator Don Cameron and Miss Beale rapped on Henry's window with their umbrellas and, of course, got in; as Miss Beale explained, 'It's better than ringing because you can't say engaged.'" [47]

So ended one year; so began another. October seemed the quickening time of year—their new year. Soon, Marian was so much in the thick of things that she said her life was like a circus, and she hated to go to bed at night, for fear of missing something.⁴⁸ She would stop for a moment at the end of a day and find herself tingling with the assault of it all upon her nerves. "When I went to bed," she said on one such occasion of rueful reflection, "I calculated that, from five to eleven, there had been no let-up except for ten minutes." ⁴⁹ It was not so much the quantity of sensation beating upon her, as the liveliness of her own reactions which exhausted her.

It was amusing for a long time. But as the years went by, it became too much. A note of weariness began to creep into her letters. She began to falter; she caught cold, had an earache or a toothache. It was as if her system rebelled and sought some sort of relief. It was as if a tightly wound watch had begun almost imperceptibly to lose time.

Neither she nor her husband apparently noticed. Year by year the Washington-Beverly swing went by. There was more good talk in the easygoing, frank, and bright companionship of the fireside at No. 1607. Here was Agassiz home from Brazil; here was Pumpelly fresh from Montana; here was Henry James on the way back to England—and writing a romantic farewell to his land in the person of Marian Adams. She was a little sniffy about it, not quite clear whether it was a compliment or not. "I had a farewell letter from Henry James, Jr., written Tuesday at midnight on the eve of sailing. He wished, he said, his last farewell to be said to me as I seemed to him 'the incarnation of my native land'—a most equivocal compliment coming from him. Am I then vulgar, dreary, and impossible to live with?" ⁵⁰ Something in Maggie Verver or Milly Theale might have answered her, years later, but she would not hear the answer.

Their door might open, too, to the great and energetic bulk of Henry Richardson, bringing them his designs for the house that he was building near them for the Nicholas Andersons. They watched it going up from the first laying of the foundations and laughed a little at the Andersons for complaining at the topsy-turviness of their existence while the great whirlwind of Richardson's creativeness blew through their lives.

The architect was not easy to endure at close quarters. His personal wants were as emphatic as his generosities. When he settled down to live with the Andersons while working on their new house, he upset their routine and their peace.

But Richardson was an easy man to forgive. "Sunday we had three or four people to dine with Richardson," wrote Marian on May 7, 1882; "he can say truly 'I am my own music,' for he carries off any dinner more or less gaily." [51] The Adamses would be engulfed very soon in the same difficulties as the Andersons had had. They had caught the fever too, and, jointly with the Hays, were planning now a double house which Richardson was to build for them.

In these social years between their settling at No. 1607 and their building No. 1603, Henry Adams had done much. His regime suited his work habits exactly. He had private time for writing, and he had other hours for a relief from writing. He had perhaps a more balanced existence than his wife, for he could retire inside himself. She lived ever so sensitively and charmingly, but always in the aspects of persons, places, and things presented to her by her senses. He had a world of thought that was more solid and more compelling than anything he saw happen on Lafayette Square. What this world of thought produced in books and ideas will be discussed more fully later. Here, it is important to stress first the range and the scope of these books of the good years in Washington.

Adams had come home from Europe and settled in residence at No. 1607 with two books recently published (*Gallatin*, in 1879, and *Democracy*, in 1880) and making their own way; one, with scholarly restraint and decorum; the other, in the midst of gossip and recrimination, rocketing along with the pace of a best seller. It probably pleased his innate actor's taste to walk Wahington's sidewalks as two men. He was Henry Adams, the historian, who had taught at Harvard, was known to be writing a history, and was to be gravely saluted for his authoritative editing of Albert Gallatin's papers, and for writing the definitive *Life*. This work was available in four heavy volumes, praised by several, read by a few. He was also—unknown, unidentified—the author of the cruel, witty, and graceful novel of satire, *Democracy*, which had stood Washington on its ear. He had a curious satisfaction in performing an act, and then stepping aside to watch himself performing. He wrote to Hay, who received his most intimate ideas. "My ideal of authorship would be to have a famous *double* with another name, to wear what honors I could win. How I should enjoy upsetting him at last by publishing a low and shameless essay with woodcuts in his name!" [52] (June 25, 1882).

What Adams remarked (as *Gallatin* and *Democracy* made their respective debuts, in 1879 and 1880) was not so much the lack of reaction on the part of the public as the inadequacy of reaction. His *Gallatin* was praised, but ignorantly.

The reviewers, for the most part, found out all they knew of their subject in the book they were supposed to be reviewing. As far as the novel was concerned (and Adams was in a position to hear frank and un-selfconscious comment) his friends buzzed mostly about the minor matter of the identification of the characters (and some were recognizable, if distorted and one sided). Few seemed to care about the idea of the book.

Adams had already reached a lonely eminence. He was writing books which had meat in them, but of a kind slow to be assimilated. His ideas would henceforth seem to go underground and come up again only generations later. He should have known—and did consciously know—that this was the common fate of any book of original or generative thought. In a tranquil, untragic regime of existence, he might have grown used to dropping ideas into a void. But he was to have his life broken in 1885 and would grow bitter. Even in 1880, 1881, and 1882, near the beginning of his career as a writer of history and biography, he was disturbed. There seemed to be a fatal lapse of connection. Here he was on one side—the writer and teacher—and there, on the other side of an unbridgeable chasm was the untouchable reader. Whether this reader was of a scholarly or frivolous nature seemed to make no difference.

Yet in the early 1880's Adams's mind was not set, not fixed, in a particular attitude; he was merely impatient. If he were sarcastic, he was sarcastic in the hope of setting things right. If he were impatient, it was because he saw far, and others did not. He worked vigorously and knew that he worked well.

By the end of 1882, Adams's phenomenal energy had accomplished two more books, both biographies, and both studies for his *History* which was his principal, continuing occupation. Marian Adams wrote on December 3rd to her father: "I'm glad you like Henry's *Randolph*; the *Burr* is much better. . . ." [53] But *Aaron Burr* never saw the light. Adams put the manuscript aside after it had been rejected by Houghton. He thought of offering it to other publishers, or of bringing it out at his own expense. He seemed originally to have had a high opinion of it, but he lost patience with his orphan, threatened to destroy it, and probably did.

If we can judge from the Aaron Burr of the *History*—a portrait which must be assembled by the reader out of references scattered throughout the work—the biography would have been an engagingly rapscallion picture, a study in intellectual depravity, but of a depravity that did not lack a sheen of charm. Burr was Adams's "ideal scamp," a scamp of whom he was rather fond, in spite of his vices; the opposite kind of villain from Randolph, who, in spite of several virtues, gave him the shudders.

By January 31, 1883, Adams could be optimistic about his *History.* He wrote to Henry Cabot Lodge: "History moves on apace. I am getting to Chase's impeachment and the close of my first four years, the easiest quarter of my time." [54] He would not publish any of the *History* until 1889, but by February, 1884, he had in his hands, and for his private use, a printed version of what he had so far accomplished.

He wrote to Charles Gaskell on February 3rd:

Yesterday I received a bound copy of the first volume of my History. I have had six copies privately printed as a first edition for my own use. When I am ready, I shall reprint and publish two volumes at once. Perhaps I may reach this point in the year '86. I admit to thinking the book readable, but to you it would be sadly dull reading. You see I am writing for a continent of a hundred million people fifty years hence; and I can't stop to think what England will read. . . . The truth is, our affairs were never in so good a condition; public opinion was never healthier; and barring a few doubtful jobs, no government was ever so economically and sensibly conducted. We have got to the point where our protective duties must be lowered, and in another ten years we shall push Europe hard in manufactures. There is a tremendous amount of activity in every direction; and another generation will see the result. I consider ours to have already done its work, and on the whole it is biggest on record.[55]

These generalizations show Adams in a mood as true to the time of his marriage as it would be untrue later. It shows in what spirit he worked; and, strange as it may seem, he carried much of this belief in America into the blacker mood and tone of the future.

Meanwhile in 1883, he was trying his hand at another novel and accomplished something with more heart in it than *Democracy,* something more precarious, a novel about belief. He wrote a note to Henry Holt on November 9, 1883, discussing some proofs he was correcting.[56] Very probably his reference was to *Esther.* The book would appear in early March of the succeeding year, 1884, under the same absurd pseudonym as he had used for *Democracy,* Frances Snow Compton.

So far as we know, Adams's wife knew nothing of this book. And, from internal evidence, one can judge that it would have been almost impossible for him to have shown it to her. For its subject was simply Marian Adams. Not in situation, not in plot, but in its study of a soul Esther is Marian. Adams exacted secrecy. There was to be no advertisement, only a bare announcement of the book's publication.

By the time the new house was commissioned—January, 1884—and by the time Richardson got to work on it, Adams could take a breath and look back on accomplishment in the years since he had come to live in Washington. Since 1877 there had been then: *Documents Relating to New England Federalism* (1877), the papers of Gallatin and the *Life of Albert Gallatin* (1879), *Democracy* (1880), *John Randolph* (1882), *Esther* (1884), and the privately printed edition of the first four years of his *History,* a gage that it was well begun, a promise that it would be well finished.

Chapter 12

Disaster

IN SPITE OF the seeming happiness and continuity of the Adamses' way of life, there was a darkness growing on them. A part of this darkness was purely intellectual, a shadow cast on them by Adams's theory of life. He had come to think of existence as rigidly determined, but without teleology, that is, without purpose. These dark views made little difference to the cheerfulness of his and his wife's daily life so long as they were both in good health, good spirits, and good fortune. But a domestic unhappiness overtook them. His dark view of the universe seemed then to be grimly applied to him personally in his own house and in his own life. Emotion as well as reason led to despair.

Passages in his letters hint at the preliminary development of his dark views. He wrote to William James on July 27, 1882, in connection with James' paper, "Rationality, Activity and Faith," *Princeton Review,* 1882, in part as follows:

You choose to assume that the will is free. Good! Reason proves that the Will cannot be free. Equally good! Free or not, the mere fact that a doubt can exist, proves that X must be a very microscopic quantity. If the orthodox are grateful to you for such gifts, the world has indeed changed, and we have much to thank God for, if there is a God, that he should have left us unable to decide whether our thoughts, if we have thoughts, are our own or his'n.

Although your gift to the church seems to me a pretty darned mean one, I admire very much your manner of giving it, which magnifies the crumb into at least forty loaves and fishes. My wife is quite converted by it. She enjoyed the paper extremely. Since she read it she has talked of giving five dollars to Russell Sturgis's church for napkins. As the impression fades, she talks less of the napkins.[1]

Adams was set against free will. He believed stubbornly and devotedly that man was not free, that all his acts were the resut of the movement of the universe. But there was a deeper abyss he was just beginning to plumb. If man's acts were determined, what meaning could there be in those acts, what meaning in his own, in Henry Adams's, acts? Yet in spite of thinking in this manner, his mood was not consistently tragic. It was, on the contrary, a jaunty impatience with easy solutions, a sort of confidence in the results of his own dangerous adventuring upon shaky ground.

A half-year after writing the letter to James, he wrote on January 24, 1883, to Samuel J. Tilden. Adams thanked the older man for his praise for the recently published *Gallatin,* explaining how relatively easy it was to do justice to Gallatin, and how relatively difficult to do justice to Gallatin's compatriots Madison and Jefferson: ". . . For they appear like mere grasshoppers kicking and gesticulating on the middle of the Mississippi River." [2]

With this instance at hand, Adams moved toward a generalization:

There is no possibility of reconciling their theories with their acts, or their extraordinary foreign policy with dignity. They were carried along on a stream which floated them, after a fashion, without much regard to themselves.

This I take to be the result that students of history generally reach in regard to modern times. The element of individuality is the free-will dogma of the science, if it is a science. My own conclusion is that history is simply social development along the lines of weakest resistance, and that in most cases the line of weakest resistance is found as unconsciously by society as by water.[3]

Almost two years later, on December 21, 1884, Adams wrote to Francis Parkman a letter strangely mixed in hope, pride and despair:

My own labor is just half done. [He was speaking of the *History.*] Two heavy volumes have been put into type, partly for safety, partly to secure the advantages of a first edition without publicity. The more I write, the more confident I feel that before long a new school of history will rise which will leave us antiquated. Democracy is the only subject for history. I am satisfied that the purely mechanical development of the human mind in society must appear in a great democracy so clearly, for want of disturbing elements, that in another generation psychology, physiology, and history will join in proving man to have as fixed and necessary development as that of a tree; and almost as unconscious.[4]

These excerpts from letters of the early 1880's indicate the direction Adams was going. It was against this intellectual background that in 1885 a personal tragedy acted itself out in his life.

In the spring of 1885 Mrs. Adams had to leave her husband, her house, and the accustomed activity of Lafayette Square to go to Boston. Her father, Dr. Robert Hooper, was gravely ill, and she was needed to help her sister, Mrs. Gurney, in nursing him.

Henry—lost, lonely, uneasy—stayed behind in Washington. He was able to see Marian only on brief visits to Boston. A letter of his written to her on March 21st indicates his disturbance. Writing to her as his "Dear Mistress" he said: "Your telegram inviting me to Cambridge arrived at half past six, and at first frightened me out of my wits; but Richardson read it and reassured me, declaring that he would give anything in the world if his wife would send such a telegram to him. After consultation and dinner I decided to take the two o'clock train with him on Monday." [5] (Richardson's home was in Brookline.)

He was disconsolate in the Washington intervals, yet saw himself in his situation there with some humor. To a friend, Rebecca Gilman Dodge, he wrote on April 8th: "I am very much obliged to you for your gracious letter, and wish that I could say that Dr. Hooper is better; but he is not. My wife has been four weeks away, and I bolt forward and back like a brown monkey. Nobody wants me in either place. They won't take me for a nurse, and I can't live all alone in a big, solitary house when it rains and I can't ride. Even the goldfish are bored, and the dogs fight to pass the time. The young women won't look at me, and as for the old ones, I am too young to win their confidence." [6]

Two days later he tried to give his wife—wrung by anxiety, worn with waiting—a gift of a picture of the spring: "After ransacking the Smithsonian" [he had been looking for a kind of marble for a fireplace for the new house] "I came back at three o'clock, and started off for a ride on Prince. The day was fine though cool (Therm. 44°), and I took my first three-hour spring excursion round by the dog-tooth violets and Rigg's farm. A few maples show a faint flush here and there, but not a sign of leaf is to be seen, and even the blood-root and hepatica hid themselves from my eyes. A few frogs sang in the sun, and birds sang in the trees; but no sign of a peach-blossom yet, and not even the magnolias and *Pyrus Japonica* have started. In 1878 the magnolias were in full flower and killed by frost on March 25, and in 1882 the frost killed them on April 10. I have not even seen the yellow Forsythia in flower, thought it should have been out as early as March 15. Last year the *Pyrus Japonica* was

156

reddening on April 2. So you have not yet lost much spring . . ." [7]

Three days later, on April 13th, Dr. Hooper died. Marian Adams could go home, after her father was buried, and should then have begun to recover from her loss. But her hurt did not heal. Mental anxiety continued long after her physical tiredness was gone. Some wound of the mind—perhaps an old one—was reopened by this grief. As in Egypt, her weakness was in her nerves. She fell into an abnormal melancholy.

Henry tried to distract her by movement. They went into the Virginia mountains in the summer and returned to Beverly to remain quietly far into the fall. There they sat close, but Marian did not improve. At last, in early winter, they returned to Washington where their new house was at last almost finished.

On November 4th Adams wrote to his friend T. F. Dwight, "We lead a quiet and very retired life at present, as my wife goes nowhere." [8] On November 13th he wrote Henry Holt, "I never had so many reasons for wishing to be left in peace as now." [9]

On December 6th Marian Adams killed herself. She swallowed some of the poisonous crystals the deadliness of which she well knew—photographic chemicals with which she had worked expertly for many years.

Henry Adams was alone on the Sunday he found his wife dead. He remained alone, offending his neighbors by refusing to see them. He stayed alone till his family could arrive from New England. There was a coroner's report. There was a funeral. There was a burial in Rock Creek Cemetery. Adams left town afterward, in a flight from horror and a flight from happiness.

It is not necessary to know all the details of Mrs. Adams's death to conceive the effect upon her husband. We have, as direct evidence, only the friendly gossip of a neighbor who watched it from the outside and the broken words of the man to whom it happened. It is sufficient.

Nicholas Anderson, who had been Henry's companion in college and in Berlin before the Civil War, had settled near the Adamses a few years before. Mrs. Adams had taken a picture of his house and given it to him at the time that he had been having difficulties with Richardson. At that time Mr. and Mrs. Adams had teased Anderson for his confusion in the face of the Richardsonian genius. In November, 1885, Anderson wrote to his son Larz, at Harvard: "I am bitterly revenged on the Adamses for the fun they had with my architect troubles, for their house is not nearly finished and Mrs. Adams is suffering from nervous prostration." [10]

A month later, on December 9th, Anderson again wrote to his son about their neighbors: "The death of Mrs. Henry Adams was a great shock to us. She and her husband breakfasted at noon on Sunday, and she had gone to her room. At two a lady called to see her, and Henry went to her room and found her, as he supposed, in a swoon before the fire. He placed her on a lounge and summoned a physician who said she had been dead on hour. I called as soon as I heard it, and offered to do all that I could, but Henry refused to see anyone. I appreciate his state of mind, but I am sorry he would not let me show my sympathy by my acts. Until his family arrived he saw, as far as I can learn, no one whatever, and I can imagine nothing more ghastly than that lonely vigil in the house with his dead wife. Poor fellow! I do not know what he can do." [11]

"I can endure, but I cannot talk," Adams wrote to George Bancroft on December 8th.[12] Ten days after the event, he wrote to William Godkin, who, after years of sadness, had married for a second time: "I am glad to think of you as in the sunshine again. Never fear for me. I have had happiness enough to carry me over some years of misery; and even in my worst prostration I have found myself strengthened by two thoughts. One was that life could have no other experience so crushing. The other was that at least I had got out of life all the pleasure it had to give. I admit that fate at last has smashed the life out of me; but for twelve years I had everything I most wanted on earth. I own that the torture has made me groan; but, as long as any will is left, I shall try not to complain." [13]

Some assumption buried beneath reason made Adams hang on. Endurance was a bare sort of existence, but he held grimly to it. For many years he endured but did not live, and for all the rest of his life he was marked by the experience. As his last word from the immediate neighborhood of his torture, here is his letter of March 8, 1886, to Henry Holt, who had evidently written to him about book business: "I am almost amused at the idea of my caring now for anything that so-called critics could say. When the only chapter of one's story for which one cares is closed forever, locked up, and put away, to be kept, as a sort of open secret, between oneself and eternity, one does not think much of newspapers. What a vast fraternity it is,—that of 'Hearts that Ache.' For the last three months it has seemed to me as though all society were coming to me, to drop its mask for a moment and initiate me into the mystery. How we do suffer! And we go on laughing; for, as a practical joke at our expense, life is a success." [14]

In this manner ended Henry Adams's marriage. He would be a different man from this time forward. What he did, what he said, what he wrote were to be curiously branded by what had happened in his house on a particular December day of 1885 when he was forty-seven years old. It is necessary to recognize the fact for any kind of comprehension of him.

Chapter 13

The Growth of a Mind

Past and Present

ADAMS'S BOOKS of the fortunate years (those years which led to tragedy) resulted from the shuttle-like movements of his thought, from present to past, from past to present. To the friends of his Washington dinner table, Adams seemed to be concerned mostly with present-day history. But in his own mind, past and present were parts of one living whole. Jefferson was as unspared and unsparing a reality to him as General Grant or President Hayes or Secretary Blaine whom he might brush in the street. By a quick, deft motion of an efficient imagination, he could put himself in the Virginian's Washington, D.C., or set up the figure of Jefferson, and Jefferson's ideas, in Chester Arthur's world. He tried to tie the two ages together. He continually refreshed the past with insights from the present, and the present with insights from the causal past.

He worked at the *History* all these years. It was the center of his intellectual life. The other books—whether of past or present—were all related to the larger work.

In 1879 he published the *Life of Albert Gallatin*; in 1880 the contemporary novel of Washington society *Democracy*; in 1882, *John Randolph*; in 1884, the contemporary novel *Esther*. Enumeration shows the restless sweep of his mind back and forth from the early part of the nineteenth century to his own decades.

Life of Albert Gallatin

As far back as those anxious months in London when, to distract himself from the war, Adams had hacked away at the story of Pocahontas and John Smith; he had thought curiously about the problems of history and biography. He had theorized about history in the teaching of it at Harvard, but he had not, even then, considered himself a practitioner. It was only on coming to Washington, and giving up the job of history professor, that he could, at last, become a historian.

The *Life of Albert Gallatin* was his first attempt to work out a justification of his ideas.

The book differed from many previous American studies of national heroes in the thoroughness of its careful, complete backing in documents. Adams had come into possession of a mass of important and unpublished material. He had hunted for and found other documents in government files and in private collections, and had set these papers in order and published them in three volumes. Then, in the *Life,* the fourth volume of the set, he attempted to show how to use such a collection of papers. The *Gallatin* was, first of all, an experiment in technique.

The documentation was what struck his contemporaries, almost to the exclusion of any other merit in the work. The casual reviewer found in his hand a heavy book, awkward to hold, with unattractive small print and narrow margins, a book studded with extended quotations from state papers and letters. The reviewer looked it over, paid superstitious reverence to Professor Adams's scholarship, which was obvious, and went no further. He saluted the author with ignorant praise and failed to discover the life hidden between the heavy covers.

In writing the biography Adams had had large ambitions unconnected with the scholarly arrangement of verified facts. Albert Gallatin was, for Adams, the most admirable figure of the Jeffersonian period. That period was the crucial one in which America discovered its permanent character. Yet the conjunction of the age and the life—in spite of great achievement—was sad. Why? Adams set out, in writing a perfectly accurate and authoritative life, to explore a question of value as well as of fact.

The theme of the *Life of Albert Gallatin* was to be stated comprehensively in the *History,* but in the biography one individual, rather than a society, bore the weight of Adams's consideration. The movement of emotion in the *Gallatin* and in the *History* was the same: from hope to disappointment to disillusionment.

With a youthful enthusiasm and idealism, Albert Gallatin had given himself to the Rousseauistic faith in his native city of Geneva. He had hated the Old World tyrannies. He had believed in basic human nature. He came to America in 1780 without money or position and threw himself upon the back country. After various hardships and the tragic loss of his first wife, he achieved a distinguished place in the new nation. He based his career on the goodness of the unspoiled common man. He adored democracy. But he was, himself, of a keen, cool, moderate, and rational temperament.

He made an excellent right-hand man for both Presidents Jefferson and Madison. He achieved much more than his offices alone would indicate. He served in the Pennsylvania Legislature, in both branches of the national Congress, and was Secretary of the Treasury under both Jefferson and Madison. He should by right have been Secretary of State under Madison, but was kept out by political chicanery. He was engaged in foreign missions from 1813 till 1829 in St. Petersburg, Ghent, Paris, and London. After this variety of distinguished public service, he retired from official life to live in New York City. There he made a decent living as a bank president, but devoted most of his energies to private and scientific research. He studied finance, and became an expert and consultant in this subject. His greatest pleasure in these later years was a study of the languages of the American Indian. He became the first American expert in this field.

Where was there room for disillusionment in this long and honorable career? In what consisted the tragedy? It was not tragedy of the outward and visible event, but of the inward life of the mind. Adams was interested in Gallatin's own estimate of himself. The book was written with Gallatin's attitudes, as well as acts, in the foreground.

The basic trouble was a bankruptcy of faith. Gallatin's faith had been democracy and he had lost it.

The *History* which Adams was writing at the same time as his *Life of Gallatin*, was to be a great tragic-comic pageant of a young society. Its theme was to be the fall of a young and naïve society from a too high, a too ideal theory of government to a more realistic and less happy conception. America of Jefferson's embargo was to wake to find itself with the same problems, the same vices, as other nations. It discovered that it too must use force, exert power, and govern, if it were to stay alive in a rapacious world.

The biography of Gallatin, the best man of the times, was planned to display this falling off from perfection as a personal as well as a national tragedy. Gallatin's disillusionment was not lessened by the fact that the new nation grew steadily into a greater prosperity during his public career. It did not help him in his bankruptcy of belief to realize that he had had a principal part in bringing about this new American complication and sophistication.

Gallatin did not falter in his efficiency as a planner or

administrator. He merely found out that he had a different nation on his hands from the one he had envisioned. America, of Jefferson's first inauguration, had thought itself different in kind and better than Europe. America, of Jefferson's embargo and of Madison's War of 1812, found that it had to cope with the same kind of ugliness, the same problems of force, with which the Old World had always struggled. Gallatin saw that the sweet simplicity of a government which governed at little as possible had been a shallow concept and would not suffice for a government which annexed all of the Louisiana Territory, which fought a sea war and a land war, and which—to his own way of thinking—needed the active planning of internal improvements.

Adams put his case in this book in extreme terms. It would have been possible to muffle the importance of the crisis. But in Adams, as in Gallatin, there was a certain stubborn honest extremity of view. The change, as between 1800 and 1816, was a real change; it was painful; it was, to Gallatin, enough of a change to warrant a melancholy loss of faith.

Adams, writing as if for Albert Gallatin, offered a personal dirge to a lost belief:

Thus the Administration of Mr. Jefferson, whose advent had been hailed eight years before by a majority of the nation as the harbinger of a new era on earth; the Administration which, alone among all that had preceded or were to follow it, was freighted with hopes and aspirations and with a sincere popular faith that could never be revived, and a freshness, almost a simplicity of thought that must always give to its history a certain indefinable popular charm like old-fashioned music; this Administration, into which Mr. Gallatin had woven the very web of his life, now expired, and its old champion, John Randolph, was left to chant a palinode over its grave: "Never has there been any Administration which went out of office and left the nation so deplorable and calamitous."[1]

It is obvious—in spite of the weight of the proud new documentation—that the story of Gallatin was a sorely personal story to its author. He identified his own disillusionment in the world after the Civil War with that of Gallatin in the first decades of the century. Adams buried his own emotion, his extreme hopes for the good to result from the war, his despairs of the wreckage of the two administrations of Grant, in that other time. Part of this identification was conscious. Perhaps a great deal of it was unconscious. At any rate, one can learn something about Henry Adams himself by listening carefully to what he has to say about Albert Gallatin at certain crucial moments in the *Life*. It would be possible to annotate the entire biography in this sense. Here it is enough to point out a few of these coincidences of character, thought, and feeling.

First there was the likeness between Gallatin's childhood home and Henry Adams's. Geneva, with its Protestant, bourgeois, and commercial aristocracy, and its strictness of morality, was the one city in Europe that could produce a mentality like Boston's. Next, there was the fact of Gallatin's espousal of the popular radicalism of his day, something similar to young Adams's fiery abolitionism in the 1850's.

There were other, more subtle and more personal likenesses that Henry Adams discovered between himself and the Swiss. Adams, speaking of Gallatin at nineteen, could have been writing autobiography: "At this time, and long afterwards, he was proud and shy. His behavior for many years was controlled by these feelings, which only experience and success at last softened and overcame." [2] "Instead of embracing his opportunities, he repelled them. . . . [He] refused to owe anything to his family. Not that even in this early stage of his career he ever assumed an exterior that was harsh or extravagant, or manners that were repulsive; but he chose to take the world from the side that least touched his pride, and, after cutting loose so roughly from the ties of home and family, he could not with self-respect return to follow their paths." [3] One thinks of Henry Adams in Berlin, of Henry Adams resenting the natural ties of Boston during the Harvard years, of Henry Adams cutting loose and getting out of New England altogether.

Gallatin's description of Hannah Nicholson, the girl who was to be his second wife, is somewhat of Adams's own deprecatory description of Marian Hooper: "I am contracted with a girl about twenty-five years old, who is neither handsome nor rich, but sensible, well-informed, good natured, and belonging to a respectable and very amiable family, who, I believe are satisfied with the intended match.' " [4] Adams's comment speaks something of himself: "The young lady was Hannah Nicholson, and the characteristic self-restraint of Mr. Gallatin's language in describing her to his friend is in striking contrast with the warmth of affection which he felt, and ever retained." [5]

The sympathy with which Adams discussed Gallatin's private occupations in his later years shows approval and a feeling of like-mindedness. He felt that Gallatin's observation of the excesses of the generation of 1830 was akin to his own observation of the excesses of the generation of 1870:

. . . the United States of 1830 was no longer the same country as the United States of 1790; it had found a solution of its most serious political problems, and its more active intellectual life was turning to the study of social and economic principles, to purely scientific methods and objects, to practical commerce and the means of obtaining wealth. Old though Mr. Gallatin might think himself, it was to this new society that he and his mental processes belonged, and he found it a pleasure rather than a pain to turn away from that public life which no longer represented a single great political conception, and to grapple with the ideas and methods of the coming generation. In fact, the politics of the United States from 1830 to 1849 offered as melancholy a spectacle as satirists ever held up to derision.

Of all the parties that have existed in the United States, the famous Whig party was the most feeble in ideas and the most blundering in management; the Jacksonian Democracy was corrupt in its methods; and both, as well as society itself, were deeply cankered with two desperate sores: the enormous increase of easily acquired wealth, and the terribly rapid growth of slavery and the slave power.[6]

Adams approved of Gallatin's character and was united with him in a related kind of melancholy. The partiality gives the book something of its flavor, yet interfered in no way with its truthfulness. Organically whole, it was a rich, full volume. Its only fault was an excess of length, details, and perhaps of documentation. It could do with an easier interest in trivialities.

Democracy

Washington, D.C., had a hold on Henry Adams from the first time he saw the city. When he finally settled there at thirty-nine, to live as a householder on Lafayette Square, he determined to get at the truth of Washington. *Democracy* was the result.

When he began to shape the book in 1879, he had a still youthful lack of fear. He was not afraid of trying something new. He decided to "do" Washington and "do" it as a novelist. He would make up characters, paint scenes, invent dialogue, and build a plot. He very nearly carried off the novel as boldly as he had planned.

The plot is contrived, the characters are not sufficiently involved in the action, and some of the circumstances, now, creak ever so slightly with age, but all this is a shadow on what he achieved. The main force is still in the book, for the author was concerned more with satire and thesis than with plot. And his eye, while jaundiced, was acute, and he had gusto.

His scene was Washington in the middle 1870's when a newly elected President from the Middle West had come into the city to await his inauguration. The public action of the novel followed the subduing of the pathetic President to the party boss. The private action followed the career of a cultivated private citizen in the social and political life of the capital. Mrs. Lightfoot Lee, weary of Philadelphia, New York, Boston, and Europe; weary of society, business, philanthropy, and culture, had come to try Washington as a last possible sphere of action.

Several passages in the early pages of the novel set the mood of Madeleine Lee's restless craving. They relate her mood to the author's: "She meant to get all that American life had to offer, good or bad, and to drink it down to the dregs, fully determined that whatever there was in it she should have, and that whatever could be made out of it she would manufacture." [7] Her discontented ambition was, for her creator, something to be explained only in simile: "It was the feeling of a passenger on an ocean steamer whose mind will not give him rest until he has been in the engine-room and talked with the engineer. She wanted to see with her own eyes the action of primary forces; to touch with her own hand the massive machinery of society; to measure with her own mind the capacity of the motive power." [8] "Perhaps after exhausting the political world she might try again elsewhere; she did not pretend to say where she might then go, or what she should do." [9]

Madeleine Lee was both beautiful and intelligent. It was not difficult for her to meet interesting people and to find herself soon involved in the push and pull of power politics. What she sought here, after all, was naked, primitive human energy. And she pushed her way toward this pulse of power in pride and high spirits.

Adams's novelistic method was to set Mrs. Lee in the center of the seemingly innocent social whirl of the city's life and show her off at parties, picnics, receptions, tête-à-têtes. In this way he had the fun of showing off Washington types and achieving a surface of light satire. And at the same time he underlined in Madeleine's fundamentally serious reactions his own deeper thoughts.

166

Diplomats and Cabinet officers, journalists and lobbyists, giddy belles and grim hostesses whirred by like the bright fall leaves of the District woods. He made them up of one or more traits from real Washington people. They were not the full creations of the born novelist, but the glancing, striking suggestions of the born satirist and critics. They lacked continuity, but sufficed for a novel of ideas.

The diplomat Jacobi was a plausible echo of one side of Aristarchi Bey. Carrington, the weary Southerner, had pathos, a trait caught from James Lowndes. Vicky Dare, the "little daredevil" was perhaps his best creation, done out of a happy and admiring malice. Miss Beale recognized herself, so there must have been something of real life in her and her impudences.

As for the Prairie Giant of Peonia, Senator Ratcliffe, the stumbling block of the new President, and the snare at the feet of Madeleine Lee, he is not to be traced to one particular model. He is not Blaine—he is too crude—yet some of his circumstances remind one of what Adams knew of Blaine. He is not any one of a number of corrupt Grant stalwarts, but almost a creation, as Madeleine Lee is almost a creation, as the novel is almost a novel.

In certain scenes the clash between the tense, dedicated woman and the powerful, concentrated man almost blazes into life. Silas P. Ratcliffe, Mrs. Lee discovers, soon after coming to Washington, is the most important man in the Capital. He is a man used to running Presidents, and getting control of the frightened new one is his natural kind of work. As a mover of power, he fascinates Madeleine, who imputes several good motives to his work. She thinks that there must be a secret virtue behind his rude exterior, and some greatness. She makes him her study and does not know that he has done the same for her.

He likes her attention. He is a little weary of the grosser aspects of power. The softness of Mrs. Lee's sophistication makes an appeal to him. He thinks that if he could succeed in marrying her, he would take on the virtues of her money and her culture. She thinks that through him she can put her finger on the throttle of power.

Up to a certain point the mutual fascination of the unlike pair is well handled. Madeleine finds out with a shock that she is not leading the bear by the nose. The Prairie Giant is not pleased to dance for her, but rather he—massive, crude, monumentally clever in practical management—has begun to manage her and to use her as a shield for a depth of corruption she has just begun to guess.

Here Adams's novelistic management rather failed. He pulled Madeleine out of her dilemma a little too easily. His solution for his heroine was too pat, too easily contingent upon the receipt of a certain letter at a certain time, and upon the heroine's merely rational rejection of the Senator. Mrs. Lee withdraws from the situation and turns down the Senator's proposal of marriage at just the point a true novelist would have begun to enjoy himself: the moment of confrontation and conflict between two vitally clashing personalities.

Meanwhile Madeleine Lee had found out democracy, or thought she had. "She had saved herself in time. She had got to the bottom of this business of democratic government, and found out that it was nothing more than government of any other kind. She might have known it by her own common sense, but now that experience had proved it, she was glad to quit the masquerade; to return to the true democracy of life, her paupers and her prisons, her schools and her hospitals." [10]

But she had been swayed to the depths by the finding out. "I want to go to Egypt,' said Madeleine, still smiling faintly; 'democracy has shaken my nerves to pieces. Oh, what rest it would be to live in the Great Pyramid and look out forever at the polar star!' "[11] Mrs. Lee's last words are prophetic of a mood her creator would soon be in.

Although the novel has a certain amount of pathos, the bright surface dominates the darker elements. The graceful, malicious satire controls the whole. The anarchic ideas merely decorate a highly amusing, sensuous impression of a small, bright, bad, and agreeable Capital, perfectly recognizable today. In a certain sense, Adams was a good novelist, for he kept a unity of mood.

Words served him well. He had learned to ride them with a light whip, to make them pace and strut and caracole. On democracy he wrote: "Democracy, rightly understood, is the government of the people, by the people, for the benefit of Senators." [12] On monkeys and evolution, " 'After all, we ought to be grateful to them, for what would men do in this melancholy world if they had not inherited gaiety from the monkeys—as well as oratory.' " [13] On women: "The capacity of women to make unsuitable marriages must be considered as the corner-stone of society." [14]

The setting was Washington, D.C., seen and felt and appreciated as a Southern city. What was there in the city of James G. Blaine to like but some memory of those who had lost: a hollow Arlington, a ragged, unrecovered Mount Vernon? Who could best criticize the corrupt activity of the place but a Southerner, Carrington who loved Mrs. Lee, and watched her love the uncouth Senator Ratcliffe. The human philosophic center was thus for Adams, the novelist, the young Southerner who had lost everything in the war, who did nothing in the alien present but practice a little quiet law, but who saw and understood—out of experience, out of tragedy. What device would best serve for perspective but to remove his characters physically from the city and have them hold a picnic with the ghostly figure of General Washington on the lawn at Mount Vernon, or go sit in despair upon the steps of Arlington and weep?

John Randolph

Henry Adams wrote *John Randolph* during the first half of 1881. It was published in 1882 by Houghton Mifflin in the *American Statesmen* series. The time of his work on it was perhaps the happiest of his life. He and his wife found Washington the most to their taste after their recent trip (their second) abroad. The city was new enough to them, and they were well enough settled in it, for them to take its life comfortably and easily. Adams was at work on his *History*, too. By the time the biography of Randolph was published, he had done the first four-year period of the *History*. The biography was, like the *Gallatin*, a study for the *History*, but it too could stand alone.

The subject of the book was as opposite a piece of human nature as he could find from Albert Gallatin. The two made an odd pair in his mind. But he took pleasure in juggling dissimilars. He was considering Aaron Burr as the subject for a third biography, and had recently—in *Democracy*—done a sketch of George Washington. Toussaint L'Ouverture teased his imagination too; a sketch of him was to be the emotional center of his essay "Napoleon I at San Domingo," to appear within two years in the Paris *Revue Historique*. He liked to think that he was a virtuoso of characters, and referred familiarly to Randolph, Gallatin, Burr, Napoleon, Tecumthe, Jefferson, and Madison, as if they were casual acquaintances of his, and not to be taken more formally.

In Adams's mind, Albert Gallatin was rational, impartial, and adaptable; John Randolph was passionate, partial, and unbending. The books about the two men differed in tone accordingly. The life of the Virginian was terse rather than ample, pointed rather than fair, and cruel in its remorseless showing up a man who, after all, did a good job of showing himself up. The *Randolph* is more readable than the *Gallatin*.

Adams's dislike was perhaps childishly simple. Gallatin served his country, even in disillusionment. Randolph, in Adams's view, helped bring his country to the wreck of Civil War. All the talent, the honesty, the incorruptibility of Randolph could not reconcile Adams to the use he made of his qualities.

Aside from the actual damage Adams conceived Randolph to have done his country, he had another ground for disapproval. This reason was perhaps below the level of consciousness. The man was a purely negative, rather than positive, force. Randolph, with a brilliance superior to all his contemporaries, had cut all his vital connections with his nation. He was altogether a critic, not at all a leader. The fact that Adams himself, in a different national context, was being forced into a similar position did not make him like Randolph better. It added a sort of personal animus to his portrait. And in the *Randolph* his personal and sectional background took hold.

The Civil War, still recent to him, got in the way of his judgment, and warped his views. He was thinking 1860 when he wrote 1830 in the book. A similar distortion of tone, if not of fact, may be seen in another New England production of the following year, *Thomas Jefferson,* by John T. Morse, Jr.

Was Adams fair to Randolph? A later biographer, William Cabell Bruce, who in 1922 wrote a comprehensive life of Randolph, thought that Adams had been grossly unfair; that writing the book had been his chance "to direct against the memory of Randolph the thrice-refined venom in respect to its subject which had filtered into his own veins from those of his great-grandfather, grandfather, and father," [15] and that Adams's biography was "really nothing but a family pamphlet, saturated with the sectional prejudices and antipathies of the year 1882." [16]

No doubt Adams treated John Randolph with merciless roughness. But there was a secret in this sadism—if his treatment can be described as such. Obviously, Adams detested the man, or the kind of man that Randolph was. But he felt a kind of fascination for the perfection of a type. Randolph fell by passions which Henry Adams also possessed—pride, impatience with dullness, desire to act—but which, unlike

Randolph, he kept under control. The tension in the book is a consequence of the fascination which Adams felt—almost as if giving in to vice—at the prospect of great gifts misused. He saw in Randolph what he might have been, or might be, if he let go.

There was indeed a trace of envy in his regard for the unselfconscious Virginian. He had not reached the point of throwing off rationalism yet. He felt obliged still to condemn merely habitual and unconscious social action—however graceful or good. Yet he was coming to the point. *John Randolph* was a last holding off from throwing over the views of his ancestors and his native place; but the strain shows. There was something painful in his treatment of the man, something lacking in frankness and self-knowledge.

This is not to say that Adams was not truthful. He was exact as to facts and quotations; he had uncovered new documentatiton in letters not used by biographers before; he used them copiously—to condemn Randolph out of his own mouth. What is more important—in painting his portrait—he furnished enough material to allow a judicious reader to come to a slightly different conclusion from the one held by the author.

The book is a provocation, not a dead end. He successfully piques the reader's curiosity as to Randolph's private character: What could have made him so perverse? In effect, Adams sends the reader on to other writers on Randolph.

These strictures should not be taken to mean that Adams did not write a brilliant book. It is a tour de force; a lively, living sketch of a man caught in the decisive moments of his life; what it lacks in breadth of humanity it makes up in pungency. Nothing of Adams is more readable.

Esther

Esther was Henry Adams's most secret production, both in its writing and publishing and in the amount of the buried life of feeling and thought which he put into it.

The book has a curious history. Adams wrote it in 1883, saw it published in 1884, and by 1885 was glad to see it forgotten. When he gave it to Henry Holt, he was more stringent about secrecy than he had been even about *Democracy* which had come out four years before under the same pseudonym, Frances Snow Compton. (The modern reprint in 1938 misspelled the name—a curious continuance of misfortune for the book.)

Holt published the book in March, 1884, as the third novel

called the Leisure Hour Novel Series. According to Adams's request it was not advertised at all, but listed only in the *Publishers' Weekly* of May 10th. *Democracy* had been popular on both sides of the Atlantic. Presumably, it had formed an audience of some size that would have liked to read a second story by the same author. Yet this audience never even heard of *Esther*, so successful was its author's campaign of non-advertising.

During 1884 only 504 copies were sold; in the next ten years, only 23 more. A few more copies were sold in England; eleven copies were given away; 200 were accidentally burned; and the remainder of the 1,000 copies printed were done way with in some unknown manner. The total sales came to $326.00. (Robert E. Spiller ascertained these facts when he edited the only modern edition of the book, in Scholars' Facsimiles and Reprints, in 1938.)

During his wife's life Adams had perhaps sufficient reasons for not wishing to be known as the author of the book. After her death he had other reasons. Yet the book came out— apparently out of depths that had, somehow or other, to be expressed. It was the production of a sensitive, abnormally shy and proud man, who would hesitate in company, in letters, in conversation, to say the most private, secret things about himself, yet felt the need for saying them somewhere, and solved his problem by writing a novel which he made almost as secret as a diary.

The book is in no literal sense a story about himself and his wife. The plot is at a remove from anything literally true. Yet there are analogies of truth in it. Anyone, with only a slight knowledge of Adams's character, his wife's, or his friends', could see something of a relationship between the actual lives and the characters in *Esther*. Adams had to create these analogies; he had even to see them in print; yet he shrank from identifying them. The book was more of a commitment than *Democracy* was.

Adams pretended to Henry Holt, and to himself, that he was simply going to try an experiment when the book came out, to see just what effect advertising or non-advertising had on the sales of a light novel. On the surface level of thought he was sincere. His legitimate disgust at the evident power of the vulgar art was a truthful reaction. Yet he had reasons for keeping the book quiet that he could not discuss. Not that the book was sensational, or revealing, in any easy way. But it had him—himself, his inner tender being—turned inside out and exposed to view. He had both to make the show; and then, to deny it.

Esther is a novel about the individual and belief. Appropriately, it starts in church. George Strong, a young geologist, had brought his cousin, Esther Dudley, to the first public service in a new church in New York City. He was a friend of the young minister, Stephen Hazard, and wanted Esther to meet him, a brave example of an intelligent and enlightened clergyman. Esther was un-churched, yet not disturbed by the fact, and not afraid to face an energetic minister.

St. John's (not to be confused with the actual church of that name) was, in fact, Trinity Church, Boston, disguised and transported, for the scene of Adams's novel, to Manhattan. Adams had watched Richardson, La Farge, Saint-Gaudens, and the other busy artisans of Trinity go about their work during the 1870's when he had lived nearby on Marlborough Street. The building of the church, and Richardson's conception of the work as a joint venture of artists, had caught his imagination. He commemorated the impression in *Esther*.

What George Strong and Esther Dudley saw of joyous color and assertive life in the first service in the not yet finished St. John's must have borne some resemblance to the first service in Trinity, Boston; and Stephen Hazard's taking possession of the congregation in the novel surely had a relationship to the authoritative manner of Phillips Brooks in that other, actual church.

"Sitting in the gallery, beneath the unfinished frescoes, and looking down the nave, one caught an effect of autumn gardens, a suggestion of chrysanthemums and geraniums, or of October woods, dashed with scarlet oaks and yellow maples. As a display of austerity the show was a failure." [17] Stephen Hazard "took possession of his flock with a general advertisement that he owned every sheep in it, white or black." [18]

The story begins to move when George presents Esther to Stephen Hazard, who admires her for her bright independence, and covets her for his congregation. "If he could not draw to himself and his church the men and women who were strong enough to have opinions of their own, it was a small triumph to draw a procession of followers from a class who took their opinions, like their jewelry, machine-made. He felt that he must get a hold on the rebellious age, and that it would not prove rebellious to him. He meant that Miss Dudley should come regularly to church, and on his success in bringing her there, he was half ready to stake the chances of his mission in life." [19]

Esther is drawn into the circle which includes Hazard, Strong, and the moody artist of the church, Wharton. Another member of the circle is Esther's young friend, Catherine Brooke, an orphaned girl from the West, whom her Aunt Sarah Murray had asked Esther to help entertain. Esther has a small talent for drawing and does a portrait of Catherine. Wharton sees a skill that he can use, and engages Esther to help finish the murals of the sanctuary. Soon there is much social coming and going in and out of the church, much easy meeting and talking, and, inevitably, a certain amount of falling in love. Catherine falls in love with Wharton, and he with her, despite the existence, somewhere, of a bitter wife. Hazard is soon enchanted with Esther, and she is, at least, disturbed by him. George Strong, who has been half in love with Esther from the beginning, finds his feelings deeper and more definite in the face of competition.

Adams has created an agreeable group. The story lingers at this early stage of friendly acquaintance to splash the reader in conversation, argument, discussion, and a friendly clash of personality. The company very much resembles that which Henry and Marian Adams were accustomed to entertaining at 1607 H Street in Washington, D.C.

The characters in the story, who are more complex than any he created for *Democracy,* have yet a marked resemblance to several of the Adamses' friends. Wharton is something like John La Farge, and, in his antecedent boyhood poverty, also something like Augustus Saint-Gaudens. George Strong is clearly an undisguisedly Clarence King. Hazard is less clearly Henry Adams's cousin, Phillips Brooks. Catherine Brooke, in her fresh and youthful impudence and beauty, resembles, perhaps, Mrs. Don Cameron, when she first came into Washington and charmed both Marian and Henry Adams. Esther's father, the retired, epicurean, and well-to-do lawyer, is surely Marian's father, the retired physician, Dr. Robert Hooper. And, of course, Esther Dudley, in her vivacity, quickness, and delicacy, as well as insecurity, is Marian Adams. But these likenesses should not be pushed too far. The resemblances are not complete, and were evidently not meant by the writer to be complete. And Adams involved these pieces of the personalities of his friends in a plot which they never lived.

What is more important to remember is that each one of these characters is, in a sense, a part of Henry Adams, their creator. Wharton clearly stands for Adams's growing responsiveness to art and for something inexpressible and noninstitutional in religion; Strong, for his belief in science and for a certain healthy, laughing skepticism; Hazard for a certain desire to master and dominate—but perhaps there is less of Adams in Hazard than in the others; and, last of all, in Esther's rock-bottom, lonely independence of soul there is something of Adams, perhaps the most precious part of him. Her anguished struggle with and against an unfair authority, in the person of her lover, seeking to remake her in an alien image, is the heart of the novel.

Adams's descriptions of his characters are lively and attractive. Here is Strong, an unmistakable likeness of King: ". . . he looked . . . like what he was, an intelligent man, with a figure made for action, an eye that hated rest, a manner naturally sympathetic. His forehead was so bald as to give his face a look of strong character which a dark beard rather helped to increase. He was a popular fellow, known as George by whole gangs of the roughest miners in Nevada, where he had worked for years as a practical geologist, and it would have been hard to find in America, Europe, or Asia, a city in which someone would not have smiled at the mention of his name, and asked where George was going to turn up next." [20]

Here is Wharton, bearing a somewhat devious and distorted resemblance to La Farge: "He was a man of their own age, so quiet and subdued in manner, and so delicate in feature, that he would have been unnoticed in any ordinary group, and shoved aside into a corner. He seemed to face life with an effort; his light-brown eyes had an uneasy look as though they wanted to rest on something that should be less hard and real than what they saw. He was not handsome; his mouth was a little sensual; his yellowish beard ragged. He was apt to be silent until his shyness wore off, when he became a rapid, nervous talker, full of theories and schemes, which he changed from day to day to another, but which were always quite complete and convincing for the moment. At times he had long fits of moodiness and would not open his mouth for days. At other times he sought society and sat up all night talking, planning, discussing, drinking, smoking, living on bread and cheese or whatever happened to be within reach, and sleeping whenever he happened to feel in the humor for it. Rule or method he had none, and his friends had for years given up attempts to control him. They took it for granted that he would kill himself with his ill regulated existence." [21]

One day Catherine asked Strong, with whom she could be impudent, and for whom she felt no awe, if Wharton were a great genius. " 'Young woman, we are all of us great geniuses. We never say so, because we are as modest as we are great, but just look into my book on fossil batrachiaps.' " [22] That is very like King, and very like the tone of the King-Hay-Adams-Richardson-La Farge set, at home, and laughing at itself, yet half believing its own pleasantries.

The three men—Wharton, Strong, and Hazard—were fascinated by Esther, the independent-minded young woman who soon became the center of their society. One day Wharton launched a discussion of her as being a rare specimen of an American type. " 'I hesitate before everything American. . . . I don't know—you don't know—and I never yet met any man who could tell me, whether American types are going to supplant the old ones, or whether they are to come to nothing for want of ideas. Miss Dudley is one of the most marked American types I ever saw.' " [23] (He echoes the Adamses' young friend Henry James in his tributes to Marian Adams.)

Wharton had, at first, pretended hesitation, but he was fluent: " '. . . in the first place, she has a bad figure, which she makes answer for a good one. She is too slight, too thin; she looks fragile, willowy, as the cheap novel calls it, as though you could break her in halves like a switch. She dresses to suit her figure and sometimes overdoes it. Her features are imperfect. Excepting her ears, her voice, and her eyes which have a sort of brown depth like a trout brook, she has no very good points' " [24] (echoing Henry Adams's description of Marian before he married her).

Wharton, warmed to his subject, found it easy to go on: " 'I want to know what she can make of life. She gives one the idea of a lightly sparred yacht in mid-ocean; unexpected; you ask yourself what the devil she is doing there. She sails gayly along, though there is no land in sight and plenty of rough weather coming. She never read a book, I believe, in her life. She tries to paint, but she is only a second-rate amateur and will never be anything more, though she has done one or two things which I give you my word I would like to have done myself. She picks up all she knows without an effort, and knows nothing well, yet she seems to understand whatever is said. Her mind is as irregular as her face, and both have the same peculiarity. I notice the lines of her eyebrows, nose and mouth all end with a slight upward curve like a yacht's sails, which give a kind of hopefulness and self-confidence to her expression. Mind and face have the same curves.' " [25]

And he went on, " 'There is nothing mediaeval about her. If she belongs to any [world] besides the present, it is to the next world which artists want to see, when paganism will come again, and can give a divinity to every waterfall.' " [26]

Meanwhile, serenely unmoved by flattering attentiveness from the others, Esther is upset by Hazard's devotion. She neither impedes nor encourages it. "To be steadily strong was not in Esther's nature. She was audacious only by starts, and recoiled from audacity." [27] Therefore, she let Hazard lead her into the tangle of a relationship, but within was uneasy and unconvinced.

At this point in the story, Esther's father falls ill and dies. The situation and the emotions connected with it would be re-enacted, with an appalling repetition, only a little more than a year after the publication of the book, in the life of the author. It was as if Adams were clairvoyant; in the book, Esther Dudley suffers fearfully in her father's dying. He was too much her only stay in life. Writing of the night before the death, Esther's creator said: "To Esther this evening was the last when the stars shone bright and clear. The next morning her glimpse of the blue sky had vanished and the rigor of the storm began." [28] "She knew that there was no hope and that her father himself was only anxious for the end, yet to see him suffer and slowly fade out was terrible." [29]

Her father said to her, " 'Its' not so bad, Esther, when you come to it.' " But, for Esther, "Now that she had come to it, she thought it was very bad; worse than anything she had ever imagined; she wanted to escape, to run away, to get out of life itself, rather than suffer such pain, such terror, such misery of helplessness." [30] (These words suggest not only Marian Adams's deepest traits, but prophesy her mood of the following year. They recall also Henry Adams's agony at the time of his sister's death in Italy in 1870.)

Stephen Hazard was kind to Esther at this time. In her rudderless state, before she realized what she was doing, she was not only in love with him, but engaged to be married to him; all this, without, as yet, surrendering one inch of her mental freedom.

After their engagement Esther tried valiantly to suit her

mind to Stephen Hazard's insistent will. She studied theology till her head ached. She even consulted her good cousin George Strong in her need and asked him for arguments to support the church's claims upon her. Strong was personally an agnostic, but he thought the church did good, and so must be supported. His reason desolated rather than comforted her, for Esther wanted not just to give in, but to believe. She was desperately eager to change her own mind. And her lover was eager for her to do so.

Strong's comment was: " 'Hazard is a priest at heart. . . . He sees nothing good in the world that he does not instantly covet for the glory of God and the church, and just a bit for his own pleasure. . . . The struggle is going to tear both their poor little hearts out.' " [31] But Strong was not neutral; he, too, had come to love Esther, and had at last some hope in the incompatibility of the two lovers.

Mrs. Murray, Esther's aunt and friend, became impatient with them all—for Wharton and Catherine were in difficulty too. She thought their troubles all imaginary: " 'Well,' said Mrs. Murray with a sigh [to Strong], 'You have lost her now, and Mr. Hazard will lose her, too. You and he and all your friends are a sort of clever children. We are always expecting you to do something worth doing, and it never comes. You are a sort of water-color, worsted-work, bric-a-brac, washed-out geniuses, just big enough and strong enough to want to do something and never carry it through. I am heartily tired of the whole lot of you.' " [32] (This is the reverse side of the humorous pride and buoyancy of the group. It should be referred back to the letters of strong hope and pride Henry Adams wrote to Charles Adams during the war years. He must, himself, in writing these words, have noticed the connection.)

The strong-minded aunt worried about her niece. " 'Yesterday, when I took her to drive, she was in tears about the atonement, and today I suppose she will have gone to bed with a sick headache on account of the Athanasian creed.' " [33]

" 'Is religion true?' " cried out Esther to George. " 'Now tell me what you would do to get faith if the happiness of your whole life hung on it.' " [34]

Worn out with trying to make her mind believe, she fled from Hazard's presence and went away for a few days to Niagara Falls. She could not bear to refuse Stephen Hazard, neither could she bear to remake her soul for him.

Esther's room overlooked the Falls. "She had already taken

a fancy to this tremendous, rushing, roaring companion, which thundered and smoked under her window, as though she had tamed a tornado to play in her courtyard." [35] She could not bring herself to Hazard's orthodoxy (it is presumed that he was an Episcopalian), but in his absence, by the side of the Falls, she found a sort of unorthodox belief of her own, typified somehow by the physical spectacle before her. She found herself wondering if perhaps the "next world is a sort of great reservoir of truth, and that what is true in us just pours into it like raindrops?" [36] (Even Esther's sojourn at Niagara has a relationship to a happening in Henry and Marian Adams's life. They went there together in January, 1879, on one of their very infrequent absences from Washington at that time of year.)

Esther's last interview with Stephen Hazard is tragic. She makes him see her mind, at last, and understand that it cannot be reconciled with his. Yet she has continued, and still continues, to love him. His last word is true of both of them: " 'I love you. I cannot help loving you. There is no friendship about it.' " [37]

What does this novel say of Henry Adams and his wife? One should not be literal. The deepest emotion in the story seems to be a celebration of the purity and bravery of Esther's truth to herself, under pressure. It is a tribute to the integrity of the lonely human individuality, even when most lost in a world it does not understand. Surely, Henry and Marian Adams were united in this attitude. And surely, too, they were united in their rejection, almost in despair, of religious orthodoxy, or even of any sureness or trust in faith itself. The book tells of the trouble of their mutual decision, but also of its honesty and immutability.

What bearing this loss of faith—or lack of it—had upon Mrs. Adams's death is not altogether clear. The analogy of character is easier to read. Esther is of a frail, delicate, and pure beauty of soul; this too could be said to be true of the proud, pathetic wife of Henry Adams—in her life and in her death. When Marian was once dead, the intimacy of the story could not be borne by the writer. He would have no one at all, if he could help it, read the book. For there were suggestions in it of insurmountable despairs, of frailties, and of a radical weakness and insecurity which, after 1885, it would be obscene for others to read and understand.

In consequence, he let darkness blot out all memory of *Esther,* and of Marian. Yet whenever he spoke of *Esther,* as he did a few times later in his life, he gave himself away, for he valued, he said, a dozen pages of that novel more than all the volumes of the *History*.[38] But it was a buried value. He only, of all the world, had the right to contemplate it. In pathetic and arrogant privacy, he constrained others from the privilege.

Chapter 14

A Toy Land

ADAMS WAS very quiet during the winter and spring of 1886. He kept his misery to himself, talked little, wrote few letters, worked if at all on his *History,* which seemed to him, as his own life had done, to have broken its neck.

In April, Henry Hobson Richardson died, not yet forty-eight. It was another ending to make a double stop in Henry Adams's life. He and Nicholas Anderson were the only friends of Richardson from Washington, D.C., who went to Boston to the funeral. Phillips Brooks preached the service in Trinity Church. In that building, under the rich ceiling which Richardson had conceived, Adams sat and listened and made himself realize that never again would his dead friend build mightily or laugh mightily.

In June, not caring greatly whether he went or not, Adams set off on a summer trip to Japan. John La Farge went with him, careless of obligations, gleefully leaving behind duties and cares. He had just signed a contract to do a mural on the altar wall of the Episcopal Church of the Ascension on Fifth Avenue in New York City. He left behind, also, an outraged publisher's agent to whom he had promised illustrations of Shelley's *Skylark.* From Poughkeepsie, La Farge, impenitent at escaping, telegraphed the agent, appropriately, "The purple evening melts around my flight." [1] The artist took an immediate and childlike delight in the various landscapes which shifted past their train windows as they crossed the continent. He stirred Adams to pay some attention to the world outside himself.

They went in some style. Henry's brother, Charles Adams, a prominent railroader now, lent them his director's car. They traveled in it in solitary splendor from Albany, New York, to San Francisco, waited on, and fussed over, Adams said, "as affectionately as though we had money to lend." [2]

A local reporter in Omaha, impressed with their state, and sure of their importance, came aboard to interview them. He asked them why they were going to Japan. La Farge told him, wide-eyed in mock solemnity, that they were both seeking

Nirvana. " 'It's out of season!' " the boy told them.[3] And they were to wonder later if he had not been right.

San Francisco was dusty and unimpressive to Adams. He hunted feverishly for the novels of Dumas, and did not find them, while La Farge searched for artists' materials. They went on board an almost empty ship and endured a rough crossing. They were both seasick but discovered that they could put up with each other in bad circumstances as well as in good.

Their ship deposited them in the steaming port city of Yokohama at the beginning of July. They slept in a hotel on the bay and commuted every day the twenty miles to Tokyo, busy with sights and curios. They went to a *No* play, and to see wrestlers. They hunted for porcelain and lacquer, and they visited temples. They laughed immoderately, or Adams said they did.

Adams's laughter was rather morbid. He wrote to Hay: "Positively everything in Japan laughs. The jinrickshaw men laugh while running at full speed five miles with a sun that visibly sizzles their drenched clothes. The women all laugh, but they are obviously wooden dolls, badly made, and can only cackle, clatter in pattens over asphalt pavements in railway stations, and hop or slide in heelless straw sandals across floors. I have not yet seen a woman with any better mechanism than that of a five-dollar wax doll; but the amount of oil used in fixing and oiling and arranging their hair is worth the money alone. They can all laugh, so far. The shop-keepers laugh to excess when you say that their goods are forgeries and worthless. I believe the Mikado laughs when his ministers have a cabinet council. The gilt dragon-heads on the temples are in a broad grin. Everything laughs, until I expect to see even the severe bronze doors of the tombs, the finest serious work I know, open themselves with the same eternal and meaningless laughter, as though death were the pleasantest jest of all." [4]

La Farge, Adams said, was a sight to see, flying through the city's streets in his rickshaw, peering out at a new world through delighted spectacles. La Farge was ecstatic over the light. "What is absorbingly new is the light, its whiteness, its silvery milkiness." [5]

From La Farge's sketches—of the word and of the hand—published later in his *Artist's Letters from Japan,* and from Adams's own personal letters, we can gain an idea of what the historian and the painter saw and how they occupied their time during the summer months they spent in Japan. La

Farge's reaction was an unaffected joy in a new scene. He liked the uncluttered, simple, even severe domestic interiors. He dreaded the closeness and stuffiness of the familiar "artistic" interiors at home after this revelation of space and light and quiet taste. He was curious about the architecture of the temples and found out their function as well as their beauty. Their columns, for instance, were set in sockets in the foundation, but not attached; so that they would shift, but not break in the expected earthquakes. La Farge entered just as joyfully and curiously into the philosophy behind the *torii* and the shrines. He was delighted to make his way into the thought he encountered entangled in the art. A calm, tolerant Catholic, sure of his own base, he was friendly with the Buddhist priests he met, seeing in them the same kind of vocation he had seen in priests of his own faith.

Henry Adams's reactions are more difficult to interpret. He had come to Japan in a state of shock. He was able, off the top of his mind, to compose racy letters to friends and relatives about the surface of the new life he observed in Japan. But he was never able, as La Farge was, to sink himself into the scene, and to rest in this new environment; he could do this no more in Japan than he could at home in Washington. But at least travel saved him from an overt expression of suffering. He could move about, see new sights and report them superficially and vivaciously; to that extent, it helped him to be away from home. But he could not afford yet to thaw out the numb core of himself. Awakening would be too painful.

After a number of hectic days in the port cities, heat and cholera drove the two men north to a cooler, healthier climate. They went to Nikko to spend several weeks of quiet in a tiny house in a temple yard. Sturgis Bigelow, the Bostonian who had turned Buddhist, had introduced them in Tokyo to the American scholar of Japanese and Chinese art, Ernest Fenollosa. The Fenollosas, who had a house in Nikko, secured a place for La Farge and Adams to settle for the worst part of the hot season.

By sitting still in one place, they learned more of Japan than by energetic touring. La Farge sketched; Adams read— the *Paradiso* of Dante; they explored the temples scattered like objects of nature through the unspoiled woods of the hilly region. They talked to calm-faced Buddhist priests and visited their neighbors, the Fenollosas and Bigelow, who was a friend of former times and a relative of Marian Adams.

The walks they took up and down the hills, through the

woods from one segment of a shrine to another, impressed the artist particularly. La Farge in his *Letters* speaks with admiration of the artifice of sculpture and architecture, bringing out the natural beauty of the forest which lapped around each temple. "There is no defiance of time, no apparent attempt at an equal permanency; it is like a courteous acceptance of the eternal peace, the eternal nothingness of the tomb." [6]

Many new images, many new ideas, teased the two Westerners. Every symbol—in temple, statue, even in domestic arrangements—brought them face to face with a new and powerful system of thought, that of the East. "Of all the images that I see so often," wrote La Farge, later, "the one that touches me most—partly, perhaps, because of the Eternal Feminine—is that of the incarnation that is called Kwan-on, when shown absorbed in the meditations of Nirvana." [7] "The Deity, or goddess, seated in abstraction by the falling waters of life represents, I suppose, more especially an ideal of contemplation, as the original Indian name indicated, I think; but her name to-day is that of the Compassionate One." [8]

It was an idea which struck Adams, too. It was an opposite to, or at least a complement to, all that he had been taught by family, school, and the conflicts of life in New England, Britain, or Washington. It was as yet only an alternative, not to be accepted, but at least to be held in mind.

Adams said little, as yet, of what most impressed him, but a few words in a letter to T. F. Dwight show the new turn of his thought. "Japan has the single advantage of being a lazy place. One feels no impulse to exert oneself; and Buddhist contemplation of the infinite seems the only natural mode of life. Energy is a dream of raw youth.[9] . . . I think as little as I can about America and my affairs and friends. If the thing sinks and disappears, I shall sit over it and learn the fact." [10]

Yet the more usual mood in which he wrote home was a sort of desperate flippancy. He spoke of their doll house; and of themselves as doll creatures whose owners would surely come soon to take them out to play with. To his eyes everything he saw was doll-like, toy-like. He could not admit that the country or its inhabitants were real. If he could deny reality to the scene and to himself, then he could laugh, deride, enjoy—all at a safe distance. His speaking of Japan as a toy land was as much a comment on his own state of mind as a comment on the scene itself. He was in no mood to write, even to close friends, about anything that moved him in a serious way.

When the danger of cholera was somewhat less, Adams and La Farge left their refuge at Nikko and went south to the Tokyo region and beyond it, by sea, to the cities of Osaka and Kyoto. They absorbed much information and many diverse impressions, and they bought "tons" of curios, as Adams claimed.

La Farge had now ideas aplenty for the Ascension mural. He had found in Japan a landscape proper for miracle. Japanese mountains and mist would be the setting for his Christ in the far-off church on Fifth Avenue. He had also material for a study of the Japanese print maker Hokusai.

Adams, as a last adventure, photographed the Great Buddha, the Daibutsu, at Kamakura. He borrowed a camera from a resident priest, climbed a roof, and, "standing on my head at an angle of impossibility, perpetrated a number of libels on Buddha and Buddhism without shame at the mild contempt of his blessed little moustache." [11]

Shortly after this last venture in alien culture, the artist and the historian took ship again for home. They carried with them various loose and unassorted ideas of the East. La Farge made immediate and magnificent use of his. Adams was slower, but the impressions and notions of the hot summer of 1886 were of a durable sort. He could not, or would not, sport them in tourist fashion. But they stayed with him and were to be evident later in attitudes and ideas. If Japan had not given him peace, it had given him, at least, distraction. He had moved a few steps further from the frozen despair of the previous winter.

Chapter 15

The Breakfast Table

IN THE LATE 1880's a certain house on H Street in Washington, D.C., began to attract curiosity and speculation. Its narrow front, sober and reserved next to its neighbor, the Hay House; its dignity of red brick and light stone; the somberness of its arched entranceway; all this inconspicuous solidity of architecture might never have caught the inquiring eye but for the seclusion and supposed inaccessibility of its owner. Just when he wanted most to be left alone, Henry Adams achieved a mild sort of celebrity. His *History*, coming out at this time, had something to do with it; his self-enforced solitude, more.

A newcomer to Washington might not realize how different the atmosphere of Henry Adams's household was now from what it had been before 1885. The newcomer might find it attractive, but he would also find it strange. What Adams had had to do was to construct a regime without his wife. The leaven of her laughter and social animation was gone. He himself thought things went haltingly now, but to one who had not a ready comparison in mind 1603 H Street seemed interesting and attractive in an odd sort of way.

Such a newcomer was Cecil Spring-Rice, who came to Washington in the service of British diplomacy in the spring of 1887. His was a fresh reaction. He had not known the earlier Adams, and his letters give an authentic impression of the dislocated Henry Adams who had just come home from Japan. The only distortion in them is one of sympathetic dramatization.

Spring-Rice had a farm heart and was prepared to be interested in Adams by what the Hays, the Lodges, and the Camerons had told him. It is interesting to see him in his letters to his brother in England progressing to intimacy through a maze of half-truths and guesses. His judgment of Adams's character was sound, although he was not always entirely correct about circumstances.

On March 22nd of his first year in the American Capital, he wrote to his brother Stephen about meeting the older man and finding him "an interesting sort of cynic." [1] Adams had evidently listened as well as talked. "I had a real jolly evening with him last night talking over England and America." [2]

Spring-Rice was twenty-eight. He had been five years in the diplomatic service. He had ambition and he probably knew that he would do well. He loved poetry, languages, good talk, and private study. He had also a hesitant sort of charm and a habit of ridiculing himself. Adams wrote to his English friend Charles Milnes Gaskell shortly after making the acquaintance of the young man: "An intelligent and agreeable fellow has turned up here at your legation; about the last place one looks for such. His name is Spring-Rice, and he has creditable wits. Mad, of course, but not more mad than an Englishman should be." [3]

Spring-Rice, shy and self-effacing, saw Adams perhaps more clearly than his older friends did at this time. They had been paralyzed into an unnatural solicitude by the tragedy that had hit him and were perhaps too careful of him to his face. Spring-Rice records the hesitancy of the Southerner L. Q. C. Lamar, who at this time was literally afraid to call on Adams and would walk unhappily past his front door rather than knock on it and confront his friend in his unhappiness.[4]

Somehow Spring-Rice got beneath Adams's guard. He was unselfconsciously kind. And he was respectful and interested. Adams lent him the privately printed volumes of the *History*, and Spring-Rice stayed away from a good many parties to sit up late in Adams's study reading his "intensely interesting history of Jefferson's administration." [5]

The book's author took possession of the young Englishman's imagination. He wrote about him often in his letters home. His new friend was first of all an Adams, and like all Adamses, clever, and like all Adamses (Spring-Rice was becoming an expert in his subject) he made "a sort of profession of eccentricity." [6] But, "I like the one here, who since his wife died has no friends and no absorbing interest and takes an amused view of life, tempered by attachment to Japanese art." [7]

In their first acquaintance, Spring-Rice put his finger on the essential. "He found his wife dead on the floor one day and the next was the first day since they had been married that they were separated. Since then he has regarded life with a frivolity which rather shocks people who don't know him well; but I can quite understand that there are griefs so great that after them one is independent of joy and sorrow or the respect of men." [8]

187

His liking for the man did not blind him. "He is queer to the last degree; cynical, vindictive, but with a constant interest in people, faithful to his friends and passionately fond of his mother and of all little children ever born; even puppies." [9]

Spring-Rice, or Springy, as his friends came to call him, was by the end of his first season of acquaintance with Henry Adams, a constant friend, one who came when he pleased at 1603 H Street. He was already a good friend of several of Adams's earlier friends, too.

In September, 1887, he described a visit to the Lodges at Nahant. "There is a peninsula running into the Atlantic and joined by a narrow road to the shore. At the extreme end of it is the house I stayed in surrounded on three sides by water with splendid rocks. There were some jolly children and I lived very quietly there playing lawn tennis and riding on the beach (which is about three miles off) and bathing off the rocks. . . . My host was Cabot Lodge, the grandson of an Englishman, but a very anti-English member of Congress. He has written several books, which I have read—one a life of Hamilton, which is very good indeed. His wife is pretty and very pleasant." [10]

He knew the energetic young Theodore Roosevelt, of New York, already, and his wife, Edith. He had, in fact, been Roosevelt's best man in London, the winter before, after having met him previously on a trip to America to visit his brother, Gerald, who had settled in Canada. By 1887 Spring-Rice and his traits were a regular subject of correspondence between the Roosevelts and the Lodges. On June 23rd of that year Roosevelt wrote to Cabot Lodge from Sagamore Hill: "Spring-Rice stayed here a week. Once, not being an over good rider, he let the polo pony Caution run off with him. On rejoining us he remarked with his quiet, cool little manner: 'I never met a pony that had such a thorough command over its rider,' as his only comment." [11]

The young Englishman was adaptable. He soon felt at home in Washington, and liked the place. He saw the bad and the good of American life with a keen and unsparing eye, but not ever from any lofty or alien viewpoint. He was aware of political skullduggery, of the uncontrolled domination of the corporations, of the shocking cynicism of the good citizens. He was personally more of a critical liberal than many of his new American friends. Yet he fitted in; he belonged; he was one of them. He was a particular favorite of Anna Lodge and Elizabeth Cameron. The untidy, pallid, charming English boy, who talked well and listened well, had a special appeal to these attractive women who enjoyed taking him in hand.

It was to these women, who had good hearts as well as manners, that Henry Adams turned, too, in these years. He was to be, from this time on, more intimate with Mrs. Lodge and Mrs. Cameron than with either of their husbands. He found them alive to shades of thought or feeling which he could not have broached in cold blood, in reasonable, rational terms, to Cabot Lodge or Don Cameron.

Taken for granted, as of long and solid duration, was his close relationship with the John Hays, next door, and with Clarence King, beginning to round out into a figure of debonaire middle age, yet still the adventurer, the wanderer of this circle. Hay told the best stories, said Spring-Rice, that he had ever heard. The Englishman heard King's good stories, too, when the geologist poured them out in profusion in front of one or another of Adams's fireplaces. King gave as little sign of writing his stories down as he gave of settling in any one spot. His health and his dubious success in business—now up, now down—caused much worry among his friends. But he could not be prevented from squandering his money, his health, and his nerves as carelessly as his stories.

Adams's life among these friends who came and went at 1603 H Street was, to his private way of thinking, a makeshift thing. His house was more charming to his visitors than to him. Yet the regime which he had created there, with only half a mind on it, had a solidity and ease which seldom betrayed the restlessness of the man who was the center of it.

The keynote at 1603 H Street was that of unpretentious friendliness. Its great lack—for which Adams's friends were grateful—was stiffness, rigidity, formality. Adams went out of the house for quiet afternoon talks with Anna Lodge or Elizabeth Cameron, or next door to the Hays. He seldom went anywhere else. He had ditched society as such. He had, in a manner, used his sorrow as a lever to get him out of his obligations to organized social life. He was out of the round of prescribed duties from 1885 on, and took his social life, as he pleased, at home. It was as if all the original unsureness, shyness and constraint he had suffered in the giant parties in London during the war had come back on him. Everyone thoroughly understood that they should expect no conformity from him to their own standards of calling, leaving cards, going to parties. Adams's procedure was tyrannical, but he made himself either indispensable enough or interesting enough to a number of people to furnish him with the only kind of society he now wanted. Whenever he wished, he shut himself away from his friends, and was granted the license of a known eccentric. He had created his own role. Others could accept the situation or give him up. Most who gained admittance were pleased to take him on his own terms.

Adams was human enough and contradictory enough sometimes to indulge in self-pity and to feel neglected and to blame others for a situation in which he had placed himself. This not so pleasing side of the man came out only when he was fatigued or particularly depressed; ordinarily he was content with his self-chosen and self-regulated position.

The house which Spring-Rice and the others soon learned to know by heart Henry Richardson had finished for Henry Adams late in 1885. Even in its furnishings it came, after a time, to partake of the man and his ideas.

There were two doors on the narrow front of the house[12] opening on H Street to the view of Andrew Jackson on his horse in the center of Lafayette Square. One door, an inconspicuous one to the left of the main entrance arch, led to the kitchen and servants' quarters; the other, under the arch, led to the main downstairs room, a large entrance hallway with an impressive fireplace in it. At the back of the house, the two parts of the main floor communicated. The left side of the house (from the front doorway) was ruled over by two Negro servants, William Gray and Maggie Wade, who, as a matter of fact, ruled the other parts too. Marian Adams had hired them. They stayed after her death. They were devoted to Henry Adams, and he to them. They kept his house while he was gone, ran it while he was there, and in a real sense took somewhat similar care of him. Maggie Wade would begin, a few years later, to correspond with his nieces and give them news of their uncle from time to time.

From the main entrance hall a broad staircase, broken by comfortable landings for easy climbing, led upstairs to the rooms where Adams actually lived. These upstairs rooms seem to have been remembered for their deep chairs, their Japanese vases, their prints and drawings, and for the richly carved fireplaces. Everything was built low to the floor, the size for a small man. The house was typical of Richardson's regard for comfort as well as for beauty. One fireplace—the material for which Henry Adams had chosen to please Marian—was of Mexican onyx of "a sea-green translucency." (He had written to her, when she was away in Boston looking after her sick father, "If you can reconcile yourself to it, please have a sea-green onyx fire-place.")[13] The fireplace was a sort of personal punctuation of waywardness in the middle of careful and appropriate dignity.

Henry Adams had come home to this house from Japan in the fall of 1886 resolved to finish up his affairs and go East again. On October 21st just after he landed, he wrote to Hay: "Japan and its art are only a sort of antechamber to China and . . . China is the only mystery left to penetrate. I have henceforward a future. As soon as I can get rid of history and the present, I mean to start for China, and stay there. You will hear of me then only as of a false pig-tail pendant over eighteen colored suits of clothes; which, I am told, is the swell winter dress of a Chinese gentleman. In China I will find bronzes or break all the crockery; five years hence, I expect to enter the celestial kingdom by that road, if not sooner by a shorter one, as seems more likely to judge from the ways of most of my acquaintances at home." [14]

But he got bogged down in work on the *History* and tangled up in personal relations. The death of a friend was his first news of home. Whitman Gurney had died of pernicious anemia just before Adams reached the West Coast. Gurney had been his sponsor at Harvard, his colleague, and his very good friend. He was also the husband of his wife's sister, Ellen. He knew that her life would be difficult now and, through sympathy, he partook of her trouble.

Only a few weeks after his homecoming from Japan, his own father died. There was something final, as of a door closing in his own life, in the death of that spare, resolute, and impeccable presence. Having worked with his father as closely as was possible in the battle of the Legation in London, Henry appreciated Charles Francis Adams better than anyone in his immediate family (except perhaps Brooks), and had a clearer view of his accomplishments.

He was to think silently of those years in London, to turn over in his mind every circumstance, every pronouncement, every hidden twist and turn of diplomacy through which his father had gone immaculate and, at last, victorious. Charles Francis was, to his way of thinking, the most efficient Adams; he had used his resources, such as they were, best. If he lacked something of lovableness in the efficiency of his person, that fact did not make it easier that the efficient weapon had been let to rust. His country had not used him after the brilliant years of the London Ministry and after the brief glory of the Geneva Arbitration. Why? wondered his son? And where was the blame?

191

After the death of her husband, Mrs. Charles Francis Adams stayed on at the Adams house in Quincy. She was a semi-invalid and needed care. Henry was held to a close orbit for several years: winters in Washington, summers in Quincy, where he helped look after his mother. He had occasional short flights during these years—to Cuba, to California, to the Carolinas, to the Virginia mountains—but his life was relatively confined and constricted.

In the house on H Street, Adams lived quietly in his own fashion. Outsiders thought he was amusing, and his breakfasts great fun. He himself had a faint pride in them and thought back to Monckton-Milnes's breakfasts as a precedent. His hour for breakfast was noon. Plates were set for more than were scheduled to eat. His privileged friends dropped in casually, as they pleased. The aroma of exclusiveness did not displease the dispenser of hospitality. Adams was not cured of pride by sorrow. He was fully conscious of a sort of invidious choice in the way he lived. Yet, once inside, the manner of it all was easy, friendly, and simple.

A half-year after his return from Japan, Adams wrote a letter which displays his continuing morbidity of thought. Congratulating John Hay on the appearance of a poem of his in the *Century Magazine,* he said:

'Tis pretty, Hay 'tis much! Perhaps the conclusion is a little weak; but I would not care to strengthen it. King says we ought to publish our joint works under the title of "The Impasse Series," because they all ask questions which have no answers; but nothing has any real answer, and when one walks deliberately into these blind alleys where Impasse is stuck up at every step, one cannot, without a certain ridicule, knock one's head very violently against the brick wall at the end. Victor Hugo did this, to the delight of Frenchmen; but, for our timider natures, let us go on, as before, and, when we see the brick wall, take off our hats to it with the good manners we most affect, and say in our choicest English: *Monseigneur, j'attendrai.*[15]

In this mood everything outside a very few and special interests had not too much reality for Adams. Public and private activities buzzed on, but he did not care. The world of politics was less vital to him than at any other time in his life. Cleveland was in the White House when he came home in 1886. Adams had been "for" him, but it did not seem to matter now. Harrison was elected in the fall of 1888, and he felt only a mild distaste. Even the fact of Blaine's being once more in the State Department did not have the power to move him. Hay might go to Republican Conventions and politick for his favorite candidate—it was all one to his friend next door.

Relatives and friends went about their business, pursuing various careers with more or less heat. Their ardor did not warm Henry Adams. His young brother Brooks wrote a brilliant, iconoclastic book about the Puritan fathers, *The Emancipation of Massachusetts,* (1886). John Hay saw his and John Nicolay's monumental biography of Lincoln begin to appear in print at last in the *Century Magazine* in November, 1886. It would run till May, 1890, and then appear in book form in ten volumes. It was popular and profitable. Carl Schurz wrote *Henry Clay* (volume one appearing in 1887) for the same series for which Adams had done *John Randolph.* Alexander Agassiz brought his scientific work before a comparatively popular audience with his narrative *Three Cruises of the "Blake"* (1888).

Henry Richardson was dead in the flesh, but his recently completed store building in Chicago (the Marshall Field Warehouse) was not. "It is, to use your own elegant phrase, a squealer from Squealerville," [16] wrote Hay to Adams, the first of the two to see it. And remarkably soon after the architect's death, a first-rate study of his work appeared in Marianna Van Rensselaer's *Henry Hobson Richardson and His Work* (1888). (Marian Adams had liked the intelligent young woman who had come to her house in 1882 to see her drawings and water colors.)

John Singer Sargent painted Isabella Stewart Gardner of Boston in a portrait that was something of a scandal in its direct statement of character. Mrs. Gardner, caught already in a passion for art, would before very many years enlist Henry Adams's occasional help as unofficial agent in buying objects of art.

Clarence King wrote his attractive Spanish Sketch, "The Helmet of Mambrino" for the *Century Magazine* of May, 1886, and a review of the Lincoln biographies for the October issue; he wrote a piece about modern education for the *North American Review* of October, 1888—faint traces of the man, but traces, none the less.

John La Farge was made a member of the French Legion of Honor in 1889 after he exhibited one of his glowing windows at the Paris Exposition. In February, 1890, his "Letters from an Artist in Japan" began appearing in the *Century*—traces of himself and Henry Adams.

E. L. Godkin went abroad for a visit in the summer of

1889. In June and July he was with Henry James in London, seeing the sights of the Old World, discovering in the process that he belonged now irrevocably to the New World. James had not yet begun *The Tragic Muse,* had done *The Princess Casamassima,* and was worrying privately about its lack of success. James wrote his hidden troubles to William Dean Howell, at home in America. There, Howells, in middle age, was slowly and painfully waking to find his America no longer beautiful. If Howells had talked to Henry Adams, he might have found an agreement with his diagnosis, but a disagreement as to ends; Adams would have found Howells's calm faith in a kind of socialism too easy and to simple for his own ferociously disturbed mind.

Things happened in the world of the arts or in the world of action. Some of these effects were ripples set in motion by oneself or one's friends. Louis Sullivan's Wainwright Building was erected, an original thought. It would not have been imagined in quite the same manner if it had not been for the preparatory work of Richardson. In 1890 the Sherman Anti-Trust Act was passed, the result of much furious reform activity in which Adams had had his share for several decades. The law had not much force as yet. It was a sign-post of change.

As for Henry Adams, he had a low opinion of himself and his doings. He looked after people who needed looking after, when no one else was handy. He worked at the finishing of a long study the beginnings of which seemed now centuries away in a kind of personal pre-history. He commissioned a monument to be set up over a grave in Rock Creek Cemetery.

He had discussed this private need for a monument for his wife's grave with La Farge in Japan. While they were there both men were influenced by Buddhist thought and Buddhist art. From the time of their summer trip in 1886, it was certain that the image to be set up would have something in it of that experience.

Adams took his problem to the sculptor Augustus Saint-Gaudens and pressed La Farge into service as adviser on ideas, meanings, significances. Saint-Gaudens contributed not only the shape and material embodying of the idea, but his share of remote influences. His own religious and artistic preconceptions entered into the monument. The work was born of the union of three minds.

Augustus Saint-Gaudens, a man ten years younger than Adams, had begun at last in the 1880's to come into his own. He had known bare poverty in his youth. The son of an immigrant French shoemaker (his mother was Irish), he was apprenticed at thirteen to a cameo cutter. He had had his first art instruction in night classes at the Cooper Union. He had been hungry and sick more than once when he went abroad to study sculpture on the encouragement of his shoemaker father. The elder Saint-Gaudens had saved the money for the trip out of the wages Augustus had given his family.[17] The young sculptor, richer in experience, came home to New York City to a studio in the German Savings Bank Building at Fourteenth Street and Fourth Avenue. Homesick for the fountains of Rome he turned on the water faucets for a faint echo of what Rome had meant to him.

Working on Trinity Church with Richardson and La Farge in the 1870's had helped him at the beginning of his career. With other young artists in 1877, he had revolted against the dry academic manner of the day and founded the Society of American Artists. He had in hand, when Adams approached him, the Shaw Commission for the Boston Common. The Farragut Statue was already set up in Madison Square, an imaginative, noble and straightforward figure. The sculptor discovered his father one midnight before it and pretended to believe the shoemaker's brusque denial of his purpose in being in Madison Square at such an hour. Adams's friends, Edward Hooper, Phillips Brooks, La Farge, and Richardson (while he lived) made Saint-Gaudens's studio on Thirty-sixth Street a regular stop whenever they were in New York. Every Sunday afternoon musicians, who were Saint-Gaudens's friends, assembled informally to play chamber music.

The sculptor was a man of a genial, racy style of talk, not ever much on his dignity, but impresive as if, one friend said, he had designed his own face, the fine, clean-cut long features marked by struggle and the reach of thought. Underneath his gaiety there was an intensely self-respecting, hard-working base. He had had to overwork all his life. Now, when he might slow down, he continued to work in spasms of nervous energy. He was undermining his health.

Saint-Gaudens had known Adams since the Trinity Church days in Boston. Since that time he had come to appreciate his house in Washington, "a remarkably attractive place, unlike any other place I know of in the feeling of elbow room and the gentle easy-going social customs." [18]

The monument for the grave in Rock Creek Cemetery had a slow growth in his mind. Its genesis can be guessed from a sketch he made of the figure and from the cryptic words he had jotted below the sketch:

Adams
Buddha
Mental repose
Calm reflection in contrast with
the violence or force in nature[19]

Reading these spare notes is like listening to the conversation of these men. With his germ of an idea firmly grasped, Saint-Gaudens set to work.

Like the artist and the sculptor, Adams himself went back to struggling with a problem in words. His main strength was engaged in the work of finishing his long-enduring *History*. Conceived at the time of his move from Boston to Washington, continued during the happy time of his wife's life in Washington, it must now be finished in loneliness.

At first he found it difficult to pick up his broken thought. But the friction of work engendered interest. And into this difficult task he poured all the best part of himself between 1886 and 1889: his virile thought, his keen sense of form, his chastened way with words.

His work went with him wherever he went, whatever he did. Whether in Washington in the winter or in Quincy in the summer, the *History* was an intermittent, but recurring, reference in his mind. In Washington Spring-Rice was set to reading the privately printed proof in the first weeks of their acquaintance in the spring of 1887. In the summer that followed, when Adams was at Quincy, the work occupied his main time.

His mother, in addition to other ills, had crushed her foot in an accident. Henry undertook to look after her. He and his dogs and his growing manuscript took up residence in the Adams house for several months.

The quiet of the place allowed him to concentrate. It also fed his melancholy. Here he seemed to be out of things physically as well as emotionally. But in his void, he was industrious. He described his situation to John Hay on June 28th in a letter in which his incorrigible wit played a sort of counterpoint to his gloom.

Hay had gone abroad to more animated scenes and was presumably having an entertaining time. As for Adams: "My gaiety has been exhausting and continuous. I have called on two old ladies of eighty or more, and have frequented various invalids and persons in bad condition. Dr. William Everett [his eccentric cousin] has called upon me. I have returned the civility. I have given rifles to my two twin nephews, with which they are as certain as possible to kill each other, or someone else; but I don't care, because they have a big new sailboat which will drown them if they escape shooting. They are twelve years old. My nieces all prefer jack-knives, an amiable taste, showing refinement and literary propensities."

". . . I write history as though it were serious, five hours a day; and when my hand and head get tired, I step out into the rose-beds and watch my favorite roses. For lack of thought, I have taken to learning roses, and talk of them as though I had the slightest acquaintance with the subject." [20]

At the end of the summer, Adams, tired out, was ready to give up his place to Brooks and leave. He was full of a bottled-up restlessness and looked around for someone to share a trip with him. "I must explode into space somewhere, after this summer of galley-slave toil," he wrote on September 12th to Elizabeth Cameron.[21] But Clarence King failed him, and an excursion to Mexico fell through. He returned home to Washington and in a spasm of energy had a wall of his house torn out to make room for a greenhouse.

It was not long before he heard more bad news. In November, Whitman Gurney's widow, Ellen Hooper Gurney, died in singularly distressing circumstances. She died, as her sister had, a suicide. Her death affected the nerves of others. Edward Hooper went to bed for six weeks; Henry was concerned for his brother-in-law. What he felt for himself he kept to himself.

The winter passed. In the early spring Adams took a short trip to Cuba with Theodore Dwight. By the time summer came, he was established once more at Quincy. His mother was not much changed and still needed care. His manuscript was longer and heavier. He was seized with a "frenzy of finishing the big book." "I hurry off chapters as though they were letters to you," he wrote to Hay on July 8, 1888.[22]

On September 9th he wrote again to Hay: "I can hardly believe my own ears when I say that tomorrow my narrative will be finished; all my wicked villains will be duly rewarded with Presidencies and the plunder of the innocent; all my models of usefulness and intelligence will be fitly punished, and deprived of office and honors; all my stupid people, including my readers, will be put to sleep for a thousand years; and when they wake up, they will find their beards grown to their waists, and will rub their eyes, and ask: 'Do crows still fly over Washington?' " [23] His occupation was gone. He was free to stay out in the soggy garden with the roses as long as he wanted. The rain drove him inside and he read Gibbon.

In the fall, once more relieved from duty at Quincy, he went on a long rummage across the American West with Robert Cunliffe, one of his old friends from England. In February he spent a few wet weeks along the Carolina coasts with William Hallett Phillips and Thomas Lee. In March he returned to Washington to sign a contract for the publication of his *History* and to begin the labor of proofreading.

A new Administration—Benjamin Harrison's—had been inaugurated. It sent Abraham Lincoln's son, Robert Lincoln, as minister to England. Adams wrote to Gaskell to be good to him. It brought Theodore Roosevelt to Washington for the first time. "You know the poor wretch has consented to be Civil Service Commissioner and is to be with us in Washington next winter with his sympathetic little wife. He is searching for a house. I told him he could have this if he wanted it; but nobody wants my houses though I offer them freely for nothing." [24] Roosevelt was to make more of his job than was expected, and to have more fun doing it.

At the beginning of June, Henry Adams, according to an old custom, went out on horseback to see the spring. There had been rains and flood, but his mood, as explorer, was high. He wrote to Elizabeth Cameron, on June 2, 1889:

At the first glimpse of sunshine yesterday, I started off on Daisy to see what was left of the universe. I found all the old bridges gone on Rock Creek, and had to come down to our new bridge to cross, where Martha's little waterfall quite roared. [Martha was Mrs. Cameron's little girl.] Rock Creek tumbled like the rapids at Niagara. I came across, and down to the Potomac about half way to the Chain Bridge. The whole thing was running loose. The canal was busted and running like an insane mule. The river was quite superb. I raced with casks and beams, but they beat me, though Daisy was going an easy seven miles. This morning, Pennsylvania Avenue is flooded and the trains and steamers can't run. I am going to try the B. & O. train at noon, for I must meet King and La Farge at dinner at seven.[25]

He was on the way, first, to New York, then to New England. He expected another summer of attendance on his mother. When he arrived at Quincy he found her dying. The change had come so quickly that those at Quincy had not been able to warn him.

In a continuation of the letter about the spring floods in Washington, and in a different mood, he wrote from Quincy, after the funeral: "Apparently I am to be the last of the family to occupy this house which has been our retreat in all times of trouble for just one hundred years. I suppose if two Presidents could come back here to eat out their hearts in disappointment and disgust, one of their unknown descendants can bore himself for a single season to close up the family den." [26]

He was wrong about the house—later Brooks Adams would live there for many years—but its loneliness and abandonment in the summer of 1899 must have struck him harshly. He settled there to close his mother's affairs and to close his accounts with the *History*. The last proofs must be read, and an index had to be made. He and his friend Theodore F. Dwight occupied themselves with this job for the rest of the summer.

The first two volumes of the *History—a History of the United States of America During the Administration of Thomas Jefferson and James Madison*—appeared this same year. Volumes three, four, five, and six appeared in 1890. Volumes seven, eight, and nine appeared in 1891. He had done what he had promised to do in October, 1886, when he came home from Japan. Now, in a manner of speaking, he was free, to go anywhere, to do anything.

As to what he had accomplished, he was more or less numb. He had had the good fortune to realize from time to time during the writing of the work that it was good and would bear the weight of generations of thought. Yet at the time of the actual finish, he understated its importance. His mother's death seems to have been a last straw laid upon his endurance. He said little directly about it, or about the other deaths strewn in his recent past. But a letter to Charles Milnes Gaskell, from Washington, on November 24, 1899, was symptomatic of his sense of dislocation:

I have lost count of our letters, and remember only that I have heard nothing from you for a very long time. Luckily time no longer affects me. I have become as indifferent as the Egyptian Sphinx to the passage of centuries, and my friends always remain young because I don't see them. You can't imagine how pleasantly I remember England, and how very much alive you all are, though you have been dead or quarrelled these many years.

I am as dead as a mummy myself, but don't mind it. As a ghost I am rather a success in a small way, not to the world, but to my own fancy, which I presume to be a ghost's world, as it is mine. Things run by with spectre-like silence and quickness. As I never leave my house, and never see a newspaper, and never remember what I am told, the devil might get loose and wander about the world for months before I should meet him, and then I should not know who he was. You can have no idea how still and reposeful, and altogether gentlemanly a place the world is, till you leave it.[27]

I have thrown upon the cold world two children in the shape of volumes, the first eight or ten of which I am to be delivered. As they lost all interest for me long ago, I cannot believe that they would interest my friends, so I have sent no copies about. If any American should ask if I sent them to you, say Yes,—and that you have read them with much pleasure. The conversation will not go further, and both of us will have made a proper appearance before posterity.[28]

By the spring of 1890 Adams was ready to set off on his travels again. He was delayed through the summer by John La Farge, who had promised to go, but who had a thousand things to do first. China was not found to be practicable. Adams decided on the islands of the Pacific: first Hawaii, or the Sandwich Islands, as they were then called, then the others to the southwestward. He had no very definite idea of the date of his return, but in his practical way made careful arrangements for two full years of absence. He had no occupation and no person to hold him, although John Hay told him that his "pleasant gang" in Washington would fall to pieces in his absence.[29]

In August he went to New York to collect La Farge by main force: He wrote to Elizabeth Cameron on the 16th: "La Farge I saw at nine o'clock He had then three pictures to paint, two windows to lead, and his packing to do, but promised to be ready at four o'clock." [30]

By evening of the same day, Henry Adams got La Farge on board a train and they were soon speeding along the Hudson River in much the same mood in which they had set out four years before for Japan. They would go much farther this time, and stay away longer. The trip would mark a divide in Adam's life, an ending and a beginning again.

Chapter 16

Time and the Sliding Rock

ON A MILD October evening in the year 1890 a middle-aged American historian, sitting under the thatched roof of a wall-less native house in a village on the island of Tutuila, enjoyed a fresh sensation. In the early dusk a kerosene lamp was lighted, and the historian and his companion asked for the native dance, the Siva.

Cautiously, the girls assured themselves that these Westerners were not missionaries. Then Wakea and her sister Siva, daughters of the village chief, and several others, ran off laughing into the dark, leaving the two men in suspense as to whether they were going to have their Siva or not.

What came next was a climax for a satisfying day. Adams and La Farge had come ashore in the afternoon. Their steamer, the *Alameda,* had brought them within reach of a native schooner. From it they were transferred to a smaller boat. A strong Samoan had picked them from it, wrapped them, one after the other, unceremoniously, in an oilcloth, and carried them through the surf to the land. They were to spend the night here and go on next day to Apia on the neighboring island of Upolu. This was their first night on the Samoa Islands.

The unspoiled appearance of the small village, the grave courtesy of the older men, the friendliness of the women, the strangeness of the food they tried to eat—all this newness had given them a unique experience. Adams made literary references and reminded himself of Melville's sailor in the valley of Typee. La Farge lost no time but set to sketching while the light lasted.

Suddenly out of the dark, five girls came into the light, with a dramatic effect that really I never felt before. Naked to the waist, their rich skins glistened with cocoa-nut oil. Around their heads and necks they wore garlands of green leaves in strips, like seaweeds, and these, too, glistened with oil, as though the girls had come out of the sea. Around their waists, to the knee, they wore leaf-clothes, or *lava-lavas,* also of fresh leaves, green and red. Their faces and figures varied in looks, some shading the negro too closely; but Siva was divine, and you can imagine that we found our attention absorbed in watching her. The mysterious depths of darkness behind, against which the skins and dresses of the dancers mingled rather than contrasted; the sense of remoteness and of genuineness in the stage-management; the conviction that at last the kingdom of old-gold was ours, and that we were as good Polynesiacs as our neighbors—the whole scene and association gave so much freshness to our fancy that no future experience, short of being eaten, will ever make us feel so new again. La Farge's spectacles quivered with emotion and gasped for sheer inability to note everything at once. To me the dominant idea was that the girls, with their dripping grasses and leaves, and their glistening breasts and arms, had actually come out of the sea a few steps away.[1]

With enthusiasm Adams wrote this description to Elizabeth Cameron. He had needed just such a drastic differentness to wake him up. Just because the Polynesian was alien to his background, he could appreciate him and like him. He could at last let go his numbness and his lethargy, and find distraction from the hardened misery in which he had lived encased for nearly five years.

His foolishness in going so far turned out to be not so foolish. As he sailed from island to island and the vivid Pacific life unrolled before him, his nerves had rest from the assumptions of Washington, Boston, London, and Paris. The memory of the trip would give him in the future a point of departure and an angle of judgment. The experience would prepare him for the important studies of his later years.

Before Adams and La Farge were lifted ashore in the arms of a handsome Samoan and deposited in a small village on the island of Tutuila, they had had their first taste of Pacific flavor in Hawaii, where they had spent the month of September. Tutuila, where they enjoyed their first Siva, was only an overnight stopping place. They came to rest at last at Vaiale, the native village next door to the port town of Apia on the Island of Upolu.

Here in their own native house set down among others in a grove near the shore, they began to take in and react to the gentle savagery of Samoa. Here they had good company: two kings, one current, one deposed, Malietoa and Mata-afa; the American Consul, Howard M. Sewall, who invested them with the prestige of great American chiefs; and nearby on his hill the Scottish writer Robert Louis Stevenson, who attracted and alarmed in almost equal proportions.

Adams could appreciate the complete otherness of the Samoans, but he could not like, or even approve, such a displaced person as R. L. S. Adams came upon Stevenson at a difficult time. He was in his pioneer stage in Samoa, hacking a home out of the tough forest in the hills above Apia. He was engaged in digging up roots, cutting down trees, building fences, and in elemental planting. He was not even sure of bodily survival; it had not yet become clear that Samoa was going to be good for his debilitated physical frame. He and his wife did not have always enough to eat, certainly not enough to serve guests munificently. Any adequate house or style of living was reserved for the future. Stevenson had not yet achieved the tranquility, the stability, nor the style that he would have as the influential and respected Tusitala.

Whenever he mounted his skittish little horse to ride down the hill through the woods to Apia to see the painter La Farge or the historian Adams (he innocently knew Adams only as "an American historian"),[2] he came tired, ill clothed, not immaculate in appearance, fresh from grubbing stumps, or (with his usual ill luck in his meetings with the critical Adams) from falling in a stream bed. If Stevenson innocently did less than justice to Adams and stung his pride, Adams, willfully, did less than justice to Stevenson. There was, in fact, a basic incompatibility between them. Yet Stevenson was an attractive person to other fierce discriminators—to Henry James, for instance, who loved Louis Stevenson, and who also found Mrs. Stevenson brave and quite acceptable, as well as interesting. Adams thought Stevenson weird, if abnormally intelligent, and Mrs. Stevenson, savage.

The grounds of his uncontrollable and instinctive recoiling seem to have been two. Stevenson was by nature, if not by birth, a bohemian. Adams mistook the source of this unhingement from society. He thought it due to family education. But he was ignorant of the other man's background. Stevenson was reared gently, but sternly, in a Scots Presbyterian household in Edinburgh, a house whose atmosphere could not have been very different from the Adams house on Mount Vernon Street in Boston. But in Apia, Stevenson seemed rootless, déclassé, exotic. This was what Adams most deeply feared for himself and, therefore, hated most bitterly when he observed it in others. He could not connect Stevenson with any stable background.

Adams could encompass the Samoan, a creature rooted in a vital community. The islander's complete differentness did not dismay him. He could adjust himself to this differentness and do justice to the integrity of the Samoan and his civilization, for significantly, he thought, the individual and the civilization were at peace in Samoa. But Stevenson was another matter. He was half like himself and half another kind of fish altogether. He could not get in touch with him, or perhaps he did not try.

Yet Adams saw him brilliantly: "I shall never forget the dirty cotton bag with its sense of skeleton within, and the long, hectic face with its flashing dark eyes, flying about on its high verandah, and telling us of strange men and scenes in oceans and islands where no sane traveller would consent to be dragged unless to be eaten." [3] Stevenson was simply an *aiku* (the Samoan word for spirit or ghost), not quite human. Although Adams was not just, he caught a valid aspect of Stevenson, one his friends rather played down. It would be too bad to lack altogether Adams's view of him.

The second ground of incompatibility was a differentness in their dearest faults. Adams was a proud, willful man, but not vain. Stevenson was a child in crowing vanity, but not proud at all. Their virtues, as well as their faults, were opposite.

Therefore, what good Adams got out of Samoa was from its native civilization, not from its most distinguished foreign resident. That good, however, was a decisive one. It promoted a whole new outlook for him.

A sign of the change was the series of long, highly colored, and poetic letters he began writing home—to John Hay, to his niece, Mabel Hooper, to Anna Lodge, to Elizabeth Cameron. He wrote most easily to Elizabeth Cameron. He had first to make her understand that he was living in a different kind of time from that they used at home. "Sunday here," he wrote on October 12th, "when it should be Saturday, but Samoa is above astronomy. Time has already made us familiar with our surroundings. I find myself now and then regaining consciousness that I was once an American supposing himself real." [4]

Apia had not spoiled Vaiale. Apia itself was an innocent, insignificant sort of place. The twin disintegrators of the Pacific—commercialism and imported religion—had not yet worked powerfully here. They had laid on only a veneer. The Samoan had not changed his manners, his arts, or his mood. He sang and danced, fished, fought, and feasted, gave princely gifts, made long speeches, all in the old way.

And it was the old way which caught the imagination of Adams. As historian and as man, he found himself admiring a society as different as possible from the one in which he had been reared.

Seumano, the chief of Apia, arranged a great *malanga*, a boat expedition to the island of Savaii, the most western of the Samoan group. Adams and La Farge went as visiting chiefs, escorted by Seumano and Sewall. Village chiefs received the party at each stop with feasts and dancing. There was much ceremonious greeting and farewelling. In each place the village maiden, the *taupo* (with her duenna in attendance), was appointed to entertain them. Adams saw *siva* after *siva:* sitting dances, standing dances, war dances, dances in imitation of every village activity. It seemed to him that he "had got back to Homer's time, and were cruising about on the Aegean with Ajax." [5]

The artist in La Farge was knocked speechless. "No one had told me of a rustic Greece still alive somewhere, and still to be looked at." [6] He and his companion became partisan, jealous of the particular island charm which seemed doomed to an early, brutal extinction. "The missionaries' good-will," wrote La Farge, "has never gone as far as to try to understand him [the Polynesian] as a being with the same rights to methods of thinking that we claim for ourselves. . . . What we call savagery was a mode of civilization." [7] La Farge caught as many aspects of the island life as he could in drawings and paintings.

They returned to Vaiale before going forth on another *malanga*, this time around Upolu. The people of the village accepted them, gracefully and casually. Adams, strolling home in the evening from Sewall's or Mata-afa's, heard greetings of "Atamu" from shadowed, glowing figures in the early dark.

A month later he wrote to Hay a lively account of a picnic he had arranged. He asked Seumano's wife, Fatuleia, to invite several of the girls for a day's expedition to the Sliding Rock. They made their way—he, La Farge, and the pretty girls Fanua, Otaota, Nelly, Fang-alo—several miles through the tangled woods and found their waterfall in a ravine. Here the shallow water dropped over a slippery stone and arched in a free fall of twenty feet into a pool at the bottom. It was a familiar place to the girls, who went there to amuse themselves by sliding with the water into the pool below. "They go like a shot," wrote Adams, "and the sight is very pretty. La Farge and I were immensely amused by it, and so were the girls, who went in as though they were naiads. They wore whatever suited their ideas of propriety, from a waistcloth to a night-gown dress; but the variety rather added to the effect, and the water took charge of the proprieties." [8]

La Farge's description of the same scene shows his awareness of color: "In the plunge and the white foam, the yellow limbs did indeed look like goldfish in a blue-green pool." [9] He wrote ruefully, as of a missed opportunity: "The whole thing was catching, and had we stayed longer, we too should have been over." [10] But they did not go over; they ate their picnic lunch off banana leaves, and rode sedately home with their covey of girls, and thought about the day many times.

The perfectly proper informality of the girls charmed Adams. Their morality, while different from that of Lafayette Square, was quite as real. He and La Farge, Adams wrote home, might quite properly have married (except that La Farge had a wife already), and when they were ready to leave could have then quite properly sent their wives home to their fathers with suitable gifts. The wives would be just as free to leave whenever they wished. But in the meantime he and La Farge—as Samoan husbands—would have incurred staggering responsibilities. The girls' families could rightfully claim shelter and food and all one's means. And the cocoanut oil, with which the girls made their bodies shine, was as yet something of a drawback, too. Adams wrote with some show of bravado as if saying: I have instincts, I have appetites. Yet neither at this time, nor later, does he seem to have been seriously tempted. The crushing out of certain emotions at the time of his wife's death seems to have been final.

Yet Adams achieved another relationship more difficult than that of sex. He achieved friendship. Even in the South Seas, Adams characteristically preferred the company of women. He enjoyed their familiarities and their impudence and gave them extravagant presents. He tried to look "as solemn as a Justice of the Supreme Court" among the chiefs, who were tremendously dignified men.[11] (He called one of them John Adams.) But "when the giants have dismissed me, and I can sprawl on the mats among the girls, I begin to be happy, and when the handsomest one peels sugar-cane with her teeth, and feeds me with chunks of it, I have nothing more to ask." [12]

While Adams enjoyed all the innocence that Samoa could show, he did not put his mind to sleep. He saw the Samoan civilization in its entirety. "Within their limitations, they are a marvelous success, complete all round, and physically a joy to look at." [13] This completeness and organic wholeness made the deepest impression. He would hold this measure up against other societies later and usually find them wanting.

But: "Now for the limitations! They are, as far as I can see, the least imaginative people I ever met. They have almost no arts or literature or legends. Their songs are mere catches; unmeaning lines repeated over and over. Even their superstitions are practical." [14] Thus Adams wrote to Hay on December 7, 1890. He had been intensely curious during the weeks he had so far spent on the islands. He had learned the kind of things that made great professors. "What I don't know about Samoa is hardly worth the bite of a mosquito." [15]

His interests spilled over in different directions. He worked effortlessly, with genuine amusement, a thing that had not happened since December, 1885. He geologized, making a hobby of coral reefs, trying his hand at refuting Darwin's theory that they had sunk. He anthropologized, insisting that these island people had come from the East, not against the trade winds, but with them. He thought too that the Polynesians had, at some remote time, been a more highly civilized people than they were today. They had then had larger boats and practiced long since forgotten crafts. Sitting among their chiefs, as a great American *ali* (chief), he studied archaic law, remarking that "Jimmy Ames and Wendell Holmes would go off their heads to find the *patria potestas* about as well-defined and as much alive as it was in the Roman Republic." [16]

During all this time, he tried too to paint. It was as if under the sensitive guidance of La Farge he peeled off skin after skin and got his perceptions on the quick. He did not become a painter, but he saw with a new intensity and was made excitably aware of light, of color, and of shadings. He looked at the sea, the sky, the people of the islands as a painter; he saw what La Farge achieved—a sense of light— as an equivalent for the emotion of a scene. He said a little later, on March 29th, "I have learned enough, from La Farge's instruction, to make me look at painting rather from the inside, and see a good many things about a picture that I only felt before." [17]

This was much to have gained on the dull misery of recent months at home. He had solved nothing of his own existence, but he let the color and animation of the temporary island life fill his conscious thoughts. "Time slides as though it were Fang-alo on the Sliding Rock." [18] So he wrote out of a dreamy involvement with the life of the island. The date was November 16th, the letter to John Hay.

But as his stay lengthened, Adams's critical sense went to work. He found blank spots in these splendid men and women. He chafed at their want of imagination. He had no one to talk to except La Farge, and La Farge, like himself, was occasionally blue. He was ready to go when he succeeded in getting a ship to go out of its way to take them to Tahiti. (Adams extravagantly paid $2,500 to gain this end.) And Tahiti, when he came to it from the simple and hearty civilization of Samoa, was a different thing altogether.

Tahiti had been much more marked and marred by Western civilization than Samoa. The Tahitians had seen their Eden ravaged, and, like Eden's original inhabitants, after the angelic devastation, they had the look in their eyes of conscious suffering. The Tahitians were subjective; they were melancholy. Their sad fate made a bridge of understanding between them and outlanders. Adams found he could communicate with them.

Perhaps Adams exaggerated the subjectivity of Tahiti. Perhaps, if he had been only the tourist there, he would not have caught the nuance. But he was never just the tourist in Tahiti. Almost, for a little while, he himself was of Tahiti. He learned from it, gained something from it, and in return, gave something of himself to the place.

The cause of this difference in his reaction to Tahiti from that he had had for Samoa was the friendship of a family. The Salmons, half English, half Tahitian, became the friends and sponsors of La Farge and Adams during their stay. In them Adams met Tahiti face to face and did not have to go out to look for her. Through coming to know the Salmonidae (as he called them), he established a personal relationship with the spirit of the place.

Adams had carried letters of introduction from Samoa to the head of the family, head of the Teva clan of Tahiti as well as of the commercial family Salmon, a man of their own generation, Tati Salmon. He received them generously and made them free of the island. There was no gap of understanding between them. He and his brother and several sisters had been educated in Europe and understood all Adams's and La Farge's references, all their points of departure. But he and his family held also a loyalty to the island and to their people, the Tevas, who were the greatest chiefs of the island, easily outranking the present King, Pomare.

Tati's European father, Salmon, was dead. But his mother, whom they all called, tenderly, Hinari, Grandmother, was alive. She was all Teva, and scorned to indulge in the European dress and habits of her sophisticated children. It was in getting to know this quiet, imperious, gentle woman that Adams got furthest into knowing Tahiti.

Tati's sisters were interesting and attractive women; they supplied Adams with a commodity he had been missing in the Pacific—witty and civilized conversation. These sisters had married variously. Marau had at one time been married to Pomare, the King, but was divorced; another had married a Scottish merchant, Brander, and after he died, had married another Scot, Darsie; a third sister had married Atwater, the American Consul. The ones whom Adams came to know best were Marau, the divorced Queen, and two unmarried sisters, Beretania and Manini.

The two travelers met the Salmons first in Papeete, the little provincial seaport capital of the island. But it was only when Tati Salmon received them as host in his country place at Papara, halfway around the island from Papeete, that Adams and La Farge found themselves involved in a growing intimacy with the family. The old-style French house of many doors and wide verandas facing a blue sea pleased Adams at once. "From the first moment, I felt contented." [19]

Tati was a grand seigneur in Papara, yet he was a modern young man, too, who handled moderately large commercial interests. He was a large man, open, freehandedly generous, reminding Adams and La Farge most strikingly of their dead friend Richardson. His sisters were complex creatures. A younger one, Beretania, enlisted Adams's susceptible sympathies. She was twenty-four; had broken down in health while studying music in Germany; had come home to Tahiti; "but she saved only her life, not her lungs. She coughs incescantly, and is bored besides. One may survive either of these afflictions, but not both." [20]

The older sister, Marau, was large, flamboyant and attractive with a sort of dormant recklessness in her nature. Like Tati, she was generous, warmhearted, intelligent. She had been forced into the marriage with King Pomare, Adams suspected; disgusted with him, she had divorced him. Adams admired her intelligence and force and also a look that told him she was capable of going to the devil in a wholehearted, reckless Polynesian fashion.

The member of the family who touched him most deeply was Tati's mother, Hinari. She was an authentic, old-style Tahitian, who had lived through the latter days of her island's ruin; but she had been little daunted by it. She lived in the island way, even in her son's European house. She remembered the old legends and songs, and as she came to trust

Adams, began to tell them to him. Then one day Hinari made a little speech to Adams in the native tongue and went through the proper and traditional form of adopting him into the Teva clan and giving him a name. He was more moved than he would have thought possible. "The whole thing was done simply but quite royally, with a certain condescension as well as kindness of manner. For once, my repose of manner was disturbed beyond concealment," he wrote in a letter to Elizabeth Cameron on April 8, 1891.[21]

It is wrong to conceive of Adams as thinking of the adoption into the Teva family as a joke. He had got rather far into the island way of thinking. While he did not lose a certain dryness about incongruities, he took Tahiti seriously. His most serious moment was saying goodbye to Hinari. He was surprised at the reality and depth of his emotion on June 4th when he said goodbye. "We had a gay breakfast; but I cared much less for the gaiety than I did for the parting with the dear old lady, who kissed me on both cheeks—after all, she is barely seventy, va!—and made us a little speech, with such dignity and feeling that, though it was in native, and I did not understand a word of it, I quite broke down. I shall never see her again, but I have learned from her what the archaic woman was." [22]

On June 5th the two travelers left Tahiti for Rarotonga, Fiji, Australia, the Torres Straits, Bali, Java, Singapore, Ceylon, the Red Sea, Egypt, and eventually Marseilles, Paris, and London. Another outlander slipped into Papeete just a few days before they left: Paul Gauguin, penniless, diseased, who would find in Tahiti something to make his unpleasant life worth having been lived.

As for Adams himself, he carried away perhaps as vivid a sense of Tahiti as Gauguin would gain. Some of it is in his letters, some of it (by implication) in future books about other places, a great deal of it in the book *Tahiti*. This volume was privately printed by him in 1893 after he had received from Marau a mass of material he had partially got together and left with her on the island, and after he had patched his personal knowledge with research in libraries. It was called, in the first small printing, *Memoirs of Marau Taaroa, Last Queen of Tahiti*. Presumably he sent the book to some members of the Salmon-Teva family. In 1901 Adams enlarged, corrected, and reprinted the book with a new title: *Memoirs of Arii Taimai e Marama of Eimeo, Terrirere of Tooarai, Terrinui of Tahiti, Tauraatua i Amo*. Arii Taimai was Hinari, Marau's mother, the last of the Tevas to play a historic role in Tahiti's story. Adams recast his history of the island to read as if it were she speaking.

Adams referred to the book as *Tahiti* as early as a letter of 1902. A modern reprint uses the island name for title, showing the more correct, more fantastic title inside on the title page.

The book was the result of a busy month or two—the last he spent with the Salmons. He had suggested to Marau that she ought to write her memoirs. Then he had used every wile and charm he possessed to get all of Marau's family talking their past to him. Kindling each other with enthusiasm, remembering events they thought they had forgotten, they were soon pouring forth not only personal remembrances, but Tahitian pre-history: myths, snatches of epics, war chants, love songs. The most remarkable performer was Hinari, the imperious grandmother, who knew island history and legendry better than her Westernized children. Adams had had to work hard during that time to keep up with her.

The result was that when he left Tahiti, his head was humming with stories, poems, bits of history and statistics. He eventually unified his material and made it into the book that he printed in 1893.

If the reader can get past the difficulty of the Tahitian names and genealogy, if he can accustom himself to the non-Western perspective which Adams insisted on, he may be able to see that this small book was a foretaste of what Adams was going to write later.

The book pictured first the healthy, primitive society whose members lived an un-selfconscious, organically whole life—a round of existence in which every member had a satisfying and functionally useful as well as beautiful part to play. It pictured next the invasion of that life by alien forces —explorers, traders, and missionaries—who infected Tahiti with unassimilable ideas. It pictured last the degraded state of society in which Tahiti lived when, at the end of the eighteenth and at the beginning of the nineteenth centuries, Western forces had done their worst. Tahiti's population was depleted and diseased, its life devitalized, its arts and crafts almost forgotten.

The opening sentence established the sound of a voice and a personality: "If the Papara family and people had any name, in European fashion, I suppose it would be Teva, for we are a clan, and Teva is our name." [23] Adams's method added both charm and a certain difficulty of belief to his book. He was unable to keep it consistently Papara's voice.

Although he could not keep to a consistent tone, he showed, as in his *History,* a gift for pulling unlike things together. He linked Tahiti's history with that of Europe and America and showed the connections between events upon the far-off island and the revolutionary struggle over ideas in the time of Rousseau, Voltaire, and Jefferson. "At that moment," he wrote in connection with this linking, "Europe, and especially France, happened to be looking for some bright example of what man had been, or might be, in a state of nature, and the philosophers seized on Tahiti to prove that, if man would only rid himself of restraints, he would be happy." [24] Europeans, of the propagandizing revolutionary generation, saw Tahiti narrowly and inaccurately. The happiness of the Tahitians, Adams says, was not the absence of restraints, but the presence of a deeply felt system of restraints that had got into the blood and bone and become almost natural. "The real code of Tahitian society would have upset the theories of a state of nature as thoroughly as the guillotine did," said Adams, making an excellent point, but losing his Tahitian voice.

Adams concluded his book with an extended passage that he indicated was almost a transcription made by him of what Hinari, Arii Taimai, had told him of her greatest moment. In 1846 the French fleet, on provocation of an island war, threatened drastic retaliation in which they would use all the efficient methods of modern Western war. The Chieftainess Arii, the head of the Teva clan, and the most influential woman of the islands, roused herself with dignity and decisiveness, interposed with both the French and the native troublemakers. She prevented the war, caused her people to face the inevitable, and by submitting, saved them from a worse intervention than they had suffered yet. At the end of her few days of action, she rather haughtily turned down the crown which the French wanted to transfer to her from the spineless Pomare queen.

In this story one recognizes the kind of person whom Adams admired—a person of integrity, force, and simplicity. He pictured her as a worthy successor to her happier ancestors. Hinari evidently did not waste sentiment on herself or her situation. But Adams made obvious through indirection the inherent pathos, not only of the woman, but of her whole people.

When Adams left Hinari and her family, he dreaded to go home. He half thought he might do better to stay in the South Seas. Among the islands he was out of the world; he could here, without bad conscience, let things slide like Fang-alo on the Siding Rock. If he went home, he would have to take up a kind of struggle with his age and his own society.

But La Farge needed to go home. His affairs would go bankrupt if he did not return soon. And La Farge would not go without Adams. Adams pretended to himself and to his correspondents that the painters' affairs were what pulled him home. But he had several reasons of his own. The worst of them was that his interest was engaged. However bad things got in Western Europe and in the United States, that part of the world was his home, and his mind fretted to cope with a change of pace which he had discerned in Western affairs. He caught up on newspapers and magazines. There was interesting news from his brother Charles, and from John Hay about politics and economics. Despite himself, he wanted to find out about Gladstone and Parnell; about the financial crash of the Barings in London, about his brother Charles's losing the struggle with Jay Gould in the inner politics of the Union Pacific Railroad. He seemed even at a great distance to discern a new trend. "If I thought I should be alive twenty-five years hence, with my full powers of mind and body, I should prepare to continue my history, and show where American democracy was coming out." [25] Thus he wrote on January 2, 1891, to Mrs. Cameron while he was still in Samoa. Even in the dreamy peace of the Samoan islands, a spasm or mental energy had seized him; it foretold the end of island peace. It indicated the nature and strenuousness of his future interests.

The strongest pull from the West was personal. He wanted to see the monument which Saint-Gaudens had by now set up over his wife's grave in Rock Creek Cemetery. One may imagine the tremor with which he read these words of Hay, who wrote to him on March 25, 1891: "The work is indescribably noble and imposing. It is, to my mind, St. Gaudens' masterpiece. It is full of poetry and suggestion. Infinite wisdom; a past without beginning and a future without end; a repose, after limitless experience; a peace, to which nothing matters—all embodied in this austere, beautiful face and form . . ." [26]

Meanwhile the islands had helped Adams. He was calmer in his nerves, slept better, was "more like a sane idiot" than he had been, he said, for the last six years.[27] This he had written to Rebecca Rae on April 27th, as the time for his departure became countable.

Therefore, Fiji, where he went from Tahiti, in midsummer, could not hold his interest. He, La Farge, Governor John Thurston, several government officials, and a crew of Fijians made a strenuous expedition over the mountain of the island of Viti Levu into territory seldom seen by white men. Adams looked on mountainsides for a raised coral reef, found one, and was briefly triumphant, but he was tired of the exotic. The Fijians lacked the charm of the jolly Samoans and the melancholy Tahitians. They seemed merely practical. He moved on. Australia was only America without scope, Bali was only a nuisance of a two-hour stopover. Java was an industrious bore; he did not want to see any more Dutch colonies; everyone worked too hard.

He found out that his *History* was not dead. In Samoa he had come upon a curiously bitter attack on the work in an anonymous article in the New York *Tribune* signed "Housatonic." [28] (The diatribe, labeled "A Case of Hereditary Bias," appeared in two parts, on September 10, 1890, and December 15, 1890. It is not clear whether Adams in the South Seas saw both numbers, but he received the printed pamphlet of the whole later as a humorous gift from Theodore Roosevelt.) The attack stems, from internal evidence, to have been the work of an arch neo-federalist. "Housatonic" thought Adams shockingly unsympathetic to Hamilton, wicked in his treatment of the federalism of the period of separatist feeling in New England, and traitorous to his section in obviously preferring a "horse-racing chevalier" of Virginia (Jefferson) to the narrow society of New England presided over by "the minister with the cocked hat." [29] He accused the author of writing out of family prejudice and stridently accused him of a "glaring perversion of facts" [30] and said that there was "hardly an honest statement relating to the motives and opinions of the men whom the historian had marked for condemnation." [31]

Besides curiosity as to the fate of his book, Adams had more private reasons for feeling a pull homeward.

Singapore, with its swarm of varied Eastern life, would have made more impression, he said, if he had come that way first, and not approached it at the end of months of sensations. Only in Ceylon did he find real attraction, in Kandy, the pretty port city, and in Anuradhapura, the dead Buddhist city in the interior.

He observed there, perhaps for the first time, that a whole civilization had flourished when its central belief flourished, and had died when that belief died. Yet he found its artistic impressiveness due to bulk alone. "The place was a big bazaar of religion, made for show and profit. Any country shrine has more feeling in it than this whole city seems to have shown. I am rather glad the jackals and monkeys own it, for they at least are not religious formalists, and they give a moral and emotion to the empty doorways and broken thresholds. Of course we went at once to the sacred bo-tree, which is now only a sickly shoot or two from the original trunk, and under it I sat for half an hour, hoping to attain Nirvana. . . . I left the bo-tree without attaining Buddhaship." [32]

But Ceylon reminded him of Buddhism as he had first seen it in Japan. His close meditation on Eastern belief crystallized into a long philosophical narrative that he set down in verse, writing it in the heat and dullness of the slow-moving boat as it crossed the Indian Ocean and streamed northward on the Red Sea, taking him closer to the West, farther from the East.

What he wrote was not careful of dogma. It reflected merely what he took to be two contrasting attitudes, both Eastern, and his choice of one of them to be appropriated into his own beliefs. He tagged one attitude "Buddha"—the attitude of complete separation from action and of complete dedication to contemplation. He tagged the other attitude "Brahma"—the attitude of a partial acceptance of life, of living in life, of acting a part in it, and yet of judging it from the angle of contemplation.

The poem *Buddha and Brahma* was a philosophic narrative. A young man, Malunka, had asked three times of Gautama Buddha what his eternal pose of contemplation meant. Buddha, for answer, only lifted his lotus and contemplated it held aloft. Malunka then went to his father, a Rajah, who, although a companion of Gautama in his youth, had lived in the world. Malunka asked the Rajah what his way meant. The Rajah's answer seems to be Henry Adams's:

> *Think not! Strike!*
>
> .   .   .   .
>
> *all my wisdom lies in these three words.*
>
> .   .   .   .
>
> *Gautama found a path. You follow it.*
> *I found none, and I stay here, in the jungle,*
> *Content to tolerate what I cannot mend.*
> *I blame not him or you, but would you know*
> *Gautama's meaning, you must fathom mine.*

He failed to cope with life; renounced its cares;
Fled to the forest, and attained the End,
Reaching the end by sacrificing life.

  .   .   .   .

Gautama's way is best, but all are good.
He breaks a path at once to what he seeks.

  .   .   .   .

But we, who cannot fly the world, must seek
To live two separate lives; one, in the world
Which we must ever seem to treat as real;
The other in ourselves, behind a veil
Nor to be raised without disturbing both.

  .   .   .   .

Never can we attain the Perfect Life.
Yet in this world of selfishness and striving
The wise man lives as deeply sunk in silence,
As conscious of the Perfect Life he covets,
As any recluse in the forest shadows,
As any Yogi in his mystic trances.
We need no Noble Way to teach us Freedom
Amid the clamor of the world of slaves.
We need no Lotus to love purity
Where life is else corruption.

  .   .   .   .

Gautama tells me my way too is good;
Life, Time, Space, Thought, the World, the Universe
End where they first begin, in one sole Thought
Of Purity of Silence.[33]

The writing of this low-keyed meditation was an exercise in solitary thought. It was Adams speaking to himself. He gave a copy of his poem to John Hay a few years later. Hay held it unpublished until 1915 when, with the silent consent of Adams, he gave it to the *Yale Review* where it appeared in the October issue.

Within a few weeks of writing these lines, Adams was restored to the jungle of the West. He had been, for months, suspended between living and dying, between pleasure and pain; now he must wake up to intensities of enjoyment and disgust. The temporary numbing of his mind had done him a kindness. But, nearing Europe again, the time of cushioning was at an end.

Even before he left the ship, a happening jarred him to the quick of life. A child died during the voyage. "I passed the cabin at the time and caught a glimpse of that white horror which becomes so terribly familiar as life goes on; but on board ship no one is supposed to die. Nothing is said, and I do not venture to ask." [34]

Pain was an awakener. Associating this stumbled-upon grief with his own muffled sorrow, he reconnected the two parts of his life which had been mercifully sundered.

Yet he had been the gainer from the temporary suspension of his passions. What the gain was he did not know as yet as he battled to keep his equilibrium in the nightmare of the active life in his own world of the West.

He remained for a time in Europe, commuting restlessly between Paris and London. Prosaically, he had his teeth fixed. And he had performed, successfully, a minor operation, the removal of a small lump from his shoulder.

He tasted and tested the Western mixture in the two capitals thoroughly. He read newspapers, magazines, books, raking them together in piles. He admired a few of the new writers, particulary Lemaître and Anatole France. He went to see Réjane act and Melba sing. He listened to Wagner, "but that damned swan bores one at last." [35]

He tried, but failed, to like his surroundings. He was extraordinarily sensitive to the malaise of the decade, and not happy enough to be sensitive to its good things. The whole achievement of the Impressionists, rounded out from tentative beginnings to completion within the last thirty years, did not touch him deeply at this time. Yet this was the kind of painting which La Farge had prepared him to like. The distinction of the Impressionists was the distinction of the scattered, single, individual view. What was good in Impressionism was finely illustrative of what Adams thought wrong with the age. He came later to speak of Impressionism as a symptom of a bad age. All the arts and all the manners which he had tasted (as if he were a lost and wandering Samoan or Tahitian or Rarotongan) struck him as sickly and detestable and altogether too clever. What he missed were simplicity, straightforwardness, and self-forgetfulness. Sophistication seemed damnable.

And it seemed to him that, in the purely mechanical arts, Europe had actually fallen behind the United States. He shivered disgustedly on a Channel crossing, no more comfortable in 1892 than it had been in 1862. "The comforts of European travel in winter fill me with admiration for America. . . . I can understand that their art should be bad and their literature rotten and their tastes mean, but why the deuce they should inflict on themselves cold and hunger and discomfort, hang me if I can understand. Actually, in Europe I see no progress—none! They have the electric light, voilà tout!" [36]

He said an oblique goodbye to his past on November 24th, when he wrote to his friend T. F. Dwight, whom he had left in charge of his house in Washington. "So little Possum has followed Marquis to the next world—I am glad I had not to see him go, but as I expected it soon, I am not surprised. Indeed I wish only that Prince and Daisy might also have a peaceful end, as they are too old ever to be used again. Whenever I come back, I would rather begin perfectly fresh, with as little as possible of decrepitude. I like youth about me now that I have not to carry its anxieties." [37]

He made a new friend in Larz Anderson, the son of his old friend Nicholas. The young man was attached to the London Legation, and listened respectfully, with just a shade of patronage, to Adams's tales of the old days. Just so Adams had listened in the 1860's to his elders. Catching sight of that likeness, he felt his age. Yet young Anderson was good to him; visited him in the hospital at the time of his operation; dined wilth him; talked with him; and, particularly, listened.

Trying to catch up with the rattling present, Adams kept going back of it, to farther and farther reaches of the past—his own, as in his reminiscences of the Civil War Legation—and his family's, as in a letter to Elizabeth Cameron. He wrote to her on December 29th that he had

hurried off to the Opéra Comique to perform an act of piety to the memory of my revered grandfather. Some people might think it a queer place for the purpose, and the association of ideas may not be obvious even to you, but it is simple. A century ago, more or less, Grétry produced his opera, Richard Coeur de Lion. A century ago, more or less, President Washington sent my grandfather, before he was thirty years old, as minister to the Hague, and my grandfather was fond of music to such an extent that, if I remember right, he tried to play the flute. Anyway, he was so much attached to Grétry's music that when he was turned out of the Presidency he could think of nothing for days together, but *"Oh, Richard, oh, mon roy, l'univers t'abandonne"*: and as I had never heard the opera, I thought I would see it now that it has been revived at the Opéra Comique. Nothing more delightfully rococo and simple could well be, than the music of Grétry. To think that it was fin de siècle too—and shows it in the words—and led directly to the French Revolution. I tried to imagine myself as I was then—and you know what an awfully handsome young fellow Copley made

218

me—with full dress and powdered hair, talking to Mme. Chose in the boxes, and stopping to applaud *"Un regard de ma belle."*[38]

When he stepped out of imagination of himself as an eighteenth century Adams, he disliked his surroundings all the more. His nerves rebelled against being replaced in their proper, but agonized, setting in the competitive, ambitious, accelerating West. It must be done, but he was not happy about it. "In all Paris—literature, theatre, art, people and cuisine—I have not yet seen one healthy new thing. Nothing simple, or simply felt, or healthy; all forced even in its effort to be simple—like Maupassant, the flower of young France—all tormented, and all self-conscious." [39]

Knowing that he must somehow replace himself in this tormented and self-conscious Western world, but not knowing as yet what interest or what object would accomplish this difficult re-establishment, he went home to the United States in February of the new year of 1892.

Chapter 17

The *History*

HENRY ADAMS'S nine-volume work, the *History of the United States of America during the Administrations of Thomas Jefferson and James Madison,* was a concentration of intellect upon a limited subject matter and a limited time area. The extremity of the case required that it be a brilliant, not merely a moderate, success. It was successful in these terms. If he had written nothing more, it would still give him a secure place among the first rank of American writers.

Acknowledgment of brilliant success does not characterize a work. It is necessary to break down what the author put together; to analyze what he fused into synthesis; to name the parts of the whole; to indicate the intent, the tone, the bias of the work; and in the end repair the damage of analysis and present the author's whole once more.

This is the attempt of the following pages which treat, in order:

a. Facts
b. Sources
c. Materials and structure
d. Framework, perspective and limitations
e. Tone, texture, and techniques
f. Themes, ideas, obsessions, bias
g. Achievement

From the time Henry Adams gave up teaching history and began to write history in 1877—when he moved from Boston to Washington—every interest and every energy of his mind pointed toward the finished *History of the United States.* He wrote its last pages in the summer of 1888 and finished correcting proof in the summer of 1889. The *History* began its public life in 1889; Scribner brought out the first two volumes of the public edition in the last part of the year. In Adams's absence from the United States during 1890 and 1891, the publisher completed the job. Volumes three through six came out in 1890; volumes seven through nine in 1891. Volume nine included the comprehensive index covering the whole work, an index Adams had compiled with the help of Theodore Dwight. Adams came home, in February, 1892, to find his *History* fully committed to the public. He himself had finished with it. It had now to make its own way—a respected, but slow way, in the beginning.

The large question to be asked is: What is the life of the work? The preliminary question: What first are the facts about it?

The *History of the United States* covers a period of sixteen years of the early life of the American nation. Its beginning is the inauguration of Thomas Jefferson in March, 1801; its end, the retirement of James Madison, and the inauguration of James Monroe in March, 1817. There is affixed at the beginning, before the commencement of the narration of the sixteen years, a prologue of six chapters, and at the end, an epilogue of four chapters. The middle part, the narration of the sixteen years of American history, covers four presidential terms, two of Jefferson's and two of Madison's. The actions of Jefferson and Madison serve as centers and references for a world-wide complication of action and reaction. The character and thought of Thomas Jefferson dominate the entire *History*. Adams relates all major actions—including the War of 1812, which was fought under Madison—to this system of thought. The sixteen years of American history are shown as a radical testing of that thought. The reaction of the nation to Jefferson's thought brought to birth a new civilization. It was Adams's thesis that the American civilization was born, not coincidently with the Revolution, but with the inauguration of President Jefferson.

What were the historian's sources? What had he been doing, in other words, in the 1870's and the 1880's when he found that preparing to write a history was as expensive as keeping a racing stable?

State papers—the finding, collating and discriminating among them—were his biggest job, his greatest pride, his most onerous duty during these years. It was for state papers of various kinds that he made an extended trip to Europe with his wife in 1879 and 1880. It was for state papers (of the United States) that he worked at the State Department, at his private desk, before and after the regime of James G. Blaine.

It was with the apparently unrewarding files of state papers that he worked most creatively, choosing the ones he needed, translating them for his own use, making quotations from them light up the darkness of history, making them refute earlier acceptances of crude half-truth, placing them for point and wit, so that his pages sparkled with incident, opinion and illustration, as well as occasionally dragged with drawn-out example. When he had done with them, he bundled a large part of these state papers into a collection of dipomatic papers and presented them as a gift to the United States Government, giving the State Department, by that act, the possession of certain materials and facts concerning the diplomatic acts of France, England, and Spain, in the period 1801 to 1817, which it had not had before.

The sheer energy which this work required, and which he possessed to the point of nonchalance during these years, was impressive. The job of going through the unattractive files of four nations was done thoroughly, and he had strength left over for the scholarly job of integration and the witty by-play of translation. He offered—in his translation from the French papers—the original French key word of each passage, side by side with his own rendering. He was rarely literal. Translation itself was used, sometimes, as a device of humor, as in the tragi-comic tone of the desperate reports of Bonaparte's brother-in-law, Captain-General Leclerc, abandoned on the island of Santo Domingo in his hopeless attempt to conquer the Negroes and the fever.

These letters of Leclerc make an interesting case in point. They had been suppressed by Napoleon as injurious to his reputation and had lain buried in the French archives till Adams dug them up. They illustrate one purpose he had— to make a complete and authentic history.

In addition to diplomatic correspondence, there were other caches of information: messages to Congress; debates of Congress and Parliament; reports of Cabinet officers and bureau chiefs—these and other kinds of state papers to be read and assessed, to be weeded for the small bright word that might throw light where he needed it. In addition he made use of the very earliest United States Government statistics— the first censuses, the earliest surveys in economics or finance. The work might thicken occasionally with the weight of this documentation; the job he had set necessitated overwhelming —not tentative—evidence on all doubtful points; but on the whole Adams used statistical material fluently and with imagination.

In addition to public papers, he used the private papers of the time. Any package of old letters, any volume of reminiscence, any document which might hold something of the life of the first two decades of the nineteenth century must be assessed to see if he could use it. Private correspondence of the time made events come to life by furnishing a warmth of immediate reaction. Whatever was pertinent, whether published or not, he used.

He persuaded various families to let him read their letters and other private papers. What Cabot Lodge unearthed about his grandfather, George Cabot; what his own father guarded of his own grandfather's journalizing, he read. He had in the end a live book, dyed deep with the eccentricities, the personalities, the virtues, and the vices of an age.

Sermons, as well as letters, were authentic relics, bearing as much a load of passion as of piety. Newspapers could not be skipped. He read volume after volume of the principal newspapers of his period. Some of them were sent to him, summer after summer, from Harvard to Beverly Farms, in an especially constructed wooden box. He read the dignified and the undignified press, the authentic journal of integrity, and the party hack, or assassin. He studied the characters of the journalists of Jefferson's day with almost as much care as the statesmen. Their motives were important, too. In the end he used them all to obtain a full coverage of the violent opinions of the day, being careful to indicate the kind of newspaper source he was quoting. It made a difference to the tone of his history that he could indicate from season to season between 1801 and 1817 just what the private citizen was reading not only in Thomas Jefferson's U.S.A., but in George Canning's England.

Since it was the birth of a new civilization that he was uncovering, the views of travelers could not be overlooked. He took delight in digging up such curious narratives, some of them more curious than true, but all valuable in presenting the strangeness of the new land.

What might be claimed as literature had to be examined too. Any pamphlet, however slight, or any book, however weighty, was scanned. Adams used the verse, as well as the statistics, of 1800 to set the stage, and in his conclusive chapters he drew his deepest reflections from the first authentic pieces of writing that the new nation had by 1817 produced. To give color and background to his battles of the War of 1812, he was not above introducing passages of descriptive matter from the fiction of the time. Jefferson's own philosophizing was made to keep step, or shown to be out of step, with the year-by-year developments.

Adams used his own personal resources, too. Whenever he could he dug into his own reservoir of memory—of scene or person—and painted from life. The aspect of Washington and its wooded hills described from volume to volume owed much to his own liking for the place. He had looked well at the familiar scene and knew it in his bones. One feels, too, in his familiarity with the earlier generations, some effect of table talk at home through all the years of his growing up. The Adamses had long memories. He had grown up in the room where John Quincy Adams sat and wrote. His father, Charles Francis, remembered the sight of Gilbert Stuart painting his grandfather, John Adams. Although Henry Adams leaned over backward to avoid the easy kind of gross partiality another writer might have been tempted to fall into, and in the early volumes went through several circumlocutions rather than mention the family name, yet the family memory could not have been anything but an aid to the imagination.

Adams used other historians, too, both specialist and general, whenever their previous work was a help. He lost no flavor through this. Although he intended the *History* to be as well documented as possible, he was not afraid of personal warmth. Personal reaction was a source for him too. His pages on Charles James Fox—however competent in analysis —have a warmth to them, giving evidence of an old hero worship with deep roots in his past. The book gained in character through his frankness of feeling. He carefully showed grounds, but did not pretend to write a *History* in a vacuum. He saw no reason to disguise his opinion that Gallatin was an admirable man, that Monroe was lucky rather than brilliant, and that Napoleon was a clever, heartless scoundrel, with several amazing blind spots.

Seeing into Jefferson's time through the windows of Adams's sources, what materials of history did he choose? What structure did he build? Like any creator, and in his *History* he was a creator, Adams had to choose. What elements of man's existence—of the American man's existence of the years 1801 to 1817—did he make use of?

Political action was the center of the work. As Adams made clear, the time was primarily a political age. In a manner of speaking, this two-decade beginning of the nineteenth century was the last political age. What Adams was describing was the end of an age. He was clearing the stage for the beginning of another age—an economic age—when other values would dominate both the common and the uncommon man.

But his emphasis upon political action was relative. It was his principal, but by no means his only, material. This fact has been disputed—Adams's *History* having been criticized as limited to political actions—executive, legislative, judicial, diplomatic, military. The actual complexity of the work should be underlined at the beginning; any discussion of it should make clear its taking notice of the mixed elements of the life of a people; their ways of making a living, or failing to; their popular, as well as literary, thought; their national temperamental characteristics which political action helped bring into being, and which, in turn, influenced political action.

Relatively, then, the most important material of the *History* was political action. Adams saw the year 1817 as ending one phase of American life—the revolutionary phase begun in 1776. The primary emphasis upon the forms, force, and methods of the new government was a truth of the period, not just a personal emphasis of the historian. Therefore, the intense importance—felt at the time, and reflected in the pages of the *History*—as to what the early Presidents, the early Congressmen, and the first military heroes did with their new powers. These powers were pristine, amorphous, indeterminate; the Constitution had to be tested before its scope or limitations could be defined and accepted; the period of Jefferson and Madison was important to Adams because it seemed to him that at just this time the American government, for better or worse, settled into permanent shape.

In the same way American temperament was being defined at this time. Hence, Adams's careful definition of the American character at the beginning of the period and his careful definition of the American character at the end when he demonstrated a definite change in the energy and aim of that character. In the narration of sixteen years of history he was watchful to show every possible fact of human life that might influence the creation of a national temperament. Therefore, he described as only slightly less important than the all-engrossing political facts, the economic developments of the country and the subtle national variations in intellectual and emotional tone.

As for scope of scene, Adams was not confined to the narrow circumstances of the thin settlement along the American coast. He needed nothing less than the whole scene of Western civilization to show the pressures exerted upon the new American civilization. He exercised choice seemingly with a free hand, bringing in such remote influences upon American fate as Toussaint L'Ouverture in Santo Domingo or the Shawnee chieftain Tecumthe in the Indiana forests. Yet in the process of tying these far-fetched examples into his story, he indicated clearly the connections—not far-fetched at all—between them and the shape that American history took under its two first Presidents of the democratic faith.

The motives of men were also materials of history. He had to indicate not only the ruling passions of a diverse gallery of individuals, but of classes and nations. Not only the motives of his principals—Jefferson, Madison, Gallatin, Napoleon, and the others—but of exotics such as Godoy of Spain or the pirates of Tripoli. He took into account not only the person, but the group. What made New Englanders restless under the embargo when eventually they profited by it; what made Virginians quit, when it ruined them? How long could the sugar growers of the West Indies endure the commercial restrictions upon their trade which were slowly starving them to death? Why did the soldiers under General Harrison, mistreated, hungry, trapped, still endure? What kept the discontented creoles of New Orleans from making Aaron Burr's plot a flaming rebellion? Adams was concerned with possibilities which, as he wrote, seemed to come alive again as real choices. He attempted to make the conditions of choice real too.

Cunningly he had to weave together the most disparate elements, the most fantastically varying characters and diverse motives. No novel could have contained more improbable elements. These incentives to action must, in his scheme, be set forth truthfully, clearly, and made to connect, one with another, and with the larger point he was trying to make.

Listed below—as an example of the way Adams worked—are the principal elements of Volumes I and II. These are not the only materials which Adams juggled as he began the *History,* but the most important ones:

    a. Jefferson's inauguration: a scene in which Jefferson, Burr (the Vice President), and Marshall (the Chief Justice) are shown face to face in surface courtesy, the author meantime exploring hidden hatreds, rivalries, and in general foreshadowing a struggle for power.

    b. The Spanish Court: an anecdotal, discursive discussion of its difficulties and its corruption; a character sketch of Godoy, Queen's favorite and Prime Minister—a hint of what the new United States will owe to this corrupt man's bravery and intelligence in his attempt to delay Napoleon's advance into Spain and the Spanish New World.

c. Toussaint L'Ouverture: the story, almost an epic, of the Negroes' rebellion on Santo Domingo, and an indication of the way in which this event would affect both Napoleon and Jefferson.

d. The Louisiana Purchase: an analysis of the debate over this turning point in American history, a thorough survey of presidential and congressional speeches and motives, both public and private.

e. The West Indies trade: a dissertation upon the island economy in which sugar had become the focus of imperial struggles between the commercial and shipping interests of England and New England—as well as the cause of the West Indians living or dying; dying more often than not, because of a particular turn that the monopoly had given to government policy in Whitehall.

f. The impressments: a survey of the archaic cruelty of the British Navy's methods of enlisting seamen—an indication that the breaking point may be here—for thousands of Americans, as well as Englishmen, had been impressed.

g. The social war in Washington: a series of scenes depicting the humiliation of Mr. Merry, the new British Minister, and his wife, in the social wilderness of Washington, suffering under the smart of the new President's rule of no rule—the rule of pêle-mêle; the tone humorous, then sinister, as the author shows the social sting turned to something more dangerous as Merry is drawn into Burr's conspiracy.

Adams united these elements under one theme—the dangers which threatened Jefferson's aims as outlined in his inaugural address. His inaugural address is the initial action of the narration. What follows, however remote, has some relation to it.

Upon arrangement depended Adams's success. Structure was essential for the good sense of the work, and for something more. Adams was as ambitious as he could conceive. He wanted the *History* to be not less good than a total creation, such as it was possible for a poem, a novel or a play, to be. But he was limited by the nature of his materials to a literalness of truth. The *History* was bound by weights, fetters, and foreign considerations which poets, novelists, and playwrights were commonly free of. Yet Adams built for drama. He intended there to be one discernible motion, one major flow of action and feeling to a large climax, and within this large movement smaller build-ups to lesser climaxes.

Organization for drama meant a careful paring of the parts for fitting together. Each chapter was planned to contain a particular topic, although the topic might have many related parts. Yet at the beginning of each of these separate parts, it was necessary to link the new subject with its previous history, or with related topics, or to indicate that it was a departure. The topic might be an individual, an action, or a generalization; it might be a congressional debate, a military campaign, a financial program, or the character of a President; it might be a dissertation upon Yankee privateers, upon the militia system, or upon Spanish character; but whatever each chapter covered, it must be properly related to the general flow of the story. From its beginning, the swearing in of Jefferson in March, 1801, to the swearing in of Monroe in March, 1817, the *History* was designed to progress chronologically from year to year, from season to season, carrying forward with some consistency a broad load of interests—political, economic, social, and intellectual.

The author undertook in his ambition not only competence, but style and flavor. He intended not only to be accurate, but to be pleasing. To do this it was necessary to vary the weight of his pages. The nature of his work caused him to be heavy with careful detail in certain matters. He seemed, in some chapters, to come to no end of certain involutions of diplomacy. Yet he intended, and on the whole succeeded, in lightening his pages.

An example of variation in weight was his alternating detail and generalization, a shifting from the particular to the general. Adams did not run on, chapter after chapter, listing one fact after another, and in false modesty refusing to draw conclusions. He knew the emotional as well as intellectual value of the pause to pull loose threads together, to make the conclusion which the facts indicated.

This, for instance, was his powerful summing up of Jefferson in action:

Within three years of his inauguration Jefferson bought a foreign colony without its consent and against its will, annexed it to the United States by an act which he said made blank paper of the Constitution; and then he who had found his predecessors too monarchical, and the Constitution too liberal in powers—he who had nearly dissolved the bonds of society rather than allow his predecessor to order a dangerous alien out of the country in a time of threatened war—made himself monarch of the new territory, and wielded over it, against its protests, the powers of the old kings. Such an experience was final; no century of slow and half-understood experience could be needed to prove that the hopes of humanity lay thenceforward, not in attempting to restrain the government from doing whatever the majority should think necessary, but in raising the people themselves till they should think nothing necessary but what was good.[1]

Adams was bold; he did not hesitate to indicate a conclusion when the facts justified one. Yet he was seldom dogmatic. He was not afraid to face a drawn conclusion. He carefully weighed evidence in doubtful cases and showed himself doing so. He assessed the weight of men, guns, morale, in both land and sea battles. He offered enough material to allow a student, in dubious cases, to come to a conclusion different from his own, but he always presented his own, with a certain exhilaration.

In building a work out of freely chosen material, the historian was yet limited. There was always the fact that his own mind worked a certain way. He saw things with a certain perspective, no matter how free he was. The bent of his own mind made a certain framework for his thought, no matter how judicious he was. One should examine Henry Adams's own limiting framework before going on.

He had first a purpose he could not controvert. He intended to write a documented history. He could not make up facts, deliberately disarrange them, or draw conclusions based on fancy. He was held to a certain authenticity which involved some heavy going, both for the writer and for the reader.

Another factor of limitation was the Adams family past. The historian made no vulgar case for the individual acts of his family—he seemed often enough to disagree with particular acts. But the consistent Adams philosophy of government through four generations could not fail to mark him and his book. Some of the elements of this family philosophy were: a loyalty to the national, above the sectional, welfare; a belief that government was a positive, and not a negative, force; a belief that government in its positive role should be a superior arbitrating force properly above and properly more powerful than all other conflicting national elements; a belief in "internal improvements"; a prejudice against perfectibility, the counter-belief that life was an adjustment of naturally warring elements. These assumptions, and others, necessarily influenced Adams's deepest levels of thought and imparted a flavor, even a bias, to his work. Yet he was never blindly loyal to that tradition, and at times strayed heretically into opposite and conflicting views.

Another limiting perspective was the tyranny of his own times. He could not help being an American citizen and writer of the period after the Civil War. His own time worked powerfully upon the past he was examining. Fortunately Adams was conscious of this fact and converted a danger into an instrument of irony. The *double-entendre* of the *History* was the unspoken comment of his own age upon that of Jefferson's, and of Jefferson's upon his own. He contrasted the feebleness and inertia of 1800 not only with the surprising change of mood of 1817, but with the almost cosmic explosion of energy which he had seen in his own lifetime. He had in mind the Civil War, the expansion of industry, the energy of reform, the multiplication of invention and communication, the growth of population, the thickening of cities, the conquest and settlement of an entire continent, the application of science to every kind of work and thought.

A further factor of limitation was his own divided loyalty. When he came to the time of writing the *History,* he was still half a radical reformer and half a skeptical observer. He was not quite sure about the efficacy of reform; he had practiced the art and had asked much of it. Part of Adams was disposed to be sympathetic with Thomas Jefferson; part of him thought him something of a damn fool. The act of writing the history was an act of self-exploration. It was an objective act, but also an introspective one. Every chapter quivers with Adams's own beliefs, struggles. It is—in spite of documentation—an intensely personal book.

The tone which Adams used toward his material was neither grand, presumptuous, nor pompous. Adams eschewed the lordly manner, although he admired it in Gibbon. He held closer to the common touch of the equally admired John Richard Green. Adams's syle was quick, terse, keen, accurate, and lithe. It held a close rein upon the nervous energy and flexibility of his thought. The thought was supple and adaptable. So was the manner. His thought ranged deftly from the factual to the expressive. So did the style. Adams's emotional bias was skeptical rather than romantic—in the sense of romanticizing. He was an asker rather than an answerer, an inquirer rather than an acquiescer, a disturber rather than a soother.

His most pervasive manner was that of wit. It touched the smallest matters and the largest and ranged from the friendly flick to the cruel cut. Yet it was not incompatible with pity or with passion. He was a skeptic who yearned for the absolute. He lashed himself as well as others in his search. The wit itself had its roots in his heart, although it was the most characteristic action of his alert mind. The mood of the *History* is a curious blend. It shifts like quicksilver from amusement to pain, from sympathy to derision. It is as if the writer were the object of all these moods, as well as the creator of them.

He thrust rapier-like at Jefferson: "The principle of strict construction was the breath of his political life. The Pope could as safely trifle with the doctrine of apostolic succession as Jefferson with the limits of Executive power." [2] He cut at the quality of Napoleon's reasoning: "as convincing as a million bayonets could make it." [3] In sarcasm—the sarcasm of self-punishment—he was bitter about the nation's going unprepared to war in 1812: "Many nations have gone to war in pure gayety of heart; but perhaps the United States were first to force themselves into a war they dreaded, in the hope that the war itself might create the spirit they lacked." [4] He directed a bitter tirade against a criminally inadequate general: "When he might have prepared defences, he acted as scout; when he might have fought, he still scouted; when he retreated, he retreated in the wrong direction; when he fought, he thought only of retreat; and whether scouting, retreating, or fighting, he never betrayed an idea." [5]

Wit was a weapon against dishonesty, against pretension and against self-deception. He admired competence, candor, and self-knowledge. Pity was reserved for those who had failed, but whose failure had had a trace of extravagant greatness in it. He had a trace of it for Randolph, although he disagreed with Randolph's every principle. He had much of it for the Indian Tecumthe, and for the Negro Toussaint L'Ouverture.

Pity for the nameless was easiest of all; for the pioneers beyond the Alleghenies: "Whatever trials the men endured, the burden bore most heavily upon the women and children"; [6] for the privates of Harrison's Army in Indiana fighting a stupid war for the vain-glory of their commander—"Men who for four months had suffered every hardship, and were still unclothed, unfed, uncared for, and sacrificed to military incompetence but hardened to cold, fatigue and danger, had no reason to be ashamed of their misfortune or of their squalor." [7]

His laughter and his pity flowed easily into a larger movement of passion. When in peacetime the English ship *Leopard* fired on the unready American ship *Chesapeake* in June, 1807, Adams wrote that the American people had for the first time "the feeling of a true national emotion. . . . The outrage committed on the 'Chesapeake' stung through hidebound prejudices and made democrat and aristocrat writhe alike." [8]

The historian's deepest feelings were awakened by the spectacle of the tragic resolving of an idea. He wrote as follows on the failure of Jefferson's embargo: "Jefferson's vast popularity vanished, and the labored fabric of his reputation fell in sudden and general ruin. America began slowly to struggle, under the consciousness of pain, toward a conviction that she must bear the common burdens of humanity, and fight with the weapons of other races in the same bloody arena; that she could not much longer delude herself with hopes of evading laws of Nature and instincts of life." [9]

Adams's admiration was aroused when some spectacle of action or of character had about it a quality of cool fitness in its bravery or beauty. He wrote one whole chapter of rhapsody upon the qualities of the Yankee privateer. The following passage suggests the kind of poetry of which he was occasionally capable:

The private armed vessel was built rather to fly than to fight, and its value depended far more on its ability to escape than on its capacity to attack. If the privateer could sail close to the wind, and wear or tack in the twinkling of an eye; if she could spread an immense amount of canvas and run off as fast as a frigate before the wind; if she had sweeps to use in a calm, and one long-range gun pivoted amidships, with plenty of men in case boarding became necessary,—she was perfect. To obtain these results the builders and sailors ran excessive risks. Too lightly built and too heavily sparred, the privateer was never a comfortable or a safe vessel. Beautiful beyond anything then known in naval construction, such vessels roused boundless admiration, but defied imitators. British contractors could not build them, even when they had the models; British captains could not sail them; and when British Admirals, fascinated by their beauty and tempted by the marvelous qualities of their model, ordered such a prize to be taken into the service, the first act of the carpenters in the British navy-yards was to reduce to their own standard the long masts, and to strengthen the hull and sides till the vessel would be safe in a battle or in a gale. Perhaps an American navy-carpenter would have done the same; but though not a line in the model might be altered, she never sailed again as she sailed before. She could not bear conventional restraints.[10]

The privateer had a personal reference for Adams. It stood as a sort of metaphor of a human quality he admired. He made it stand, in his novel *Esther*, for his heroine, lightly and dangerously rigged, beautiful but frail. Presumably behind Esther was Marian. There was a depth of emotion in the chapter which strained the limits of his words.

What tied his prejudices of emotion to the service of his cool brain was the guidance of his imagination. Imagination showed in every joist of the work. It entered into the small choices as well as into the large ones. Two techniques illustrate it well enough: that of writing history in scenes, and that of psychologizing.

Scenes added variety to the movement of the work. The visual element varied the stiffer going of statistics, analysis, and generalization. One saw as well as heard about the new President as he was inaugurated in March, 1801: "With Aaron Burr on his right hand and John Marshall on his left, the assembled senators looked up at three men who profoundly disliked and distrusted each other." [11] One saw Aaron Burr as he ran away from the failure of his conspiracy: "Disguised in the coarse suit of a Mississippi boatman, with a soiled white-felt hat, he disappeared into the woods." [12] At every moment of high pressure, Adams resorted to the scenic. His lips curled at the British Admiral Cockburn's "personal incendiarism" [13] and he showed him and the other Admiral Ross gathering together the draperies of the White House and setting the fire going, as well as, later the same night, attending personally to the American press: "Mounted on a broad mare, white, uncurried, with a black foal trotting by her side, the Admiral attacked the office of the 'National Intelligencer,' and superintended the destruction of the types. 'Be sure that all the C's are destroyed,' he ordered, 'so that the rascals cannot any longer abuse my name.' " [14]

As for the other technique of the constructive imagination —psychologizing—it was ever present. No person was introduced, however unimportant, without some attempt to make him live. The subtle study of the principals went on, stroke by stroke, through nine volumes. There was material enough for a dozen biographies to be dug out of the work.

Here was Madison—"his willingness to irritate and his reluctance to strike." [15] Here was Pickering—"respectable seditiousness," [16] and here was Burr—"veneered profligacy." [17]

233

Here was Jackson—"He thought rightly only at the moment when he struck." [18] And Adams's grandfather: "Anxious by temperament, with little confidence in his own good fortune, —fighting his battles with energy, but rather with that of despair than of hope,—the younger Adams never allowed himself to enjoy the full relish of a triumph before it staled, while he never failed to taste with its fullest flavor, as though it were a precious wine, every drop in the bitter cup of his defeats." [19]

Examples of the analysis of the individual could be multiplied endlessly. He did a more difficult kind of psychologizing too, that of class, region, and nation. Here he differentiated between the efficacy of insult: "Virulence against virulence, aristocracy had always the advantage over democracy; for the aristocratic orator united distinct styles of acrimony, and the style of social superiority was the most galling." [20]

A passage showing him moving from the particular to the general, from a matter of passing importance to a conclusion significant for his whole work, is the following one. His starting point was an analysis of the qualities of the Pennsylvania Congressmen:

That men like Sloan, the butt of the House, and like Smilie and Findley, the ordinary representatives of an intellectual mediocrity somewhat beneath the Pennsylvania average, should habitually end in carrying their points, in singular and unexpected ways, against the ablest leaders of New England Federalism and the most gifted masters of Virginian oratory; that they should root up everything in their path, and end by giving to the whole country the characteristics of their own commonplace existence,—was partly due, not to their energy or their talents, but to the contempt which their want of genius inspired. Not their wisdom, but their antagonists' errors decided the result, and overthrew successively Church and State in New England and a slave-owning oligarchy throughout half the continent. . . . Punishment of Pennsylvania Democrats was waste of time and strength; sarcasm did not affect them; social contempt did not annihilate them; defeats made no impression upon them. They had no leaders and no well-defined policy, but they gravitated like inert weights to an equilibrium. What they wanted they were sure in the end to get.[21]

A passage of this type did several things. It accomplished psychological differentiation. It marked a national tendency. It predicted the future. Its prediction concerned not only the future of the United States, but the future of the historian. He was here making a tentative move toward allying history with science.

The historian—with his limitations and his ability—was hunting the truth of a segment of time. What did 1801–1817 signify to the men who lived then; what, to himself in 1889; what to the future? Adams started an idea in every incident, and chased it like a hare, but his main concern can be suggested under three headings: the transformation of America, the differentness of America, and the drawn conclusion.

Adams chose a particular sixteen years because it seemed a real unity. It was not a haphazard time bloc; it was a period of crisis. He thought the American character was achieved at that time—therefore, the concentration of attention and the careful staging.

Adams presented first a picture of the inertia of 1800. The emphasis was on the pathos of the human situation—the slender string of states along the seabord, the wilderness at their rear, the land yet to be farmed, the roads and waterways of the interior yet to be explored, the minerals of the land yet to be mined, inventions, ideas, even the national personality yet to be found. The American dream in 1800—beginning to operate already—was arrogant, unlimited, out of touch apparently with the facts of the case.

Adams put the problem of the year 1800 in as strong terms as he could: "With the exception that half a million people had crossed the Alleghanies and were struggling with difficulties all their own, in an isolation like that of Jutes or Angles in the fifth century, America, so far as concerned physical problems, had changed little in fifty years. . . .[22] The valley of the Ohio had no more to do with that of the Hudson, the Susquehanna, the Potomac, the Roanoke, and the Santee, than the valley of the Danube with that of the Rhone, the Po, or the Elbe.[23] . . . No civilized country had yet been required to deal with physical difficulties so serious, nor did experience warrant conviction that such difficulties could be overcome."[24]

Piling scenes of economic, social, and temperamental sluggishness upon basic physical sluggishness, Adams presented a picture of a society which was both "sober and sad."[25] In 1800 there was little evidence in American society of what we have come to think of as the particularly American virtues—inventiveness, quickness, energy, the liking for the new thing. He put his case as strongly as he could, for the sake of drama, for the whole work was constructed on dramatic principles.

Adams presented next, in analysis and in picture, the Virginians, who were—against their better principles—to work a great and astounding transformation in this sober and sad society. He showed them in their environment, in their character, in their ambition. "To escape the tyranny of Caesar by perpetuating the simple and isolated lives of their fathers was the sum of their political philosophy." [26]

Positively, they represented a better chance for the so-called common man—a sort of genial, optimistic encouragement of individual abilities among those who had been used to being disregarded or even oppressed. This was their strength and their support; this was the revolution they were bringing in; this was the reason for the fears, the denunciations, the hatred of their opponents who were resigned to a society of status and of limited opportunities.

Negatively, the Virginians wanted the government (which they were taking over in their revolution of March, 1801) to govern very little; to be a pure government, to let people be. They wished for the United States to remain largely agricultural (as Virginia was), for commerce merely to supply needs, for industry to be kept at a sort of handicraft level, for the cities to stay small, for war to be avoided. Taxes were to be reduced or abolished, the debt paid up, and all the departments of government run on as limited a scale as possible. The positive side of government would be handled by the states; the negative, with the possible exception of foreign affairs, would be handled by the Federal Government.

Jefferson was the principal Virginian. It was important for Adams's story that his reader understand Thomas Jefferson. the first description of the man prepared the way. The book was to be a continuing portrait, a picture to which Adams added stroke after stroke through nine volumes. If the *History* was to be an exercise in irony, the irony was to have as its hero and its victim the best man of the age. There could be little complaint made of the minuteness of Adams's attention to Jefferson after he had set him in action in the inauguration scene. One could complain, however, that he neglected to assess the weight of the man in his pre-presidential phase. He indicated the direction of the Jeffersonian thought up to that time, but possibly understated the effect that that thought had before and after the Presidency.

The career of Jefferson as President was to be a tragicomedy. History's solution of the nation's problems was to go counter to every dogma of the Viriginian, and he was to be history's instrument. The advocate of negative government was in the end to increase government's scope and strengthen both the executive and the federal character of the government. Every sincere attempt to follow out repubican ideals

236

was to lead to national danger and personal humiliation: The good that he would do in almost every case contradicted his own received belief. He did not, for instance, believe that the Louisiana Purchase was constitutional. Yet it was undoubtedly one of his great creative acts. It illustrated early in the course of his presidential career how, in spite of himself, he accumulated power and then used it.

"Jefferson might honestly strip himself of patronage, and abandon the receptions of other Presidents; he might ride every day on horseback to the Capitol in 'overalls of corduroy, faded, by frequent immersions in soapsuds, from yellow to dull white,' and hitch his horse in the shed,—he alone wielded power." [27] The *History* was a study in power, how accumulated, how held, how transferred. But the study was broad— its focal points not only persons, but whole societies.

What was the element of England's survival and strength in its situation on the edge of Napoleon's new accumulation of energy? What was Napoleon's real weight, Spain's, Russia's? How would a new, naïve and unformed society behave once it had been drawn into the whirlpool of these tragic, time-old aggressions and habits? What would become of its new liberty?

Tied in with the problem of power was that of the stability of the new American society—democracy—as men were just beginning to call it. Was democracy a source of weakness, or of strength? And did this kind of society best develop the force that meant national survival and national expressiveness in every field from politics to the fine arts? By force, Adams meant social vitality. He was thinking of a high, intense quality of effort as well as of a broad basis of quiet, effortless, unconscious at-oneness in the social body.

Jefferson's period (which included Madison's) was the period of the open question. Issues were sharp and real. The third President was an honest man. He carried his experiment far enough to be tested, far enough for danger. He made the drama. The historian only pointed out the elements, limits, and dénouement.

Two points of high climax occurred in these years. One of these, in Jefferson's administration, was the failure of the Embargo—the attempt to substitute commercial for military war. This act marked the extreme reach of the President's republican theories. The other point of climax, in Madison's Presidency, was the act of going to war. Both the failure of the Embargo and the going to war demonstrated that the new republic could not avoid, as Jefferson had hoped it could avoid, the ugliness, the brutality, the tragedy of other times, and other societies.

Jefferson had thought the United States of America to be an exception. He intended for her to avoid the evils endemic in other types of nations. He intended that the unfettered individual of his new country—preferably an agricultural person—enjoy peace, prosperity, and a new kind of freedom without paying for it in blood, in struggle, and in corruption. Yet blood, struggle, and corruption had existed since time began. They seemed to be built into every previous civilization. Was his experiment a failure when he had to give up the peaceful coercion of the Embargo; when his chosen successor, Madison, had to raise reluctant armies, build and supply a navy, and fight a hazardous war?

History's solution was an irony. It was a showing up of life as a tragi-comedy, not a scene of possible perfectibility. Jefferson's career (in which his ideas were at cross-purposes with his acts) was an example of an immature set of beliefs, a naïve conception of human nature.

A system of thought which had no patience with tragedy was superficial. But Adams was not setting up the figure of Jefferson as a target to be knocked down. He was stressing a quality in the man common to human nature. Jefferson's view of life was inadequate; life was not a scene of easy and progressive perfectibility; it was a corrupt mixture where tragedy was inevitable. Therefore, government must take cognizance of man's lower nature, as well as higher; it must be more than neutral.

After stressing the tragi-comedy of Jefferson's two administrations, the twistings and turnings by which the President tried to make his federalist acts match his republican thought, Adams showed at the end of eight years a Jefferson beaten by events, whipped by public scorn, no longer popular, no longer loved, leaving the White House in bitter unhappiness and disappointment, not to regain his hopefulness for many years. In presenting the humiliated Jefferson, Adams accomplished a turnabout of emotion. Without effort he turned a corner, and showed the dignity and pathos of Jefferson in defeat.

Jefferson's failure—failure only to make his philosophy agree with his acts—was comparative. In the long run his acts gained the enthusiastic concurrence of history, and his thoughts continued, however incongruously, to operate as a power. His story in the *History* was not set up as an isolated kind of drama. Jefferson was made to stand for a quality of ingenuous hopefulness and idealism which history did not seem able to stamp out of men. Jefferson's failure was his own, but also America's, also Henry Adams's. His was the fall of much—the disproof of the dearest, not the least, of one's illusions. It was as if one laughed at oneself for sharing the too easy belief. Adams had been inside the hope; he was not unscathed. He trusted that his reader was not unscathed either.

Jefferson's self-contradiction, self-deception, his wanting more from life than life would be likely to give, his wanting happiness to be an arrangement and not a quality—all this was displayed as indigenous to humanity. There was bitter fun at Jefferson's damn foolery, but it was seen, after all, to be the damn foolery of all mankind, particularly of American mankind.

And concurrently with the bitter laughter at Jefferson's expense, there was, throughout the *History,* a consistent allegiance to one of Jefferson's assumptions—that America was an exception to the world. America was different; not different enough to escape tragedy, but different enough, perhaps, to create a new kind of society, almost a new kind of man. There was a subtle contradiction here between two leading ideas, making a kind of internal argument in the work and stirring the narration of objective events with a current of vital dialectic.

This idea of American differentness might be a contradiction to the irony—that Jefferson's America must deal in tragedy like other civilizations, must "bear the common burdens of humanity," [28] and not be free for nothing. But, in Adams, it was a fruitful contradiction. In a way, it was subtle vindication of Jefferson, for it showed the historian falling sway, in spite of himself, to the kind of influence Jefferson had exercised upon his time—the sway of unreasonable hopefulness.

America was different enough—not to escape tragedy—but different enough to create a new society and a new man. Adams's technique throughout the *History* was to emphasize to the point of pain and frustration the difficulties, even the impossibilities, of the new society as it entangled itself in Canning's world, in Napoleon's. And then his technique was to show how, making use of a new kind of force or energy, it burst its bonds, broke through impossibilities, and, in effect, worked miracles. It seemed incredible that the ill prepared, badly managed American war could end with the military victory at New Orleans and the diplomatic victory at Ghent;

that it could have come out creditably both in warfare and in negotiation. Adams gave due credit to the individual force of Jackson and the fine intelligence of Gallatin to whom these victories were principally due, but he tried to show that there was some broad basis in the whole society for a kind of success. This was the illusive matter of American different-ness. The whole work was a probe for that quality.

It took the whole scope of the work, the whole sweep of the sixteen years to demonstrate the differentness.

Even the most elevated of Englishmen saw little to admire. Wordsworth, for instance, spoke of the New World as a scene of "Big passions strutting on a petty stage," [29] and felt only "poignant scorn" [30] for the human situation of the American. Adams, having introduced Wordsworth as a shallow critic of America, went on with growing passion:

> Some misunderstanding must always take place when the observer is at cross-purposes with the society he describes. Wordsworth might have convinced himself by a moment's thought that no country could act on the imagination as America acted upon the instincts of the ignorant and poor, without some quality that deserved better treatment than poignant scorn; but perhaps this was only one among innumerable cases in which the unconscious poet breathed an atmosphere which the self-conscious poet could not penetrate. . . . If the Englishman had lived as the American speculator did,—in the future,—the hyperbole of enthusiasm would have seemed less monstrous. "Look at my wealth!" cried the American to his foreign visitor. "See these solid mountains of salt and iron, of lead, copper, silver, and gold! See these magnificent cities scattered broadcast to the Pacific! See my cornfields rustling and waving in the summer breeze from ocean to ocean, so far that the sun itself is not high enough to mark where the distant mountains bound my golden seas! Look at this continent of mine, fairest of created worlds, as she lies turning up to the sun's never-failing caress her broad and exuberant breasts, overflowing with milk for her hundred million children! See how she glows with youth, health, and love!" [31]

Energy in the new social structure welled from below: "Reversing the old-world system, the American stimulant increased in energy as it reached the lowest and most ignorant class, dragging and whirling them upward as in the blast of a furnace." [32] The historian thought more highly of the privates of Harrison's army than of its general. The tough resistance of Joshua Barney's sailors and their futile battery which faced and delayed the British raiders on their way into the Federal City—these men who died while the commanding

240

general retreated—this too signified a kind of social cohesiveness which was strongest where it was most unreflective. The unity of the trans-Allegheny West—in contrast to the divisiveness of the older, more Europeanized East—all this spoke for the strength of the American when he was most completely American. The energy of the younger generation of 1812— Henry Clay, John C. Calhoun, and others—was representative of the new social order. The new man faced forward; 1800 was almost forgotten in 1817.

Adams rated consistently high the instinctive and constructive intelligence of the people. "The conduct of England, which caused Jefferson his most serious difficulties abroad, worked in his favor among the people of America, who were more patriotic than their leaders, and felt by instinct that whatever mistakes in policy their Government might commit, support was the alternative to anarchy." [33] The quiet change which the anonymous citizen brought about was the great one: "Every day a million men went to their work, every evening they came home with some work accomplished; but the result was a matter for a census rather than for history. The acres brought into cultivation, the cattle bred, the houses built . . ." [34] And at the end of the war, in contrast to the unsettled state of Europe, the new American society was stable, in a workaday mood, broadly based upon the shrewdness of the bottom of society. Jefferson, the Jacobin, had not brought in anarchy after all.

Not stability alone, but distinction in certain fields had revealed itself amazingly in the new American society. Considering the unpreparedness of the United States for war, the wretched administration of the war, and the disproportionate strength of the nation's enemies, survival alone would have been cause for surprise. But here and there were uncalled-for eruptions of expertness. There was a lyrical inventiveness united with practicality in the design and the utility of the Yankee privateers. There was a high and consistent superiority in American gunnery. There were intelligence and smartness in the building of breastworks, forts, and other engineering structures.

And aside from an ingenuity and deftness in the conduct of the war, there were signs, in civil life, of other kinds of distinction. "In the course of sixteen years certain Americans became distinguished. Among these, suitable for types, were Calhoun and Clay in Congress, Pinkney and Webster at the bar, Buckminster and Channing in the pulpit, Bryant and Irving in literature, Allston and Malbone in painting. These men varied

241

greatly in character and qualities. Some possessed strength, and some showed more delicacy than vigor; some were humorists, some were incapable of a thought that was not serious; but all were marked by a keen sense of form and style." [35]

Adams's further discussion of his list of distinguished men did two things. He established their Americanness—the fact that they were the first growth of a non-colonial intellect—and he marked and emphasized what seemed almost an excess of refinement in them. He seemed to point the way to an indigenous but isolated kind of art, the future native high-brow. Yet at this point he stressed primarily the fact that this art was a native growth.

Adams surveyed other growths, other changes in the intellectual fields. Religion was turning away from rationality, in the direction of a new emotional warmth. Political questions no longer pressed; they were avoided rather than faced. The great change which seemed well under way in 1817 was a shift of interest. This was to be an economic age, rather than a political age.

The sign of the great change was an event which took place on the 17th of August, 1807. It was simply "the beginning of a new era in America,—a date which separated the colonial from the independent stage of growth; for on that day, at one o'clock in the afternoon, the steamboat 'Clermont,' with Robert Fulton in command, started on her first voyage. . . . Compared with such a step in her progress, the mediaeval barbarisms of Napoleon and Spencer Perceval signified little more to her than the doings of Achilles and Agamemnon." [36]

The discussion of the steamboat was of a piece with a principal theme of the four conclusive chapters, that, as of 1817, America had reached a turning point, a place where a signpost pointed to 1870, 1890, in other words, to his own age, which was surely an economic age. "The continent lay before them, like an uncovered ore-bed." [37] The fields of endeavor of the new society were to be two: the filling up of the continent with settlers and the making of "practical devices for popular use, within popular intelligence." [38]

The new society produced in the historian both a malaise and a sense of challenge. He was both sorry and glad to say goodbye to political man and political society with its heroes and entrenched institutions. Since this was for him the last American political age, he was free to portray heroes—Toussaint and Napoleon, Jefferson and Canning—who had, by the slightest pressure of the individual will, affected the whole of society. But he indicated, too, the ground swell of a new age when power would inhere in the inarticulate common man. It was as if Adams moved over a broad arc of thought from Carlyle to Tolstoi and covered all the space between them.

The new society would demand of historians a new treatment. "Should history ever become a true science, it must expect to establish its laws, not from the complicated story of rival European nationalities, but from the economical review of a great democracy. North America was the most favorable field on the globe for the spread of a society so large, uniform, and isolated as to answer the purpose of science." [39]

His words foretold his own future. The last pages of the *History* point to what he would try to do in 1894 in *The Tendency of History*, in 1904 in *Mont-Saint-Michel and Chartres*, in 1907 in *The Education of Henry Adams*, and in 1910 in *A Letter to American Teachers of History*.

The future was a question, both as it concerned the new society and as it concerned the historian. The final paragraph bore a double emotion:

With the establishment of these conclusions, a new episode in American history began in 1815. New subjects demanded new treatment, no longer dramatic but steadily tending to become scientific. The traits of American character were fixed; the rate of physical and economical growth was established; and history, certain that at a given distance of time the Union would contain so many millions of people, with wealth valued at so many millions of dollars, became thenceforward chiefly concerned to know what kind of people these millions were to be. They were intelligent, but what paths would their intelligence select? They were quick, but what solution of insoluble problems would quickness hurry? They were scientific, but what control would science exercise over their destiny? They were mild, but what corruptions would their relaxation bring? They were peaceful, but by what machinery were their corruptions to be purged? What interests were to vivify a society so vast and uniform? What ideals were to ennoble it? What object, besides physical content, must a continent aspire to attain? For the treatment of such questions, history required another century of experience.[40]

The conclusion of the work was a question and a challenge.

One faces, at last, the validity of the whole effort. What had Adams done with the years, the skills, the ambitions spent upon the *History*?

One could question many matters without affecting the integrity of the whole. Certain of Adams's emphases seem too sweeping. His notion that the political age had definitely

243

closed in 1817 might be said to be an overstatement. He knew very well that the ideological struggle going on in his childhood and leading to the Civil War was, at least, as important as the economic struggle between the two sections. Yet his over-statement only emphasized a truth and pointed out the leading motives of two ages.

Adams was so intensely interested in relating Jefferson's age to his own that he was occasionally guilty of a rash foreshortening in order to gain the perspective he wanted. It was the kind of vice into which he would inevitably fall, for he wanted the *History* to cast a shadow on the future. Nor was he altogether fair to Jefferson as a human being. By stripping him of his life before 1801, he stripped him of some of his greatness. But the segment of Jefferson's life which he chose to treat—the Presidency—was that part of his life which had the greatest material effect upon the United States. That fact, he thought, justified him in cutting, shaping, and emphasizing. Deliberately simplifying, he succeeded in relating Jefferson's time to his own, and by darkening certain details, made doubly clear the significances of these relations. His own age —the United States of Grant, Hayes, Garfield, and their successors—was surely an economic age, in which government abdicated its authority and let other forces plunder the national resources. Where was the root of this national fault? In Jefferson's age; extraordinarily, Jefferson led to Grant.

It would be more serious to accuse Adams of distorting the facts of history to suit his theories. Upon examination, one can exculpate him of this accusation. He did something more ingenious, and more difficult to manage successfully, a thing that was also more honest. He invented alternative theories: (*a*) America was subject to the same tragic necessities as other nations; (*b*) America was an exception in some manner of speaking. He offered the indisputable facts in full enough detail to allow agreement or disagreement. The detail was full enough for the reader to carve out theories of his own, if he wished. Adams's technique was that of a passionate, but undogmatic, thinker swayed by honest doubts, which doubts he did not, even as a historian, try to disguise. But he tried to share with the common reader the reasons for the wavering, to convey the idea of two poles of loyalty, to show that life was not easily resolved into axioms.

It would be possible to say from one set of quotations that Adams was enthusiastically "for" democracy, and from another set of quotations that he was "against" democracy. Neither statement would be quite true. He hoped, but he also doubted. Since the outcome for him was not a dead thing of a dead past, but involved his own and his nation's untold future, his book had some of the uncomfortable dubiousness of life, where choices opened at every turn and no guarantees were offered to the chooser.

His *History* did two things. It caught permanently and portrayed a segment of American time. This was the book's static function. Doing this, Adams did as much as the historian is usually required to do.

But he did more. What makes the *History* a permanently interesting work is its dynamic function. He placed certain disturbing ideas before his own generation and succeeding ones. Was the society of 1817 worth the agony which had gone into its creation? And by implicit reference, was the society of 1870, or 1900, or 1950? And he asked: Which virtues were best, those of the archaic, political society before 1817, or those of the present-day, scientific and democratic world, a world begun in Jefferson's time? Adams tried to admire the virtues of the new man and the new world but did not altogether succeed. He admired more easily the personal heroism of Tecumthe, or Toussaint, the personal force of Perry, of Brock, and the personal gallantry of the Spanish lieutenant who died defending a defenseless fort which the forward-looking Americans captured under Madison's dubious authority.

As a student of history, Adams knew he had uncovered important beginnings. He felt within himself that he had put his finger upon the pulse of the future. "That Europe, within certain limits, might tend toward American ideas was possible, but that America should under any circumstances follow the experiences of European development might thenceforward be reckoned as improbable." [41]

Thus he wrote in the last chapter of the last volume. His curiosity had impelled him to follow the scent he had raised and trace the process of a leveling democracy into the future. A partiality of emotion inclined his sympathies in another direction—toward the contemplation of personal drama in recognizably human limits. His *History* represented a crossing point—where both his curiosity about the democratic future and his partiality for human drama could be indulged. The moment was crucial for him, as he thought it was for the nation.

Where could he go beyond this point? He could not know as yet. This was one end. He must make another beginning to reach another end beyond this one.

Chapter 18

Dos Bocas

ON FEBRUARY 2, 1894, Henry Adams met Clarence King in Tampa, Florida. They had bright weather for a passage to Havana. There they did not stay long, but crossed Cuba southward to the town of Batabanó and went aboard a small coasting steamer, the *Josefita,* for four days of lazy eastward movement along the south shore of the island.

They sailed among green islands in protected waterways most of the way and had glimpses of the mountainous coast, a coast as beautiful as any Adams had ever seen. Their progress—from Cenfuegos, to Trinidad, to Manzanillo— along the shore of a decadent and ruined Spanish Cuba, was a way out of their own world. And at this moment theirs was a world they were glad to leave. The ship was indifferent in its accommodations. The food was mostly fried and out of cans, and whenever they hit open water they were seasick. Yet it was not a bad trip. Their progress was enlivened by the presence on board of the matador Minuto of Spain, who was bright and winning although both drunk and seasick most of the time. Santiago de Cuba, where they were tumbled ashore at five o'clock in the morning, was as archaic and out of the world as any place they could have sought. King knew the British Consul, F. William Ramsden, who gave them breakfast on their second day in the city, and told them of a vacant house they could have, that of his partner, Ernest Brooks. The place was called Dos Bocas.

Dos Bocas was high, cool, and dry, eight miles above Santiago in a narrow mountain valley. An eccentric railroad carried them uphill to their house for the first time, but the more usual mode of travel was by muleback. Mule caravans, tinkling with little bells, passed by their door going higher up the mountain, or downward to the coast. Adams and King settled here to live several weeks. The house was large, square, cool, with a garden, a stream, and a green forest all around.

They were alone except for Alexander, King's friend and servant, and for Pepe, hired as cook. Pepe's food was a continual surprise, being composed of elements hitherto not thought by New England minds as capable of being mingled.

They passed day after day at Dos Bocas in comparative isolation. Adams liked to go out early in the morning to climb to the high ridges where there were a few farms and a clear look toward the sea. King, as if by instinct, geologized the rocks, or fixed the height of the two rock buttresses at the top of their valley. Adams tried to sketch. King collected specimens from nine miles of railway cutting. Nearly every day their neighbors, the farmers, brought in one or more pairs of fighting cocks, and the courtyard of Dos Bocas was the regular scene of cockfights. One night, soon after their arrival, the young people of the Brooks family came up to have a party in the moonlight and to make the house gay with their dancing. They made a pretty sight for Adams's acute eye as they left, winding down the mountain trail below the house, their cries and laughter lessening bit by bit as they disappeared among the trees.

King's restlessness—for he was restless in the midst of peace—almost dragged them into trouble. He probed the calm and found the revolution smoldering just under the surface. He stopped casually at every cabin door he found in his way and got along with the Cubans as easily as with Adams. "If a woman was only old enough and ugly enough, and wore a red bandanna round her head, King was sure to be in her cabin, drinking coffee, and talking negro-Cuban dialect that was invented for the occasion, and getting from her all the views of creation in which she was rich." [1] So, Adams remembered it.

King had no trouble making up his mind about the wrongs of these people. He was with them in their desires, and in his easy-going way soon got to know all the brigands in the neighborhood. Adams, later, remembering their surprising freedom of movement, suspected that he and King were kept from kidnaping and ransom only because of the royal courtesy of the principal brigand, Daniele, who took it into his head to protect these two middle-aged sympathizers. Daniele was betrayed later to the Spaniards, and "shot where he stood. . . ." [2] Meanwhile King went to the outlaws' dances and wound himself into all their affairs. He would set to writing propaganda for the Cuban revolution during the next year—before the cause had been contaminated by commercial interests, or settled by the United States Navy. And Adams would make his house on Lafayette Square a sort of lobbying center for Cuba, working energetically to get Cuba free from Spain without war and set up with a workable government before the sugar interests could dominate the affair. He was to fail, but at least he would not have spared his energies between 1894 and 1898.

The weeks went by, February into March. King wanted a larger scope for his geologizing, and there was a mountain, La Gran Piedra, at this eastern end of Cuba that he wanted to climb. It was tamer than Whitney, but not to be passed by. Ramsden got up a party for them and arranged transportation by iron-train and ponies. Their little one-unit train took them eastward along the coast under cliffs of coral rocks. Every time King saw anything along the rock wall that he wanted to examine, he gave the signal to the engineer, and they all got off while King chipped off his specimen. The train took them by nightfall to a remote mining camp where they spent the night.

Adams wrote a circumstantial letter of an evening which he must have relished. By firelight, with deep shadows thrown round them, they sat while a few newcomers slipped in to join them. There was a man with a guitar, a youthful priest, a rural guard officer, and a private, as well as their own party. "The entire company, except myself, then set to drinking rum, singing and dancing, and kept it up till twelve o'clock. I was amused, especially by the private soldier, who danced the Bull-fight and the *Culebra* with as much spirit as my Samoan friends used to put into their dances, which were quite the same sort of thing. The *Cura* danced less well, but took his rum like a Saint, and applauded a variety of the very least spiritual songs I ever heard. They would have gone on all night, if at twelve o'clock, our host had not sent us to bed, for we had to be up at five." [3]

They set out on horseback next morning and traveled rough trails all day long, climbing at last, at sunset, the cold rock peak of La Gran Piedra. There they spent the night in the open, sleeping on fern beds, fortified by doses of rum and water. They climbed down even worse trails next day in another direction, Adams pitying his horse and leading it much of the way. Only at sunset, after twenty-five miles of going, did they reach the *cafetal* which was their goal. Adams wrote simply of that trip, "We were uncommonly happy." [4]

There is much poignancy in those words, for Dos Bocas was only a moment of serenity in a time of stress. The time spent there on the mountainside above Santiago was like the quiet eye in the middle of a hurricane. Even the reason for coming there was an unhappy one.

King's health had broken down. The trip was an attempt to mend it. The year before, he—among many others of

Adams's friends—had lost money and equilibrium in the violent financial crisis of 1893. His nerves were affected. It is not perfectly clear whether King's ailment was organic or non-organic, but a violent affliction of the backbone—allied with almost unbearable pain—broke him down completely for several months. He committed himself to the Blooming-dale Asylum in New York, and after several months of torture, improved. Adams had written to King at Blooming-dale, as soon as he had heard of his trouble, and offered to go with him anywhere southward as soon as King would be able to travel. Therefore—Dos Bocas.

King was better in Cuba. Certainly, as Adams said, per-fectly sane. But Adams invented a paradox. It was his con-tention that, of course, King, in contradistinction to society, was mad, and he, Adams, was mad too; they should both have been locked in Bloomingdale from youth. This was his back-handed way of accusing the present age of madness. For, as of this time in Cuba, he realized his role for the future. He was to be a sort of Cassandra, a truth teller in an inimical society, eccentric, perhaps mad, and utterly unable to leave off his discomforting thoughts.

He had come to this realization of role only gradually after his return from the South Seas. He had come home in Febru-ary, 1892, resolved to face things—but what things he did not quite know. His wife had been dead for seven years, and his *History* was finished. He had no over-ruling personal rela-tionship to which to defer, and no exorbitant occupation. When he went to the cemetery near the Soldiers' Home to see the monument which Saint-Gaudens had made for his wife's grave, he was very much alone. He had reached a loose end of existence.

He was, at first, after the strange difference of Samoa and Tahiti, abnormally withdrawn. In June, 1892, a sprained ankle, sustained on one of his rides to the cemetery, when his horse rolled on him on soft ground, emphasized his moral withdrawal by a period of physical immobility. He showed, in this same season, a morbid sensitivity in refusing to accept an honorary degree from Harvard. He wrote to Charles Eliot: "I cannot stand alone before a great crowd of people, in such a position. . . . No work of mine warrants it in itself," [5] and he pointed out Hay and Nicolay's *Lincoln* as more worthy of notice.

He could judge others properly, but not himself. Parkman, after years of difficult devotion, had finished his great history of the French empire in North America and sent Adams a copy of the last volume (as he had sent him the others). Adams celebrated the occasion with a letter to Parkman in which praise for him was as marked as dispraise for himself in his letter to Eliot. He seemed perversely to insist (although he knew better somewhere inside himself) that his work was of no account; yet next year, on July 12, 1893, Frederick Jackson Turner would matter-of-factly use the *History* as one of several solid blocks on which to build, when he developed and presented as a paper before the American Historical Association, his new idea: "The Significance of the Frontier in American History."

For a full year and a half Adams marked time. In the early spring of 1892 he made a short visit to South Carolina with the Camerons and John Hay for a few days of crabbing on the coast. In the late summer he engineered a prolonged stay on Deeside in Scotland with his five young Hooper nieces. His own pleasure was in the restful void and perfumed emptiness of the moors.

In November he was at home again and host on Lafayette Square to his Tahitian brother Tati Salmon. He enjoyed the successful incongruity of the occasion. He made much of Tati and showed him off to Lodge and Cameron, Hay and Theodore Roosevelt. Roosevelt, writing to Spring-Rice at this time about dining at Henry Adams's, said of him, "exactly the same as ever." He commented on the good company to be found there—"pretty Mrs. Cameron," perhaps, or Hay or King or La Farge, and went on: "Did I write you that he had staying with him a delightful Polynesian chief, and adopted brother? a polished gentleman, of easy manners, with an interesting undertone of queer barbarism."

Adams made much of Tati, but little of himself. He continued to be restless. He went to Cuba with William H. Phillips in February, 1893, and to the Columbian Exposition in May. Its unexpected images of white unity and its pulse of latent power puzzled him. He would go back again in the fall.

In midsummer he was in Switzerland, looking at the mountains with Mr. and Mrs. Cameron, when the storm broke. Messages from two of his brothers (Charles and Brooks) were dire. It seemed that the sky was falling, and he must come home at once to pick up the pieces.

Boston was frantic. At Nahant gentlemen of the respectable investing and speculative kind were daily "walking into the water with their clothes and hats on." [6] Adams stayed over a month at Quincy with his brother Brooks, to help settle the family finances. Henry, in his own immediate affairs, righted himself quickly. Through good sense, or merely through lack of interest he had not over-extended himself. He had lost no money, although in the immediate banking crisis, when he asked for one hundred of his own dollars, he was given only fifty. His brothers John and Charles were harder hit. The effects for Charles Adams were long-lasting and chastening, as he has told in his *Autobiography*. For the eldest, John, they were to be within a year fatal. But the family, acting as one in the financial crisis, bailed itself out of obvious and immediate trouble.

It was through his imagination that the crisis of 1893 hit Henry Adams. He brooded over personal tragedies and over the general tragedy. He descended into a sort of purgatory of meditation. Almost the worst of it was that he was interested. However much he was harrowed, his hurt told him that he was alive again. What had happened to his brothers, his friends, his country was a problem to be worried with all the power of mind he could muster.

His younger brother, Brooks, had a manuscript to show him. It was an early draft of the book he was to call *The Law of Civilization and Decay*. In the midst of the panic, the brothers sat down together to tear the heart out of their troubles and the troubles of civilizations. Certain of Brooks's ideas fell in with earlier ones of Henry's and stimulated him powerfully. Henry's interest gave steam to Brooks's ideas. They excited each other and, working together, thought more powerfully than either had done before alone. Henry was fifty-five. He had thought that his life was over, but now found a new life beginning. Brooks was forty-five—still a young man to his brother Henry—just beginning to exercise the full force of an eccentric but powerful mind.

"If I live forever," wrote Brooks Adams in 1919, "I shall never forget that summer. Henry and I sat in the hot August evenings and talked endlessly of the panic and of our hopes and fears, and of my historical and economic theories, and so the season wore away amidst an excitement verging on revolution." [7]

Henry really saw his brother for the first time as a mature individual. The fifteen-year-old boy whom he had taken to the Isle of Skye had become a colleague and a powerful stimulator of thought in a time of trouble. Trouble became a source of interest. For the suffering which he, his brothers, his friends, and the whole population endured was, in these hours of talk with Brooks, transmuted into idea. The two men constructed in words a kind of vision of human society.

251

The suffering was real enough. Henry, in this cruel season, burst out in invective—he hated, he despised his age. Later he would put on a mask of irony and indirection; just now he was passionately direct. But in this season of suffering at Quincy, in talk with Brooks, he began also to see his own time, his own nation, and himself in a sort of long perspective. Henry had earlier pre-figured—in his *History* and in *Tahiti*—a conception of political ages and economic ages, of archaic societies and modern societies. Now his brother's thought chimed in with his. Brooks had threaded a succession of economic ages and imaginative ages upon a series, an alternation of centralization and decentralization from Rome to their own period. And with keen psychological insight he had made vivid the human types who succeeded in each age.

Brooks and Henry—sitting in séance over humanity—agreed in mordant laughter tha their particular society (as Rome had been, as Tudor England had been) was an economic age rather than an imaginative one, and that the usurer, the lender, the financier was its chief and triumphant type. They had both suffered from the temper of the age. Now making out how and why, they turned their thought into a kind of revenge upon their age.

They agreed about the foreground—about 1893—that the "goldbugs," as they named the financiers, had squeezed society deliberately; that "silver" (a metaphor for a complex of attitudes and loyalties) was their own personal side, as it was the side of the farmer-debtors of the American West; but they thought, too, that "silver," as well as free trade, as well as a decent balance of industry and agriculture, as well as a small-scale individualism (all old dogmas of their family), were on their way out, being crushed out by the gigantism of combination, trust, and protection. They ran on in thought, traversing ages and continents, diagnosing disaster eagerly, almost gaily.

Henry saw, in better perspective, his Samoans and Tahitians, who were people living in what Brooks would call an imaginative society. There, priest, warrior, and artist predominated, and the economic mind was quiescent. He saw now why he had liked them and their archaism, and in what significant detail these doomed peoples differed from his own contemporaries.

He was now caught on the sharp hook of curiosity. The weeks of crisis went on. He finished his sessions of talk with his brother and went home to Washington. People there were as troubled as in Boston, and the least pinprick became a savage personal affront. He was half humorous, but also genuinely angry, at one innocent provocation. "Everyone looks on his neighbor as a dangerous lunatic. My neighbor is Dan Lamont [Cleveland's Secretary of War], who has cut down my old Virginia Creepers that my wife planted on 1607, and is painting it fresh and pretty. I want to assassinate him." [8] This was his first recorded reference to his wife in eight years.

In October he went back to the Columbian Exposition. "The Midway Plaisance," he wrote to Hay on the 18th, "was a sweet repose. I revelled in all its fakes and frauds, all its wickedness that seemed not to be understood by our innocent natives, and all its genuineness which was understood still less. I labored solemnly through all the great buildings and looked like an owl at the dynamos and steam-engines. All the time I kept up a devil of a thinking. You know the terror of my thought." [9]

Adams wondered if the remarkable brightness and surface charm of the Exposition was promise or not; and if, next time, the remarkable energy of the Midwest would be able to express itself, and not make a brilliant copy of Europe. Louis Sullivan might have told him that the Exposition, for all its surface shine, was a tragedy for architecture, a turning away from the robust native tradition of Henry Hobson Richardson, Sullivan, Root, and the young Wright, a foretaste of a regime of refined eclecticism. After Chicago, 1893, American architecture would ignore genius and let it die heartbroken, as Sullivan would die, and would elevate mediocrity for many years to come.

In the same letter in which he told Hay about the Columbian Exposition Adams wrote his worries about Clarence King. "His bank busted with the rest, and I fear he has gone under." [10] On November 5th he told Hay that he had seen a report in two newspapers of King's having suffered a breakdown. "The sum of it is that, for whatever reason, King has either chosen, or consented, to go to Bloomingdale for a time. Apparently he is sane enough, as far as sense goes, and, if off his head, the trouble is physical rather than mental; but the inevitable asylum has swallowed him too." [11]

Adams had further news on November 8th on the bank failure which had precipitated their friend's trouble and on December 15th he told Hay that he had heard more news of King and "that he is getting on well, and that his friend Gardiner is always with him. If anything can drive him to sanity, I think Gardiner can do it; he would drive me to a much further region. Townley [another of King's friends] tells me that King talks now of going to Nassau. I have sent him word that I will go with him either to Nassau or the West Indies in January." [12]

Hay was hurt that King had, so far, not written him, but Adams told him with brutal good sense one reason why. On January 16th, from Beaufort, South Carolina, where he was poised, ready to meet King farther south, he wrote: "That he has not written to you is just what I should expect. I never owed money to any one, but I imagine how it must alter relations. If I owed you money, could I entertain for you other sentiments than those which, as a conservative anarchist, I am bound to entertain towards all bloated bondholders." [13]

Adams joined King at Tampa, and reported to the third member of the old friendship. "I have at last effected my junction with King here," he said on February 3rd, "where I arrived last night. He feels better, and seems fat, bright and active; so we start for Cuba this evening to find out where to go. He says he is writing to you now." [14]

And King wrote that same day to Hay: "Letter writing has been next to impossible to me during all my illness and strange to say next to impossible to those for whom I have the most feeling—my Mother and you.[15]. . . I am still a very bruised and battered old hulk but wonderfully improved. . . . Looking back to last July when my spinal trouble with its reflex effect began, I cannot understand how I ever lived through the merciless agony which crazed and nearly killed me. It seems as if the human organism could not survive such suffering. But here I am gradually but apparently surely recovering with the promise from the doctors of a new lease of life, and health as good as I ever had in my life. This I cannot believe but who am I that I should doubt Weir Mitchell?. . . I have a world to say to you but that must wait a little while longer. I have to avoid business and anything serious and keep in shallow waters." [16]

The detail of quotation from the letters of this crisis in the lives of the three friends is justified by the sense it gives of the warmth of concern and interest they had for one another. It was just such support of friendship on which Adams lived at this time of the "terror" of his thought. He had no household. He had twice the need of friends. Giving to them time, trouble, and support, as he gave to Clarence King in Cuba, was the way he kept his own keel even.

Adams returned to Washington in April, 1894. He was interested now in trouble—financial, economic, agricultural, and cultural—as he had not been interested when he first came back from the Pacific. He sat back in his house and kept his eyes open. He quietly read Karl Marx—and Petronius Arbiter—pursuing the lines of comparative thought which Brooks Adams had laid out. Part of the time he had King with him in the house, and occasionally Cecil Spring-Rice. When they were gone, he set up what he called "a girls' boarding-house" [17] for several of his nieces. He would do this regularly, year after year, for weeks or months at a stretch, enjoying the innocence and fun of the girls' growing up. Their coming and going, their falling in or out of love, made a kind of music in the house. And he was soothed by their frivolity, even while keeping up the "terror" of his thought.

His apparent inactivity was deceptive. His attempt to understand his society was a truer relationship, and a more strenuous one, than that of many of the captains of the age—whether in industry, education, or politics. The rest of his life would be spent pursuing one or another of the lines of thought he perceived now—all rigorously related to the leading currents of the age. Yet he seemed a quiet man, somewhat inactive and retiring, difficult in his attitudes, rather prone to shocking or eccentric statement.

He could not stick to his chosen struggle, internal and solitary, for more than a certain length of time. When he sickened of mental exertion, he flung himself off from the centripetal whirling centers of modern civilization (Washington, London, Paris) to the edges and fringes of civilization—to such places as the Yellowstone or the Scottish Highlands, or to "rotten" Spanish islands of the Caribbean, whose relationship was with another time and another culture.

One such rest from civilization was a trip to the Yellowstone and Teton country in the summer of 1894. He had with him John Hay, whom he had teased into going with him; Hay's son, Del; the geologist Joseph P. Iddings; and William H. Phillips.

The big country was unchanged from 1871; only he himself was changed. It was almost as easy in 1894 as in 1871 to get away from roads and telegraph lines, beyond the reach of news from home. Adams and his friends carried their camp with them and set out on Western ponies for a wandering of several hundred miles.

Adams was not so easily moved to enthusiasm as he had once been, but his first sight of the Grand Teton was worth the coming. It was "almost a Matterhorn; much the finest of

American mountains." Adams confided to Mrs. Cameron: "We have an illusion that we are the first white men who ever crossed into the source of the Yellowstone. We did it by climbing up to eleven thousand feet, and sliding down a mountain-side. It was queer country up there, all striped with snow like a crazy-quilt, with grass between the stripes. A very queer, mad, hoodoo, drunken landscape." [18]

Hay—on his side—enjoyed as much the sight of Adams in the wilderness as he did any of the mountains or canyons. He described with much relish several aspects of Adams's appearance to his wife: his attire, "white flannels and wide-brimmed sombrero, . . . very cool and Cuban," [19] his poor face swollen from mosquito bites, his ineradicable sketching habit which caused him to ignore most of their shooting and angling chances, and his Adams manner, as cool on the banks of the Yellowstone as on the shoals of Lafayette Square. Hay's letter on August 19th told how Adams "gave Billy his orders to-day that there must be no more stops. 'I am bored,' he said in his most royal tone." [20]

Adams came out of the mountain wilderness to face bad news. At Livingston, Montana, he received a wire that his brother John Quincy had died on August 14th. Here was another delayed result of last year's crisis. It seemed that escape from the deadly problem of one's native culture was to be brief—as this one had been—as Dos Bocas had been.

After Dos Bocas, Adams had written to Charles Gaskell: "One effect of years I can now take as constant. I love the tropics, and feel really at ease nowhere else. A good, rotten tropical Spanish island like Cuba, with no roads and no drainage, but plenty of bananas and brigands, never bores me. . . . Every time I come back to what we are pleased to call civilized life, it bores me more, and seems to me more hopelessly idiotic." [21]

He was to be regularly faithful to the tropics. In December, 1894, he went on a long rummage through some of the roughest territory in Mexico, happiest in the little provincial towns, most contented when got up in peon manner, astride a mule, starting off on a foredoomed attempt to ride from the city of Mexico to Acapulco. In January he moved eastward from Mexico to the islands. He liked best the Spanish ones, and least, the British ones.

There was something compulsive about these swings to the south. The attraction he had felt first with King at Dos Bocas continued to exert a strong pressure on him. The charm of these ruined Spanish lands had a latent relation to the problem of his own civilization, but he had not yet fully worked it out.

He went home again to Washington, and on April 25th wrote to Gaskell again: "We have but two political elements. One, the most powerful, is the money-lending class, with its dependent interests; the other is the money-borrowing class, with the whole body of cultivators. We are Rome of the Gracchi You can safely ignore everything in politics which is not a candid expression of one or the other of these forces. As I have a foot in both stirrups, I am alternately kicked off on both sides." [22] He would not be surprised when in the following election year these two forces arrayed themselves for battle and set up, as symbols, McKinley and Bryan.

The provocation of the American situation was too great for him to remain quiet. He made use of his job as president of the American Historical Association (unsought by him and hitherto unfilled) to make a statement in the form of a communication to the association which, whether the members liked it or not, took the place of the customary annual address.

Apparently he wrote the letter while still in Washington in the fall of 1894, but dated it carefully to seem to come from Mexico, thus excusing him from personal attendance at the meeting, held that year in Washington, D.C. This "communication to the American Historical Association," later labeled "The Tendency of History," was more of a challenge than a solution, more of a questioning than a definition.

He was vitally conscious of a drift toward disaster. For the first time he felt a compulsion to share that insight, and his paper was an attempt to arouse the historians to join him in the definition of doom, or in the exploration of live alternatives. He knew that his brother Brooks Adams had done spadework in his as yet unpublished book *The Law of Civilization and Decay*. His own paper was intended to be a sort of preparation for that bold document. Brooks needed a sort of herald—something or someone to kick open airtight doors and let in a little brutal fresh air into academic ways of thinking. The paper was a series of questions. But the questions were those that he intended to spend his life, and that, he hoped, others would be spending their lives, trying to answer.

Here follow a few disconnected sentences from the "communication":

You may be sure that four out of five serious students of history who are living to-day have, in the course of their work, felt that

257

they stood on the brink of a great generalization that would reduce all history under a law as clear as the laws which govern the material world. As the great writers of our time have touched one by one the separate fragments of admitted law by which society betrays its character as a subject for science, not one of them can have failed to feel an instant's hope that he might find the secret which would transform these odds and ends of philosophy into one self-evident, harmonious, and complete system. He has seemed to have it, as the Spanish say, in his inkstand. Scores of times he must have dropped his pen to think how one short step, one sudden inspiration, would show all human knowledge; how, in these thickset forests of history, one corner turned, one faint trail struck, would bring him on the highroad of science.

But what will be the attitude of government or of society toward any conceivable science of history? We know what followed Rousseau; what industrial and political struggles have resulted from the teachings of Adam Smith; what a revolution and what vehement opposition has been and still is caused by the ideas of Darwin. Can we imagine any science of history that would not be vastly more violent in its effects than the dissensions roused by any one or by all three of these great men?

If it pointed to a socialistic triumph it would place us in an attitude of hostility toward existing institutions.

If, on the other hand, the new science required us to announce that the present evils of the world—its huge armaments, its vast accumulations of capital, its advancing materialism, and declining arts— were to be continued, exaggerated, over another thousand years, no one would listen to us with satisfaction.

If, finally, the science should prove that society must at a given time revert to the church and recover its old foundation of absolute faith in a personal providence and a revealed religion, it commits suicide.

A science cannot be played with . . . we must follow the new light no matter where it leads.[23]

Adams pleased few and puzzled many with his letter to the American Historical Association. He could only indicate, and not explain, that he was in the grip of a merciless search. He had the motive, the energy, the means, and a kind of tragic ruthlessness to ensure his continuing search for answers to questions that society, at this time, did not even want to hear posed.

Chapter 19

The Cathedrals

THE SUMMER OF 1895 was to be a momentous one for Henry Adams, as important for him as 1858, 1872, or 1885. But he had no forewarning. Going to Europe with Senator and Mrs. Lodge and their two boys promised to be, at most, a distraction. The company would be good, the pace steady, the scenes varied. Another summer would be got through.

Adams did not agree always with Cabot Lodge as a public man, but he got along very well with the private man, especially when the senatorial quality in him was relaxed. In 1895 Lodge had been Senator for two years, but seemed to have been so forever. With Mr. Lodge—Sister Anne, as Adams called her—he was fondly easy. This summer he became acquainted with their sons, George and John, and enjoyed them in their ingenuous initiation into Europe.

John, the youngest, was the more sensible, being almost too full of good common sense for his age—nineteen. George, whom everyone called Bay, was twenty-two, full of difficult ambition and unexpressed ability, hard on himself and on others. He was a splendidly athletic creature, handsome, with fine manners. He had hunted with Theodore Roosevelt on the Little Missouri, in his summer vacations from Harvard, and he had sailed, with passionate enthusiasm, off Nahant. But he was burdened in his handsome body a brooding, philosophic soul. His father regarded his son wonderingly and wrote to Roosevelt during the course of their trip that he "sits about absentmindedly a good deal and then writes." [1]

As the party set off to do London and then Normandy, Touraine, and Paris, it seemed to Adams that he could congratulate himself on the prospect of an undistressful season. To his great surprise, the experience of this casual summer expedition was the opposite of distraction. It was concentration, intensification, and a kind of highly wrought peace, stumbled upon when the busy mind was looking backward at trouble.

Trouble was what had engaged his mind since the crash of 1893. It was what he and Brooks, with a kind of bitter relish, had tackled in their conversations, and letters since that time.

Trouble was the subject of his brother's book, which at last had a title, *The Law of Civilization and Decay*. And in London it was with this book that Henry was most concerned. He visited Brooks's publisher, Sonnenschein, to check on the progress of the printing, to correct proof, and to make sure that the book would come out in early fall as promised. On August 3rd he wrote to his brother. "Whatever the public may think—or not think—or say—or not say,—you may take my word for it that the book is a great book." [2] And Henry carried on his and Brooks's joint interests by calling on financiers in the City and listening to their confirmation of the Adamsian diagnosis of trouble.

He stepped to one side, with a reserve that had an element of pride in it, and left London society to the elder Lodges. He wrote sardonically to Brooks that "Cabot and Sister Anne are flopping on royalty and following the servile steps of the heathen." [3] He preferred walks with the boys and with Cecil Spring-Rice, who was in London preparing to go to Berlin. The four of them sat upon various park benches and "wondered at the women who paint themselves more than ever and wear all sorts of English tastes." [4] They got on well despite a queer assortment of ages. Uncle Henry—he was Uncle to Cecil as well as to Bay and John—was fifty-seven, Spring-Rice was thirty-six, Bay was twenty-two, and John, nineteen.

Adams enjoyed too the subtle company of La Farge and the more robust energy of Henry Higginson as each one passed through London. He went alone to Wenlock Abbey to see the Gaskells and north to Tillypronie to see the Clarks. "Here I am," he wrote from Scotland to John Hay, "swung once more to the northern limit of my pendulum." [5]

All seemed customary, familiar, and somehow unimportant. The political interests of the English seemed as out of touch with reality as the same activities in America. "The causes of every political revolution nowadays are cosmic, not to be reached by legislation; but we all go fussing and buzzing about beer and bishops as though the parish were still the centre of human competition." [6]

It seemed as if the very satisfactory and distracting trip would successfully carry him through the summer and fall without breakage and without sensation, until he came to France. There, all at once, he was bowled over by a sensation he had not foreseen. It was the northern cathedrals of that country which stunned and delighted him. He had known about them, intellectually; he had been earlier to Amiens; but, until now, he had never felt them. Something in him was ready for the experience, and in the middle of dust and heat and bustle of tourists he discovered a new world. From this time forward, to the end of his life, he had a home and a center and an unending source of interest.

He lost his pride, his studied indifference, his darkness of mood. He found instead, in the wash of pure sensation, humility and joy. He was able to keep the full force of this overturn to himself. But in his inmost being, he succumbed to an assault of emotion and emotion-colored thought which changed, permanently, the direction and tone of his life.

Amiens, Bayeux, Coutances, Mont-Saint-Michel, Vitré, Le Mans, and Chartres—that was the order of their going, from one spire to another. The effect of the spires was cumulative. Adams did not himself at first realize the importance of the experience. He knew only that at Coutances he felt as if he were a native.

His historical imagination, which was his greatest quality, set to work to reveal to him his own essential at-oneness with the men who had built this church. He walked about at Coutances, and at Saint-Michel, going from the beach to the abbey with the enthusiastic boys, talking, laughing, cursing the tourists. But inside himself he carried on a kind of private passionate dialogue (partly revealed by his subsequent letters), in which he worked his way back into a past that had raised such buildings.

First came the knocking away of pride. He wrote later, from Paris to several intimates something of what he felt. His letter of September 1st to his niece, Mabel Hooper, said, in part:

The Norman Cathedral there [Coutances] was something quite new to me, and humbled my proud spirit a good bit. I had not thought myself so ignorant or so stupid as to have remained blind to such things, being more or less within sight of them now for nearly forty years. I thought I knew Gothic. Caen, Bayeux, and Coutances were a chapter I never opened before, and which pleased my jaded appetite. They are austere. They have, outside, little of the vanity of Religion. Inside, they are worked with a feeling and a devotion that turns even Amiens green with jealousy. I knew before pretty well all that my own life and time was worth, but I never knew before felt quite so utterly stood on, as I did in the Cathedral at Coutances. Amiens has mercy. Coutances is above mercy itself. The squirming devils under the feet of the stone Apostles looked uncommonly like me and my generation.[7]

At Saint-Michel it was the unanticipated force and majesty of the place that took his breath—"The Saint Michael of the

Mount is as big as Orion and his sword must be as high as Sirius." [8] And before they turned away from the churches to go into the more bourgeois atmosphere of Touraine, there was Chartres—"last of all, two long hours at Chartres on a lovely summer afternoon, with the sun flaming behind Saint Anne, David, Solomon, Nebuchadnezzar, and the rest, in the great windows of the north transept. No austerity there, inside or out, except in the old south tower and spire which still protests against mere humanity." [9]

Adams wrote to Gaskell, rather shy of disclosing too much emotion:

As for my impressions, all of them are so familiar to you that you would be bored by hearing them. Being by no means an imaginative or emotional animal, but rather a cold and calculating one, I think I can appreciate Norman architecture better than average tourists, who are either emotional, stupid or ignorant. I am sure that in the eleventh century the majority of me was Norman,—peasant or prince matters nothing, for all felt the same motives,—and that by some chance I did not share the actual movement of the world but became a retarded development, and unable to find a place. Going back now to the old associations seems to me as easy as drinking champagne. All is natural, reasonable, complete and satisfactory. Coutances and St. Michel show neither extravagance nor want of practical sense. They are noble, both in spirit and execution, but they are not, like the latter Gothic, selfconscious or assuming. They knew their own force perfectly well; measured it to a hair; gave to the ideal all it had a right to expect, and looked out for the actual with a perfectly cool head. So we conquered England, which was a pretty dull, beer-swilling and indifferent sort of people.

Undoubtedly you and I were there, which accounts for us. I rather think the most of me were vassals of the Church; respectable farmers, doing military service for their fiefs. They also helped to build the churches of Coutances and Bayeux and Caen.[10]

Adams's letter to Gaskell was written from Paris, where he and the Lodges settled for several weeks. They had been in Normandy, and in Touraine. Now they kept close to Paris, going out from the city on short tether. In this fall of 1895 Adams was more at peace with his environment than at any time in years. "Paris is the best summer-watering-place in Europe. It is the only city in the world which understands the world and itself. That I hate it is of course; it hates itself; but it at least amuses the pair of us," he wrote to Mrs. Cameron.[11]

A whole new world of sensation and idea filled his mind

as he went about the city with the others. Thought seethed. His was the plight of the man with more to say than he knew how, as yet. It would take him eight seasons of asociation, counting this as the first, for him to pull feeling and thought into the coherency of words.

But he had social duties to perform. He had undertaken to be a guide to the younger members of the party. He devoted day after day to showing them the great and varied city. Paris, so new to them, was almost new to him this season as he looked at it through their eyes. He wrote to John Hay on September 7th: "Bay Lodge and I go about together a good deal; so do Cabot and I; but I prefer Bay who is a nice fellow, with only one failing, which is the kind of ambition and aspirations which you and I had fifty years ago." [12] (Adams exaggerated his age; fifty years earlier he was seven years old.)

External matters pressed. Contemplation was pushed below the level of surface activity, Adams went to Fontainebleau to Beauvais, and back to the Loire. There he forgave the vulgar Valois for the sake of Blois and Chaumont. One day in Paris he called on Rodin and tried to choose a piece of work to buy. He felt the force of Rodin's greatness, but—with Coutances in the back of his mind—it was a greatness of a kind he did not like. The very fact that Rodin's work faithfully partook of the most intense and the best of contemporary consciousness made it distasteful to Adams.

Each individual of the family group intruded upon his imagination. He was easiest with Mrs. Lodge, and wrote in a happy mood to Elizabeth Cameron, "I elope with Sister Anne alone, when she is tired, and take her to dine in the Bois among hair-curdling society, or in the astounding Hotel of Madame de Paiva, described by Goncourt in his Diary." [13]

As for Bay, Adams made himself his aider and abettor in his desire to stay on in Paris, after the others should have gone home. Bay wanted to try his quality against the city. The pretext would be a year of study at the Sorbonne. Modern languages would be his formal subject, but modern literature and philosophy and poetry would engulf his time. The young man's ardor appealed to Henry Adams. He wanted to see that ardor given its scope, whether for failure or success. He helped Bay carry his point with his father, who was proud of his son, yet somewhat helpless in his relationship with him.

Adams went home even before Senator and Mrs. Lodge and John. He was back in Washington by the middle of

October, burdened with a load of sensation and thought, unsorted, inexpressible, as yet. He wrote on November 3rd to his faithful English friend Charles Milnes Gaskell: "The autumn is very beautiful here—quite marvellously beautiful—and like the spring, more ideal and logical in expression than almost any other form of nature I have ever seen, in mere vegetation. I cling to the days as they pass." [14]

Chapter 20

Twelfth Century—and Twentieth

ONLY A FEW MONTHS after he had seen the northern cathedrals of France—home again in Washington—Henry Adams wrote to his brother Brooks: "As for your ailments, I suppose, like the rest of us, that you are breaking up. I am. It is time. So let's enjoy ourselves and not bother." [1] This was bravado, but Adams was engaged in a hidden battle that required bravado.

The casual acquaintance's notion that Mr. Adams was a fortunate man was superficial. He had enough money, a comfortable house, and friends; he was free to travel; he had no burdens, no ties, no irksome job to deaden his days. All true enough. And Adams had, by this time, developed a high skill at eliminating the useless friction from everyday existence. Some of his facility was devoted to making his life seem superficial. He did not seem to be doing anything of particular importance and did not wish to seem so.

He was the valued companion of several interesting and entertaining men; he was an inconspicuous chaperon for an increasing number of young people to whom he regularly lent his house for their social amusement; he was a good talker and an excellent letter writer. Apparently, he read a great deal, although he took pains to deny the fact. Yet nothing seemed to come of it. He produced nothing. He published nothing.

(An exception—proving the rule—was a piece of historical research, "Count Edward de Crillon," which appeared in the *American Historical Review* in the October, 1895, issue. It was an ironic yet serious discussion of the room for error in history. He illustrated his point by a blunder in his own *History*.)

But Adams's serious interrogation of his own historical work was almost entirely private. Such an article as "Count Edward" had a limited circulation. And most of his questionings of the *History*, as well as his undaunted belief that it had quality, were pursued in silence.

It is worth emphasizing: Adams cultivated the manner, not of a historian, but of a man of the world. It is worth emphasizing, too, that the exterior, seeming to reflect only quiet good fortune, hid a battle. Adams led, during these years of the end of one century and the beginning of another, an interior life of high velocity of thought and violence of sensation. It would be years before he would be able to shape this chaos into coherency. In his letters one can catch only glimpses of this disturbed inner life.

He lived his outward daily life on the edge of great events, events in which some of his friends took a prominent part. He shared their experiences, imaginatively, to the extent that he was almost a part of John Hay's or Theodore Roosevelt's political careers; or Alexander Agassiz' or Samuel P. Langley's scientific explorations; or John La Farge's or Augustus Saint-Gaudens's artistic creations. The private meditations to which he retired were necessarily colored by these personal relationships, and by the national events of the time. Yet he was not completely dominated by his environment. He saw the figures and actions of the present as exemplars in an interior dialogue in which the present was only one part of the scene. The historic past and the historic future were as great a portion of the same flowing picture. It was no wonder that, to some of these others, in the heat of their immediate concerns, Henry Adams might seem somewhat remote. But he was not remote; it was only that he had the imagination of a longer view. As the years went by, he gave himself to these meditations with increasing fervor.

The battle was in the mind, the debris was piled up interiorly, the damage was done to nerves and sinews. Life was painful, yet Adams knew himself alive again after having spent more seasons than he might care to recall in a semi-drugged condition. He was not particularly happy, in his changed condition, but he was intensely, almost fanatically interested, and he had occasional moments of joy.

The prerequisite for this life of thought was freedom. Yet the freedom was not altogether a boon. He was free, but horribly, pitiably, free. No wife, no child, no drag of necessary responsibility held him back from making choices. Adams did not really approve of a person like himself. He had come to think that man best off who was so deeply engaged in the round of existence that his joys and duties were almost unconscious, who was so in tune with his time that he never bothered to be subjective. And here he was—disengaged, intensely individual, critical, and self-conscious. All his traits of character became more sharply pronounced

His virtues, and his faults, became more prominent. There was a margin of morbidity around even his sharpest insights. Unballasted, his freedom pushed him further in various directions than he would have gone if he had been more engaged, more enmeshed in everyday life.

His freedom made him more lonely. Therefore, he grappled his friends to him. He was constant in his devotion to the boring or hateful small duties of friendship. He would do anything for John Hay, Clarence King, Bay Lodge. Friendship was his anchor, his substitute for the other bondages in which he could not noose himself. If he could not be anything but free in the mind, he would be bound in his love. Yet he was a difficult man even for his friends.

All his eccentricities intensified in these later years. Morbidity hardened into a system, and his vagrant prejudices, gathered from sources he could not remember, or had never noticed, stiffened into habit. His trait of identifying the Jews with a group he detested—the bankers who he was convinced were running society along the lines he least liked—crystallized into a verbal ugliness. He was not consistent. There were exceptions, even in prejudice. The Salmons of Tahiti were half Jewish; he loved Tati as his brother and Marau and Beretania as his sisters. And he did not act from the prejudice; the trait was verbal entirely, yet it was ugly.

Another trait which made him difficult was another habit of the tongue. He had grown accustomed to speak with a certain cruelty of language. As for himself, it was a rough defense; he was more cruel of quip when the point was applied to himself than to another; yet some acquaintances might not take cognizance of that fact and soon cease to be acquaintances. As dear parts of himself, he treated friends as he treated himself. Intimates had to know him well to understand the blistering sarcasm, the exaggeration of debility, the shortness with excuses. Seeing beyond the sharpness, some of them saw the love in the manner and the man. Others, who could not see so far, came to detest him.

What was more corroding than prejudice and sharpness was a certain growth of cynicism in him. He had treated Cabot Lodge to a dose of it years before in advising him to take to the literary life in Boston as profitable. And he had treated another, more innocent correspondent to a touch of it once in giving advice on the writing of biographies, saying that it consisted totally of the chronological arrangement of documents in a folder.

These were early, comparatively harmless examples of the

tendency. But in the later years of the nineteenth century, and in the early years of the twentieth, the trait became flamboyant. It was a symptom of despair; it was despair made desperately amusing, of despair tricked out as superficiality. Yet try as he would, he could not kill in himself the root of an innocent and ardent belief. Year after year, as he outraged others, as he outraged himself, he found within himself —despite himself—the capacity to believe.

Freedom warped him, no doubt; freedom and loneliness and the unceasing movement of a mind that would not rest. Yet freedom, loneliness, and unfettered cerebration gave him also the great virtue of these years: a relentless grasp upon the chosen matter of his meditations. He followed his light where it led him with patient and tenacious faithfulness. The purgatory of his existence gave him a proper edge.

Adams's routine of physical movement became almost regular during these years. Each year he spent several of the winter months in Washington. In spring or summer he crossed the Atlantic and went by habit and choice to Paris. There he spent summer after summer, sometimes a fall, sometimes a winter. He arranged his eastward and westward migrations so that he could travel with his friends. When he could gather some of his friends around him in Paris or its neighborhood, he would set up housekeeping with some elaborateness. At other times, he lived very much alone in the heart of the city, looking out from an attic window, perhaps, at the Place de l'Étoile, spending his strength and time on books.

Regular as he became in his mode of life—winter in Washington, summer in Paris—there was in him still an almost insensate desire to fling off this regularity, to bound off beyond the civilized circle he had built. His friends would hear from him from the marshy coast of South Carolina, the dry upper reaches of the Nile, archaic Damascus, or under the northern lights at Hammerfest. Getting away toward the outer fringes of civilization, he saw civilization better.

It would seem that these years were not the best for achieving perspective. They were full of spectacular achievement by some of his friends, and spectacular failure by others. Yet Adams kept clear as to what was big and what was little. During these years of Bryan and McKinley, of Hanna and Hay and Roosevelt, he knew perfectly well what mattered to Henry Adams—a long stretch of history in which these gentlemen had their place, but not perhaps the place they imagined.

Adams was, in fact, a man obsessed. His obsession had two faces: one, that of modern disaster; the other, that of medieval harmony. He remained faithful to these two poles of interest while yet talking to his friends the jargon of the present moment. He had known, since 1893, that waiting somewhere ahead of them all—in spite of the alleviation of prosperity, and in the late 1890's American prosperity seemed considerable and important—not to be got around, was some kind of ultimate and colossal disaster. It was a disaster that would not be accidental, but would be caused in part by this very contemporary and exhilarating activity in which he and his friends had their being. And since 1895, on the other hand, he had been held by the fascination of a historical alternative, that of the eleventh, twelfth, and thirteenth centuries. Ever since he had first walked into the cathedral of Coutances, he had perceived that this other way of life was personally important: perhaps he could find out its general importance, too. His life, from 1895 to 1902, when he began to write again, and beyond, to the end of his life, was an attempt to fill in the abyss between these opposites.

And in spite of his proud temper and irritable nerves, he made also the attempt to relate himself in some significant way to these two poles of existence. He stretched himself upon the rack to do so; and all the time, seemed to be leading a suave and fortunate existence.

More fitting now than when he first wrote them were these lines from his poem *Buddha and Brahma*:

> *But we, who cannot fly the world, must seek*
> *To live two separate lives; one, in the world*
> *Which we must ever seem to treat as real;*
> *The other in ourselves. . . .*[2]

The world moved and made its noise, and he was still incorrigibly interested. As he looked, it began to be something new. The year 1895, the year of the cathedrals for him, was also the year of the first X-rays, the first wireless message, the first Diesel engine. Not that Adams was aware at the very moment of each such discovery, but he was aware of a new world, both outside himself, and within.

Meanwhile his friends performed in their various circuits, and he looked on. Agassiz planned a new ocean trip for 1896, a voyage to the Great Barrier Reef off Australia for more research on coral. La Farge, calmly and shrewdly, his eyes on unalterable things, but humorously so, blandly so, planned to bring out, as a little book, his *Considerations on Painting,* the talks he had given three years before at the Metropolitan Museum.

In politics Carl Schurz, in much misery, would have to give up support of Bryan in the presidential campaign already brewing. It was the wicked money question that caused him to be groaningly for McKinley. Brooks Adams, vociferously opposite, launched a book, *The Gold Standard,* as a blast against McKinley and a push for Bryan. Hay, quaintly regular in Republican dogma, as Adams thought, was to be pro-McKinley, but not without his jokes with his neighbor next door; jokes which made it possible for them, in undisturbed devotion to each other, to agree to disagree.

Meanwhile John Hay's next-door neighbor—before the Cuban misery threatened war or became a plaything of the sugar interests—tried to help Cuba. He and Clarence King had had the idea ever since their spring retreat on the mountain above Santiago in the spring of 1894.

King was still "broke," as Adams reported to Hay, but stubbornly refused to take money from his friend for "new stories or old Turners";[3] he was squeezed, but "not yet squeezed enough to write except for the Cubans." [4] He was preparing two inflammatory articles for the *Forum* magazine: "Shall Cuba Be Free?" September, 1895; "Fire and Sword in Cuba," September, 1896. William H. Phillips, a lawyer, and an amiable, humorous man, was one of the conspirators of H Street, too.

Adams was deeply disgusted with the Democratic gentleman across Lafayette Square who had refused to touch the Cuban issue at a time when he thought it might have been adroitly handled without bloodshed. Already contemptuous of Cleveland for his knuckling under to the bankers' policy of hard money, Adams washed his hands of him over Cuba. As usual Adams was out on a limb, liking no standard-bearer of either party.

All the winter of 1895–1896 Adams worked for his Cubans. On November 14th he wrote to Hay, who was away from the city at this time: "Come and revolute Cuba. We are going to have a gay old circus. Unluckily my relations with Dupuy [the Spanish Minister] are so friendly that I cannot openly embrace his enemies." [5] To Brooks, on February 7th: "I am kept here by Cuba, which I appear to be running, for the faculty of bungling is the only faculty a legislative body possesses in foreign affairs. Of course, my share in it is wholly behind the scenes. Even Cabot keeps aloof from me, or I from him; for I can't control him, and want no ally whom I can't control. So please do not allude to my doings either in letter or conversation." [6]

It is not clear how much Adams and his friends accomplished. Their amateur plotting was swallowed soon in the larger, more selfish interests of 1898. Yet, afterward, many of Adams's conspirators, who had come and gone quietly at 1603 H Street, held high office in the Cuban Government that resulted from the war.

Adams seemed to be, and was, up to his neck in an immediate tangled contemporary problem. Yet his eye, as always, scouted beyond the momentary: On February 18th he wrote to Brooks his grim large view: "As a religious and conservative anarchist I have had much to thank God for. We have done well on massacres this last year, and counting the deaths from exposure this winter in Armenia, I doubt whether civilisation has ever had such reason to be proud. It must have killed, or allowed to be killed, more people not soldiers, than have ever been massacred before in the same time, since the middle-ages, if then, within the range of European influence." [7]

In March he went to South Carolina; in April, to Mexico; and in the summer, at last, to Europe. His companions were John Hay and his daughter Helen, and her friend Elizabeth Warder. They rattled a little too vigorously over the face of the continent to suit Adams. He valued most the seeing of the Byzantine art of Ravenna, Torcello, and Murano, a seeing that came off to his deep satisfaction. Hay, shortly afterward, had to go home to campaign for McKinley. Adams was left alone in a ringing solitude after much vigorous talk and movement. Alone, he sank effortlessly into that other world he had discovered the year before.

On a Sunday he went to Chartres again, and sat there through the afternoon service, finding his ideas of the previous year reinforced. But he would not speak well of himself, even in this relationship: "I am myself somewhat like a monkey looking through a telescope at the stars; but I can see at least that it must have been great." [8]

It was impossible to stay in the twelfth century. In a continuation of the letter to Elizabeth Cameron, in which he told her about going to Chartres, he wrote to her on the next day about American politics: "Yesterday I went to Munroe's and read through a whole week of American papers. Frankly, my impression was that Bryan could not

271

destroy anything worth preserving, if he makes a clean sweep of all we have. Always, hitherto, I have hated revolutions, not so much on account of the revolutions as on account of the subsequent reaction; but at last I am getting to think that rot and moral atrophy are worse than revolution or reaction. . . . Still believing that McKinley will certainly win, I trust that, like most such men and such regimes, he will create more hostility than revolution itself; but at any rate all my sympathies and all my best wishes are for his opponent, and the larger his support, the better I shall be pleased." [9]

Adams hid his grimness from Hay. The two friends stuck out their tongues at each other and jeered. From shipboard on August 4th Hay wrote: "The boat is filled with highly respectable New York Democrats who say they are going to vote for McKinley, and then go below and are sick at the thought of it. Poor things! Poor things! I am sorry for them— I, who would die for McKinley and the Old Flag. Why can't they vote for him and like it." [10] But in case Bryan should win: "Please buy me a house in Surrey, and a couple of palaces in Venice—name of Bryan Debs Smith, if you please." [11]

Adams retorted, when he got home: "Hurry to Washington! Together we will burn incense in my last Japanese incense-burner before the Major's shrine." [12]

After making the required pilgrimage to Ohio to see the Major, and taking the stump, Hay wrote again to Adams: "You are making the mistake of your life in not reading my speech. There is good stuff in it—to live and die by. If you read it in a reverent and prayerful spirit, it might make you a postmaster." [13]

Adams took up the banter again on October 23rd: "We are all right for the Majah here. Die for him daily." [14] But he was weary of the campaign, of a national life in which the only solvent seemed to be money. He turned to Cuba with a sense of relief. It, at least, seemed real to him. He wrote a report on Cuban affairs to be turned in by Senator Cameron to Congress as his own.

Another Virginia fall crumbled slowly into winter and winter warmed into spring—Adams trying through these months to adjust himself to the new era of McKinley. Unreconciled as yet in January, 1897, he spoke of the incoming Administration as "dust and ashes with a slight flavor of dish-water." [15]

Hay awaited his assignment; England seemed to be indicated. Theodore Roosevelt was to be Assistant Secretary of the Navy. Bay Lodge, a sorry fate for a poet, but welcome as a friend, was coming to Washington as his father's secretary. Cameron, in stiff-necked disgust, was retiring from the Senate.

Outside politics, Brooks Adams's American edition of *The Law of Civilization and Decay* was out, and being read. Henry's younger brother was not hanged, nor pilloried. He seemed even to impress the impressible; Theodore Roosevelt reviewed it in the *Forum*.

La Farge prepared his modest study *Hokusai*; it appeared inconspicuously in 1897. Alexander Agassiz planned a long sea-researching trip to the Fiji Islands where Adams had once hunted a raised coral bank upon a muddy mountainside. Near by, Samuel P. Langley launched his seemingly futile "aerodromes" and came to H Street to talk to Adams about the theory of flight and other scientific matters.

It seemed inevitable, when spring came, to go to France once more. He had had the good luck to cross with the Hays, on the way to London. Hay was McKinley's Minister to England, rewarded very tardily by his party in his friend's opinion. Hay wrote home humorously to Senator Lodge about their arrival: "If you had been at Southampton, you would not have had the pleasure of seeing Oom Hendrik gloating over my sufferings. He so thoroughly disapproved of the whole proceeding that he fled to the innermost recesses of the ship—some authorities say to the coal-bunkers —out of sight and sound of the whole revolving exchange of compliments. Henry James stood by, and heard it all, and then asked, in his mild, philosophic way, 'What impression does it make on your mind to have these insects creeping about and saying things to you?' " [16]

Adams deposited Mr. and Mrs. Hay in the echoing and empty house in London where he himself had spent many miserable days and nights long ago. He laughed at them over his shoulder as he said goodbye, seeing them "sitting solemnly in the midst of their grandeur, having lost all the keys of their trunks." [17] Adams did not, after this, because he was a friend, agree with all of Hay's acts. He disapproved, in one instance, of Hay's energetic tying of England and America together internationally, preferring himself a closer relation with the Latin nations of Europe. But he had an unquenchable loyalty to Hay as a person and a growing admiration for his dexterity and subtlety in office.

With Hay safely established in London; and a month later,

Mrs. Cameron—shaken and ill—met at the boat and brought to London and moved to Paris; Adams could turn to his own unimportant personal existence. That life seemed to flourish best in Paris and Parisian neighborhoods. He found congenial companions this season in Sturgis Bigelow and Bay Lodge. The three of them set up housekeeping together and Adams enjoyed himself in their stimulating company, writing to Hay:

EMINENCE: Yours has served to lift for a moment the clouds and to soften the east wind. In spite of clouds and winds I am again in my twenties, lodged in a correct attic with Sturgis and Bay, imperially indifferent to dynasties and *dynastys,* even in the days of the good Napoleon when the world was young and intelligible. Nothing has changed in Paris in forty years except that there are several Frenchmen more.[18]

The reference was to the days of Louis Napoleon's France when John Hay was one of the youngest and gayest diplomats of the American Ministry in Paris. Adams had come to have a settled opinion that the date of Louis Napoleon's fall was a kind of slamming of the door upon his own and Hay's youth when the world was small and bright and manageable.

Conscious of being much older, Adams could enjoy another person's similar season of happy illusion. Bay Lodge's enthusiasms were warming. William Sturgis Bigelow was not youthful in years, but by a certain narrowness of idealism and rigidity of optimism he seemed curiously untouched by the kinds of despair which swept over Henry Adams. Bigelow was an earnest Bostonian idealist of the Buddhist persuasion, somewhat too insistent upon the dogma of his belief to suit Adams, yet of a mannerly presence, in appearance even foppish, with a brushed and shining and decorative beard. He was, besides, a cousin of Adams's dead wife, and patches of their past were similar. They had links which Adams could not break despite his habit of vocal disgust at Bigelow's too easily made up mind. Bigelow was a close friend of the Lodges and had been something of a mentor to Bay in his reading and thinking.

The youngest member of the attic trio, Bay Lodge, oppressed by other men's misfortunes, troubled by his own good luck, faced the world questioningly, yet ardently. His glowing mind and animal health floated the three of them, this season, in a mood of exhilaration as they saw sights, went to plays, ate out, strolled late along deserted streets, and talked continually.

Adams, writing home to Anna Lodge, quieted her fears for her son's well-being in the disastrous city. He wrote with a certain ruefulness. The truth was that in the presence of these two innocents, he himself felt old and wicked and frivolous. "They try to improve my moral nature," he wrote to his niece Mabel.[19]

His fun with Bay Lodge and Sturgis Bigelow hid a new trouble: the death of William H. Phillips, the unassuming good friend of many quiet Washington evenings. He had died in a sailing accident, the news of which Brooks Adams wired him on May 10th. Phillips had been an ally in the Cuban plotting at 1603 H Street; he had been with him and Hay in the Tetons in 1894; he had, at home, his certain window where he would customarily sit. He would sit there no more. Here was another hole in one's personal world. It seemed to grow more and more fragile.

In midsummer, after the attic ménage broke up, he tried to build up another fabric of life, almost as if he were another Prospero. He rented a house at Saint-Germain-en-Laye, sharing it with the Hooper nieces. He hired horses for forest rides and teased them into studying French and French history with him. Mrs. Cameron was in another house nearby, her health not yet recovered, but energetic and vivacious. When Adams wished to get free of adolescence, she was close at hand for talks.

The woods were all around, for rides and walks and mushroom hunts. Caressing their eyes, a broad curve of the Seine made a border for their view. Paris was not far away, but it did not tempt them as summer passed. It was a precious suspension of time.

Sooner or later, in these visits abroad, everyone else went home. This summer, as in others, Adams was at last left alone. He returned to Paris and solitude. It was in such periods of intense aloneness that he began to synthesize his errant thoughts. One part of him fastened on news and events of the present moment. The other part of him waved all that aside and sank itself in another age. He studied the kinetic theory of gases *and* the *chansons de geste*. The age which had written the *chansons* was accessible just below the surface noise of this rattling city of modernity.

He did not go home to the United States in the fall or in the winter. Mr. and Mrs. Hay had a vacation from diplomacy; they asked Adams to go with them to Egypt for a boat trip up the Nile. Afraid of memories, he went. He wrote to Elizabeth Cameron an unguarded cry, awakened by these

275

memories, as he saw the river and the desert again: ". . . the sudden return to the boat came near knocking me quite off my perch. I knew it would be a risky thing, but it came so suddenly that before I could catch myself, I was unconsciously wringing my hands and the tears rolled down in the old way, and I had to get off by myself for a few minutes to prevent Helen, who was with me, from thinking me more mad than usual. She could hardly know what it meant, in any case, and it would not have been worth while to tell her. A few hours wore off the nervous effect, and now I can stand anything, although of course there is hardly a moment when some memory of twenty-five years ago is not brought to my mind." [20]

It was in Egypt, in February, that the boat party heard the news of the sinking of the *Maine*. Theodore Roosevelt was indignant that Hay should have taken himself so far off from the field of diplomatic action. Hay could not stay long now away from trouble, but Adams continued to wander alone. He had a rough sea voyage across the corner of the Mediterranean to Beirut, making himself comfortable during a storm by renting the engineer's cabin down near the stable center of the ship. He laughed at himself for being able so easily, after all these years, to make himself comparatively comfortable on any kind of trip. He got from Beirut to Damascus with some difficulty and stayed a week there, liking it for its archaic quality. In April he moved northward to Greece and saw what he wanted of Greece with his friend William Woodville Rockhill, who was American Minister in Athens. Only slowly he made his way from the outer perimeter of his world toward its center, working his way from Athens to Budapest, to Paris, and to London. There he was surprised by the fact that the trouble had come to the shedding of blood. He had not expected that.

A revelation of the perverse workings of his mind would have been an abomination to the hotheads at home. He worried about Spain. He feared the results of victory. On June 11, 1898, he wrote to Brooks:

. . . I never was quite such a blockheaded as to believe Spain would fight. At times I have been staggered by the apparent convictions of our military people that Spain had formidable fighting power; but my own knowledge was all the other way, and my whole anxiety for two years has been to keep Spain on her legs long enough to make peace after the shock of losing Cuba. That is my anxiety still. In my eyes, Spain is too rotten to hold together, and I fear her total extinction. Western Europe is in a parlous state. If we do not take care, we shall drag the whole rotten fabric down on our heads.[21]

As for Cuba, he assumed that the true American policy should be to "save Cuba from the sugar planters and syndicates whose cards McKinley will play, and who are worse than Spain." [22]

At home, Bay Lodge put on the becoming uniform of an ensign in the Navy and prepared to go to sea for a few months. Theodore Roosevelt resigned as Assistant Secretary of the Navy, ruining his political career, as Brooks Adams thought, and prepared to assemble his Roughriders.

During the summer of the war Adams remained in England with the Camerons in a country place in Kent. The Camerons and their guests pretended to be lazy and comfortable, but were touched to the quick by every piece of news that came to them at Surrenden Dering. It was there that John Hay received the cable from the President calling him back to be Secretary of State.

Hay and his status changed before Adams's eyes at that moment; he knew that the two of them could never again be quite the same. When he went home, in November, 1898, he found many other changes in the fortunes of his friends.

Theodore Roosevelt, it seemed, had not hurt his career. He very easily became Governor of New York. Cabot Lodge was stronger than ever in the Senate. The city itself was different. The very air of Lafayette Square had a new kind of vibration. Adams's friends—for good or ill—seemed to be propelling not only the United States, but several large segments of the world, into some unknown future. Adams was fascinated, but disturbed.

The most personal problem was that of his new relationship with John Hay, catapulted into prominence and power. Their old easy-going relationship was squeezed by public pressures. The fun at first seemed to go out of their old irresponsible banter about men in power, for Hay was one of them now. Adams feared that he would not be able to talk to Hay as he had. Slowly he felt his way.

Every afternoon the Secretary would collect Adams for a long walk and rambling talk. Afterward, coming into the Hay house and the quiet luxury which Mrs. Hay was able to spread round her, they sat down with her to tea. During a winter of such walks, Adams found a new use for himself. Not asking total agreement, not expecting it, Hay yet exacted sympathetic understanding. He threw on the friend the burden of his difficulties and successes. Adams found that he was to be Hay's sounding board.

Thus, the two men found a new cement for their old relationship. Hay wanted Adams's sympathy. He did not expect, or ask, him to help make up his mind. Adams, too, pursued his own way of thought, a lonelier, more unconventional way, and did not let Hay change him in any essential respect. Their friendship was not wrecked, but strengthened by its new circumstances.

Adams was generally considered by their mutual friends to be the cynic of the two. Roosevelt quite frankly thought Adams bad for Hay. Looking back at them, one might doubt this accepted fact. Adams was the more loyal to his own conceptions but, tragically, less used. Hay served well his masters, but he laughed at them, and never altogether respected them. He had the harder role. In time, it killed him.

Adams with the private burden on him of thinking out his relations with the universe, found the close pressure of Hay's career an extra weight. He was interested, but tired, before the winter ended. He was glad to return to Europe and sink into his other century.

He located it in Sicily in April. There, pursuing his medieval Normans, he appraised their southern works, comparing Monreale with what they had built in northern France. The Lodges and Winthrop Chanler were his company on the trip. Stopping at Assisi on the way northward, he gathered indelible impressions of that other time that now seemed almost his own.

He led his two lives dexterously. He was contentious with Cabot, sympathetic with Sister Anne, slightly mad with Winty Chanler, whom he christened "the Faun," and serious perhaps only with Bay. The young veteran, sobered and matured by war, was bringing out his first volume of verse, *The Song of the Wave and Other Poems*. Lodge had taken so surprisingly well to the naval life that Adams wondered if he would not have been happier in some more permanently military era when the discipline and simplicity of the sailor's life would have given him a role and a place. Bay was statusless, almost a younger version of himself; Adams did not like to see him so, but comforted himself with the assurance that Lodge was going to be great in some relevant, splendid fashion to the new society of the twentieth century.

After he parted from the Lodges, Adams settled again in Paris. During the warm summer months he saw something of Sturgis Bigelow, as he had the year before, and of Bigelow's and Bay Lodge's friend Stickney.

Joseph Trumbull Stickney in 1899 was twenty-five. He had been Bay Lodge's companion in the year young Lodge spent in Paris. Poet and scholar, he was to be the first American to receive the French University's highest degree, the Doctorat és Lettres. He was at this time engaged in his studies for that degree. He would bring out his *Dramatic Verses* in 1902; he would go to Greece in 1903; he would teach at Harvard; and in 1904 he would die, his death one of the bitterest and richest experiences Bay Lodge would endure in his own only slightly longer life.

Stickney's gift was curiously opposite to his friend's. Lodge's focus was idea; Stickney's, emotion. Lodge's aim was a definition of belief; Stickney's, an attainment of a state of being. Lodge's tone was cool; Stickney's, warm. Trumbull Stickney was the more simple, the more passionate in his writing. His gift as a poet was greater. Lodge, if he had lived to any age, might have recognized that his own talent was discursive and thoughtful rather than lyrical. Yet in their fortunate youth the two young men shared much. Not least was a despair at the way the world went.

Stickney and Lodge found in Henry Adams their own ardors and despairs pushed beyond their focus into something frightening but interesting. And he was good to them; a good listener, a good reader of their verses. On his side, Adams liked the two young men for the freshness of their notions. Even their disillusionment was dazzlingly young. He hoped for much for them and quenched some of his unhappiness in their tonic desires.

In his own despair—for he was in despair—he had yet a desperate openness. He cultivated those who seemed to do something, or think something. "St. Gaudens is drudging away, up on Mont-Parnasse, and every now and then I drag him out of his dreary den where he creates nothing but nightmares, and I bring him here for a change. Joe Stickney comes down every week from the stars. . . . I study French four hours a day in order to be sprightly." [23]

Pretending to frivolity, he led his second life behind a screen of superficiality. He spoke a deeper word or two to Brooks on August 8th: "I am still in the religious epoch of blind and silent recognition of the will of God—or of the Devil—anyway, of the helplessness of insects and polyps like us." [24] His sadness was that of finding God an equation for fatality.

His use of the name of God was not orthodox by any standard of the church whose works he was studying in these hot and dusty days of fall. But he fell more and more into a trick of speech that echoed the diversions and controversies of his favorite age. "Nothing can be more cloister-like than my life in this haunt of iniquity. It approaches closely to my ideal of retirement from the world, if not of devotion to God and the Saints. As a matter of fact, I am also rather devoted to religion, because I always drift back to the eleventh and twelfth centuries by a kind of instinct which must be terribly strong." [25] He read the verse of the time, the popular legends and songs, the mystics and the philosophies. And every good day away from his books, he collected church spires in the region of the Île de France and to the northward in Normandy.

It is interesting to watch the prick of the desire to write begin to bother him. He asked Brooks in October if his book-dealer had any book on Eleanor of Guienne. Two summers earlier, he had busily read Valois history, almost as if he were going to use the fifteenth century as a foil for the twelfth. But in November of 1899 he wrote to Charles Gaskell: "What I do want is to write a five-act drama, of the twelfth century, to beat Macbeth." [26] Adams had uncovered in himself another ambition, when he thought ambition was dead. He wanted to do justice to the medieval mode of act and thought. He was groping for a form, but failed to find it.

Meanwhile he had his daily being in the new twentieth century. He came home in January of the new year, and by luck caught both Hay and King in New York City. They were all conscious of the rarity of the occasion. To another friend Hay wrote, "We had a merry little dinner with what is left of the gang." [27]

In the early days of the new century, Adams fell into the habit of remembering, weighing, and judging not only himself, but his friends. He thought of Richardson as he littered his rooms, as Richardson had done, with photographs and books about medieval buildings. Mentioning him in this respect to Elizabeth Cameron, he added, in parenthesis, "the only really big man I ever knew." [28]

Back in Washington, Adams saw that Hay might not be able to endure the pressure his work put upon him. Another friend, Edward Hooper, fell ill; he would no longer be a prop. More and more direly he felt that he must outface the new time nakedly and unprotectedly. His friends were too busy, as Hay was; or too distressed in their own affairs, as King was; or too ill, to help him.

Sometimes in Washington, bustling with activity and a heady new importance, Adams thought that the friend who was closest to him in mood and preoccupation was Cecil Spring-Rice, who was physically in Persia. Spring-Rice, enduring difficult and even dangerous times for the British Legation in Persia, was lonely too. His and Adams's letters, exchanged across the world, had at this time an unusual atoneness of mood.

Translating Persian medieval verse, finding for Adams a Persian Nicolette to put beside the French one, contemplatively climbing the 19,000 feet of Mount Demavend, Spring-Rice had yet as keen a grasp of contemporary power rivalries as any diplomat of the time. In Europe, two years before, he had given Hay a quick and accurate review of German power and restlessness before Hay went home to head the State Department. Now he educated Henry Adams on the Asiatic strength of Russia. It was a force he saw and felt in Persia.

Spring-Rice had, besides, a vein of personal melancholy congenial to Adams, who had initiated him into his own fantastic and imaginary political party—that of the Conservative Christian Anarchists. Soon Springy promised to outstrip even Adams and the other charter member, young Bay Lodge, in devotion to its understood perversity—a bitter rejoicing in the success of foreboded evil ways.

Spring-Rice sent Adams his greetings for the New Year and a picture of a still living medievalism in Persia, and told him he must come to see it soon or it would be gone: "The poor, harried and robbed as they are, are not unhappy. There is the sun and charity, no one starves and life is passably amusing. And for the rich, if this world is too harassing, one can become a Dervish, exchange one's robe of honour for a rag, buy a filthy tent and a brass bowl and live happily ever after, begging and thinking of the Infinite." [29]

In answer, on February 1st, Adams told the younger man how the world wagged in Washington: "To you, in Persia, Russia looms over the whole horizon. To us, in America, ourselves are the center of the Milky Way." [30]

After spending the winter and spring in the manner that had now become habit—watching Hay struggle with the Senate, reading Mr. Dooley for relief, corresponding with Spring-Rice—Adams set forth for France again. This first summer of the new century was to be a busy time, a season when he would begin to sort out many straggling impressions and set them in place in his mind.

He continued to collect church spires and windows of innocent bright color. He extended his conquest of the medieval in his reading. Aquinas was his summer companion. Just as characteristically, Adams all the long summer studied another kind of presentment of an age. The age was his own; the scene, the great Paris Exposition. He went again and again, and devoted himself particularly to the bright new machines. In them he saw not only the present, but the future.

A letter of November 7th to John Hay said:

Of personal matters I have very little to say. The Exposition is closing. To me it has been an education which I have failed to acquire for want of tutors, but it has been an immense amusement and only needed you to be a constant joy. It has brought me so near the end that I hardly care to wait for the last scenes. There are things in it which run close to the day of judgment. It is a new century, and what we used to call electricity is its God. I can already see that the scientific theories and laws of our generation will, to the next, appear as antiquated as the Ptolemaic system, and that the fellow who gets to 1930 will wish he hadn't. The curious mustiness of decay is already over our youth, and all the period from 1840 to 1870. The period from 1870 to 1900 is closed. I see that much in the machine-gallery of the Champ de Mars. The period from 1900 to 1930 is in full swing, and, gee-whacky! how it is going! It will break its damned neck long before it gets through, if it tries to keep up the speed. You are free to deride my sentimentality if you like, but I assure you that I,—a monk of St. Dominic, absorbed in the Beatitudes of the Virgin Mother—go down to the Champ de Mars and sit by the hour over the great dynamos, watching them run as noiselessly and as smoothly as the planets, and asking them—with infinite courtesy—where in Hell they are going.[31]

Adams's forebodings were not a comfortable kind of mental equipment to carry about with him. He made not only his friends uneasy; he made himself uneasy, too. Yet he could not shut down completely on verbal expression of his uncanny insights.

He was most frank with Brooks. He wrote to him on November 23rd:

Doubtless we are somehow wrong; but there is a chance, perhaps one in five,—that we are right; and, you know, some of my cards occasionally have turned up like that. But if I am right now, —I gasp!

It's a queer sensation, this secret belief that one stands on the brink of the world's greatest catastrophe. For it means the fall of Western Europe, as it fell in the fourth century. It recurs to me every November, and culminates every December. I have to get over it as I can, and hide, for fear of being sent to an asylum. Curiously enough, I think the people, way down, have here a sense of it something like mine; but society is absolutely sane,—like Rome in the year 300.[32]

Yet—from day to day—in the company of his twelfth and thirteenth century saints and thinkers, and of the Virgin, who was becoming personally dear to him, Adams was not too unhappy. "The world rocks, but I am far above it," [33] he wrote from an attic apartment on the Avenue de Bois, in December.

Out of this quiet, private world, Adams brought home to America, in January, 1901, a meditation in verse. He showed it to no one at first, and mentioned it at last, diffidently, to Elizabeth Cameron in a letter in February. "By way of relief from boredom, I have returned to verse, and have written a long prayer to the Virgin of Chartres, which I will send you presently, to put in your fire. It is not poetry, and it is not very like verse, and it will not amuse you to read it; but it occupies me to write; which is something—at sixty-three." [34]

He could speak of it only with crooked words because it held so much of him. It was all that he was at that moment; all that he had achieved of thought, emotion, and spirituality; all that he had learned, through the whippings of discipline, of the simplicity and exactitude of truth.

The *Prayer* which Adams sent to Elizabeth Cameron had the wholeness of a complete act of the imagination. He would not be able to surpass it except in some larger work which, in fear and trembling, in ambition and pride, he saw now that he would have to write. The *Prayer* contained the essence of two parts of his thought which, splitting into two streams, would become *Mont-Saint-Michel and Chartres* and *The Education of Henry Adams.*

The *Prayer* was a form pulled into shape by contradictions, a positive achieved by contraries. Really two prayers in one, it had, like a piece of music, three movements of mood with subtle modulations from one part to another.

First Adams set himself in the attitude of an assumed ancestor of seven hundred years ago, praying to the Virgin of Chartres. But himself of 1900 was a shadow visible behind the earlier man:

Simple as when I asked your aid before;
  Humble as when I prayed for grace in vain
Seven hundred years ago; weak, weary, sore
  In heart and hope, I ask your help again.

You, who remember all, remember me;
  An English scholar of a Norman name,
I was a thousand who then crossed the sea
  To wrangle in the Paris schools for fame.

When your Byzantine portal was still young
  I prayed there with my master Abailard;
When Ave Maris Stella was first sung,
  I helped to sing it here with Saint Bernard.

When Blanche set up your gorgeous Rose of France
  I stood among the servants of the Queen;
And when Saint Louis made his penitence,
  I followed barefoot where the King had been.[35]

"As when I prayed for grace in vain" is the link of emotion with the present. For Adams is here tracing a movement and development of thought:

For centuries I brought you all my cares,
  And vexed you with the murmurs of a child;
You heard the tedious burden of my prayers;
  You could not grant them, but at least you smiled.

If I then left you, it was not my crime,
  Or if a crime, it was not mine alone.
All children wander with the truant Time.
  Pardon me too! You pardoned once your Son![36]

"Truant Time" had changed men's loyalties and turned them toward other objects of worship. But a deeper trouble troubled the writer, that even in that other time she "could not grant" the prayers. A deeper disbelief than first apparent was stirring to expression.

The verses which follow trace the movement of peoples in their abandonment of the Virgin, and their finding of new energies, new worlds, new gods. The present condition of her beseecher, among like-minded men, is not happy or fortunate:

Strong as we are, our reckless courage shrinks
To look beyond the piece-work of our tasks.

Listen, dear lady! You shall hear the last
Of the strange prayers Humanity has wailed.[37]

There follows then the Prayer within the Prayer, "Prayer to the Dynamo." Here Adams has captured in intimate psychological self-knowledge the pulse of the modern world in its worship for the infinite and, in particular, of infinite power.
He begins:

Mysterious Power! Gentle Friend!
Despotic Master! Tireless Force!
You and We are near the End.
Either You or We must bend
To bear the martyr's Cross.

We know not whether you are kind,
Or cruel in your fiercer mood;
But be you Matter, be you Mind,
We think we know that you are blind,
And we alone are good.

What are we then? the lords of space?
The master-mind whose tasks you do?
Jockey who rides you in the race?
Or are we atoms whirled apace
Shaped and controlled by you? [38]

A nothingness, a *No*, has answered modern man. "A curious prayer, dear lady! is it not?" [39] the poet remarks, as he resumes his conversation with the Virgin.
Here begins the third movement of the poem. The search has faltered, the will has stumbled, the answer has not been found:

Strangest of all, that I have ceased to strive,
Ceased even care what new coin fate shall strike,
In truth it does not matter. Fate will give
Some answer; and all answers are alike.[40]

The Virgin has been victimized, as surely as the verse maker; she has been abandoned too by fate. Without belief, without hope, the verse maker, at the end, expresses, never-theless, a preference:

> *So, while we slowly rack and torture death*
> *And wait for what the final void will show,*
> *Waiting I feel the energy of faith*
> *Not in the future science, but in you!* [41]

Adams's subject has been energy. Its superior form and greatest potency he has found in an irrational, rather than a rational, form. Adams, as verse maker, reaffirmed his allegiance, in despite of fate, to Her, who was once the potent center of all effort, imagination, and belief. The Virgin was his symbol for the highest at which man had aimed, the center which had called forth his most ingenious and most beautiful social organization, art, and thought. He could not assert, or believe, literally; he was convinced, however, that for a time, that force had worked.

His conception hid a generalization, but its form was intensely personal and dramatic, as can be seen in his final ardent plea:

> *Help me to see! not with my mimic sight—*
> *With yours! which carried radiance, like the sun,*
> *Giving the rays you saw with—light in light—*
> *Tying all suns and stars and worlds in one.*

> *Help me to know! not with my mocking art—*
> *with you, who knew yourself unbound by laws;*
> *Gave God your strength, your life, your sight, your*
> *heart,*
> *And took from him the Thought that Is—the*
> *Cause.*

> *Help me to feel! not with my insect sense,—*
> *with yours that felt all life alive in you;*
> *Infinite heart beating at your expense;*
> *Infinite passion breathing the breath you drew!*

> *Help me to bear! not my own baby load,*
> *But yours; who bore the failure of the light,*
> *The strength, the knowledge and the thought of*
> *God,—*
> *The futile folly of the Infinite!* [42]

So ended the verse maker, and then hid the verse. Only two others, besides himself, saw the *Prayer* before he died. The piece of paper on which he had written it was found secreted in a wallet like Pascal's statement of salvation which he kept sewed to his person all his life. Adams read Pascal. He knew the story. Perhaps he saw the likeness.

Coming from such thoughts, Adams found himself something of a foreigner among his contemporaries. He tried to disguise his sense of strangeness. Sickness and death and change stirred the circle of his friendships; he had need of equanimity, but had it only by stoicism.

The spring of 1901 found him worrying about his brother-in-law, Edward Hooper,[43] lately ill, and about Clarence King, who was yet "fairly gay even in paroxysms of coughing." [44] He heard from Spring-Rice, now in Egypt, and laughed aloud at a letter, "more Spring-Ricey than ever, and absolutely reeking with despair." [45] "He is my best disciple. He shall be my successor as Chief of the C.C.A. Since Bay deserted, and fell victim to the old snare of Satan, only Springy remains." [46]

Reporting on his friends to Elizabeth Cameron, Adams ticked them and their moods off one by one.[47] Saint-Gaudens had dined, and was gloomy, without cause. La Farge had dined, and was gay, without cause; he should have been gloomy, for his health was precarious and his friends regularly buried him in their imaginations, with all the rites of the Church. Agassiz had "flashed by"—and "more conservative than I" was worried about the state of business. Hay, of course, came in every day, frightening his friend by some illness, but whether of the eyes, the brain, the heart, no one as yet seemed to know. Yet he did his work, and still was angry with Senators.

Adams was a sort of sounding board for each of these men. He could be counted on to be not too sympathetic, but caustic and invigorating. He had need of his own armor of toughness as the season went on. He went to Europe in his customary fashion, and had hardly arrived when bad news began to arrive with almost every mail.

Edward Hooper died on June 26th. Adams wrote to Mabel (who was now Mabel Hooper La Farge, having married Bancel La Farge) on July 11th, trying to make her focus her mind upon her child, recently born. As for himself: "I have been for thirty years more dependent upon your papa than on any other man. The time is passed when I could have supplied his loss. In fact, it is another part of myself that I lose." [48]

Four days after Hooper's death came another. Del Hay, John Hay's oldest son, tumbled to his death out of a college window at Yale where he had sat and grown drowsy during the evening of a class reunion. He was a young man of promise, had been American Consul in South Africa, and had just been named one of President McKinley's secretaries. John Hay had not known, until that moment, that he had had a happy life. His letters to Adams were cries of agony.

Adams wrote to both John and Clara Hay. His letter to Mrs. Hay was naked in its sympathy.

Of course, all turns on you. If you break down, John will break down. . . .

John will have told you why I have not written to you before. Anyone who has been through a shock that crushes one's life, knows that friends count then most for what they feel, rather than for anything they can say; though one is grateful enough for what is said, too, and still more for the sense of companionship in suffering. My deepest regret was, as I telegraphed to John, that I could not be with you; for I remembered the awful horror of solitude, for the hours before friends could reach one, in the first instants of prostration, and I thought that perhaps my knowledge of suffering might make me more useful than another friend could be. For that I was too far away. For writing, I knew that you would be overwhelmed with letters. I knew too that almost anyone would say more than I knew how to do, for I never have learned yet that anything could be said, when silence is all that is left. I was afraid even of doing harm; for the one idea that was uppermost in my mind was that when I was suddenly struck, sixteen years ago, I never did get up again, and never to this moment recovered the energy or interest to return into active life. The object of all others is now to prevent John or you from breaking down that way.[49]

After a quiet time in France, from whence Adams wrote letters home to those distressed by death, he joined the Lodge family for a summer of travel. They went first to Bayreuth to hear Wagner. Afterward, Adams satisfied a long-standing desire by going, with the others, eastward to Warsaw, Moscow, and St. Petersburg. When the others turned back, he continued to travel alone, going first to Sweden. In Stockholm he heard the news of the shooting of President Mc-

Kinley and discerned a new Washington awaiting him. Meanwhile, he boarded a mail steamer for Hammerfest on the North Cape and went northward as far as it was possible to go, glaciers and fiords on the right, the sea smooth beneath, himself engaged, as he had once called it, in the terror of his thought.

He got off the boat in New York in December to go immediately to Clarence King's funeral, a sad conclusion for the year. In Washington he was needed more than ever as a support for Hay, shaken by this year of deaths—his son's in June, his chief's in September, King's in December.

King, knowing that there was no help for him and his diseased lungs, had gone to the Southwest desert country to die without any fuss. He was incorrigible to the end. A friend, James D. Hague, learned of King's final pun. The doctor, having given him heroin the day before he died, explained to King that the medicine had been responsible for a temporary wandering of his mind. "I think the heroin must have gone to your head." "Very likely," King replied. "Many a heroine has gone to a better head than mine is now." [50]

Clarence King's death affected Adams powerfully, but he said little. He had occasion, these days, to sit quietly and think of himself and his friends, remembering ambitions, looking at outcomes. Only the mildest of emotions appeared in his letters. The deeper feelings were stifled of expression until, a few years later, he found a literary form in which to state them.

The new Washington of President Theodore Roosevelt was something he could discuss. And discuss it he did, with some sharpness in his humor. On January 12th he dined in the White House, and wrote about the occasion to Mrs. Cameron. This was the first time he had been there to dine since 1878, "under the reign of Mrs. Hayes . . . the happiest time of my whole life, associated with everything—and the only things— I ever cared for." [51] Dinner for eight, with the Roosevelts, was comfortable and easy, yet he could not prevent ghosts from rising in his mind, ghosts of his own past, ghosts of his family's past. And Roosevelt depressed him that evening, by treating him and John Hay as "sages." [52] Adams preferred impudence to pontification, and failed to enjoy being a sage.

For revenge, he read Mr. Dooley in his squibs about Theodore, and thought the better of Roosevelt when he found out that he laughed at Dooley, too.

Of his own circle, Brooks Adams alone seemed, in a back-handed sort of way, to be having a success, but he was not really "catching on" as he should. "He is like Clarence King, Richardson, La Farge and all my crowd whom cleverer and richer men exploit and rob. It is the law of God! It is also the law of common-sense. Every now and then the victim comes back on the victor and squashes him, which is why the bourgeois is afraid. Brooks is too brutal, too blatant, too emphatic, and too intensely set on one line alone, at a time, to please any large number of people." [53]

Interested, entertained by Washington, Adams in the spring of 1902 could not keep his full mind upon the place or its people. He was gathering his energies for the writing of his book. He had evidently made a beginning when he wrote to Elizabeth Cameron on April 27th, but disguised the seriousness of his effort, telling her that he had "started a historical romance of the year 1200." [54]

He carried his work abroad and steeped himself, for the eighth summer of concentration and meditation, in the color and line of the twelfth and thirteenth century cathedrals of France. He found an instrument of the twentieth century which increased his twelfth century pleasure. "My idea of paradise is a perfect automobile going thirty miles an hour on a smooth road to a twelfth-century cathedral," he wrote to Mabel La Farge from Paris on June 17th.[55]

He carried his papers to Scotland in midsummer and continued the writing of his first draft of *Mont-Saint-Michel* in a strangely incongruous setting. Don Cameron had grandly rented a Scottish castle, Inverlochy, at Fort William, and invited Adams to be his guest for the summer months. There, in a cool gray atmosphere which was saturated, as Adams imagined, with Calvinist feeling, he pursued his study of the Catholic civilization of the eleventh, twelfth, and thirteenth centuries. He was able to be alone when he wanted, and in the large house, sequestered from other guests, worked steadily and well week after week.

He did not lose his hold on his second theme in his close attention to his first: writing to Brooks Adams from Inverlochy on August 10th, he said:

I apprehend for the next hundred years an ultimate, colossal, cosmic collapse; but not on any of our old lines. My belief is that science is to wreck us, and that we are like monkeys monkeying with a loaded shell; we don't in the least know or care where our practically infinite energies come from or will bring us to.[56]

290

By the first day of December, 1902, Adams was in Paris again, inquiring in a noncommittal way of his brother, "Can you tell me who is the best printer about Boston of books of your kind, with foreign languages and ideas to set up and correct?" [57]

More frankly, he wrote to Mrs. Cameron two days later: "I've finished Thomas Aquinas and the thirteenth century. I'm dying to know how it would look in type—one copy, for me alone." [58]

On December 27th he sailed for home.

Chapter 21

Mont-Saint-Michel and Chartres

AFTER SEVEN YEARS, Henry Adams had made something of his visits to certain buildings in France. In the summer of 1902—in a house of H Street, at a castle in the Scottish Highlands, in a hotel in Paris—he wrote *Mont-Saint-Michel and Chartres.* Its appearance in print was long delayed. Only in January, 1905, did the first reader receive from him a copy of the privately printed volume, accompanied by a semi-humorous letter of self-depreciation.

The first reader—however sympathetic—must have been puzzled. Groping, he found few facts to guide him. The book was ostensibly about the Middle Ages, but only about a part of that time. Only the eleventh, twelfth, and thirteenth centuries seemed concerned. The scene was limited too: northern France—but there was an exception: Assisi and St. Francis were pulled in by main force. The author said: "We set out to travel from Mont-Saint-Michel to Chartres, and no farther; there we may stop, but we may still look across the boundary to Assisi." [1]

Groping still, the first reader, and the hundredth, or the thousandth, might discern that the book was possibly about architecture—about the cathedrals and abbeys of Normandy and the Île de France. There were photographs of some of these buildings and there were diagrams of vaulting. Also, somewhat confusingly, the book seemed to be about literature. The *Song of Roland* was linked to the Abbey of Saint-Michel, and *Aucassin and Nicolette,* the *Roman de la Rose,* and Francis's *Canticle of the Sun* entered the narrative after the architectural discussion of Chartres. The book would not stay put: philosophy seemed to be included too. There were, toward the end, chapters on Abelard, on the mystics, on St. Thomas. The first reader, and the last, might puzzle himself to discover what Mr. Adams was up to.

The book seemed to be a large bite for any but an athletic digestion. The first reader might have been dubious whether to tackle it or not. Adams was a good friend—although difficult—but then who, of his friends, read him? One hadn't an idea what the famous *History* was like, and one never could remember who Albert Gallatin was.

Yet at first glance the book began easily enough. There was a thoroughly enjoyable Preface, with Mr. Adams pretending that he was embarking one on a touristic excursion. He joked in it about one's carrying a Kodak; about one's being a niece or a nephew; and he an uncle. He hooked one's interest before the first reader, or the thousandth, or one hundred thousandth, realized how deep it was possible to get in.

For the opening words of the book proper rang with a different note. The first sentence of the first chapter was a challenge: "The Archangel loved heights." [2] The Preface had been seducement. Chapter I, and the chapters that followed, were all challenge, pulling one into a passionate, sensuous involvement in another world, the reader dragged in by the hair of his head, let swim if he could, left far behind if he gave up.

Yet the way Mr. Adams pushed one on imperiously, showed one the sights, made one see and understand, and even take part in these scenes of the past, made it easier to follow than to give up. His words were simple, his assaults upon the senses straightforward, his questioning of one's verities done in such a way as to arouse curiosity, anger, but always interest. He pulled the present age backward into the past, and jammed the past into the present.

He kept an easy, conversational tone even on the heights. He made one move: not only with him into the past, but along his chosen road in the past. Each early chapter ending was a simple command or signpost. Chapter III ended: "One may move on." [3] Chapter IV: "Now let us go straight to Chartres!" [4] Chapter V: "Now let us enter!" [5] Chapter VI: "Now let us look about!" [6]

Before the first reader, or any later reader, could realize it, this player upon his feelings had opened his organ stops. Command melted into allurement. The re-creation of the great scenes of the Abbey and of the Cathedral made one feel at home. One was ready for a more complex emotion.

At the end of Chapter IX, having made one sit down under the windows of Chartres and imagine there the presence of its Queen, Adams mused passionately, personally, yet encompassingly:

—You, or any other lost soul, could if you cared to look and listen, feel a sense beyond the human ready to reveal a sense divine that would make that world once more intelligible, and would bring the Virgin to life again, in all the depths of feeling which she shows here—in lines, vaults, chapels, colours, legends, chants—more eloquent than the prayer-book, and more beautiful than the autumn sunlight; and any one willing to try could feel it like the child, reading new thought without end into the art he has studied a hundred times; but what is still more convincing, he could, at will, in an instant, shatter the whole art by calling into it a single motive of his own.[7]

The reader should be ready by the end of the next chapter, the tenth, to recognize a certain largeness in a writer who could bring the casual tourist from frivolity—and without a false touch or a misstep—to the tragic pathos of this close:

It was very childlike, very foolish, very beautiful, and very true—as art, at least; so true that everything else shades off into vulgarity, as you see the Persephone of a Syracusan coin shade off into the vulgarity of a Roman emperor; as though the heaven that lies about us in our infancy too quickly takes colours that are not so much sober as sordid, and would be welcome if no worse than that. Vulgarity, too, has feeling, and its expression in art has truth and even pathos, but we shall have time enough in our lives for that, and all the more because, when we rise from our knees now, we have finished our pilgrimage. We have done with Chartres. For seven hundred years Chartres has seen pilgrims, coming and going more or less like us, and will perhaps see them for another seven hundred years; but we shall see it no more, and can safely leave the Virgin in her majesty, with her three great prophets on either hand, as calm and confident in their own strength and in God's providence as they were when Saint Louis was born, but looking down from a deserted heaven, into an empty church, on a dead faith.[8]

After beguilement, there is shock. Adams's purpose was to whip one more alive rather than to lull one into agreement. The reader, stung wide awake, and alert for what was to come, found Adams next turned suave in Chapter XI, "The Three Queens." Here was almost pure entertainment in a bringing to hot life again of earthly queens and the Heavenly Queen, too. Succeeding discussions—of the letters of the age, and of its thought—alternately charmed and stung. Adams, even in his most difficult pages, held onto his reader's hand with a sure grip.

Pride, humility, love, hate—all the intermingled qualities of his resurrected poets, thinkers, sinners, and saints—were recreated in his pages. And an extra element, an urgency mixed with an unalterable sadness, was present too. Before he got well into the book, the reader was perhaps quizzical; afterward, surely half stunned and shocked by sensation and idea.

But he may have marked, along the way, a few signposts. First, the book was divided into sixteen chapters. These chapters had titles, not just numbers. Chapter I was "Saint Michiel de la Mer del Peril." Chapter V was "Towers and Portals"; XI, "The Three Queens"; XVI, "Abelard"; and so forth. And looking back upon these chapters, one could see a rough grouping; the first three chapters were about the eleventh century, about the building of the Abbey of St. Michael and about the great epic song, Roland's, which was sung so many times in its halls. Chapter IV was a kind of survey of the ground yet to be covered. Chapters V through X concerned Chartres. Chapters XI, XII, and XIII were a tapestry of history with the women of the age as foreground figures. Chapters XIV, XV, and XVI were about the great men of thought or faith, about Abelard, Francis and Thomas—a sounding of the mind of the time.

There was a sense of time in the book and of the passage of time. From the setting in place of the first stone of the Abbey of the Mount to the setting in place of the first stone of Beauvais Cathedral, there was a slipping away of days and years. Adams made one know the mood of the beginning and the end, and the mood which held together, for a moment, the conflicting energies of that time's people. He made one know that the harmony was always precarious, always threatened, and that, in the end, it failed. He made visible the primitive heroism of the Mount; the mental and emotional ardor of the Virgin's reign at Chartres; and the sophistication of both feeling and thought in the last moment before the harmony of the age dissolved. The unit of time was held as if in the hand. Yet, paradoxically, it was seen not as small, but as large, tumultuous, full of the flavor of life and of death.

It should have been evident to the first reader that this unit of time was not presented in the purity of isolation. It was treated as a living time and not a dead time; it had relations with the past and the future, that future which was the reader's, and of the writer's, present. There were tentacles of thought, tendrils of reference, growing out toward one's own time, making the knowledge of the past time uneasy with meaning for one's own time. It came to seem, in the course of the sixteen chapters, that Henry Adams was writing as much about the present time as he was about that other time.

Nearly everything he had to say about the eleventh, twelfth, and thirteenth centuries seemed to have meaning for the twentieth.

The intense emotion and wroght-up thought of Henry Adams's first summer of the cathedrals had not gone to waste. Seven successive summers had deepened and matured the first brilliant impression. Yet the first sight had been important. The sensuous impression had acted as a catalyst. Seeing these buildings of northern France had transformed whole areas of thought in the mind of the beholder. The cathedrals—and the poems, the works of philosophy, the treatises of theology belonging to the same time as the cathedrals—had had a retroactive effect. They had sluiced the viewer's past with light and sent a glare into the future. The book *Mont-Saint-Michel and Chartres* was the outcome of seven years of mental activity, but also of a lifetime. The whole man wrote the book.

The book was a vision of the past. It was a comment on the future. It seemed a decided shift of balance in the writer. Yet its essential framework belonged to a point of view the writer had had from earliest maturity. The book could be taken as contradiction or as fulfillment. It was something of both.

Adams had grown up in an atmosphere of ardent faith, a faith of the present moment, the faith that science could change the world, and that science's agent was the patient, industrious effort of the good man. *Mont-Saint-Michel,* on the contrary, seemed a mocking of science and modern men, and a turning toward another kind of faith. It painted the culture of the other belief with sympathy, understanding, and enjoyment. Yet, try however he might to escape his own age, Adams's picture was framed in a perspective which betrayed the modern man in him. His way of looking at the past was scientific. The past, however lovable, was a finite sequence of time. He saw the time and the passing of time; its growing to fullness; its passing away. The study of the past in *Mont-Saint-Michel* was a study of sequence.

Adams had come a long way to the writing of this book. Yet one can look back, across his life, and see him, in the midst of other interests, coming to this other late interest. He had had, from the beginning, the sense of color. He had had, inborn, a deep respect for the non-rational. He had had, from the beginning, imagination. Family training, city training, school training, the life of the journalist, reformer, teacher, and scientific historian had not killed these useless susceptibilities; it had only sidetracked them.

Growing in him at the same time as the approved virtues—honesty, industry, respect for the good work that the good man could do—were others more vagrant. Certain scenes, certain persons, certain pieces of good or bad fortune aggravated these useless traits. Washington, D.C.—as a physical scene—first shocked the child out of the sureness of all juvenile prepossessions. He found out, at twelve, that other peoples had manners and morals different from those of New England, and just as satisfactory to them. The Southern boys at Harvard continued this teasing of his sense of rightness and propriety. In Dresden, in 1859, he went through something of that stimulating demoralization which Henry James would soon describe in his novels of the young American in Europe. In London, a variety and range of possibility—or life and of living—opened before him. In Washington, after the war, in addition to reform, there was the uneasy charm of irresponsibility and fun.

Harvard, in the early 1870's, might seem to have reinforced his oldest associations and obliterated the impressions of the years between, but this was so only superficially. He carried methodology in history to an extreme at first, but his later historical work was more upsetting than reassuring to his inherited dogmas. He found out how small a part the rational had played, how great a part, the non-rational, in the working out of American destiny. He found out how helpless his heroes had been; how ironical the dénouements of the career of President Jefferson.

German tribal history, in his early years of teaching, had been a sort of brain teaser, a game for logic and method. American history, in his later years of teaching, was something different, something more human, a kind of drama in which good and bad could not be neatly sorted out, as he had been taught they should be, but inextricably woven together into the fabric of life. The work did on the *History of the United States* reoriented his own thought. While using his efficient mind to its utmost, he undermined in himself his trust in the infallibility of the mind alone. He saw that societies were cemented together by sub-rational bonds, as well as rational ones. He suspected that the sub-rational bonds were stronger.

Work done, places seen, the general friction of the life he had lived, and the people he had known and loved—these things made the book of the summer of 1902 possible. Henry

Hobson Richardson, Clarence King, and John La Farge taught him to see as an artist saw. In their company, he refound his five senses, and relearned a fresh delight in color, line, and pattern. It was preparation for the undiscerned book he could write.

He came to his unclassifiable relationship with the Virgin of Chartres by way of a series of close relationships with other women. The earliest influence of any importance upon him was his sister Louisa. Her death was the first great tragedy in his life. Another woman, his wife, helped to remake him during the fortunate and happy years of his life.

Marion Hooper came out of the same New England that had made him, and was even more bound by its laws and shaped by its mores than he had ever been. His experience was wider, his knowledge larger; yet she tempered him and formed him during their years of marriage as surely as he changed her. In her was a nature not of strength but of delicacy, not of vigor, but of fineness. She made little of logic; she relied upon the judgments of sensibility. Adams's wife taught him respect for a side of human nature which had had scant praise in his bringing-up.

And with his wife, he underwent further unsettling of certain religious and moral dogmas of his childhood. In his case, the teaching of the inherited belief had been perfunctory. Questing uneasily together, dissatisfied with easy solutions, groping, half lost, yet not willing to seize upon the pat answer, Henry and Marian Adams wandered. They relied each upon the other for more than half a universe while presenting to the world only the bright assured gaiety of a fortunate union. The loss of this wife bereft Adams of personal, as well as dogmatic, support for his own existence. Every wall of his life fell down. If he went on at all, he had to reframe even the reasons for existence.

If Adams had lived in a stable age; if he had had an undisturbed personal life—if Lincoln had not been murdered, if his wife had not killed herself—he might never have written his later books. But disaster in two regions—public and private—overturned his outer and his inner worlds. The bankruptcy of the national life and the bankruptcy of his own personal life struck him down all at one time. And when he got up, he was a different kind of person. After 1885 he was unhinged from his earlier aims and ambitions, wrenched out of contentment, estranged from complacency. Unhappiness, disillusionment, and disgust made him think more deeply and see further than he might ever have done if he had been lucky.

Intellectually, he was ready for his new study long before he was ready in his emotions. At Cambridge in the 1870's he had developed tentatively a theory of history which divided time into ages which differed qualitatively. Jefferson's age was the last American *political* age, he thought. The following age would be an *economic* age: the *History* was a foretelling of one as much as description of the other.

Then, in 1893, in a time of trouble, he fell in with his brother Brooks Adams, and found he could talk to him. They could be vigorous and free, hit hard without being polite, and find out things together. Brooks's theories, more elaborate than his own, went far toward explaining the social trouble in which they were all embroiled. The brothers came to see that the financial crash was only the outward sign of a deeper inward trouble.

For several years Henry sank his interests in Brooks's. Brooks only at this time published; Henry took his thought out in talk and letters. Brooks was the more aggressive theoretical analyzer. He had, perhaps, the more clear-cut sinewy mind, yet was capable of great compassion; he was more easily partisan, more single-minded. Henry acquiesced in the theory, although he was quite cruel in his criticism of Brooks's manner of expressing it. He held back something of himself. He continued to look at history more complexly, more esthetically. Brooks was the more interested in the moment of transition from one age to another; Henry, in the intuition of the texture and mood of a certain age. Wherever he went— to Samoa, to Greece, to Norway—he tried, at least in letters, to put into a kind of picture the very bedrock of each civilization through which—dissociated yet sympathetic—he journeyed.

Henry took over much of Brooks's terminology. Their thinking was so close during these years that perhaps he shared with Brooks something of the origin of these terms, but Brooks's mind was the kind that enjoyed the provocative imaginative label. Ages (or societies) were then, for the two brothers, either those of centralization or decentralization. Ages were either economic or imaginative. Force, or energy (its source inexplicable), channeled itself through the men who best expressed the age: through the soldiers, priests, and poets of the imaginative age whose subconscious motivation was fear, or through the lenders, traders, and manufacturers of the economic age whose subconscious motivation was greed.

What struck Henry particularly was the difference between imaginative ages and non-imaginative ages. His own was, of course, the latter. And he came to see himself in all his socially approved ambitions as helping to make his own society even more a non-imaginative one. The positive, evolutionary, reforming faith of science—in which he had ardently believed, although always with some nagging doubts —had transformed the world. But it had led away from the virtues, as well as the evils, of the imagination. Now, in disillusionment, he doubted more sweepingly than he ever had before. The malfunctioning of American society, the malfunctioning of his own personal life, made him stumble and halt. He had to look about again to see what he did, after all, believe.

Yet he could see little point in revolt. His and Brooks's unhappy theory was necessitarian. And whatever an age was —whether economic or imaginative—he could see little virtue in mixing these two modes. His own age, to excel, must be ever more intensively itself. Yet personally, in the depths of his being, he experienced a revulsion both from the virtues as well as from the vices of his times. On his travels he looked for the imaginative society, and was comfortable and happy only when he was surrounded by people who lived by other standards than those of London, Paris, New York, and Washington, D.C.

Japan was the first imaginative society he came upon after 1885. Here, for the first time, he saw the power of religion as a base for the social order. Buddhism had created the organism whose superficial decoration was the forest temple. That energy was fading in 1886, but it was still the cement that held the organism together. As he and La Farge explored the temples together, he saw that what would come next in Japan would be completely alien to the *torii* and stone Buddhas, something akin to what he had left behind in the United States.

Samoa and Tahiti were the most complete and unspoiled examples of the imaginative society. Both were archaic in relation to the West, but almost absolute in fulfilling his preconception of an imaginative society. These Pacific civilizations had qualities of cohesiveness, proportion, order, unity, and vitality that the West seemed to him to have lost long ago. He had a strong desire to sit down on those islands and give up the problem of the West.

Coming home reluctantly at the end of 1891, Adams felt only a kind of horror at the swirling disorder of the West. He got away from its centers as often as he could. He found rest in wildernesses where social man was unimportant, or in decadent islands of the West Indies where the struggle to find a solution was in abeyance. In Cuba he found little vitality, but discerned a shape beneath the wreckage—the shape of a once vital community.

By the time he wandered into the first of the Norman cathedrals in the company of the Lodge family in 1895, he was ready for the large experience which, during that summer, he underwent. He saw this other age—which had built the cathedrals—as centrally relevant to his own time. It was its predecessor, its ancestor. Here was an organic society which had not been exotic, narrow, or decadent, but strong and vital. It still mattered.

It is important to state here that Adams never revolted against the deepest assumption of his background. The fundamental drive of his mental motor was the same all through his life, and it was the same as his father's, his grandfather's, and his great-grandfather's. The Adamses had all concerned themselves with a practical matter: man living, not alone, but in society. The good life for an Adams—for Henry, as for his family predecessors—was the social life of the human being. It is important to notice that he was not an individualist as many of the great Americans of his period were. His contribution to knowledge was not theirs. It was fitting that he was a historian. Man fixed firmly in the political, social, and economic condition of life—no matter how tragic—was his subject. There was a deep movement of thought in him that was never disturbed. Below surface changeability, below despair and disgust, this movement of thought held its course. In this deepest level of belief, almost unnoticed by himself, his integrity of motive persisted. One can see now, in his interest in the cathedrals, the same basic drive which had led him all his life. The motive which took him to Chartres was the same as that which had led him on other, superficially incompatible pilgrimages.

Practical, flexible, ingenious—the Adamses had used various methods; had fallen in with various factions and parties, had been, in other words, adaptable. But their end, from one generation to another, never changed. Not one of them could conceive of the individual as living in a vacuum. To live well as a human being, man must live well in society. And the Adamses were born to set man right.

Henry Adams never practiced the political art of his ancestors, but in his teaching, reforming, writing he had, unconsciously, the same aim: he wanted to grasp in his mind, and grapple, the condition, the vital *why,* of a properly functioning social order. In this social order there should be sufficient freedom and sufficient order. It should be alive from top to bottom, vital enough to spill over its superabundance of life into appropriate laws, traditions, and arts.

Adams discerned that what created an age was its basic motive. The motive of an age was simply primal physical energy taking a particular form. The motive might not be the god to whom men paid lip service; it was, nevertheless, the god that ruled their lives.

The motive of the age of Mont-Saint-Michel, of Chartres, Coutances, Caen, and of Abelard, Thomas, and Francis was a very different one from that of his own age. Its very differentness gave it a high visibility as he looked back at it from the early twentieth century. It was the motive of faith, a particular kind of faith. "Europe was unity then. . . . Christianity was the unit." [9]

But even that unity was subdivided. In the eleventh century it was faith in God the Father—God the Seigneur to whom Roland, dying, proffered his glove. Man's business then was war, glory, masculine heroism, with no nonsense about grace, chivalrous love, or any but manly courtesy.

The faith of the age of transition, 1140 to 1200, the age that built Chartres, was already different. This was the moment of balance between primitive energy and rational judgment, the balance of the reign of love as personified in the Virgin whose shrine Chartres was. It was a sunny time— "whatever Chartres may be now, when young it was a smile." [10]

The Virgin had, by 1200, engrossed God the Father, God the Son, and God the Holy Ghost. She was more important than the Trinity. However incorrect the fact was as doctrine, it was a fact, and accepted uneasily by the Church. This was Adams's favorite moment of the two hundred years he had chosen to study, a moment full of contradictions, but of contradictions lulled to sleep by love. It was a unity that contained multitudes but it was indisputably a unity. And being a strong, healthy, un-selfconscious unity, its parts were vigorous and lively.

It was, supremely, one of Brooks Adams's great ages of the imagination—imagination which put to its service all the other useful qualities, science among them.

After the transition came the last part of the age crowned by such far-stretching efforts as the unfinished Beauvais Cathedral. It was a time that went to extremes and still, somehow, held together. St. Francis's repudiation of formal thought, and the proliferation and sophistication of the Schools were extremes, pushing outward from the still center of the age's harmony. Capping the age, and its intellectual climax, was St. Thomas's masterful synthesis of thought.

Adams did Thomas full justice, but was not warm toward him. He found Thomas's cool scientific brain too modern; it sacrificed too much spontaneity to suit him. Adams was really on the side of the foolish mystics. He saw that their findings could never be overturned, and that St. Thomas's structure, solid as it seemed and was, could be by-passed, if not overturned. There it stood: majestic, impenetrable, noble, praising man in the fullness of his powers, as well as God and God's world; yet just beyond St. Thomas's achievement, and very near too, was the ruin and wreckage of all this remarkable age. "Nothing is sadder than the catastrophe of Gothic art, religion and hope." [11]

Adams meant the book to cover the time between William the Conqueror's sitting down to dine in the refectory at Mont-Saint-Michel and St. Thomas Aquinas's sitting down at his writing desk to compose the *Summa Theologiae*. It was a journey in time through three centuires, and a journey in space across the northern provinces of what would one day be France. But it could countenance a leap across boundaries to bring in the Italian, Francis of Assisi. The book's honesty of scholarship and scope of design ensured a kind of balance of the more important factors of the age. Yet it was saturated with the personal. Its personal tone was not a matter of the obvious parading of the ego of the writer, but of the choice of material, motive, arrangement of sequence; what he put in mattered; what he left out mattered. He saw the age as a unity, but what he saw in that unity betrayed the personal bias and gave the book its flavor.

The qualities which he particularly valued were those which he thought had died out in modern man. They were the qualities he had enjoyed in minor civilizations. These qualities were (1) of the will, (2) of the senses, and (3) of the imagination.

The will of the time was strong because its belief was simple, undivided, and so assured as not to think about itself at all. It was the will of direct action. The earliest part of the great age exhibited best these pure traits of the medieval will.

Simple, severe, sturdy—both in its architecture and in its poetry—this was an age of act, that did not need the preparation or accompaniment of thought. Its heroes were so bedded in their faith that act could be all. Adams's affection for these men of the Abbey, and for their poetic exemplars, the heroes of the *Song of Roland,* was intense to the very extent that he was weary and sick of the excessive argumentation and self-consciousness of his own time. He saw in William and Harold what he would have liked to be, and what he never could be. This time of the building of the Abbey was a singularly pure example of Brooks Adams's age of the priest and the soldier.

Yet Brooks's brother did not analyze; he followed his own temperament, and demonstrated. He praised in picture. His translation of parts of the *Song of Roland,* set down side by side with the original old French, had the same rude strength, if not the music of the original. He tried, particularly, to set down in his roughly literal translation just the strength of the unconscious and therefore mighty will. These chevaliers of God the Father did not meditate; they acted; but their acts were fit subjects for other's meditations.

Comparatively speaking, the age of the Abbey was the age of will. But Adams showed the trait, though diminishing slightly, carried through the building of Chartres, where the architect resigned his means as well as his end into the hands of the Virgin. Adams recreated, in a charmingly life-like dialogue, the conversation of the builder and his Queen, in their joint discussion of the decoration of the building. Paradoxically, the will was strongest where it was least one's own.

The senses were as vital and innocent as the will. The direct intuition of color was a kind of key experience for Adams, standing to him for all the other experience of the senses. the naïve directness of the flat and flaring colors of the windows of Chartres stood for a whole side of man's life which had been grayed out in recent centuries. (Adams's passionate espousing of color was his own unconscious prophecy of the return to color of the artists of the late nineteenth and early twentieth centuries. He was, in his way, as much of his age as it was possible to be, but slightly ahead, so that deceivingly he did not seem to be so.)

Color stood for all the kinds of sensuous pleasure which the conscientious rationalistic nineteenth century had weeded out of human nature, or had tried to weed out. Adams, in the shock of tragedy, had cleared away the dead debris of his century and seen through the ruin the reality of other ages. Color was a reality and a finality. He won back in color something remembered from his childhood. And in the twelfth century he found not just the child playing with color, but a whole civilization of passionately intelligent adults playing gigantically and powerfully with color. Color stood for what that age's people had had; for what he and his age had lost; for a special richness in the quality of living.

And color, in the great age of Chartres, not only brayed out its own trumpet blasts, but served the greater whole, served the glory of the Virgin who was the goddess of the age, whose love, grace, and mercy presided over all its productions. The taste of the age, even in color, was a unity. In the cathedral of Chartres, there was "no difference in taste between the Virgin in the Choir, and the Water-Carriers by the doorway." [12]

The imagination was as naïvely alive as the will and the senses. Imagination gave the age variety, fire, passion. Its people were more alive than those of one's own time. Life was bolder, deeper, went to extremes. Yet the extremes had a line cast round them which defined and tempered the whole.

The character of Abelard, as Adams showed him in the book, was a striking example of imagination: in the writer, in the character, and in the age. Adams was unsentimental and somewhat severe in his presentation of the scholar. This was not a softened, vulgarized Abelard, but a man, proud, unbending, arrogant; yet a man of his age, as sincerely devoted to the Virgin as any one of his enemies who thought him dangerous in his skepticism.

Abelard enters the book twice; once in the chapters on Chartres, and later in a particular chapter devoted to him. In a discussion of one of the windows of Chartres, Adams brought in Abelard by analogy. He saw him as a possible contemporary model for the window of the Prodigal Son. For Abelard was indeed a sort of prodigal son of his age. With great virtuosity Adams described the window literally and, in counterpoint, Abelard's prodigal career, stressing here the color and pathos of the life.

In the chapter properly devoted to Abelard and his ideas, Adams treated the great and arrogant teacher more roughly. He was a great individualist in an age when individualism (not individuality) might be the fatal note which would shatter the whole structure of living. One realizes, slowly, in reading Adams on Abelard, that his severity toward him was a kind of intimacy. It was as if he saw something of himself in Abelard, and were, for that reason, all the harder on him. The full-length picture resulting—scratchy with contempt, dislike, reluctant admiration, and a secret sense of kinship—had all the more of life. Abelard was one of the great imaginative characters of an age that for a few years held all the warring qualities of the imagination in a sort of passionate equilibrium.

The central place which Adams gave the Virgin in his study of the high Middle Ages resulted not only from his objective study of the age, but from a subconscious assumption of his own. The Virgin was an underlining of the high place he assigned the sensuous, the unconscious, the feminine, the non-rational in his scheme of things. But she was more. She stood for his deepest revolt against the way he thought the universe was organized. He made her stand for a similar revolt which he discerned in the people's upraising of her in the twelfth century.

The Trinity, the official objects of the age's worship, stood for One, and One for justice. Justice could not be kind—look at life around one. The Virgin, on the other hand, stood for kindness, for mercy, for love—qualities which had little to do with justice. Her business was to tamper with justice, to blunt it, turn it aside, to laugh it to scorn. No one could escape whipping at the hands of justice; man did not want justice. The dispensation of the Virgin might be a way of getting around justice.

Justice, for Adams, was the same thing as fate, and as coldly to be regarded. Fate had no personal regard. He stated his point thus:

Mary concentrated in herself the whole rebellion of man against fate; the whole protest against divine law; the whole contempt for human law as its outcome; the whole unutterable fury of human nature beating itself against the walls of its prison-house, and suddenly seized by a hope that in the Virgin man had found a door of escape. She was above law; she took feminine pleasure in turning hell into an ornament; she delighted in trampling on every social distinction in this world and the next. She knew that the universe was as unintelligible to her, on any theory of morals, as it was to her worshipers, and she felt, like them, no sure conviction that it was any more intelligible to the Creator of it.[13]

Adams was aware of the fact that behind Mary stood the shadowy figures of the other great goddesses of the past: "Astarte, Isis, Demeter, Aphrodite . . ." [14] and that she stood for power, energy, instinct back of and below both medieval Christianity and modern rationality. He thought that the Middle Ages, in Mary, coped with sex in a way in which his own age had so far failed, or dodged. (This intuition was another almost unconscious cast into the future. He seemed to be looking back, but was looking forward, too, to a change in attitude.)

Adams did not lose his historical perspective even in the quick of his sympathetic feeling for the age. The fact that he was able to look before and after, to accept the mortality of Mary's great age, had a curiously dramatic effect in the book. His own hesitancy, his own thwarted passion of belief entered into the book and made it more potent with emotion.

The two motives—the historical truth about the age and his own attitude toward it—both tragic, made a kind of internal drama. He set the stage for the downfall of the great idea at the moment he began to re-create it. He said in Chapter I, "The Normans stood more fully in the centre of the world's movement" [15] than any of their descendants, but also, "In 1020 Norman art was already too ambitious." [16] He would not let the reader be at peace, letting him glimpse, but only glimpse, the deep personal trouble he had experienced in discovering and re-creating the age.

About the Virgin, the true center of his study, Adams experienced the same conflict of emotion: she of "the large mind," [17] of "the strong will," [18] the pivot of "an intensity of conviction never again reached by any passion, whether of religion, of loyalty, of partiotism, or of wealth, perhaps never even paralleled by any single economic effort except in war." [19] Yet—"she is gone." And worse, he finds her now, "looking down from a deserted heaven, into an empty church, on a dead faith." [20]

The age went bankrupt as his own age undoubtedly would, or had. That Mary's age was the best, not the worst, of ages, did not seem to matter. Concluding ostensibly upon the subject of the poem *The Romance of the Rose,* he spoke his last word upon the age: "The deepest expression of social feeling ended with the word: Despair." [21]

The book, written with an unfailing vivacity of color and manner, might seem on first reading to be cheerful, even gay, certainly bright. Yet it rests upon a bedrock of somber prepossessions. Its premises might be stated as follows:

a. The universe is unintelligible and inimical to man.

b. Society is a fiction—an attempt to make the universe intelligible and bearable.

c. There are various possible fictions on which society may rest.

d. The fiction of the twelfth century was one of the best.

e. It too failed—life is tragic.

Chapter 22

Multiplicity

IN HIS middle sixties—fretful at what he thought of as approaching old age, angry at the world, impatient with himself —Henry Adams accomplished a great and original work, the writing of two books, *Mont-Saint-Michel and Chartres* and *The Education of Henry Adams*. They were the two halves of one whole.

By the close of the year 1902 he had done his main work on the cathedral book and would take home with him from Paris a completed first draft. Although he tinkered with it for three more years before publication, he lived from this time until the spring of 1907 in the mood of its successor, sequel, and antithesis, *The Education*.

Adams seemed quiet, set, placed and passive; near great events yet not of them. But inside him, hidden from all but his closest friends, was a turmoil of explosive thought. This period of the imagination of *The Education*, and of writing it, was one of agonizing stimulation. Stimulation had to stand in the place of hope, for his thought seemed to lead him into darkness.

"I am lost but not untrue," Adams wrote to a friend.[1] He put his case as a joke, but stated it fairly. He diagnosed multiplicity in the life around him and in himself. It seemed to him that there was a general shattering, a splintering, and a diffusion of all purpose and all design in contemporary existence. Yet by defining multiplicity, in an act of the imagination, he achieved a kind of unity. In deep trouble, he kept hold of himself and his materials.

As for the general conditions of his living during the time that his thought grappled darkness, he moved in a fixed circuit, quietly and predictably. His big travels were over. He spent some time each year in Paris, some time in Washington. He saw the same friends in a regular rotation of the seasons. The same scenes met his eyes year after year: Lafayette Square outside his winter windows, the Place de l'Étoile, humming with life, outside his summer windows.

Out of this quiet life, there issued disquieting phrases.

308

Before he came home with the rough manuscript of the cathedral book achieved, he wrote to his niece Mabel: "The world becomes more amusing every year. I am always in greater hopes of living to see it break its damn neck, which I calculate must happen by 1932." [2]

Adams carried home, in December, 1902, in addition to his manuscript, another piece of baggage, a portrait of Clarence King done by King's half-brother, George Howland, for the Century Club. The keen, humorous glance of that picture, directed outward at a world that did not care how wrong the life behind those eyes had gone, must have haunted Adams even after the picture was safely stowed away. He could not stop thinking of King. King's case, he came to see, was not so very different from his own, or his generation's, only more melodramatic in its contrasts of ambition and achievement.

He had much in mind both the success and failure, the strength and weakness of his friends, as of himself. Had there been some common vice in them that, so full of promise and opportunity, they had done so little? Would time wash away the dross of circumstances and leave some residue of good they had done? He chewed the cud of the problem.

He widened the range of his thought by linking himself to the fate of his friends, his generation, and his country. His bitterness was no longer entirely personal. It had something in it that transcended his private fate. He began tentatively to frame and phrase the circumstances of his own life in larger terms, to set himself up as an object of thought, to see his life, as if from the outside, in reference to a greater whole.

Some of his friends, unlike King, still troublesomely involved in life, squirmed under his steadfast gaze. For he had transferred the searchlight of his attention from the twelfth to the twentieth century, and now studied his friends as attentively as he had Eleanor of Aquitaine or Francis of Assisi. He looked at his contemporary environment as curiously as if it were a strange territory he had just discovered. He had an occupation now: an ever continuing dialogue with his age.

He came home at the beginning of 1903 to find his next-door neighbor, Hay, embroiled in exasperating items of foreign business: the Samoan question, the Alaskan boundary question, and the engineered revolt of Panama against Colombia. Hay, so good a listener, had little time to listen. He was absorbed in his own troubles.

Adams could not stop his mind, and sought outlet in letters. On January 8th he wrote to Henry Holt, "I'm deep in actualities." [3] Next day he wrote to Brooks, "Everything behind 1900 is already bric-a-brac." [4]

Adams's mood fluctuated between practical impatient concern for government's getting good works done—what might be called his *new-dealism*—and a seeming opposite, a sweeping belief in the anarchism of all modern affairs, governmental and philosophic.

This fluctuation was not really a contradiction. A phrase in a letter written to Brooks on March 8th shows the connection: "If civilisation were science . . ." If civilization were science, then government as the instrument of civilization would, as a matter of course, perform good works for the whole of society. And, "We should be able to make some roads, pave some cities, build some docks, have some outfit for science, and perhaps keep a little nearer our pace, instead of falling daily behind." [5] This is exactly his grandfather, John Quincy Adams, speaking again, for his great obsession: internal improvements.

Civilization not being science, and the fact proved to him beyond a doubt, he gave up *every* result and let himself be swept into an absoluteness of denial beyond compromise. The sad fact for him, in the early 1900's, was that he could not be happy in denial, nor satisfied. Therefore, he was restless, angry, provocative, dangerous, but, in the end, creative.

His contemporaries went their own various ways. John La Farge had a new book coming out, *Great Masters*. It was paler, as all his books were paler, than he was. Henry James published his biographical study *William Wetmore Story and His Friends*. It was to be the book of James that would mean the most to Henry Adams. It struck him as a parable of their generation (although actually Story belonged to a generation before his and James's). It seemed to stand for that generation's good intentions and its actual non-delivery of the goods.

In the same year, 1903, Trumbull Stickney (familiarly, Joe Stickney to Adams and the Lodges) got away to Greece and in three months there achieved a brief glory of lyricism. This time his friend Bay Lodge stayed home. Young Lodge found himself fettered by the people he loved and by the responsibilities he had chosen. He was anchored, yet still rebellious.

The most fortunate of Adams's friends this year was Raphael Pumpelly. The greathearted, generous man achieved in 1903 a life-long ambition, a scientific expedition into the uplands of Central Asia to find there, if he could, the traces of earliest man and the high-water marks of a prehistoric lake bed. He had talked over the purposes of his trip many times with both Henry and Brooks Adams, and with his fellow scientist Alexander Agassiz. When he left Boston in March, 1903, he took with him the ardent interests of these men. Adams wove into his interior dialogue the figure of the seeker, Pumpelly, who cared so little (so lightheartedly) what the men of his time did, but did instead his own abstruse work. He invited Henry to go with him and almost had his consent. Adams hesitated and the chance was gone. "Fifteen years ago," he wrote to Pumpelly, "I should have gone like an automobile." [6]

It was an accepted idea among his friends now that Adams was morbid. Yet in himself Adams never quite fitted the category. Each time he returned to Washington, something in the place infected him with an exasperating hope. Things went so exceptionally well there. There was such an air of easy power in the air. He found himself contradicting his own dogma. "Only I fear that, with their confounded practical commonsense, our people will invent some practical working-system." And: "As yet nothing is broken. Our people are quick and practical, and have not yet lost their heads." [7] His mood was a perverse gloom, crossed by an impish heretical glee at the glimpse of doom outwitted.

Meanwhile he hung onto the tail of science which was galloping into a future he dreaded and was yet curious to see. By intuition, rather than by knowledge, he studied gases and atoms.

In May, 1903, Adams returned to his "summer watering place," Paris. In June he wrote to Gaskell:

Every generalisation that we settled forty years ago, is abandoned. . . .

Poor old nineteenth century! It is already as far off as Descartes and Newton.

You have not answered my question about our breakfast at Sir Henry's [Holland] and William Everett's dinner, if it was a dinner, at Cambridge. What year was it, '62 or '63; and what year did you come up to read law? I want to make some calculations of figures on it. [Not a word about a book that, by this date, must have had a definite shape in his mind.] What will the next term of an equation or series like this:—$1823: 1863::1903:X$. Figure it out in coal-production; horsepower; thermodynamics; or, if you like, just simply in fields—space, energy, time, thought, or mere multiplicity and complexity. My whole interest is to get at a value for that X before I break up, which is an x more easily calculated. . . .

Science has given up the whole fabric of cause and effect. Even time-sequence is beginning to be threatened. I should not at all wonder if some one should upset time. As for space, it is upset already. We did that sixty years ago with electricity. I imagine that in another sixty years, if my X sequence works out regularly, we must be communicating throughout space, by X rays, with systems infinitely distant from us, but finitely distant from each other; a mathematical problem to be solved by non-Euclidean methods.[8]

No wonder that John Hay, who received regularly a quota of Adams's more imaginative speculations, should address him from afar as, "O Mirror of Excellence and uncle to the Cosmos!"[9] As for Adams, he entertained for Hay's own public world a curiously mixed emotion, part fascination, part repulsion. The public world was, after all, the Adamsian true world; yet it seemed as seriously awry as any private world of thought. Perhaps, deep down, he entertained a desire to get into that world, and to do something about its confusions. But the impulse was pushed far down and almost squelched. He enjoyed genuinely his sidelines seat, where he could be irresponsible and smile and gesticulate at others' failures.

It was only in creating the structure of the book, which now more and more occupied his thought, that he resolved in a manner many conflicts in himself. Building that work in his imagination, he used, and in using them, transformed, his own bitterness, his own frustrations, his own fears and hopes. He found that he could integrate all that he had seen or done. He found that he could place his life in a kind of perspective. Doing this, Adams transcended something of jealousy in his character, something of malignancy, something of fruitlessness. The creation of the book was an act in as full a sense of the word as the political acts of his public friends. He did not fully understand this fact himself. He apprehended it only dimly and at times. it remained for a later generation to whom he seemed to be speaking directly to see more clearly than he could what he had done.

It was as if Adams saw the world perversely. He was like the boy in Andersen's fairy tale *The Snow Queen*. He had got a monstrous sliver in his eye and saw things differently. Some events were large to him that were small to others; others, small. Both the big happenings on the horizon of the future and the small ones near at hand were apt to strike him with a certain singularity.

In the year 1904 it was important to him that Bay Lodge's verse-drama *Cain* appeared in print. In it the young poet fastened a social and philosophical radicalism upon the Bible story. *Cain* promised more than it delivered; its verse was more thoughtful than poetic; and its thought, more youthful than deep. Yet it had a grave kind of charm.

To Adams it was important in 1904 that Pumpelly was able to achieve a second expedition to Asia, and that Alex Agassiz sailed for the Easter Islands. It was important that the Clarence King *Memoirs* came out, containing his usual revealing chapter. It was important to him that in May he went with John Hay to St. Louis to the great Exposition; and that, on the way, he suffered almost a revelation of what the mid-American continent had become, and how its empty spaces had been filled up, urbanized and industrialized during his own lifetime.

Aggravating, interesting, and important during the summer of 1904 in Europe was his acquisition of an automobile, a Mercedes of eighteen horsepower[10] and a driver. He indulged, all the long summer and fall, his taste for cathedrals, and collected them, one by one, triumphantly, in spite of trouble with the car, and his own humorous supposition that he might kill someone, or be killed himself, at any moment.

While Adams ransacked France for glass, John Hay in America quietly visited Augustus Saint-Gaudens at his studio-home at Cornish, New Hampshire. He went to him for a portrait bust—a work Saint-Gaudens had been interested a long time in attempting—making out of Hay a sort of snub-nosed, bland, and humorous latter-day Socrates. Hay's sitting for the bust was a gesture consciously looking forward to his own death. If it was to be done, it would be done well. Hay looked curiously at Saint-Gaudens's place, finding it, as he wrote to Adams on August 17, a mixture of "Greek, Gascon, and Yankee." [11] He was disturbed by the obvious fact of Saint-Gaudens's own failing health.

But Hay had still a capacity for a joke. He was an instigator of another less serious work by the sculptor, a medal of Henry Adams as *Porcupinus Angelicus*—a caricatured head with little stiff wings and barbs. Adams received the medal in Paris and wrote his acknowledgments to Saint-Gaudens on September 3, 1904: "Your winged and pennated child arrived yesterday by the grace of God and his vicar the Secretary of State. . . . I'm sorry you can't give Hay wings too, he needs them more than I who live in holes." [12]

News from home was not all banter. Trumbull Stickney died in Boston very suddenly of a brain tumor on October 11, 1904. Adams, in Paris, must have sensed an empty space open out before him. He could imagine vividly the personal loss to Bay Lodge, who had sat by Stickney's side and who had seen him die. As in the case of other deaths, Adams could sit still by his Paris window and see another promise wither, and see also the future look smaller. Stickney's being gone would be noticeable in several spheres. He had been poet, teacher, and critic. There was no one to take his place. He was humanly and artistically unique.

In the late fall, under November skies, Adams crossed the Atlantic and settled once more for a winter at 1603 H Street. The American Capital was again a stimulation. "Washington is now rather more amusing to me than other places, because I can laugh at all my friends who are running what they call a government. . . . This country is terribly interesting. It has no character but prodigious force." [13] So he wrote to Gaskell on December 30, 1904. Adams was dreadfully fascinated by force. He was half in love with it, and half afraid of it. It was killing all that he loved. Yet he thought that as a proper historian, he must discard morality and set off on the track of mindless, heartless energy, and trace its course as truly as he could across the lonely void of the universe.

Interlined between reactions to the present, in his letter to Charles Gaskell, was news of a particular reaction he had undergone to a particular past. He told Gaskell he had completed the work on his cathedral book. "Talking of Thomas Aquinas, I have just finished printing my *Miracles de la Vierge* [that is, his *Mont-Saint-Michel and Chartres*]. This book will run up to a pretty bulky size, but I print only a hundred copies, one of which will be for you. It is my declaration of principles as head of the Conservative Christian Anarchists; a party numbering one member. The Virgin and St. Thomas are my vehicles of anarchism. Nobody knows enough to see what they mean, so the Judges will probably not be able to burn me according to law." [14]

The *Chartres* book was Adams's strongest movement of reaction against the amoral force or energy which seemed in the modern world to be running them all into the ditch. The book to come, *The Education*, was to be an attempt to chart the course of force as it seemed to him to have developed and accelerated. Having finished with the twelfth century, Adams now turned the full battery of his attention upon the twentieth. He saw now, with some distaste, but also with a kind of deadly fascination, that his own life, seen in a certain perspective, was to be the peg on which to hang his thought.

In January, 1905, he sent out the first privately printed

copies of *Mont-Saint-Michel and Chartres*. Copies went to Anna Lodge, to Margaret Chanler, to his brother Brooks, and others. His letter, with a copy to his former student, the historian H. O. Taylor, has the value of tying together the two books. "I am trying to work out the formula for anarchism; the law of expansion from unity, simplicity, morality, to multiplicity, contradiction, police. . . . The assumption of unity which was the mark of human thought in the middle-ages has yielded very slowly to the proofs of complexity." [15]

An early and ingenuously enthusiastic response to the book came warmingly to Adams from the sculptor, Saint-Gaudens, in April:

You dear old Porcupinus Poeticus!
You old Poeticus under a Bushelibus:
I thought I liked you fairly well, but I like you more for the book you sent me the other day. . . . You have revealed to me the wonder of the Twelfth Century in a way that never entered my head. . . . the general guts and enthusiasm of the work . . .
Thank you, dear Old Stick in the Mud.
Your brother in idiocy.[16]

In the new year of 1905, Adams had two visitors for whom he cared: Henry James and Cecil Spring-Rice. Friends warmed the cold universe.

Spring-Rice came *sub rosa*. His attendance in Washington was requested of the British Government by President Roosevelt, who wanted him at hand (but not officially) for the preliminary discussion of a Russo-Japanese peace.

Roosevelt had written to the American Minister in London, Henry White, on December 27, 1904: "Now I wonder if you could arrange to have the Foreign Office send Spring-Rice over here to see me for a week. I understand he is to be in London for a little while. There is no one in the British Embassy here to whom I can talk freely, and I would like to have the people at the Foreign Office understand just my position in the Far East, and I would like to know what theirs is." [17]

The American Government had found a use for Henry Adams. He was a friend of Spring-Rice. The Englishman's stay at his house would not arouse suspicion of secret diplomacy, as would his stay at the White House. Roosevelt communicated the plot to John Hay on January 13, 1905, requesting him to ask Henry Adams to house Spring-Rice when he arrived the following week. "Won't you ask Henry if he can put up this distinguished member of the kitchen ambassadorial circle—if there are members of the kitchen Cabinet, why cannot there be kitchen ambassadors?" [18]

It was no wonder that Adams remarked, one time, that he could overhear the talk at the House across the square, so near he was to its whisperers.

Roosevelt's scheme to prepare the way for his role as negotiator between the Japanese and Russians in their forthcoming peace conference was pure personal gain for Henry Adams. During the last two decades he had seen very little of his friend Cecil Spring-Rice, a man who had a special talent for catching his thought on the wing. Since the late eighties Spring-Rice had become more and more important to the British Government. But he had been important in places a long way off from Lafayette Square, and Adams had had to do without him. They wrote good letters to each other, but talk was better.

Here was at last a chance to sit and open themselves to each other. Late at night, sunk deep in the low chairs of the library at 1603 H Street, the two men exchanged words and silences. They were comfortable together. They could share face to face a mutual consolatory melancholy.

In February, Spring-Rice had to go. He said goodbye to both Roosevelt and Adams and set off for Russia. He looked back appreciatively, carrying with him a copy of Adams's new book. He wrote about it to Anna Lodge on February 14, 1905: "I departed with a cold and it developed into fever, which I enjoyed on ship in bed with the *Antiquary* and Uncle Henry's book. They really didn't go badly together which is good for Uncle Henry. It is a fine production—I fancy, a little bit like the monument at Rock Creek, in memoriam. There is the real voice of passion so that the very stones cry out." [19]

Overlapping Spring-Rice's visit was Henry James's, and the Winthrop Chanlers'. Adams had written to his niece, Mabel La Farge, the previous November that he was expecting "various nieces, but am also looking for some companions more mature; like Harry James and Mrs. Winty Chanler whom I passionately love, we being both children of the twelfth century." [20]

Adams's acquaintance with Mrs. Chanler (Margaret Terry Chanler) had begun not much earlier than the spring of 1899 when he met the Chanlers in Europe. Its progress into intimacy dated from 1904 and 1905. She was sensitive, intelligent, Catholic, but not narrowly so. He could talk to her and write to her in quick flashing allusions which she could catch and send back to him.

Adams's acquaintance with Henry James was of long duration, but it was patchy. They had not seen each other with any regularity for many years. James had kept himself close to his burgher's house in Rye, while Adams restlessly ranged the world. Yet they had met occasionally in London and Paris. Now James was coming to Washington after a fall stay with his brother, William, in New England.

Although Adams and James looked out at much the same world, they looked at it from different angles. James could endure better than Adams the corruption and dissolution of their common world. He had the artist's ability to make matter of tragedy. Adams, as historian and philosopher recognized the tragedy, but could barely endure it. He wanted to cure it.

Although they saw each other seldom, for Adams there was something inviolable in the tie that bound him to Henry James. James belonged to Marian Adams's dead past. He had been an acquaintance of the circle which had included, long ago in Cambridge and Boston and Newport, not only Miss Marian Hooper and her sister and brother, but John La Farge, Margaret and Thomas Sergeant Perry, Wendell Holmes, and Henry and William James. To it had belonged, too, Henry James's beautiful and doomed cousin, Minny Temple. Both men looked back upon that time with regret. And although Adams read very little James, and James perhaps knew little of Adams, yet they were closer in their sixties than they had been in their forties or fifties.

Adams welcomed a chance to be with this old acquaintance, changed as he himself was changed by the years, no longer the slender, quiet young man of Adams's wife's dead past, but the portly, deep-browed, weighty writer of the three great and passionate novels *The Wings of the Dove, The Ambassadors,* and *The Golden Bowl.* Yet still, behind the protective façade, he was the shy and gentle Harry, who could not bear to hurt anyone.

After the quiet years at Lamb House which had at last given him, in a rush, the three great novels, James had come to America as if playing truant. This was an adventure for him—an adventure of the senses and of the mind. His unobtrusive steady gaze on all objects, persons, scenes, situations never let go. He saw Washington as the City of Conversation,[21] a place that was out of the current of national life, almost an eddy. Washington was a relief to his nerves, which had been beaten upon by the tornadic energy of the building, making, transporting, digging of New York City. Yet with his cruel insight, he saw too that Washington, D.C., was also somewhat futile in going against the grain of American life.

The city, for him, was made up of two parts, with an official background and a personal foreground. The background made "a general impression of high granite steps, of light grey corniced colonnades, rather harmoniously low, contending for effect with slaty mansard roofs and masses of iron excrescence, a general impression of somewhat vague, empty, sketchy, fundamentals, however expectant, however spacious, overweighted by a single Dome, and overaccented by a single Shaft." [22] But, "The foreground was a different thing, a thing, that, ever so quaintly, seemed to represent the force really in possession; though consisting but of a small company of people engaged perpetually in conversation." [23]

James saw acutely the actuality of Washington in the present moment. He failed to see the future of Washington, as Adams did, who, in January, 1905, lived as much in that future as in its present. James had marvelously acute perceptions. Out of them, he could organize a powerful present truth. But he did not have Adams's political or economic imagination, the reach of which into the future was as important as its diagnosis of the present.

Among the foreground figures—the conversationalists—not one of them interested him more than Henry Adams. According to Mrs. Winthrop Chanler's recollection, it was at Henry Adams's house that he stayed while in Washington. James was reminded powerfully of an earlier time when Mrs. Henry Adams was vividly alive and had laughed at him, teased him, and won from him a dazzled admiration. But he was too shy to speak of her to Henry Adams and had to ask their mutual friend Margaret Chanler to go with him to Rock Creek Cemetery to see her grave. While they stood before Saint-Gaudens's hooded figure, he told her about Marian Adams; how attractive she had been; how Henry Adams, in her lifetime, had kept himself in the background for her wit to show better; how they had not known how wonderful Henry was till after she died.[24]

To his guests Adams's situation in Washington seemed mellowy secure. But the house and its physical security were no refuge. Trouble invaded the mind. Just next door John Hay was gravely ill, less and less able to support his job, hadly able to negotiate a halting afternoon walk. Clara Hay, in despair at her husband's acceptance of his illness, appeared to Henry Adams for help. In the spring of 1905, he undertook to get the Hays to Europe and to establish Hay—still scoffing—at Bad Nauheim for a course of waters and treatment there. Privately, Hay discussed with Adams the probable date of his death. But for the moment he seemed better, and Adams went on alone. He saw Hay again only briefly in Europe before the Secretary of State went home. Adams precariously balanced himself in a moment of peace. "I rather like these late autumns of life," he wrote to Gaskell.[25]

John Hay stopped by Washington to report to the President; in reality to say goodbye. And in his diary, in utter candor he said goodbye to life itself, to all that living had been for the fortunate John Hay:

> I say to myself that I should not rebel at the thought of my life ending at this time. I have lived to be old. . . . I have had many blessings, domestic happiness being the greatest of all. I have lived my life. I have had success beyond all the dreams of my boyhood. . . . I know death is the common lot, and what is universal ought not to be deemed a misfortune; and yet—instead of confronting it with dignity and philosophy, I cling instinctively to life and the things of life, as eagerly as if I had not had my chance at happiness and gained nearly all the great prizes.[26]

Hay dragged himself away from Washington to New Hampshire to his house at Lake Sunapee. There he died on July 1, 1905. Adams heard of it in France and felt the world rock beneath him. To his acquaintances he said either nothing at all, or something desperately casual: "I urged Hay to live long enough to make peace, but he shook his head." [27] But the event dyed indelibly all his daily acts and thoughts. It put its mark upon the book he was writing.

Adams returned to the United States in February, 1906, in time to face another death, the scientist's, Samuel Pierpont Langley. "I helped to bury Langley yesterday," he wrote to Mabel La Farge on March 4th, "and now have not a man left whom I can ask to dinner. . . . Except the Bay Lodges. I am lost." [28]

Another casualty of this season was Carl Schurz, whose charmingly irritative leadership Adams had acknowledged in the late sixties and early seventies when he himself had been a strong and not yet daunted reformer. Schurz died on May 14, 1906, saying, *"Es ist so einfach zu sterben"* (It is so simple to die).[29]

One by one the major figures of Adams's imagination were dropping around him. And to him, with the fatal sliver in his eye, each one was marked with tragedy. Langley, in his experiments with flight, had been chillingly neglected. Schurz, so jaunty, so cheerful, had been ludicrously alone. Adams was somber in his solitary meditations. "What is the end of doubling up our steam and electric power every five years to infinity if we don't increase thought power?" [30] Yet Adams was one-sided. Langley's calculations helped the Wright brothers. Flight came. And Schurz, although alone, was influential in New York in his later years, and happy.

Adams was left more than ever alone. He could, perhaps, have reneged and found a sort of rest for his old age in intellectual neutrality, but he did not, or could not. With a bleak and stoic courage, he followed his thought where it led him. Yet where it led was no happy destination. He wrote, in an unpublished letter on December 19, 1906, to Brooks, about the almost finished *Education*, "I fear it is wicked." [31]

In the early part of 1907 he sent copies of the book, still in proof, to certain friends and relatives. Blandly he asked each one to strike out of it whatever displeased him, or seemed incorrect. One can imagine the wonder with which each one—the President, the Senator, the brother—read his copy. One cannot imagine any one of them daring to correct. Not one did. Very few returned the copy. Adams's innocent-sounding request was taken as rhetorical. The book was greatly successful in its first private reading.

Yet probably each one of these first readers—frightened entranced, amused, irritated—read the book for what it contained about himself. He saw it in segments, in purple patches. And very few of these early readers saw it as more than an eccentric autobiography of a gifted but soured contemporary.

Chapter 23

The Education of Henry Adams

A QUALITY which was a liability in everyday living helped Adams write his *Education*. A vital discontent with himself and his age was an agent of creation in that book. He had a notion of another kind of life, preferable to his own. He saw an image of a more vital kind of society than the one in which he had his existence.

He would have been happy, he thought, to have lived in an age which had solid and unshakable values. He would have been content, he thought, to have lived without criticism. He would have been satisfied, he thought, to have been used— used mercilessly—by such a society all of a long, productive, unsubjective life.

The Samoans and Tahitians of the Pacific made him know that such a society could exist upon the earth. He could not live as they did, although he could sympathize with them. He could grasp the fact that their kind of unity was the kind needful for any vital community. Yet these people, who had solved their own problem as long as they were left alone, could not stand whole against moral invasion by another people. He saw them being broken by cultural incursions from his own world. They were losing their old ways; unable to adopt new ways. Suffering from a kind of moral nihilism, he might have stayed and shared their gentle easygoing ruin. Only an angry curiosity drove him back to his own world. His return was important. It re-directed his despair into a kind of action—action in thought.

The Pacific Islanders prepared him for an even more decisive experience. This was his first real seeing of the French cathedrals. Here Western culture had achieved an early measure of organic unity, and to this culture he felt himself and his world directly related. Here was his world's ancestor. Yet bitterly, he realized, too, that he could grasp this world of the twelfth century only in his imagination. If he had been entirely the artist, he might have been content. But Adams, despite his lifelong habit of the pen, was by nature a man of action. He desired, imperiously, the good society functioning here upon the earth at this present moment.

His own age, as he stood upon the ground of his life and looked at it, was the very reverse of his unassuaged idea. The book he wrote, then, was a review of a life and a time, the opposite of which he desired. Yet Adams was deeply contradictory. There was something in him deeply akin to, and at home in, his own disturbed age. There was something of the innate, as well as fortuitous, critic in him. It is hard to imagine him living in thoughtless harmony with any kind of imaginable social order. He wanted to be the man who acted intuitively, without thought; he admired the man of action; but he was incorrigibly the observer, the objector, the critic. A part of his preference for another kind of time and another kind of life was a trait of romanticizing in him. But only a part.

The actual living world around him was one which, all his life, was continually cracking up, shifting its foundations, changing, transforming itself again and again, and yet not once finding stability. His own sensibility was a battleground. He never reached an equilibrium of thought, and he never saw his world reach one. The ruthless reasoning faculty in him had only too free a field in which to operate.

Yet the acid of his thought etched a pattern across this shifting contemporary chaos. In the unwanted and undesirable habit of introspection, he raked together the pieces of his life and the fragmented scenes of his time and made them into a pattern. The pattern was to be the book he called *The Education of Henry Adams.* The book was not to be a representational portrait, either of himself or of his times. It was to be a study of history. His life would show in the context of the larger study, but only obliquely and distortedly, in a kind of perverse brilliance. Yet the flavor of the book would be that of the life.

One has to get into the book as best one can, pushing aside Adams's own explanations, as well as carefully considering them. His first Preface, the one he signed for the privately printed edition, spoke in an inappropriate tone as prelude to the book which followed. Coolly and dryly, it presented the book as something possibly "useful" [1] in that it might "fit young men, in universities or elsewhere, to be men of the world." [2] Not a word to prepare the reader for the agonies, passions, tensions of the actual book itself. It was as strange an introduction to the *Education* as he had written for the *Mont-Saint-Michel,* when he had commended that work to his nieces.

In the so-called "Editor's Preface"—not released till after

his death and signed by Henry Cabot Lodge—he wrote more warmly. Adams could be franker when he stood behind the mask of his friend's name. Here he quoted an important passage from his own book, indicating where to look for significance and putting labels on both the cathedral book and *The Education*. These labels should be considered carefully upon every reading of the two books. *Mont-Saint-Michel and Chartres,* he said, should be subtitled "A Study in Thirteenth-Century Unity," and *The Education of Henry Adams* should be subtitled "A Study of Twentieth-Century Multiplicity." [3]

The use of his friend's name allowed him to show the iron rigor of his ambition. In his second Preface he compared himself to St. Augustine, and his book, to Augustine's *Confessions.*[4] Elsewhere, he wrote that he and Augustine, of course, had *both* failed. This furnished the high and mighty measure of his idea of failure. He wished, and sometimes thought, that the book might be as adequate a signpost of the twentieth century as Augustine's was of the fifth century. He wanted his book to record the exact and painful moment of a dire and awful inner transformation in civilization itself.

Setting aside, for the moment, the shape of the book and its texture, its eccentricity of charm, its poetry of intellectuality, one should follow through its leading idea, a notion of force. Begging the question of ends, one might consider that of means. And for Adams the one mighty motive was force, the energy or vitality which attracted and caused each particular age to shape itself into a special pattern of existence.

His study was of man as a force, and more particularly, of man among the forces, nearly all of them stronger than he. It was a view of life subjected to force, hypnotized by it. He stared at the world and saw in it only that force which dominated his own mind.

Force is the continuing theme:

The object of education for that mind should be the teaching itself how to react with vigor and economy.[5]

Ch. XXI (1892)

True science was the development or economy of forces.[6]

Ch. XXV (1900)

A dynamic theory . . . defines Progress as the development and economy of Forces.[7]

Ch. XXXIII (1904)

But there is a counter-theme:

As Nature developed her hidden energies, they tended to become destructive. Thought itself became tortured, suffering reluctantly, impatiently, painfully, the coercion of new method.[8]

Ch. XXXIII

History is not obliged to decide whether the Ultimate tends to a purpose or not.[9]

Ch. XXXIII

He was devoted to the truth of his diagnosis. But he did not like that truth.

Adams's diagnosis could be set forth starkly, without reference to antecedents:

a. Below everything, sustaining everything, there is something which is not God or good, but which one might call energy or force.

b. Force pulls society along the way it must go, not the way it wants to go.

c. Individual man cannot choose, except to agree with this force, or to be wrecked by it.

d. He should, in loyalty to life, *will* to go with force, or to react to it efficiently, not lie across its path as an encumbrance.

e. And yet, there is something in individual man that kicks against irresistible force and will not agree to agree.

The antecedents of Adams's idea of force were a mixture of theories which had touched his intellect and experiences which had touched his emotions. The idea derived partly from elements of the evolutionary theory which had attracted his imagination (Darwin and Louis Agassiz, the fossils of Wenlock Edge, glaciers and mountains and Clarence King, coral reefs and ocean bottoms and Alexander Agassiz); partly from a dabbling in physics (the lines of force emanating from a magnet, the kinetic theory of gases); and partly from a personal experience of the resistless, remorseless change in the society around him which seemed hurrying toward an unknown and probably unpleasant destination. The *tone* of his theory derived from the shock he had experienced in the tragedy of his wife's death.

The terms in which Adams expressed himself (the use of the word "force" itself) belonged to his generation. But his insights, even taking into account his off-center perspective, were exceptionally keen, surpassing the words he used to phrase them. The truth of his *description* has as great an impact now, as when he wrote, perhaps greater.

"Which was he—the murderer or the murdered?" [10] Adams wanted to know, and was never quite sure. He had a sense of awe before the majesty, mass, and weight of life (history) as it passed before his attentive eyes. He tried to put himself at the disposal of that primal energy. He thought that attitude was "scientific." He tried to approve what seemed necessary. But to have been in complete agreement with the flood of life of his own time would have meant betrayal of his own integrity. And, despite his theory, his integrity seemed to live somewhere in himself apart from the rest of life. He was not, and could not be, a tame acquiescer. And the weight of inherited and acquired values developed in the air of another kind of time continued to bear upon him.

Therefore, he did not adjust. His misfitted personality assumed, not a heroic cast, but something limpingly, lamedly great. He found a vein of truth and worked it without sparing either himself or his world. He disliked being a lone wolf. The result: an impassioned criticism, a poetic criticism.

"He knew no tragedy so heartrending as introspection," [11] but he practiced the tragic art: "Every man with self-respect enough to become effective; if only as a machine, had had to account to himself somehow, and to invent a formula of his own for his universe, if the standard formulas failed." [12]

He decided to make as serious a study of his own life as he had of Thomas Jefferson's. The two studies were related. Jefferson had initiated, by his policies and attitudes, that American culture in which Adams was born and reared. Now Adams, in his own later years, saw that culture becoming something else again. The way in which he, who had been born in Jefferson's culture, had become unhinged in the new one might well say something important both to himself and to other unknown persons who woud be more accustomed to the new culture.

In comfort and consideration he had had a good life. In certain elemental satisfactions, it had not been so good. He had seen a chasm break open in the ground upon which he stood, and separate him from any satisfying participation in the life of the whole community. He had disapproved heartily of himself for this fact, as well as of the community. He had a notion that the individual could live well only when he made some sort of contribution to the whole, and was generously served by that whole, too. Something in himself, or in the age—perhaps both—was seriously wrong.

And he was not alone in feeling this sense of maladjustment. It affected most seriously those who should have worked best to enrich the whole: scholars, artists, statesmen. He saw his contemporaries suffer, as he suffered, from isolation and frustration.

Adams perceived that he could make something universal out of his own case. Yet he disliked self-revelation and writhed at a naked show of feeling. The peculiarity of the book would result from this contradiction: the urge to display his life, the urge to hide it.

In the interior chronology of the book, the time—the present moment—is 1905. Hay is just dead. Adams stands upon that event and casts a long look backward; first, to 1892, when he returned from the Pacific, as if from the dead; to 1885, a year he will not discuss, but reverberations of which will be felt all through the book; to 1871, when the active life of his maturity was just beginning; and beyond that, beyond the Civil War, to that almost legendary time of his childhood and adolescence.

The sequence of scenes, events, and reactions to events was to flow in a contradiction of profusion and clarity from his pen. He told his life in picture, dialogue, and reflective meditation—all intermingled and shaped for a narrative of variety and strong continuity. Adams's two strongest abilities as writer were by this time fully developed, and complemented each other; one, a supersensitive reaction to the stimuli of the senses; the other, a disciplined, strengthened reasoning ability. The book doubled its argument with the image of what the argument was about.

"The intense blue of the sea, as he saw it a mile or two away, from the Quincy hills; the cumuli in a June afternoon sky; the strong reds and greens and purples of colored prints and children's picture-books" [13]—this quotation makes vivid to the senses what his innocent boy's mind found pleasurable.

A remembered agony, his sister's death in 1870, lives again, not in statement, but in a kaleidoscope of images:

The hot Italian summer brooded outside, over the market-place and the picturesque peasants, and, in the singular color of the Tuscan atmosphere, the hills and vineyards of the Apennines seemed bursting with mid-summer blood. The sick-room itself glowed with the Italian joy of life; friends filled it; no harsh northern lights pierced the soft shadows; even the dying woman shared the sense of Italian summer, the soft, velvet air, the humor, the courage, the sensual fulness of Nature and man. She faced death, as women mostly do, bravely and even gaily, racked slowly to unconsciousness, but yielding only to violence, as a soldier sabred in battle. For many thousands of years, on these hills and plains, Nature had gone on sabring men and women with the same air of sensual pleasure.[14]

His pages were full of imagery. He found himself best able to relay an idea in a picture. American society in 1868 offered "the profile of a long, straggling caravan, stretching loosely towards the prairies, its few score of leaders far in advance and its millions of immigrants, negroes, and Indians far in the rear, somewhere in archaic time." [15]

His good life in France was a picture, too. "In the long summer days one found a sort of saturated green pleasure in the forests and gray infinity of rest in the little twelfth-century churches that lined them, as unassuming as their own mosses, and as sure of their purpose as their round arches." [16]

The emphasis upon the sensuous might seem too great. But there was a correction by wit. The book was not lax for all its livingness of color, image, taste, and even smell. The sharpness of epigram, the sting of wit, accompanied the passage of the life across the decades. The whiplash of words applied not only to persons, but to scenes, cultures, ideas.

He called Robert Louis Stevenson, whom he had seen briefly in Samoa, "a tropical bird, high-crested, long-beaked, quick-moving, with rapid utterance and screams of humor." [17] He said: "Strictly, the Southerner had no mind; he had temperament." [18] He said: "No woman had ever driven him wrong; no man had ever driven him right." [19] He said of modern woman too: "She must, like the man, marry machinery." [20] He did not spare Henry Adams. He showed pitilessly his fear of competing, his pride, his touch of snobbery. He overemphasized and overstated his "failure." He spoke of himself as "a cave-dweller in Lafayette Square" [21] and as "a pilgrim of power, without constituency to flatter." [22]

Adams's style was an intense concentration. Idea and emotion were squeezed into the narrow space of a word or a phrase. Such a concentrate could be expanded into an essay or a book. His remark about the Southerner, for instance, was a two-edged sword. The cut was not all directed outward. It was *temperament* above all, not mind, that the New Englander, including himself, lacked, and desperately needed.

And often there was a perverse tenderness in his most outrageous statement. One rule could be adopted for reading Adams: where he was most harsh, most cruel, most unkind, he was writing of something for which he cared bitterly, in his very bones.

"Images are not arguments, rarely even lead to proof, but the mind craves them, and, of late more than ever, the keenest experimenters find twenty images better than one, especially if contradictory; since the human mind has already learned to deal in contradiction." Thus, in Chapter XXXIV, Adams ushered in his discussion of a possible "law of acceleration," [23] indicating by his prelude how he intended it to be taken. The statement applies to the whole book. The life is to be taken as an image of truth, a figure of truth, not as the literal truth. Adams intended that the meaning which was in the book should be deciphered from similes, metaphors, images. He displayed his life (as much as he wished, being amazingly frank in many ways, and unobtrusively secret in others) in order to exhibit a line of direction in history.

He showed his childhood as archaic, his schooling at Harvard as merely negative, his experience in London a waste, his life as a reporter in Washington a dead end. He muted the productive years (they detracted from his thesis), but carried his reader past them silently to demonstrate his arrival in the mid-nineties at a state of complete cross-purposes with his environment. The interior chronology of the book, from the time of his return home from the Pacific, corresponds rather closely to the sequence of events he had actually undergone since that time. He follows, almost, from month to month, the wrestlings, the ups and downs, of his srtuggle to make his world conform to his idea of unity, and his acceptance of its failure to do so. This last portion of the book, following Chapter XX, *Failure*, is thought-saturated, its mood an acceleration of somberness.

It is important to remember that *The Education of Henry Adams* is a sequel to *Mont-Saint-Michel and Chartres*. The two books make one whole. It is helpful to keep the cathedral book in mind while reading the other. Its scene, twelfth and thirteenth century France, represented to Adams an approximately successful social unity. Yet in spite of his sympathy for that particular age, he might just as well have used another, and made the same point of comparison. If he had had a different experience of life, he might have used Ikhnaton's Egypt or Justinian's Byzantium as his base of comparison. He very nearly used classic Greece.

The cathedral book was a description of a unified world. *The Education* was a description of a multiple world, a world of vitality and energy, which had in it much that was congenial to Adams. But it was also an age of fatal disunity, an age which was accelerating and splintering, rushing toward dissipation, and possibly toward explosion.

His most successful comparison of the ages was in his Virgin-dynamo comparison, a comparison he had made earlier, privately, in his verses *Prayer to the Virgin of Chartres.* (It was a prayer to the dynamo, too.)

His comparison was simple and graphic, gathering into metaphor all the vital differences of the two societies. He had done justice to the Virgin in the cathedral book. His business now was to do justice to the dynamo, which, in 1900, seemed his own time's most fitting symbol. If he had lived in 1950, he would have chosen another symbol, possibly the atomic pile; the meaning would have been the same.

The image itself shows where he looked in the modern world; at 1900's most splendid concentration of energy. The dynamo's motion, form, and soft purr of sound awed him, as all power awed him, in whatever age. But Adams, as critic, refused to worship without question, although he badly wanted to do so. He could not make out the machine's meaning, or, dimly making it out, the meaning frightened him. It seemed to leave out all the values that had heretofore made human life worth living. So Adams, man and historian, with all his errors upon him, stood and confronted the dynamo, the age's symbol. All that had happened to him—his "education"—had only succeeded in strengthening his sense of values, of traditions, of purposes; had only served to prevent him from worshiping this modern show of energy. Therefore, he frustrated himself. His sense of values negated his sense of function.

This visible impressive energy, standing for all the power of modern society, seemed to be whirling, before his eyes, ever faster and faster, and whirling to no discernible purpose, human or divine. It distressed Adams to be disconnected from a valid purpose. It distressed him to find out that his own personal disconnection stood for a larger and more general disconnection between modern man and modern power. But he saw this confrontation of man and power (whose symbol was his own ironic questioning of the inscrutable dynamo) as the great question of the age. He knew that he had caught hold of something basic.

His failure was not failure. His book, which should have concluded with despair, concluded, instead, with excitement, anger and, in general, stimulation. Adams made the reader look beyond this stated impasse, and cry out, No! No!

Such was the typical doubleness of Adams's thought. There

was irony at the expense both of himself and of his age. There was, on the other hand, challenge for the sake of challenge. He allowed himself, at the end, the hazard of a guess designed to push the reader beyond him toward conclusions. His educated hazard was that the outcome (of all this splintered accelerating energy in the modern world) would be a "toss-up between anarchy and order." [24] The social mind, if it were going to come out on top, "would need to jump." [25] But, perhaps, "The new forces would educate." [26]

Chapter 24

Science, History, and Imagination

ADAMS HAD achieved his greatest reach in *Mont-Saint-Michel* and *The Education*. After this, he never attempted anything so big. The cast of his thought was still as deft and as quick as ever, but he worked in a smaller area. The raw material of his writing, his personal anguish, was perhaps less controlled. He was off, now and again, tilting madly against windmills, choking on his spleen, sinking momentarily beneath the blackness of his unhappiness.

Yet the two late major works, the historical essays *The Rule of Phase Applied to History* (1909) and *A Letter to American Teachers of History* (1910), were ingenious and controlled efforts of the imagination. They were further efforts to make history conform to science. He was still stubbornly sure that such an effort should be made. Yet the spectacle of himself, Henry Adams, as historian, was a demonstration of the individual somehow outside the flow of force, and commenting on it. And although there is even today something excitingly suggestive in the near science of the two essays, there is in them a residual value which is greater and of another kind than scientific.

The scientific inadequacies in these works are perfectly visible now: Adams's retailing of an "ether" theory, for instance, has a strangely old-fashioned ring. And his historical bias, too, in the direction of a stubborn determinism, does not so much convince the reader as delineate the writer. Yet these inadequacies are not as important as they would be if the essays were actually what they seemed: dry historical monographs, with a stiffening of scientific terminology. They are, instead, a curious kind of work, a type of tone poem of the historical mind.

The first of them, *The Rule of Phase Applied to History* (written during 1908, dated by Adams January 1, 1909, and published only after his death), displays all of Adams's virtues as well as his vices. It is shorter, madder, more jauntily impudent than the *Letter*. It is gaily doomful, announcing the end of the apparent world as a sort of joke. It was a surprisingly youthful work for a man of seventy to write.

His method, in *Phase* and in the *Letter,* was simple but subtle. He seized upon a salient, definable point of a scientific theory—a point definable in non-mathematical terms. After sketching it in boldly for a non-scientific audience, Adams then modulated, deprecatingly, from science to history. In the process, he established an emotional equivalent for his stated theory. He applied, then, not the exact scientific theory, but an emotional equivalent, to the contemplation of history. And Adams meant to do just this. He knew, consciously, what he was doing, both to science and to history.

Adams began the forty-four-page essay *The Rule of Phase Applied to History* by identifying Willard Gibbs's phase theory as his starting point. "In 1876–1878 Willard Gibbs, Professor of Mathematical Physics at Yale, published in the Transactions of the Connecticut Academy, his famous memoir on the 'Equilibrium of Heterogeneous Substances,' containing the short chapter 'On Existent Phases of Matter,' which, in the hands of the Dutch chemists, became, some ten years afterwards, a means of greatly extending the science of Static Chemistry." [1] Adams ended his first paragraph, "But his Phase was not the Phase of History." [2]

Adams proceeded, then, to make it so. He said, within two pages, "The Rule of Phase is to serve for clue." [3] The analogy was worked from a particular understanding of Gibbs's very abstruse theory, of whose ramifications Adams probably caught only a very generalized and literary version. In his own version, Phase began almost at once to take on a warm, human coloring. He invented for it an applicability to social equilibriums and human change. The idea he had got from Gibbs—"Every equilibrium, or phase, begins and ends with what is called a critical point, at which, under a given change of temperature or pressure, a mutation occurs into another phase" [4]—was soon, in his pages, trailing historical examples from medieval, Renaissance, and modern history. Urged on by his own personal harsh and perverse necessitarianism, Adams had the will to work out his applications.

Adams applied the Rule of Phase not merely to the gross movements of man organized into society, but to man's thought. Man's thought perhaps was determined, but that thought determined everything else. Adams's Phase Rule ran as follows: "Under the Rule of Phase, therefore, man's Thought, considered as a single substance passing through a series of historical phases, is assumed to follow the analogy of water, and to pass from one phase to another through a series of critical points which are determined by the three factors Attraction, Acceleration, and Volume, for each change of equilibrium." [5]

Skating over the thin ice of his assumptions, going faster and faster, and with more and more dash, as his analogy grew more and more tenuous, Adams traced one phase after another in the working out of history. It was a succession suitable to his dark mood, and his dark view, of a catastrophic future. The fact that Adams's mood has turned out to be congenial to the mid-twentieth century proves nothing. History works out its solutions over exceedingly long blocks of time. Yet the reader of today finds his admiration, if not agreement, provoked by Adams's intuition of near developments. This intuitional judgment had nothing to do with making history into a science. Even science is not so "scientific" now as it was in Adams's time, certainly not so scientific as Adams thought history should be. Yet Adams's feeling for the near future was marvelously acute and accurate.

In order to arrive "scientifically," by the Rule of Phase, at the jumping-off place of the present, Adams had to find a past to stand on. The bloc of time known as the Renaissance was his starting point. He worked both backward and forward from that "phase"of history.

Adams noted the period of the European Renaissance as a clear-cut, observable case of a radical new phase in human thought. The people of that time were even self-consciously aware of themselves as belonging to a different kind of order from that which had gone before. That black of time which had preceded the Renaissance Adams named as the Religious Phase; that time begun by the Renaissance as the Mechanical Phase. The end of the Mechanical Phase seemed to have come, he said, very recently: perhaps about the year 1900. Another Phase had already begun; one felt the rush of its acceleration around one. Each of these Phases seemed to move faster than the one before it. What was most noticeable now was speed. And his corollary was that the way man was going was an irreversible direction.

"Thus it seems possible that another generation, trained after 1900 in the ideas and terms of electro-magnetism and radiant matter, may regard that date as marking the sharpest change of direction, taken at the highest rate of speed, ever effected by the human mind [here Adams had been using the figure of the comet's path]; a change from the material to

333

the immaterial,—from the law of gravitation to the law of squares. The Phases were real: the change of direction was measured by the consternation of physicists and chemists at the discovery of radium which was quite as notorious as the consternation of the Church at the discovery of Galileo." [6]

Fixing a hypothetical, fanciful, but provocative mathematical rate (the law of squares) to marke the acceleration of phase in human thought, Adams carried his theory to the point of conscious absurdity: "Supposing the Mechanical Phase to have lasted 300 years, from 1600 to 1900, the next or Electric Phase would have a life equal to $\sqrt{300}$, or about seventeen years and a half, when—that is, in 1917—it would pass into another or Ethereal Phase, which, for half a century, science has been promising, and which would last only $\sqrt{17.5}$, or about four years, and bring Thought to the limit of its possibilities in the year 1921." [7]

How ridiculous! Yet not entirely so. The First World War, and its aftermath, coinciding approximately as they did with his figures, seem not so inappropriate as new phases. Adams's positiveness of date and preciseness of figure may seem as ridiculous as one may state, yet his *emotional* intention carries one with him, particularly to the generation that has lived beyond his fixed dates. He cannot seem entirely foolish or irrelevant to a society living out of bounds; in a manner of speaking, outside all the markable limits of any previous human experience, not knowing what to expect except the unexpectable, accepting as an everyday truth its existence in some totally new phase (to beg Adams's pardon for the word) of life upon earth.

A Letter to American Teachers of History, printed at his own expense in 1910, and distributed to professors of history throughout the United States, pursued a similar course to the *Rule of Phase.* His starting point was the second law of thermodynamics, the law of the degradation of energy. His manner in this essay was somewhat more sober, and more detailed; his purpose the same as in *Phase.*

The *Letter* reveals the fact that Adams had at least a slim hope for human control of acceleration. The fact of his printing the work, and distributing it to teachers of his own subject, history, shows that the Adams who was close to despair was still considering the possible ways of fighting the forces which were causing the despair.

It was a paradoxical position. Adams considered control to have a thin chance, but wrote the two late essays in the interest of control. He believed, or professed to believe, that human control of human affairs was impossible, and yet he was willing to call attention to that need, and to share that thought with those he believed to be among the more responsible members of society, his colleagues, the American teachers of history.

Chapter 25

Satanic Gentleman

HENRY ADAMS's fatalism was contradictory. He was, at seventy, still consistent with the younger self who had written in 1870, "The Administration—A Radical Indictment!" In 1907 he was indicting not the administration of the Republican party, but the administration of the universe. The conviction, the intensity, and the fundamental desire to ameliorate the condition of the human animal were the same. He could still, in his imagination, construct a world fit to live in, and he was still, in a manner, trying to bring that world into being.

In his daily life he was very much alone. He lacked supports both in his outward relations with the world of men and in his interior relations with himself. The outward world had, in his view, but two alternatives: a consistent capitalism or a consistent socialism. Both possibilities displeased him. Either kind of society flattened out the mind and over-organized the individual.

And within himself, believing in the creativity of worship —he did not worship.

Alone, then, he went on trying to grasp, at least in his imagination, an alien present and an alien future.

Adams lived eleven years after passing out copies of *The Education* among his friends, and pretending not to care about their reactions. These late years break sharply in half as to character. The ones from 1907 till 1912 were difficult, harsh, unreconciling years. Those after 1912 had an entirely different tone.

In all of these later years Adams sustained himself only by creating a role and living it—that of satanic gentleman. He would be kind, he would be courteous, yet he would not be mild—"The role of a green old age does not appeal to me." [1] There would always be a hint of sulphurous smoke about him. His eyes would show that he *knew:* that he had not been fooled; that he would not acquiesce to the enemy Life.

In the spring of the year in which he had distributed the copies of his *Education,* Adams in Paris wrote to Gaskell in England: "Once more I find myself pitchforked across the ocean into this inconceivable kettle of absurd humanity, and the only change is that I feel each time more bewildered than before by the fact of my own continued existence, which seems now to connect back with nothing. This world has no relation whatever with my world, and I go on living in dreams." [2]

Yet Adams lived always with at least one foot out of his dream. The following summer (1908), in Paris, he worked hard to edit for Clara Hay a selection of John Hay's diaries and letters which she was planning to print privately. Working with this material, Adams felt his dead friend's attitudes come alive again in his hands. He experienced again Hay's gift for nonsense and also his gift for somberness. He was disappointed when Mrs. Hay, printing what he had selected, cut out all full names of people mentioned by her husband and used initials only for identification. Adams annotated his own copy of the book and offered it to other friends for revision of their copies.

He continued his private studies, both those of a scientific, mathematical, and statistical nature and those of a historical and sociological nature. And although he attempted to tame his mind to like the future, he could not.

To his old and constant friend Gakell, he wrote bitterly, "The assimilation of our forms of government to the form of an industrial corporation—a railway or bank—seems to me steady though slow." [3] He reverted more and more, in his sympathies, to the eighteenth century. He was closer now to Jefferson than he had been when he wrote his *History*. And yet he saw the type of individuality of a Jefferson (or an Adams) more and more blocked by the development of society along "scientific" lines. With a ghastly sort of acquiescence he worked out the death of all individualities in a "scientific" future.

In Paris he saw something of Edith Wharton, Henry James, the Henry Whites, and the Wayne MacVeaghs. They too seemed disconnected from the present. Mrs. Wharton, like himself, was fascinated by the eighteenth century. She inhabited several Parisian salons which might well have existed two hundred years before. James was consciously out of place, his great creativity seeming to be at cross-purposes with the pace and mode of the age. Adams and he talked more and more of their mutual past when they sat down together.

One sees Adams's conscious groping for a role in some words he wrote from Washington in January, 1908, to his brother Charles: "Seventy years are a chemical solvent of the strongest kind. One thinks of life only as a thing to quit, and one is quite absorbed by the wish to quit it with an air of a gentleman. The first pose of a gentleman is, I am told, consideration of others. If you can help me to a *beau geste,* pray do so." [4]

Meantime his friend Saint-Gaudens had died. Adams collected what letters he had received from that gentle, humorous, simple man and sent them to the son, Homer Saint-Gaudens, who was preparing a memorial volume of his father's letters and recollections. Adams was very conscious now of his friends' dying.

Although he seemed to be outliving all his friends, and enduring into a new kind of world, he could not escape laughing at seeing his own views in the words of others. It was somewhat cruel of him to say, laughing, of Brooks: "As for Brooks, he has now reached the point where he sees the end of the world within touch, and calculates that it will fall on him before he can escape." [5]

Yet for all his sharpness, Adams, like other intense natures, experienced poignant pleasures. He wrote to his niece Mabel La Farge about returning to Chartres: "I was at Chartres yesterday," he wrote on the 15th of September, 1908, "to see whether I myself had changed. The day was gorgeous, and the sun too strong for the glass. I saw nothing to correct. After some ten years of reflection, it seems to me I got it pretty right." [6] He had his satisfactions.

Whenever he was in France, and the weather passable, he continued to go to see abbeys, village churches, and great cathedrals until he had collected almost all the medieval specimens. And then he went again where he had been before.

He continued to derive satisfaction from the literary daring of his friend Bay Lodge. Upon reading his narrative poem *Herakles,* he wrote a tribute which, if Bay read closely, he would see as a tribute more to his courage than to his finish. Adams genuinely liked the figure of Creon in the poem. Creon, one can judge today, is very much Henry Adams himself.

On February 3, 1909, he sent Brooks his *Rule of Phase.* This intense and disturbing work was written while Adams, to outward view, was simply playing the gentleman. And, characteristically, he spoke of it to Brooks as "my last plaything." [7]

At about the same time, anticipating Theodore Roosevelt's leaving the White House, he asked if he might step across

338

the Square to see him and say goodbye. "After this spring, Andrew Jackson and I will be the solitary monuments of the Square." [8]

It was at this time, too, that he pursued a long and intense private study, in partnership with his brother Brooks, which only indirectly, and not through Henry Adams, got into publication. The two brothers used up, for many months, their principal moral and intellectual energies on a study of their grandfather, John Quincy Adams.

Brooks had written a long essay on their grandfather which he submitted to his brother for criticism. Henry wrote Brooks several letters, including an excessively long one, which was not just a critique of Brooks's work, but a revelation of himself. These letters have been held unpublished among the Henry Adams and Brooks Adams papers in the Houghton Library at Harvard. They reveal no completely new element of Henry Adams's character, but add a dimension to anyone's conception of him.

Henry's main letter to Brooks on this subject was dated February 18, 1909. The character of his criticism should have been apparent to his brother from his opening words. Directing an intimate, agonized vent of wrath at his grandfather, he was really criticizing himself. Writing a character of J. Q. A., he wrote his own. The double criticism was lopsided, but acute:

Much water has swept down the Potomac since then, but the meanest refuse it has swept along is I,—Ego,—to wit, the grandson of J. Q. A.—who am a blind beetle employed by you to sprawl over the history of the grandparents, whom I pity with the keenest sympathy, and wish had never been born.[9]

Giving advice on form, he told Brooks that the study should be properly a history, and not a biography. "Your book is also bound to be a History, but you cannot make J. Q. A. the center of it. He was always fighting on the outskirts,—a kind of free lance, following the march of forces which he never commanded." [10] The last sentence could stand as epitaph for the writer.

Henry advised Brooks, too, on tone: "You are, in reality, writing a romance, a political novel, and you need above all else, Form." [11] He wrote revealingly, "I have no scruple, in my own theories, about handling my material in view of a climax, and for artistic purposes, the climax must always tend to tragedy." [12]

Henry Adams was also speaking of himself in a discussion of J. Q. A.'s doubleness of nature:

You say that J. Q. A.'s *double* was not, as I thought, a Puritan with the usual puritanic self-confidence, but a sentimentalist so feeble that, under a great strain (as in 1809 and 1829) he lay down and invited the world to walk over him; or ran away and abandoned his friends and supporters. I am the more inclined to admit the truth of this theory because I have always felt in myself the sentimental weakness, and have always avoided responsibility in consequence. The likelihood is great that I inherited some share of the old man's nature because I loathe it so heartily.[13]

Adams castigated both J. Q. A. and himself with his scornful use of the words *sentimentalist* and *sentimental*. He meant to denote weakness whereas the truer descriptive word, applicable to grandfather and grandson, might have been *passionate*. He derogated something of the best in J. Q. A. and himself, deriving a self-torturing pleasure in doing so.

The remote consequence of this exchange between the two brothers would be a piece of writing Henry Adams would never see. Brooks Adams did not publish a book on John Quincy Adams. But he made use of Henry's self-revelation, after Henry's death, in writing a double study of J. Q. A. and H. A. as introduction to Henry's historical-scientific essays. His title for the study was *The Degradation of the Democratic Dogma*.

Even while sparring with Brooks, Henry had more than ever a "detached feeling." Martha Cameron, the child who had played with dolls he had given her, was suddenly grown and planning to be married. Maggie Wade, friend as well as servant, died.

Hardest of all facts to accept, Bay Lodge died. Alone on Tuckernuck Island except for his father, the apparently well young man had a heart attack and died within twenty-four hours of his first illness. Adams heard the news in Europe and was afraid to write to the Lodges, and yet did write.

His hesitant words touched the Senator and his wife. They asked him to undertake a life of their son. Adams did not want to, but agreed. The aborted career of the likable younger man had got mixed in his mind with his own earlier days and symbolized too much something of his own position in another generation. A letter to Henry James said:

Bay Lodge's experience last winter completed and finished my own. When his *Herakles* appeared absolutely unnoticed by the literary press, I regarded my thesis as demonstrated. Society no longer shows the intellectual life necessary to enable it to react against a stimulus. My brother Brooks insists on the figure of paralysis. I prefer the figure of diffusion, like that of a river falling into an ocean. Either way, it drowned Bay, and has left me still floating, with vast curiosity to see what vaster absence of curiosity can bring about in my Sargasso sea.[14]

Adams's view was not just disgruntlement. Henry James had felt the chill of a similar discouragement in the silence accorded his three greatest novels. And their common experience was echoed in the careers of many others of the lonely creative men of their generation.

Like James, Adams was not only consigned to the past, but spoken of as actually, in the body, belonging to the past. A newspaper mentioned him as the "late Mr. Adams." Yet, like James, he continued to write and to look for some sort of audience.

He asked his friend the historian John Franklin Jameson, on December 5, 1909, to get him up a list of all the university professors and tutors of history, and of all the presidents of universities—to be used, presumably, in sending out copies of his *A Letter to American Teachers of History*.[15]

He wrote to Barrett Wendell on January 10, 1910, "I think I shall try once more, for the last time, to test the power of reaction among our readers." [16]

The catalogue of his friends' deaths swelled. James Lowndes died. Alexander Agassiz died. "He was the best we ever produced," [17] Adams wrote of Agassiz, "and the only one of our generation whom I would have liked to envy." [18]

In June, 1910, Adams and William James had an illuminating, good-humored argument by mail. The *Letter to American Teachers of History,* sent to James, had touched off the exchange, which was a live one, pointing up irreconcilable but fructifying differences of viewpoint. James hit Adams hard on his use of the second law of thermodynamics. (Adams had tried to show that human history, like energy, was running down, running out.) James rejoined that the law was irrelevant to history; that the intensity of the century, of the moment, was of importance, not its terminus. "Though the *ultimate* state of the universe may be its vital and psychical extinction, there is nothing in physics to interfere with the hypothesis that the penultimate state might be the millennium." [19]

William James's best criticism was of Adams's closed system of history. His falling below Adams was his failure

341

to grasp the largeness of the contemporary crisis in history. The two men saw things from near parallels that never met. And, in spite of a high tension of temperament, James was luckier than Adams. He was more flexible.

James's viewpoint was intensely individualistic. For him, each individual center of consciousness was a world. It was well and good if those centers could unite for various purposes. But James's reality was always and only in those tiny centers of life. He saw what was real in life as groping outward from those centers into the wild darkness of the universe, extending its reality only so far as each sensuous thinking center could extend its rational and imaginative grasp.

Adams, on the other hand, saw a man as only a part of a community which consisted of infinitely complex and interrelated political, social, and religious realities. In the course of centuries these relationships were built into structures called civilizations. And such structures could only be created by men living together as civil, and not altogether solitary, creatures.

James's viewpoint has only been degraded by his followers (pragmatism's course following perhaps Adams's law?), but James's outlook—as he phrased it—as he himself lived it— was honest, without sham, and serviceable for its time and place.

Adams himself was more pragmatic than he thought. He was pragmatic about the Virgin. He described the people of the thirteenth century as creating a belief, a dogma, to buttress an emotion and a way of living. James had said: "The truth of an idea is not a stagnant property inherent in it. Truth *happens* to an idea. It *becomes* true, is *made* true by events." [20]

Adams admired James for having kicked. He wrote to Gaskell on August 2, 1910: "My poor dear old friend and fellow William James alone has put up some sort of fight. Society is ready for collectivism; it has no fight left in it." [21]

But Henry's brother Brooks had still some fight in him. He had just published in the July, 1910, *Atlantic Monthly* an impolite, vigorous article, "A Problem in Civilization." In it he posed the need of the broad flexible administrative mind in government to cope with the complexities of modern life, especially as exemplified by the gigantism of the corporation. This was only one more application of the Adams hereditary conception of a national government which actually governed, which was capable, responsible, and positive, as the

Republican administrations since the Civil War had not been. Brooks Adams published within the next few years one after another of a series of vigorously worded, pointed, and pugnacious articles. In 1913 he brought out his book *The Theory of Social Revolutions.*

Brooks Adams doubled many of Henry's ideas (or Henry, his), but the younger brother was simpler and terser in expression, and more practical than Henry cared to be. Henry brooded more upon the imaginative complexities of the human situation.

Yet Henry, contemplating the human situation, and seeing it mostly as tragedy, never quite gave up the conception of a saving remnant. "My idea," he wrote to Albert S. Cook, in August, 1910, "is that the world outside—the so-called modern world—can only pervert and degrade the conceptions of the primitive instinct of art and feeling, and that our only chance is to accept the limited number of survivors—the one-in-a-thousand of born artists and poets—and to intensify the energy of feeling within that radiant centre." [22]

Adams had somehow regained a childlike love of color, and of vibrant life itself. He resembled once more the child who, decades before, in the Old House at Quincy, had stared at a yellowed, sunlit floor. He had come full circle, completing the journey he had traveled all his life since childhood.

Yet in the midst of triumphant syntheses, he was lonely. He intensified in his own person the loneliness of a whole generation, and was achingly conscious that he did so.

"My friends die daily," he cried out to Gaskell in December, 1910. "John La Farge dropped out, the other day. William James preceded him a week or two." [23] La Farge, who had shared so much with him, would never again make him see where he had been blind. And William James, with whom he had so recently argued, would never again gaily contradict him, and please him in so doing.

He brought himself at last to write to William's brother Henry:

I did not write to you about your brother William, because I fancied that letters were a burden to you. The other reason is that I felt the loss myself rather too closely to talk about it. We all began together, and our lives have made more or less a unity, which is, as far as I can see, about the only unity that American society in our time had to show. Nearly all are gone, Richardson and St. Gaudens, La Farge, Alex Agassiz, Clarence King, John Hay, and at last, your brother, William; and with each, a limb of our own lives cut off.[24]

Adams finished his elegy for a younger death too. He completed his *Life of George Cabot Lodge*. It was published in 1911 as a companion book to the two volumes of Lodge's poetry, three stones cast into an unechoing sea.

But Adams was not too old to start new hares. He interested himself in France in the hunt for prehistory in the caves of the Dordogne. He sent money to M. Henri Hubert to help support the digging, and wrote that he hoped to have word soon of prehistoric elephants and even of prehistoric babies.

The world outside changed. Its lurching acceleration carried it into a future strange to Adams. Peary reached the North Pole; Amundsen, the South. The Panama Canal was dug, and Panama was wrenched into the North American orbit. A Democratic President was installed in the House across the Square. And, most ominously, a World War broke out.

In the meantime, Henry Adams's own life almost ended.

Chapter 26

"Remember My Music"

THE GREAT *Titanic* traveling on its maiden voyage from England to the United States, was sliced open by an iceberg and sank on April 14, 1912. This happening was an unusual shock to Henry Adams. He had booked passage for the ship's return voyage to England. Characteristically, he saw in the event the whole shipwreck of modern life. He wrote to Mrs. Cameron, on April 21st, "Only in history as a fairy tale, does one like to see civilization founder, and to hear the cries of the drawning. My sole compensation is denied me. I can't even tell them:—'I told you so!' The sum and triumph of civilization, guaranteed to be safe and perfect, our greatest achievement, sinks at a touch, and drowns us, while nature jeers at us for our folly. I said it all, seven years ago, in my *Education,* and nature has beaten me by fifteen years on my mathematics." [1]

At his age, it was too strong a metaphor. His jibes against old age were suddenly no longer jokes. This particular shock and a long accumulation of fatigue undermined him. On April 24, 1912, in his Washington house, he suffered a stroke. [2]

The proud, articulate man was down. Oblivious of himself and of his disastrous world, he balanced perilously between living and dying. On June 16th his brother Charles had him moved from Washington to South Lincoln, Massachusetts, where he established him in a small house on his estate. [3] The two brothers, for a time, reverted to their childhood roles of elder and younger brother. Charles Adams and his family devoted themselves for months to pulling Uncle Henry slowly back toward life again.

Uncle Henry was not sure that he wanted to return. He was not fooled about the limited kind of life he would regain. Almost in spite of himself, he got better. His tongue was still sharp. He wrote in a dictated letter to Mrs. Chanler on July 29th, "If you see anybody who tells you that I am all right, you tell them with my compliments that they are liars." [4]

At first all his letters were dictated. When he began to write his own letters laboriously again, his handwriting more than any other trait showed the seriousness of his illness. It had been of a beautiful copperplate perfection. It was shaky and straggling now, the world formed with difficulty, but the thought, as tart and as indelibly Henry Adams as ever. He hated the weakness of the body, but accepted it better than his friends might have expected him to do. By the end of summer he had recovered enough physical stamina to receive friends, to take short walks, and to go on drives with nieces.

By October 31st he had improved enough to return to his house in Washington. He was stubbornly determined to be as independent as he could. That independence could not be complete, but he managed to work out a graceful and livable compromise. A young friend of his nieces, Miss Aileen Tone, agreed to stay at least for a while as companion—to run his house, sing to him (she was a talented musician) and, tacitly, look after him. One or another of the nieces supplemented Miss Tone, from time to time. He was in league with the younger generation, or they with him, to go on in a makeshift life of his own.

Sitting once more in one of the low, comfortable chairs before his fireplace, surrounded by the prints and porcelains of Japan and France, he faced the fact that he had had a reprieve and nothing more. Here in the fortress of his own house, he looked ahead the short way he had yet to go. Something in his situation made it possible for him to let go the weights and fetters of responsibility. Since he had received a few more years as a free gift, he felt that he owed no debt on them. Since this was so, why should he not enjoy what was left of sweet, sensuous existence and of contemplation? A sterner note of endurance still chimed below this mood of late innocent receptiveness, but the stoic attitude was not the everyday one. He spoke of this late life without bitterness as his posthumous existence. The clenching of the will toward achievement, rebuttal, rebuke was finished forever. He found a kind of rest in being at last really old, tired, and ready for death. He was as candid as ever, but less bitter. He was as direct, but less cruel. He had had great ambitions, he had had hot desires, he had yearned for a controlling touch. Now he could sit still and let that procession of competition pass him by. What real success he had had, and what real failure, belonged to his past, not to him. His life was truncated, but he found he could devise a mode of living which had its own muted satisfactions and its own quiet joys.

The spring following the year of illness saw the new life tested and proved. Against family advice, he decided to go to

France again. Two of his nieces, Looly (Louisa Chapin Hooper) and Elsy (Elizabeth Ogden Adams), as well as Aileen Tone, went along. They entertained him, and he them. They sailed on March 27, 1913, on *La France* and arrived in Paris on April 2nd.[5]

Adam's prefatory remarks set the tone of the summer: "Of course, I expect two or three more paralytic strokes before autumn, but I might as well have them in Europe as here. I am not made for Boston, Mass., and would rather go to heaven another way." [6]

After a time in Paris, the four of them set up housekeeping in the country. Their house was the Chateau de Marivault, Saint-Crépin (Oise), and his near neighbors seemed to be Richard Coeur de Lion and King John. They were more real to him than the others whom he saw occasionally. He was surrounded by a twelfth century world. He visited its remnants and ruins every day, and had more difficulty in remembering the twentieth century than in recreating the twelfth. This is what he wrote to Gaskell on August 7th:

It is a pleasant mode of wasting one's last summers. My nieces discover and sing to me my favorite twelfth-century songs, which they dig out of manuscripts where they have lain undisturbed for six hundred years, and where the professors of the conservatories transcribe them for us. My chief joy is to guard them from anyone else. I wish Walter Scott were alive to share them with me, but he is my only companion in these fields, and I fear that even he never heard a note of music for Rebecca or Ivanhoe, or knew that it existed. He would have enjoyed the fun of Coeur de Lion and Blondel quite fresh from the Crusades, as good as the west front of Chartres.[7]

Even in his dream world, Adams was thorough. He worked and made the nieces work. Although no one knew exactly how these medieval songs should be sung, he determined that the four of them, but particularly Miss Tone, should make a sporting effort to devise a way to sing them, so that they could live again and become a daily part of their daily lives. There was nothing in this of the dry researcher's pride in research alone. This was imaginative re-creation.

Of course there were lapses from the joyful mood of the summer of 1913. But that season was a touchstone. Again and again in these last years, in spite of an increasing outward fulfillment in the world of nations of all his worst fears, he could still find joy. When he could not find joy, he held on grimly to endurance.

He referred many times with increasing respect in these years to stoicism. He showed a passionate intuition of the attitude of the stoic, and a particular sympathy for its late Roman Empire adherents.

He had need of stoic support. Clara Hay died in 1914. "Poor Mrs. Hay has actually gone and died, which is to carry to joke too far." [8] Charles Adams died in 1915. So did Anna Lodge. Henry James died in 1916. Cecil Spring-Rice, recalled in a particularly abrupt and cruel way from his ambassadorship in Washington, died suddenly of heart failure and heartbreak in Canada on the way home. Adams died a little with each one. And a particular cluster of attachments, memories, associations raveled out with each dying.

A great part of his life consisted in sitting still and remembering. He turned more and more to his wife's short life. He cried out passionately to Elizabeth Cameron in a letter of September, 1912 (when he was still struggling back to life from near death), "Those years 1880-85, when she and you were so much, and so young, and so bright, were my last of life, when I loved and hated, and the world was real." [9]

A picture of Adams—a photograph—of these later years catches him in this attitude of watchful stillness. The hands folded, the head stoically high, the eyes far-gazing out of their deep sockets, the pose breathes stillness, steadiness, and a sort of in-gathered purpose. Henry Adams must have looked thus often, unconscious of others, unconscious of self, watchful only of that past that had receded so far behind him.

He discussed the stoic resource with H. O. Taylor in 1915. It was stoicism, he said, or an unendurable alternative. He had been reading his former student's book *Deliverance: the Freeing of the Spirit in the Ancient World,* and proceeded to sketch in his own version of the thought contained in it:

Marcus Aurelius would have been my type of highest human attainment. Even as it is, I would give a new cent to have a really good book on the Stoics. If there is one, lend it to me. I need badly to find one man in history to admire. I am in near peril of turning Christian, and rolling in the mud in an agony of human mortification. All these other fellows did it—why not I? [10]

He talked this Stoic strain to Charles Gaskell three years later. He had heard from his faithful English friend just three days before, on his eightieth birthday (February 16th), "of all birthdays the most momentous." [11] And in his long answering letter, written just a month before his death, he looked a long way back and a long way ahead:

The various horizons which you and I have passed through since the '40's are now as remote as though we had existed in the time of Marcus Aurelius, and, in fact, I rather think that we should have been more at home among the Stoics, than we could ever hope to be in the legislative bodies of the future. I derive a sort of stale satisfaction from having the wisdom of our philosophic President, Mr. Woodrow Wilson, read to me, but I certainly do *prefer* that of Marcus Aurelius and I am quite sure that if I were fool enough to live ten years longer, I should find myself in an atmosphere stranger still.[12]

Surprising what joy he could, buttressed by what stoic pride and resolution he could scrape together, Adams lived out his "posthumous existence"—six years of life. He knew that he had had his life, seen much, endured much, enjoyed much. He had stretched his mind to try to understand what he had experienced, and he had tried to fashion that understanding into a lasting shape in books.

He lived to see the beginning of the First World War. He did not live to see its end. Having attained his eightieth birthday a few days more than a month before, Henry Adams died peacefully, without pain or further debility, upon the morning of March 27, 1918.[13] He had gone to bed in his own house, waked up, felt a slight weakness, lain down again, gone to sleep, and died.

The life was finished. But the living quality—Henry Adams —perhaps was not. Six years before, writing to March Cameron Lindsay, mixing humor with pointed meaning, trying to communicate across the generations, he had said, "If you ever have to dance in the quadrille, you can remember my music." [14]

The form, the force, the memorability of the "music" remain.

NOTES

Notes

CHAPTER 1

STARTING PLACE

1. *The Education of Henry Adams* (New York: The Modern Library, 1931), p. 5.
2. C. F. Adams, Jr., *Autobiography* (Boston: Houghton Mifflin Co., 1920), p. 8.
3. *The Education*, p. 8.
4. C. F. Adams, Jr., *Autobiography*, pp. 7-8.
5. *Ibid.*, p. 7.
6. *Ibid.*, p. 18.
7. *The Education*, p. 22.
8. J. Q. Adams, Diary, Jan. 10, 1820, in *The Selected Writings of John and John Quincy Adams*, Adrienne Koch & William Peden, eds. (New York: Knopf, 1946), pp. 301-302.
9. *Ibid.*, Feb. 6, 1842, p. 390.
10. *Ibid.*, Dec. 39, 1844, p. 409.
11. *The Education*, p. 44.
12. *Ibid.*
13. *Ibid.*, p. 47.
14. *Letters of Charles Eliot Norton* (Boston: Houghton Mifflin Co., 1913), I, 114.

CHAPTER 2

NEGATIVE HAPPINESS

1. General background, Harvard, 1854-1858, a composite from various sources, the principal ones being the memoirs of Nicholas L. Anderson and Benjamin C. Crowninshield.
2. *The Letters and Journals of Gen. Nicholas Longworth Anderson: Harvard, Civil War, Washington, 1854-1892*, Isabel Anderson, ed. (New York: Fleming H. Revell Co., 1942), March 19, 1855.

3. *Ibid.*, Feb. 29, 1856, p. 73.
4. Benjamin W. Crowninshield, *A Private Journal, 1856-1858*, privately printed by his son, Francis B. Crowninshield (Cambridge, Mass.: Printed at the Riverside Press, 1941), Dec. 3, 1856, p. 7.
5. Anderson, *op. cit.*, Oct 15, 1857, p. 116.
6. *Ibid.*, April 15, 1857, p. 102.
7. *Ibid.*, Jan. 7, 1858, p. 121.
8. Crowninshield, *op. cit.*, Jan. 15, 1858, p. 100.
9. *Ibid.*
10. *Ibid.*, June 25, 1858, p. 147.
11. Vol. II, Sept., 1856, pp. 290-297.

CHAPTER 3

MAIDEN VOYAGE

1. C. F. Adams, Jr., *Autobiography*, p. 19.
2. W. C. Ford, ed., *Letters of Henry Adams* (2 vols., Boston: Houghton Mifflin Co., 1930), I, 7, Dec. 17-18, 1858.
3. *Ibid.*, p. 6.
4. *Ibid.*, p. 4, Nov. 3, 1858.
5. Harold Dean Cater, ed., *Henry Adams and His Friends: A Collection of Unpublished Letters* (Boston, Houghton Mifflin Co., 1947), p. 2, Dec. 22, 1858.
6. "Henry Adams Reports on a German Gymnasium," Harold D. Cater, ed., *American Historical Review*, Oct., 1947, p. 67.
7. *Ibid.*
8. *Ibid.*, p. 68.
9. *Ibid.*, p. 73.
10. *Ibid.*, p. 66.
11. *Ibid.*, p. 68.
12. *Ibid.*, p. 68-71.
13. *Ibid.*, p. 70.

14. Ford, *op. cit.*, I, 27, April 6, 1859.
15. *Ibid.*, p. 36, May 15–17, 1859.
16. *Ibid.*, p. 37.
17. *Ibid.*, pp. 37–38.
18. *Ibid.*, p. 44, July 3, 1859.
19. *Ibid.*, p. 46.
20. *Ibid.*, p. 49, Nov. 8, 1859.
21. *Ibid.*, pp. 53–54, Nov. 23, 1859.
22. *Ibid.*, p. 50, Nov. 8, 1859.
23. *Ibid.*, p. 50, Nov. 23, 1859.
24. *Ibid.*, I, p. 51.
25. *Ibid.*, I, p. 51.
26. Boston *Courier*, April 30, 1860.
27. *Ibid.*, May 9, 1860.
28. *Ibid.*, June 1, 1860.
29. *Ibid.*, June 29, 1860.
30. *Ibid.*, July 6, 1860.
31. Reprinted as "Henry Adams and Garibaldi, 1860," *American Historical Review*, Oct. 1919; July, 1920, Vol. 25, pp. 241–255.
32. *Ibid.*, p. 245.
33. *Ibid.*
34. *Ibid.*, p. 247.
35. *Ibid.*
36. *Ibid.*
37. *Ibid.*, pp. 248–249.
38. *Ibid.*, p. 246.
39. Ford., *op. cit.*, I, 56, March 10, 1860.
40. *Ibid.*, p. 621, July 1, 1860.

CHAPTER 4

THE WINTER BEFORE THE WAR

1. C. F. Adams, Jr., *Autobiography*, p. 43.
2. Ford, *Letters of Henry Adams*, Jan. 2, 1861, I, 75.
3. *Ibid.*, p. 62.
4. *Ibid.*, p. 81, Jan. 17, 1861.
5. *Ibid.*, p. 66, Dec. 18, 1860.
6. *Ibid.*, p. 88, Feb. 13, 1861.
7. *Ibid.*, pp. 88–89, Feb. 13, 1861.
8. C. F. Adams, *Autobiography*, p. 90.
9. *A Poet in Exile: Early Letters of John Hay*, Caroline Ticknor, ed. (Boston: Houghton Mifflin Co., 1910), p. 35.
10. W. R. Thayer, *The Life and Letters of John Hay* (2 vols., Boston: Houghton Mifflin Co., 1915), I, 7.
11. John Hay, "With Lincoln at the White House," *Harper's Magazine*, Vol. 130, pp. 168–170.
12. *Ibid.*, p. 167.
13. W. D. Howells, *Literary Friends and Acquaintances* (New York: Harper & Bros., 1900), p. 81.
14. *Memoirs of Gen. William T. Sherman*, 2nd ed., rev. (2 vols., New York: Appleton & Co., 1931), I, 196.
15. *Ibid.*
16. C. F. Adams, Jr., *Autobiography*, p. 107.

CHAPTER 5

OUTPOST

1. *The Journal of Benjamin Moran, 1857–1865*, Sarah A. Wallace and Frances E. Gillespie, eds. (2 vols., Chicago: University of Chicago Press, 1948–1949), II, 1125.
2. *Ibid.*, p. 973.
3. *Ibid.*, pp. 830–831.
4. New York *Times*, Aug. 12, 1861.
5. *A Cycle of Adams Letters, 1861–65*, W. C. Ford, ed. (2 vols., Boston: Houghton Mifflin Co., 1920), I, 24.
6. *Ibid.*, Sept. 7, 1861, p. 40.
7. "Henry Adams' 'Diary of a Visit to Manchester,' " Arthur W. Silver, ed., *American Historical Review*, Oct., 1945, Vol. 51, p. 83.
8. Moran, *op. cit.*, Jan. 10, 1862, II, 940.
9. *Cycle of Adams Letters*, I, 93.
10. Cater, *Henry Adams*, p. 14.
11. *Cycle of Adams Letters*, I, 119, 12. *Ibid.*, pp. 134–135. March 15, 1862.
13. *Ibid.*, p. 136.
14. *Ibid.*, p. 233.
15. Ford, *Letters of Henry Adams*, I, 95.
16. *Cycle of Adams Letters*, I, 282, May 1, 1863.
17. *Ibid.*, p. 245, Jan. 23, 1863.
18. *Ibid.*
19. *Ibid.*, pp. 245-246.
20. *Ibid.*, II, 46–47.
21. *Ibid.*, p. 47.

CHAPTER 6

A LONDON BACHELOR

1. Ford, *Letters of Henry Adams*, I, 103, Sept. 3, 1863.
2. *The Education*, p. 139.
3. *Ibid.*, p. 204.
4. *Cycle of Adams Letters*, II, 89–90.
5. *Ibid.*, p. 90.
6. *Ibid.*, p. 201, Oct. 7, 1864.
7. Ford, *op. cit.*, I, 115, March 3, 1865.
8. *Ibid.*, p. 119.
9. *Ibid.*, p. 121.
10. Thayer, *John Hay*, I, 222.
11. Mariana Van Rensselaer, *Henry Hobson Richardson and His Works* (Boston: Houghton Mifflin Co., 1888), p. 18.
12. From a facsimile of Henry Adams's Engagement Book, Preface, *The Letters of Mrs. Henry Adams, 1865–1883*, Ward Thoron, ed. (Boston: Little, Brown & Co., 1936).
13. *The Letters of Henry James*, Percy Lubbock, ed. (2 vols., New York: Charles Scribner's Sons, 1920), I, 26, to William James, March 8, 1870.
14. *Letters of Mrs. Henry Adams*, p. 3, May 26, 1865.
15. Cater, *Henry Adams*, p. 32, Aug. 23, 1866.
16. Cater, *op. cit.*, p. 29.
17. *Ibid.*, p. 30.
18. *North American Review*, Oct., 1868, Vol. CVII, p. 494.
19. *Ibid.*, p. 467.
20. *Ibid.*, p. 470.

CHAPTER 7

WASHINGTON REPORTER

1. M. A. De Wolfe Howe, *Portrait of an Independent: Moorfield Storey, 1845–1929* (Boston: Houghton Mifflin Co., 1932), p. 124.
2. *Ibid.*, p. 129.
3. Cater, *Henry Adams*, p. 48, to

J. D. Cox, Nov. 17, 1870.
4. Ford, *Letters of Henry Adams*, I, 148, Nov. 5, 1868.
5. *Edinburgh Review*, April, 1869, Vol. 129, p. 524.
6. *Ibid.*, pp. 531-532.
7. *North American Review*, April, 1869, Vol. CVIII, pp. 620–621.
8. Ford, *op. cit.*, I, 164, July 11, 1869.
9. *Ibid.*, p. 157, April 29, 1869.
10. *Ibid.*, p. 163, June 22, 1869.
11. *Ibid.*, p. 169, Oct. 5, 1869.
12. *Ibid.*, p. 172, Nov., 23, 1869.
13. *Ibid.*, p. 174, Dec. 7, 1869.
14. *Ibid.*, p. 183.
15. *Ibid.*, p. 185, April 29, 1870.
16. *Ibid.*, p. 186.
17. *Ibid.*, p. 184, March 28, 1870.
18. *Ibid.*, p. 186, April 29, 1870.
19. *Ibid.*, p. 189, July 8, 1870.

CHAPTER 8

PROFESSOR ADAMS

1. Ford, *Letters of Henry Adams*, I, 195.
2. *Ibid.*, I, 195–196, Oct. 25, 1870.
3. From Harvard catalogues in Ernest Samuels, *The Young Henry Adams* (Cambridge: Harvard University Press, 1948).
4. Brooks Adams, *The Degradation of the Democratic Dogma* (New York: The Macmillan Co., 1919), p. 6.
5. Ford, *op. cit.*, I, 203, March 27, 1871.
6. *Ibid.*, p. 193.
7. *Ibid.*, p. 200.
8. Cater, *Henry Adams*, p. 44.
9. *Ibid.*, p. 45.
10. *Ibid.*, pp. 45–46.
11. *Ibid.*, p. 48.
12. *Ibid.*, p. 50.
13. *Ibid.*, p. 51, Nov. 28, 1870.
14. *The Life and Letters of Edwin Lawrence Godkin*, Rollo Ogden, ed. (2 vols., New York: The Macmillan Co., 1907), II, 100.
15. *Ibid.*, p. 101.
16. Ford, *op. cit.*, 1, 209, May 22, 1871.

17. *Ibid.*, p. 211
18. *Ibid.*
19. *The Education*, pp. 310–311.
20. "King," *Clarence King Memoirs* (New York; published for the King Memorial Committee, New York, G. P. Putnam's Sons, 1904), p. 159.
21. *Ibid.*, p. 161.
22. John Hay, "Jim Bludso," in *Poems* (Boston: Houghton Mifflin Co., 1899), p. 10.
23. Henry Watterson, *"Marse Henry", An Autobiography* (2 vols., New York: George H. Doran & Co., 1919), p. 253.
24. *Ibid.*, p. 242.
25. Ford, *op. cit.*, I, 216.
26. *Ibid.*, p. 221.
27. *Ibid.*, p. 222.
28. *Ibid.*, pp. 223-224.
29. *Letters of Mrs. Henry Adams*, pp. 473–474.
30. Quoted by Edward W. Emerson, "Edward William Hooper," *Later Years of the Saturday Club*, M. A. De Wolfe Howe, ed. (Boston: Houghton Mifflin Co., 1927), p. 261.
31. Ford, *op. cit.*, I, 227, May 30, 1872.
32. *Ibid.*, p. 229.
33. *Ibid.*

CHAPTER 9

MR. AND MRS. ADAMS

1. *Letters of Mrs. Henry Adams*, p. 14.
2. *Ibid.*
3. *Ibid.*, p. 18, July 26, 1872.
4. *Ibid.*, p. 26, Aug. 23, 1872.
5. *Ibid.*, p. 28.
6. *Ibid.*, p. 34, Sept. 5, 1872.
7. *Ibid.*, p. 58, Nov. 17, 1872.
8. *Ibid.*, p. 29, Aug. 23, 1872.
9. *Ibid.*, p. 38, Sept. 8, 1872.
10. *Ibid.*, p. 52, Oct. 20, 1872.
11. *Ibid.*, p. 60, Dec. 15, 1872.
12. *Ibid.*, p. 65, Jan. 1, 1873.
13. *Ibid.*, p. 66, Jan. 3, 1873.
14. *Ibid.*, p. 75, Feb. 16, 1873.

15. *Ibid.*, p. 80, March 11, 1873.
16. *Ibid.*, pp. 81–85.
17. *Ibid.*, p. 89, March 22, 1873.
18. Ford, *Letters of Henry Adams*, I, 255, Aug. 12, 1873.

CHAPTER 10

MARLBOROUGH STREET

1. *Letters of Mrs. Henry Adams*, p. 54.
2. James Laurence Laughlin, "Some Recollections of Henry Adams," *Scribner's Magazine*, May, 1921, Vol. 69, p. 576.
3. In Ernest Samuels, *The Young Henry Adams*, and Lindsay Swift, "A Course of History at Harvard College in the Seventies," *Mass. Historical Society, Proceedings*, Dec., 1918, Vol. 52, pp. 69–77.
4. Henry Cabot Lodge, *Early Memories* (New York: Charles Scribner's Sons, 1913), p. 186.
5. Swift, *op. cit.*, p. 72, 75.
6. Laughlin, *op. cit.*, p. 579.
7. H. O. Taylor, *A Layman's View of History* (New York: The Macmillan Co., 1935), p. 68.
8. Lodge, *op. cit.*, p. 240.
9. "Henry Adams as Editor: A Group of Unpublished Letters Written to David A. Wells," John Eliot Alden, ed., *New England Quarterly*, March, 1938, Vol. XI, No. 1, p. 148.
10. *North American Review*, Vol. CXVII, p. 223.
11. *Ibid.*, Vol. CXVIII, p. 425.
12. *Ibid.*, p. 326.
13. *Ibid.*, "The Platform of the New Party," Vol. CXIX, p. 58.
14. "Henry Adams as Editor," *op. cit.*, p. 150, April 16, 1875.
15. *Ibid.*, p. 151, April 20, 1875.
16. Cater, *Henry Adams*, pp. 63–64, Feb. 22, 1875.
17. *North American Review*, Vol. CXX, p. 424.
18. *Ibid.*, Vol. CXXI, p. 216.

19. Cater, *op cit.*, p. 66.
20. *Ibid.*, p. 68.
21. Louis H. Sullivan, *The Autobiography of an Idea* (New York: Press of the American Institute of Architects, Inc., 1924), p. 118.
22. *Ibid.*, pp. 118–119.
23. *Democracy, An American Novel* (New York: Henry Holt & Co., Inc., 1925), p. 17.
24. Ford, *Letters of Henry Adams,* I, 292, June 30, 1876.
25. Cater, *op. cit.*, p. 67.
26. Ford, *op. cit.*, I, 273.
27. *Ibid.*, p. 278.
28. *Ibid.*, p. 279.
29. Carl Schurz, from his speech "An Address to the People," quoted in John Bigelow, *The Life of Samuel J. Tilden* (2 vols., New York: Harper, 1895), I, 298.
30. Ford, *op. cit.*, I, 288.
31. "Henry Adams as Editor," *op. cit.*, p. 151.
32. Ford, *op. cit.*, I, 267–268.
33. M. A. De Wolfe Howe, *A Venture in Remembrance* (Boston: Little, Brown & Co., 1941), p. 225.

CHAPTER 11

LAFAYETTE SQUARE

1. Ford, *Letters of Henry Adams,* I, 302, Nov. 25, 1877.
2. *Ibid.*
3. *Ibid.*
4. *Documents Relating to New England Federalism, 1800–15,* Henry Adams, ed. (Boston: Little, Brown & Co., 1905), pp. v, viii.
5. *Ibid.*, p. vi.
6. Ford, *op. cit.*, I, 304.
7. Cater, *Henry Adams,* p. 89, Feb. 20, 1879. to Mary Eliot Dwight Parkman.
8. Ford, *op. cit.*, I, 340.
9. *Ibid.*, 355, April 30, 1882.
10. Henry Holt, *Garrulities of an Octogenarian Editor* (Boston: Houghton Mifflin Co., 1923), p. 136.
11. Ford, *op. cit.*, I, 321.
12. *Letters of Mrs. Henry Adams,* p. 178.
13. *Ibid.*, p. 185.
14. *Ibid.*, p. 224.
15. Holt, *op. cit.*, p. 137.
16. *Ibid.*
17. *Ibid.*
18. *Alice James: Her Brothers—Her Journal,* Anna Robeson Burr, ed. (New York: Dodd, Mead & Co., 1934), p. 43.
19. *Letters of Mrs. Henry Adams,* p. 332.
20. *Ibid.*, p. 201 and note, pp. 204–205.
21. *Ibid.*, p. 212.
22. *Ibid.*, p. 232.
23. *Ibid.*, p. 251.
24. Ford, *op. cit.*, I, 325.
25. *Letters of Mrs. Henry Adams,* p. 234.
26. *Ibid.*, pp. 234–235.
27. *Ibid.*, p. 258.
28. *Ibid.*, p. 277.
29. *Ibid.* p. 240.
30. *Ibid.*, pp. 240–241.
31. *Ibid.*, p. 248.
32. *Ibid.*, pp. 256–257.
33. *Ibid.*, p. 259.
34. *Ibid.*, p. 263.
35. *Ibid.*, p. 264.
36. *Ibid.*, p. 267.
37. *Ibid.*, p. 271.
38. H. O. Taylor, *A Layman's View of History, op. cit.*, p. 67.
39. *Clarence King Memoirs,* p. 1220.
40. *Ibid.*, p. 129.
41. *Ibid.*, p. 404.
42. *Letters of Mrs. Henry Adams,* p. 272.
43. *Ibid.*
44. *Ibid.*, p. 273.
45. *Ibid.*, p. 280.
46. *Ibid.*, p. 294.
47. *Ibid.*
48. *Ibid.*, p. 334.
49. *Ibid.*, p. 413.
50. *Ibid.*, p. 384.
51. *Ibid.*, p. 379.
52. Ford, *op. cit.*, I, 337.
53. *Letters of Mrs. Henry Adams,* p. 405.
54. Ford, *op. cit.*, I, 334.
55. *Ibid.*, pp. 356–357.
56. Cater, *op. cit.*, p. 128.

Chapter 12

DISASTER

1. Cater, *Henry Adams,* pp. 121–122.
2. *Ibid.,* p. 126.
3. *Ibid.*
4. *Ibid.,* p. 134.
5. *Ibid.,* p. 144.
6. *Ibid.,* p. 145.
7. *Ibid.,* p. 147.
8. *Ibid.,* p. 156.
9. *Ibid.,* p. 157.
10. *The Letters and Journals of Gen. Nicholas Longworth Anderson,* p. 250.
11. *Ibid.,* p. 252.
12. Cater, *op. cit.,* p. 157.
13. *Ibid.,* pp. 157–158.
14. *Ibid.,* p.158.

Chapter 13

THE GROWTH OF A MIND

1. *Life of Albert Gallatin* (Philadelphia: J. B. Lippincott Co., 1879), p. 391.
2. *Ibid.,* pp. 18–19.
3. *Ibid.,* pp. 25–26.
4. *Ibid.,* p. 99.
5. *Ibid.,* pp. 99–100.
6. *Ibid.,* pp. 635–636.
7. *Democracy,* p. 5.
8. *Ibid.,* p. 10.
9. *Ibid.,* p. 11.
10. *Ibid.,* p. 342.
11. *Ibid.,* p. 370.
12. *Ibid.,* pp. 30–31.
13. *Ibid.,* p. 103.
14. *Ibid.,* p. 288.
15. William C. Bruce, *John Randolph of Roanoke* (2 vols., New York: G. P. Putnam's Sons, 1922), p. v.
16. *Ibid.,* pp. v–vi.
17. *Esther, a Novel,* by Francis Snow Compton, with an introduction by Robert E. Spiller (New York: Scholars' Facsimiles and Reprints, 1938), p. 1.

18. *Ibid.,* p. 6.
19. *Ibid.,* pp. 62–63.
20. *Ibid.,* pp. 19–20.
21. *Ibid.,* pp. 22–23.
22. *Ibid.,* p. 88.
23. *Ibid.,* p. 26.
24. *Ibid.,* pp. 26–27.
25. *Ibid.,* pp. 27–28.
26. *Ibid.,* pp. 28–29.
27. *Ibid.,* p. 66.
28. *Ibid.,* p. 147.
29. *Ibid.,* p. 148.
30. *Ibid.,* p. 149.
31. *Ibid.,* p. 184.
32. *Ibid.,* p. 186.
33. *Ibid.,* p. 191.
34. *Ibid.,* pp. 198, 201.
35. *Ibid.,* p. 257.
36. *Ibid.,* p. 273.
37. *Ibid.,* p. 288.
38. Ford, *Letters of Henry Adams,* I, 468, Feb. 6, 1891.

Chapter 14

A TOY LAND

1. Ford, *Letters of Henry Adams,* I, 366.
2. *Ibid.,* p. 365.
3. *Ibid.,* p. 366.
4. *Ibid.,* p. 367.
5. John La Farge, "An Artist's Letters from Japan," *Century Magazine,* Vol. 39, p. 485.
6. *Ibid.,* p. 869.
7. *Ibid.,* Vol. 40, p. 570.
8. *Ibid.,* p. 573.
9. Cater, *Henry Adams,* p. 168.
10. *Ibid.,* p. 169.
11. Ford, *op. cit.,* I, 378.

Chapter 15

THE BREAKFAST TABLE

1. *The Letters and Friendships of Sir Cecil Spring-Rice: A Record,* Stephen Gwynn, ed. (2 vols., Boston: Houghton Mifflin Co., 1929), I, 59.
2. *Ibid.*

3. Ford, *Letters of Henry Adams,* I, 383.
4. Spring-Rice, I, 67.
5. Ibid., p. 77.
6. *Ibid.,* p. 68.
7. *Ibid.*
8. *Ibid.,* p. 78.
9. *Ibid.,* p. 81.
10. *Ibid.,* p. 76.
11. Theodore Roosevelt, *Selections from the Correspondence of Theodore Roosevelt and Henry Cabot Lodge* (2 vols., New York: Charles Scribner's Sons, 1925), I, 56–57.
12. The description of the house paraphrases Mariana Van Rensselaer, *Henry Hobson Richardson and His Works,* p. 107.
13. Cater, *Henry Adams,* p. 146.
14. *Ibid.,* p. 174.
15. Ford, *op. cit.,* I, 383.
16. *Letters of John Hay and Extracts from Diary* (3 vols., Washington, D.C.: printed, but not published, 1908, c. Clara S. Hay), II, 150.
17. Details of the sculptor's life, from *The Reminiscences of Augustus Saint-Gaudens,* Homer Saint-Gaudens, ed. (2 vols., New York: The Century Co., 1913).
18. *Ibid.,* II, 281.
19. *Ibid.,* I, 362.
20. Ford, *op. cit.,* I, 384.
21. *Ibid.,* p. 385.
22. *Ibid.,* p. 389.
23. *Ibid.,* pp. 391–392.
24. *Ibid.,* p. 398.
25. *Ibid.,* p. 399.
26. *Ibid.*
27. *Ibid.,* p. 401.
28. *Ibid.,* p. 402.
29. *Letters of John Hay,* II, 193.
30. Ford, *op. cit.,* I, 404.

CHAPTER 16

TIME AND THE SLIDING ROCK

1. Ford, *Letters of Henry Adams,* I, 418–419.
2. R. L. Stevenson, *Vailima Letters*
(New York: Charles Scribner's Sons, 1918), p. 23.
3. Cater, *Henry Adams,* p. 202.
4. Ford, *op. cit.,* p. 420.
5. Cater, *op. cit.,* p. 215.
6. John La Farge, "Passages from a Diary in the Pacific," *Scribner's Magazine,* Jan.–June, 1901, Vol. 29, p. 672.
7. *Ibid.,* Vol. 30, p. 72.
8. Cater, *op. cit.,* p. 218.
9. John La Farge, *Reminiscences of the South Seas* (Garden City, N.Y.: Doubleday, Page & Co., 1912), pp. 209–210.
10. *Ibid.,* p. 212.
11. Cater, *op cit.,* p. 211.
12. *Ibid.*
13. Cater, *op. cit.,* p. 225.
14. *Ibid.*
15. *Ibid.,* p. 224.
16. *Ibid.,* p. 232.
17. Ford, *op. cit.,* I, 477.
18. Cater, *op. cit.,* p. 220.
19. Ford, *op. cit.,* I, 470.
20. *Ibid.,* p. 472.
21. *Ibid.,* p. 480.
22. *Ibid.,* p. 489.
23. *Tahiti: Memoirs of Arii Taimai e Marama of Eimeo,* R. E. Spiller, ed. (New York: Scholars' Facsimiles and Reprints, 1947), p. 1.
24. *Ibid.,* p. 53.
25. Ford, *op. cit.,* I, 457.
26. *Letters of John Hay,* I, 216.
27. Cater, *op. cit.,* p. 243.
28. Ford, *op. cit.,* II, 29.
29. Housatonic (pseud.), *A Case of Hereditary Bias, Henry Adams as a Historian, Some Strictures on the 'History of the U.S.'* (New York: 1891, reprinted from the New York *Tribune,* Sept. 10, Dec. 15, 1890), p. 17.
30. *Ibid.,* Preface, iii.
31. *Ibid.,* p. 22.
32. Ford, *op. cit.,* I, 526.
33. "Buddha and Brahma, a Poem," *Yale Review,* Oct., 1915, Vol. 5, pp. 82–89.
34. Ford, *op. cit.,* I, 530.
35. Cater, *op. cit.,* p. 261.
36. *Ibid.,* p. 263.
37. *Ibid.,* p. 255.
38. Ford, *op. cit.,* I, 533–534.
39. *Ibid.,* p. 535.

Chapter 17

THE HISTORY

1. *History of the United States of America during the Administrations of Thomas Jefferson and James Madison* (9 vols., New York: Charles Scribner's Sons, 1921), II, 130.
2. *Ibid.*, p. 89.
3. *Ibid.*, V, 231–232.
4. *Ibid.*, VI, 210–211.
5. *Ibid.*, VIII, 153.
6. *Ibid.*, I, 58.
7. *Ibid.*, VII, 97.
8. *Ibid.*, IV, 27.
9. *Ibid.*, p. 289.
10. *Ibid.*, VII, 318–319.
11. *Ibid.*, I, 196.
12. *Ibid.*, III, 327.
13. *Ibid.*, VIII, 146.
14. *Ibid.*, p. 147.
15. *Ibid.*, III, 188.
16. *Ibid.*, p. 218.
17. *Ibid.*
18. *Ibid.*, VIII, 342.
19. *Ibid.*, V, 419–420.
20. *Ibid.*, I, 291.
21. *Ibid.*, III, 366–367.
22. *Ibid.*, I, 5.
23. *Ibid.*, p. 8.
24. *Ibid.*, p. 16.
25. *Ibid.*, p. 159.
26. *Ibid.*, p. 138.
27. *Ibid.*, p. 266.
28. *Ibid.*, IV, 289.
29. *Ibid.*, I, 170.
30. *Ibid.*
31. *Ibid.*, pp. 172–173.
32. *Ibid.*, p. 160.
33. *Ibid.*, III, 207.
34. *Ibid.*, p. 212.
35. *Ibid.*, IX, 216.
36. *Ibid.*, IV, 134–135.
37. *Ibid.*, IX, 173.
38. *Ibid.*, p. 194.
39. *Ibid.*, p. 222.
40. *Ibid.*, pp. 241-242.
41. *Ibid.*, p. 221.

Chapter 18

DOS BOCAS

1. Henry Aadms, "King," *Clarence King Memoirs*, p. 173.
2. *Ibid.*, p. 177.
3. Ford, *Letters of Henry Adams,* II, 41.
4. *Ibid.*, p. 42.
5. *Ibid.*, p. 8.
6. Cater, *Henry Adams*, p. 287.
7. *The Degradation of the Democratic Dogma*, p. 94.
8. Cater, *op. cit.*, p. 289.
9. *Ibid.*, p. 291.
10. *Ibid.*, pp. 293–294.
11. *Ibid.*, p. 294.
12. *Ibid.*, p. 298.
13. *Ibid.*, p. 304.
14. *Ibid.*, p. 305.
15. *Ibid.*, p. 305n.
16. *Ibid.*, p. 306.
17. *Ibid.*, p. 321.
18. Ford, *op. cit.*, II, 55.
19. *Letters of John Hay*, II, 304.
20. *Ibid.*, p. 333.
21. Ford, *op. cit.*, II, 46.
22. *Ibid.*, p. 67.
23. Henry Adams, "The Tendency of History, *The Degradation of the Democratic Dogma*, pp. 127–131.

Chapter 19

THE CATHEDRALS

1. *Selections from the Correspondence of Theodore Roosevelt and Henry Cabot Lodge*, I, 185.
2. Cater, *Henry Adams*, p. 342.
3. *Ibid.*, p. 341.
4. Ford, *Letters of Henry Adams,* II, 72–73.
5. Cater, *op. cit.*, p. 343.
6. *Ibid.*

7. *Letters to a Niece and Prayer to the Virgin of Chartres, with a Niece's Memoirs,* by Mabel La Farge (Boston: Houghton Mifflin Co., 1920), pp. 79–80.
8. *Ibid.,* p. 80.
9. *Ibid.,* p. 81.
10. Ford, *op. cit.,* II, 79.
11. *Ibid.,* p. 81.
12. Cater, *op. cit.,* p. 348.
13. Ford, *op. cit.,* II, 81.
14. *Ibid.,* p. 89.

CHAPTER 20

TWELFTH CENTURY—AND TWENTIETH

1. Cater, *Henry Adams,* p. 356.
2. "Buddha and Brahma," *Yale Review,* Oct. 1915, Vol. 5, pp. 82–89.
3. Cater, *op. cit.,* p. 351.
4. *Ibid.*
5. *Ibid.,* p. 352.
6. Ford, *Letters of Henry Adams,* II, 96.
7. Cater, *op. cit.,* p. 361.
8. Ford, *op. cit.,* II, 113.
9. *Ibid.,* p. 114.
10. *Letters of John Hay,* III, 69.
11. Thayer, *John Hay,* II, 148.
12. Cater, *op. cit.,* p. 387.
13. *Letters of John Hay,* III, 78–79.
14. Cater, *op. cit.,* p. 392.
15. *Ibid.,* p. 395.
16. Thayer, *op. cit.,* II, 159.
17. Cater, *op. cit.,* p. 402.
18. Ford, *op. cit.,* II, 127.
19. Cater, *op. cit.,* p. 408.
20. Ford, *op. cit.,* II, 149.
21. Cater, *op. cit.,* p. 437.
22. *Ibid.*
23. Cater, *op. cit.,* pp. 469–470.
24. *Ibid.,* p. 471.
25. *Ibid.,* pp. 475–476.
26. Ford, *op. cit.,* II, 249.
27. *Letters of John Hay,* III, 173.
28. Ford, *op. cit.,* II, p. 240.
29. Spring-Rice, *Letters,* I, 297–298.
30. Ford, *op. cit.,* II, 259.
31. *Ibid.,* p. 301.
32. Cater, *op. cit.,* p. 502.

33. *Ibid.*
34. Ford, *op. cit.,* II, 317.
35. *Letters to a Niece and Prayer to the Virgin of Chartres,* p. 125.
36. *Ibid.,* p. 126.
37. *Ibid.,* pp. 127–128.
38. *Ibid.,* pp. 128–129.
39. *Ibid.,* p. 130.
40. *Ibid.*
41. *Ibid.,* p. 131.
42. *Ibid.,* pp. 133-134.
43. Ford, *op. cit.,* II, 326.
44. *Ibid.,* p. 327.
45. *Ibid.,* p. 326.
46. *Ibid.*
47. *Ibid.,* pp. 327–328.
48. Cater, *op. cit.,* p. 514.
49. *Ibid.,* pp. 515–516.
50. *Clarence King Memoirs,* p. 409.
51. Ford, *op. cit.* II, 365.
52. *Ibid.,* p. 366.
53. *Ibid.,* p. 367.
54. *Ibid.,* p. 387n.
55. Cater, *op. cit.,* p. 526.
56. *Ibid.,* p. 529.
57. *Ibid.,* p. 532.
58. Ford, *op. cit.,* II, p. 392n.

CHAPTER 21

MONT-SAINT-MICHEL AND CHARTRES

1. *Mont-Saint-Michel and Chartres* (Boston: Houghton Mifflin Co., 1933), p. 329.
2. *Ibid.,* p. 1.
3. *Ibid.,* p. 45.
4. *Ibid.,* p. 60.
5. *Ibid.,* p. 86.
6. *Ibid.,* p. 103.
7. *Ibid.,* p. 177.
8. *Ibid.,* p. 195.
9. *Ibid.,* p. 32.
10. *Ibid.,* p. 88.
11. *Ibid.,* p. 45.
12. *Ibid.,* p. 180.
13. *Ibid.,* pp. 273–274.
14. *Ibid.,* p. 196.
15. *Ibid.,* p. 4.
16. *Ibid.,* p. 6.
17. *Ibid.,* p. 127.

18. *Ibid.*
19. *Ibid.*, p. 143.
20. *Ibid.*, p. 195.
21. *Ibid.*, p. 248.

CHAPTER 22

MULTIPLICITY

1. Cater, *Henry Adams*, p. 584.
2. *Ibid.*, p. 533.
3. *Ibid.*
4. *Ibid.*, p. 534.
5. *Ibid.*, p. 538.
6. Ford, *Letters of Henry Adams,* II, 400.
7. *Ibid.*, pp. 404, 405.
8. *Ibid.*, pp. 407–409.
9. *Letters of John Hay*, III, 276.
10. Ford, *op. cit.*, II, 437.
11. *Letters of John Hay*, III, 307.
12. Quoted in *The Reminiscences of Augustus Saint-Gaudens*, II, 338.
13. Ford, *op. cit.*, II, 443.
14. *Ibid.*, p. 444.
15. Cater, *op. cit.*, p. 558.
16. *The Reminiscences of Augustus Saint-Gaudens*, II, 343–344.
17. *The Letters of Theodore Roosevelt*, III–IV, p. 1082.
18. *Ibid.*, p. 1102.
19. Spring-Rice, *Letters*, I, 450.
20. Cater, *op. cit.*, p. 556.
21. Henry James, *The American Scene* (New York: Charles Scribner's Sons, 1946), p. 341.
22. *Ibid.*, p. 339.
23. *Ibid.*, p. 340.
24. Margaret T. Chanler, *Roman Spring* (Boston: Little, Brown & Co., 1934), p. 301.
25. Ford, *op. cit.*, II, 446.
26. *Letters of John Hay and Extracts from Diary*, III, 350.
27. Ford, *op. cit.*, II, 455.
28. Cater, *op. cit.*, p. 581.
29. *The Reminiscences of Carl Schurz*, III, 455.
30. Ford, *op. cit.*, II, 469.
31. From an unpublished autograph letter held in the Houghton Library, Harvard University: quoted through the kind permission of Mrs. Robert Homans.

CHAPTER 23

THE EDUCATION OF
HENRY ADAMS

1. *The Education*, p. ix.
2. *Ibid.*, p. x.
3. *Ibid.*, p. vii.
4. *Ibid.*, pp. vii–viii.
5. *Ibid.*, p. 314.
6. *Ibid.*, p. 379.
7. *Ibid.*, p. 474.
8. *Ibid.*, p. 486.
9. *Ibid.*, p. 487.
10. *Ibid.*, p. 472.
11. *Ibid.*, p. 432.
12. *Ibid.*, p. 472.
13. *Ibid.*, p. 8.
14. *Ibid.*, p. 288.
15. *Ibid.*, p. 237.
16. *Ibid.*, p. 369.
17. *Ibid.*, p. 139.
18. *Ibid.*, p. 57.
19. *Ibid.*, p. 85.
20. *Ibid.*, p. 447.
21. *Ibid.*, p. 438.
22. *Ibid.*, p. 467.
23. *Ibid.*, p. 489.
24. *Ibid.*, p. 495.
25. *Ibid.*, p. 498.
26. *Ibid.*, p. 497.

CHAPTER 24

SCIENCE, HISTORY, AND
IMAGINATION

1. *The Degradation of the Democratic Dogma*, p. 267.
2. *Ibid.*
3. *Ibid.*, p. 269.
4. *Ibid.*, p. 277.
5. *Ibid.*, p. 281.
6. *Ibid.*, p. 307.
7. *Ibid.*, p. 308.

CHAPTER 25

SATANIC GENTLEMAN

1. Cater, *Henry Adams*, p. 724.
2. Ford, *Letters of Henry Adams,* II, 476.

3. *Ibid.*, p. 482.
4. *Ibid.*, pp. 486–487.
5. *Ibid.*, p. 493.
6. *Letters to a Niece*, p. 121.
7. Ford, *op. cit.*, II, 515n.
8. Cater, *op. cit.*, p. 635.
9. From autograph letter held in the Houghton Library, Harvard University; quoted through kind permission of Mrs. Robert Homans.
10. *Ibid.*
11. *Ibid.*
12. *Ibid.*
13. *Ibid.*
14. Ford, *op. cit.*, II, 522.
15. Cater, *op. cit.*, p. 671.
16. Ibid., *p.* 674.
17. From a letter dated April 2, 1910, to Henry L. Higginson, quoted as a tribute—"Envoi"—to Alexander Agassiz in *Letters and Recollections of Alexander Agassiz*, G. R. Agassiz, ed. (Boston: Houghton Mifflin Co., 1913).
18. *Ibid.*
19. *The Letters of William James*, ed. by his son, Henry James (2 vols., Boston: Atlantic Monthly Press, 1920), II, 346.
20. *The Philoophy of William James*, Horace M. Kallen, ed. (New York:

The Modern Library, n.d.), p. 165.
21. Ford, *op. cit.*, II, 546.
22. *Ibid.*, p. 547.
23. *Ibid.*, p. 555.
24. *Ibid.*, p. 558.

CHAPTER 26

"REMEMBER MY MUSIC"

1. Ford, *Letters of Henry Adams*, II, 495.
2. *Ibid.*, p. 597.
3. *Ibid.*
4. Cater, *Henry Adams*, p. 738.
5. Ford, *op. cit.*, II, 611.
6. Cater, *op. cit.*, p. 752.
7. Ford, *op. cit.*, II, 615.
8. Cater, *op. cit.*, p. 764.
9. Ford, *op. cit.*, II, 603.
10. Cater, *op. cit.*, p. 769.
11. Ford, *op. cit.*, II, 648.
12. *Ibid.*
13. Cater, *op. cit.*, pp. 778–779, and Ford, *op. cit.*, II, 650–651.
14. Ford, *op. cit.*, II, 601.

SELECTIVE BIBLIOGRAPHY

SELECTIVE BIBLIOGRAPHY

I. Primary Material

A. Manuscripts

Brooks Adams letters. Library of Harvard University, The Houghton Library, Cambridge, Mass.

Henry Adams letters and miscellaneous papers. Library of Harvard University, The Houghton Library, Cambridge, Mass.

B. Published Writings of Henry Adams

1. IN PERIODICALS

In *Harvard Magazine*, 1855–57 (undergraduate college writings)
"Holden Chapel." Vol. 1 (May, 1855), pp. 210–15.
"Resolutions on the Death of William Gibbons." Vol. 2, (Dec., 1855), p. 46.
"Resolutions on the Death of Hazen Dorr." Vol. 2 (June, 1856), p. 223.
"My Old Room." Vol. 2 (Sept., 1856), pp. 290–97.
Review of "Conquest of Kansas," by William Phillips. Vol. 2 (Nov., 1856), pp. 395–96.
"Paul Fane." Vol. 2 (Nov., 1856), pp. 440–41.
"Retrospect." Vol. 3 (March, 1857), pp. 61–68.
"College Politics." Vol. 3 (May, 1857), pp. 141–48.
"Reading in College." Vol. 3 (Oct., 1857), pp. 307–17.
North American Review, 1873–1877, inclusive.
"American Finance." *Edinburgh Review*, Vol. 129 (April, 1869), pp. 504–33.
"British Finance in 1816." *North American Review*, Vol. CIV (April, 1867), pp. 354–86.
"Buddha and Brahma, a Poem." *Yale Review*, Vol. 5 (Oct., 1915), pp. 82–89, prefaced by a letter to John Hay.
"Civil Service Reform." *North American Review*, Vol. CIX Oct., 1869, pp. 443–75.

"Count Edward de Crillon." *American Historical Review,* Vol. I (Oct., 1895), pp. 51–69.

"The Great Secession Winter of 1860–61." Massachusetts Historical Society, *Proceedings,* Vol. 43 (1910), pp. 656–89.

"Harvard College; 1786–87." *North American Review* (Jan., 1872).

"Henry Adams' 'Diary of a Visit to Manchester' "; ed. Arthur W. Silver. *American Historical Review,* Vol. 51 (Oct., 1945), pp. 74–89. Appeared in the Boston *Courier,* Dec. 16, 1861, as "A Visit to Manchester, Extracts from a Private Diary."

"Henry Adams as Editor; a Group of Unpublished Letters written to David A. Wells," ed. John Eliot Alden. *New England Quarterly,* Vol. XI, No. 1 (March, 1938), pp. 146–52.

"Henry Adams and Garibaldi, 1860." *American Historical Review,* Vol. 25 (Oct., 1919–July, 1920), pp. 241–55. Reprinted from the Boston *Courier,* July 10 and 13, 1860.

"Henry Adams Reports on a German Gymnasium." Ed. Harold Dean Cater, *American Historical Review,* Vol. 53 (Oct., 1947), pp. 59–66, 67–74.

"The 'Independents' in the Canvass." *North American Review,* Vol. 123 (Oct., 1876), pp. 426–67.

"The Legal-Tender Act." With Francis A. Walker. *North American Review* (April, 1870).

Letters. *Boston Advertiser.* 1860: Dec. 10, 13, 20, 27; 1861: Jan. 1, 11, 15, 16, 17, 22, 24, 26; Feb. 2, 6, 8, 11.

Letters. *Boston Courier.* 1860: April 30; May 9; June 1, 29; July 6, 10, 13.

Letters. *New York Times.* 1861: June 3, 7, 17, 21; July 4, 15, 19; Aug. 2, 12, 15; Sept. 14, 26; Oct. 20, 28; Nov. 2, 7, 18.

Review of "Mountaineering in the Sierra Nevada," by Clarence King. *North American Review,* Vol. 114 (April, 1872), pp. 445–48.

Review of "The Principles of Geology," by Sir Charles Lyell. *North American Review,* Vol. 107 (Oct., 1868), pp. 465–501.

"The Session." *North American Review,* Vol. CVIII (April, 1869), pp. 610–40.

"The Session." *North American Review* (July, 1870).

"Seventeen Letters." Ed. Frederick Bliss Luquiens. *Yale Review,* Vol. 10 (Oct.–July, 1920–21), pp. 111–30.

"Six Letters." Ed. Albert Stanburrough Cook. *Yale Review,* Vol. 10 (Oct.–July, 1920–21), pp. 131–140.

2. BOOKS

The Administration—a Radical Indictment! A reprint of "The Session," *North American Review* (July, 1870), published as a campaign document by The National Democratic Executive Resident Committee. Washington, 1872.

The Degradation of the Democratic Dogma, with an introduction by Brooks Adams. (Includes: The Tendency of History, 1894, The Rule of Phase Applied to History, 1909; and A Letter to American Teachers of History, 1910.) New York, The Macmillan Co., 1919.

Democracy; An American Novel. New York, Henry Holt and Co., Inc., 1925.

Documents Relating to New England Federalism, 1800-15, ed. Henry Adams. Boston, Little, Brown & Co., 1905.

The Education of Henry Adams; An Autobiography. New York, The Modern Library, 1931.

Essays in Anglo-Saxon Law, ed. Henry Adams and including his "The Anglo-Saxon Courts of Law." Boston, Little, Brown & Co., 1905.

Esther, a Novel, by Francis Snow Compton, with an introduction by Robert E. Speller. New York, Scholars' Facsimiles and Reprints, 1938.

Henry Adams and His Friends; A Collection of His Unpublished Letters, compiled with a biographical introduction by Harold Dean Cater. Boston, Houghton Mifflin Co., 1947.

Historical Essays. New York, Charles Scribner's Sons, 1891.

History of the United States of America during the Administrations of Thomas Jefferson and James Madison. 9 vols. New York, Charles Scribner's Sons, 1921.

John Randolph. Boston, Houghton Mifflin Co., 1910.

A Letter to (American) Teachers of History, privately printed at the press of J. H. Furst & Co., Baltimore, 1910.

Letters of Henry Adams, ed. Worthington Chauncey Ford. 2 vols. (1858–91 and 1891–1918). Boston, Houghton Mifflin Co., 1930.

Letters in *Life and Letters of Henry Lee Higginson,* ed. Bliss Perry. Boston, The Atlantic Monthly Press, 1921.

Letters to a Niece and Prayer to the Virgin of Chartres, with a niece's memoirs by Mabel La Farge. Boston, Houghton Mifflin Co., 1920.

Life of Albert Gallatin. Philadelphia, J. B. Lippincott Co., 1879.

"The Life of George Cabot Lodge," in Edmund Wilson, ed., *The Shock of Recognition* (Garden City, L.I., Doubleday and Co., Inc., 1943), pp. 747–852.

Mont-Saint-Michel and Chartres. Boston, Houghton Mifflin Co., 1933.

The Selected Letters of Henry Adams, ed. Newton Arvin. The Great Letters Series. Farrar, Straus and Young, Inc., 1951.

Tahiti; Memoirs of Arii Taimai e Marama of Eimeo . . . . ed. R. E Speller New York, Scholars' Facsimiles and Reprints, 1947.

The Writings of Albert Gallatin, ed. Henry Adams, 3 vols. Philadelphia, J. B. Lippincott Co., 1879.

C. Autobiographies, Diaries, Letters, Memoirs, and Other Source Material

1. IN PERIODICALS

Bishop, Joseph Bucklin, "A Friendship with John Hay." *Century Magazine,* Vol. 71 (March, 1906), pp. 773–80.

Bronson, Edgar Beecher, "A Man of East and West, Clarence King, geologist, savant, wit." *Century Magazine,* Vol. 80, pp. 376–82.

Chapman, A. S., "The Boyhood of John Hay." *Century Magazine,* Vol. 78 (July, 1909), pp. 44–54.

Frewen, Morton, "The Autobiography of Henry Adams." *Nineteenth Century* (Vol. 85), pp. 981–89 (May, 1919).

Hay, John, eight excerpts from unpublished diaries, William R.Thayer, comp. and ed. *Harper's Magazine* (Vols. 130, 131) (1915).

"With Lincoln at the White House." 130: 165–75.

"Washington After the War." 130: 327–36.

"John Hay in Politics and Diplomacy." 130: 735–42.

"John Hay as Secretary of State." 130: 836–42.

"John Hay's Statesmanship." 131: 25–35.

"John Hay and the Panama Republic." 131: 165–75.

"Close of John Hay's Career." 131: 362–68.

"John Hay's Years with Roosevelt." 131: 577–85.

Howells, William Dean, "John Hay in Literature." *North American Review,* Vol. 181 (Sept., 1905), pp. 343–51.

La Farge, John, "An Artist's Letters from Japan." *Century Magazine,* Vol. 39, pp. 712–20, 859–69; Vol. 40, pp. 195–203, 566–74, 866–77; Vol. 42, pp. 442–48; Vol. 46, pp. 419–29, 571–76.

———, "The Man Behind the Painting." *Golden Book Magazine,* Vol. 6 (1927), pp. 691–98.

———, "Passages from a Diary in the Pacific." *Scribner's Magazine,* Vol. 29, pp. 537–46, 670–84; Vol. 30, pp. 69–83.

———, "Said by John La Farge" *Golden Book Magazine,* Vol 7, pp. 647-50.

La Farge, Mabel, "Henry Adams, A Niece's Memories." *Yale Review,* Vol. 9 (Jan., 1920), pp. 271–85.

Laughlin, James Laurence, "Some Recollections of Henry Adams." *Scribner's Magazine,* Vol. 69 (May, 1921), pp. 576–85.

Mitchell, Stewart, "Henry Adams and Some of His Students."
Mass. Historical Society, *Proceedings*, Vol. 66 (1936–41),
pp. 294–310.

Morison, Samuel Eliot, "A Letter and a Few Reminiscences
of Henry Adams." *New England Quarterly* (March, 1954),
pp. 95–97.

Swift, Lindsay, "A Course of History at Harvard College in
the Seventies." Mass. Historical Soc., *Proceedings*, Vol. 52
(Dec., 1918), pp. 69–77.

Wharton, Edith, "George Cabot Lodge." *Scribner's Magazine*,
Vol. 47 (Feb., 1910), pp. 236–39.

2. BOOKS

Adams, Abigail, *Letters of Mrs. Adams*, 4th ed., rev. and enl.
Boston, Wilkins, Carter & Co., 1848.

Adams, Brooks, *Charles Francis Adams: An American Statesman.* Boston, 1912, from *Proceedings*, Mass. Hist. Soc., for
Dec., 1911.

Adams, Charles Francis, Charles Francis, Jr, Henry, and John
Quincy, Jr., *A Cycle of Adams Letters*, 1861-65, W. C.
Ford, ed. 2 vols. Boston, Houghton Mifflin Co., 1920.

Adams, Charles Francis, Jr., *Charles Francis Adams.* Boston,
Houghton Mifflin Co., 1900.

————, *Autobiography.* Boston, Houghton Mifflin Co., 1920.

Adams, John, *Correspondence of John Adams and Thomas
Jefferson*, 1812–26, selected with comment, by Paul Wilstach.
Indianapolis, The Bobbs-Merrill Co., 1925.

————, and Adams, John Quincy, *The Selected Writings of
John and John Quincy Adams,* selected and ed. with an
introd. by Adrienne Koch and William Peden. New York,
Alfred A. Knopf, Inc., 1946.

Adams, John Quincy, *The Diary of John Quincy Adams,*
1794–1845, Allan Nevins, ed. New York, Longmans, Green
& Co., 1928.

Adams, Marian Hooper, *The Letters of Mrs. Henry Adams,*
1865–1883, Ward Thoron, ed. Boston, Little, Brown & Co.,
1936.

Agassiz, Alexander, *Letters and Recollections of Alexander
Agassiz,* G. R. Agassiz, ed. Boston, Houghton Mifflin Co.,
1913.

Anderson, Larz, *Letters and Journals of a Diplomat,* Isabel
Anderson, ed. New York, Fleming H. Revell Co., 1940.

Anderson, Nicholas Longworth, *The Letters and Journals of
Gen. Nicholas Longworth Anderson; Harvard, Civil War,
Washington,* 1854–92, Isabel Anderson, ed. New York,
Fleming H. Revell Co., 1942.

Barnes, Thurlow Weed, *Memoir of Thurlow Weed;* Vol. II of

Life of Thurlow Weed, Including His Autobiography and a Memoir. 2 vols. Boston, Houghton Mifflin Co., 1884.

Becker, Carl, *Everyman His Own Historian.* New York, F. S. Crofts, 1935.

Berenson, Bernard, *Rumor and Reflection.* New York, Simon & Schuster, Inc., 1952.

————, *Sketch for a Self-Portrait.* New York, Pantheon Books, Inc., 1949.

Bigelow, Poultney, *Seventy Summers.* New York, Longmans, Green & Co., 1925.

Bishop, Joseph B., *Notes and Anecdotes of Many Years.* Charles Scribner's Sons, N.Y., 1925.

Blaine, Mrs. James G., *Letters of Mrs. James G. Blaine,* Harriet S. Blaine Beale, ed. 2 vols. New York, Duffield & Co., 1908.

Chanler, Margaret T., *Autumn in the Valley.* Boston, Little, Brown & Co., 1936.

————, *Roman Spring.* Boston, Little, Brown & Co., 1934.

Chapman, John Jay, *John Jay Chapman and His Letters,* M. A. De Wolfe Howe, ed. Boston, Houghton Mifflin Co., 1937.

————, *Memories and Milestones.* New York, Moffat, Yard & Co., 1915.

Cooper, Lane, *Louis Agassiz as a Teacher.* Ithaca, N.Y., Comstock Publishing Co., Inc., 1945.

Cortissoz, Royal, *John La Farge, a Memoir and a Study.* Boston, Houghton Mifflin Co., 1911.

Crowninshield, Benjamin W., *A Private Journal,* 1856–58, privately printed by his son, Francis B. Crowninshield. Cambridge, Mass., Riverside Press, 1941.

Eliot, Charles W., *Harvard Memories. Cambridge, Mass.,* Harvard University Press, 1923.

Godkin, Edwin Lawrence, *The Life and Letters of Edwin Lawrence Godkin,* Rollo Ogden, ed. 2 vols. New York, The Macmillan Co., 1907.

Harlow, Virginia, *Thomas Sergeant Perry, a Biography; and Letters to Perry from William, Henry, and Garth Wilkinson James.* Durham, N.C., Duke University Press, 1950.

Hay, John, *Letters of John Hay and Extracts from Diary.* 3 vols. Washington, D.C., 1908. Printed, but not published (*c.* 1908, Clara S. Hay).

————, *A Poet in Exile; Early Letters of John Hay,* Caroline Ticknor, ed. Boston, Houghton Mifflin Co., 1910.

Higginson, Henry Lee, *Life and Letters of Henry Lee Higginson,* by Bliss Perry. Boston, Atlantic Monthly Press, 1921.

Higginson, Thomas Wentworth, *Letters and Journals of Thomas Wentworth Higginson,* 1846–1906, Mary Thacher Higginson, ed. Boston, Houghton Mifflin Co., 1921.

Hoar, George Frisbie, *Autobiography of Seventy Years.* 2 vols. New York, Charles Scribner's Sons, 1903.

Holmes, Oliver Wendell, *Holmes-Pollock Letters; The Correspondence of Mr. Justice Holmes and Sir Frederick Pollock, 1874–1932,* Mark De Wolfe Howe, ed. 2 vols. in 1. Cambridge, Mass., Harvard University Press, 1946.

——, *The Mind and Faith of Justice Holmes,* Max Lerner, ed. Boston, Little, Brown & Co., 1943.

——, *Touched with Fire: Civil War Letters and Diary of Oliver W. Holmes, Jr.,* 1861-64, Mark De Wolfe Howe, ed. Cambridge, Mass., Harvard University Press, 1946.

Holt, Henry. *Garrulities of an Octogenarian Editor.* Boston, Houghton Mifflin Co., 1923.

Howells, William D., *Life in Letters of William Dean Howells,* Mildred Howells, ed. New York, Doubleday & Co. 2 vols. 1928.

——, *Literary Friends and Acquaintances; A Personal Retrospect of American Authorship.* New York, Harper and Brothers, 1900.

James, Alice, *Alice James; Her Brothers—Her Journal,* Anna Robeson Burr, ed. New York, Dodd, Mead and Co., Inc., 1934.

James, Henry, *The Letters of Henry James.* 2 vols. New York, Charles Scribner's Sons, 1920.

——, *Notes of a Son and Brother.* New York, Charles Scribner's Sons, 1914.

——, "Pandora," in *The American Novels and Stories of Henry James,* F. O. Matthiessen, ed. New York, Alfred A. Knopf, Inc., 1947.

——, "The Point of View," in *The American Novels and Stories of Henry James,* F. O. Matthiessen, ed. New York, Alfred A. Knopf, Inc., 1947.

James, William, *The Letters of William James,* ed. by his son Henry James. 2 vols. Boston, Atlantic Monthly Press, 1920.

King, Clarence, *Clarence King Memoirs; The Helmet of Mambrino.* New York, Published for the King Memorial Committee, New York, G. P. Putnam's Sons, 1904.

La Farge, John, *Reminiscences of the South Seas.* Garden City, N.Y., Doubleday, Page & Co., 1912.

La Farge, John (1880–   ), *The Manner Is Ordinary.* New York, Harcourt, Brace & Co., Inc., 1954.

Lodge, Henry Cabot, *Early Memories.* New York, Charles Scribner's Sons, 1913.

Long, John Davis, *America of Yesterday, As Reflected in the Journal of John Davis Long,* Lawrence Shaw Mayo, ed. Boston, The Atlantic Monthly Press, 1923.

Lowell, James Russell, *Letters of James Russell Lowell,* Charles Eliot Norton, ed. 2 vols. New York, Harper and Bros., 1893.

Matthiessen, Francis O., *The James Family; A Group Biography, Together with Selections from the Writings of Henry James, Sr., William, Henry, and Alice James.* New York, Alfred A. Knopf, Inc., 1947.

Moran, Benjamin, *The Journal of Benjamin Moran, 1857–65.* 2 vols. Sarah A. Wallace and Frances E. Gillespie, eds. Chicago, University of Chicago Press, 1948–49.

Norton, Charles Eliot, *Letters of Charles Eliot Norton, with Biographical Comment by His Daughter,* Sara Norton and M. A. De Wolfe Howe, eds. 2 vols. Boston, Houghton Mifflin Co., 1913.

Perry, Thomas Sergeant, *Selections from the Letters of Thomas Sergeant Perry,* ed., with an introd. by E. A. Robinson. New York, The Macmillan Co., 1929.

Pumpelly, Raphael, *My Reminiscenses.* 2 vols. New York, Henry Holt & Co., Inc., 1918.

Roosevelt, Theodore, *Letters from Theodore Roosevelt to Anna Roosevelt Cowles, 1870–1918.* New York, Charles Scribner's Sons, 1924.

———, *The Letters of Theodore Roosevelt;* selected and ed. by Elting E. Morison, John M. Blum, and John J. Buckley, 8 vols. Cambridge, Mass., Harvard University Press, 1951–54.

———, and Lodge, H. C., *Selections from the Correspondence of Theodore Roosevelt and Henry Cabot Lodge.* 2 vols. New York, Charles Scribner's Sons, 1925.

Saint-Gaudens, Augustus, *The Reminiscences of Augustus Saint-Gaudens,* ed. and amplified by Homer Saint-Gaudens. 2 vols. New York, The Century Co., 1913.

Schurz, Carl, *Intimate Letters of Carl Schurz, 1841–1869,* tr. and ed. by Joseph Schafer. Madison, Wis., State Historical Society of Wisconsin, 1928.

———, *The Reminiscences of Carl Schurz.* 3 vols. New York, The McClure Co., 1907–08.

Sherman, Thomas H., *Twenty Years with James G. Blaine; Reminiscences by His Private Secretary.* New York, The Grafton Press, 1928.

Sherman, William T., *Memoirs of Gen. William T. Sherman,* 2nd ed., rev. and corrected. 2 vols. New York, Appleton & Co., 1931.

Spring-Rice, Sir Cecil Arthur, *The Letters and Friendships of Sir Cecil Spring-Rice: A Record,* Stephen Gwynn, ed. 2 vols. Boston, Houghton Mifflin Co., 1929.

Stevenson, Robert Louis, *News Letters,* Sidney Colvin, ed. New York, Charles Scribner's Sons, 1918.

———, *Vailima Letters: Correspondence Addressed to Sidney Colvin, November* 1890-*October* 1894. New York, Charles Scribner's Sons, 1918.

Sullivan, Louis H., *The Autobiography of an Idea.* New York, Press of the American Institute of Architects, Inc., 1924.

Taylor, Henry O., *A Layman's View of History*. New York, The Macmillan Co., 1935.

Watterson, Henry, *"Marse Henry," an Autobiography*. 2 vols. New York, George H. Doran & Co., 1919.

Wharton, Edith, *A Backward Glance*. New York, Appleton-Century-Crofts, Inc., 1934.

Wright, Chauncey, *Letters of Chauncey Wright, with Some Account of His Life* by James Bradley Thayer, privately printed. Cambridge, Mass., Press of John Wilson & Son, 1878.

Wright, Frank Lloyd, *An Autobiography*. New York, Longmans, Green & Co., 1932.

————, *Genius and the Mobocracy*. New York, Duell, Sloan & Pearce, 1949.

II. Secondary Material

A. Material Bearing Directly on Henry Adams and His Contemporaries

1. IN PERIODICALS

Adams, James T., "Henry Adams and the New Physics." *Yale Review*, Vol. 19 (1929–30), pp. 283–302.

Baym, Max I., "Henry Adams and Henry Vignaud." *New England Quarterly*, Vol. 17, no. 3 (Sept., 1944), pp. 442–49.

————, "Henry Adams and the Critics." *American Scholar*, Vol. 15 (Winter, 1945–46), pp. 79–89.

Blackmur, R. P., "Henry Adams, Three Late Moments." *Kenyon Review*, Vol. 2 (1940), pp. 7–29.

Dickason, David H., "Henry Adams and Clarence King, the Record of a Friendship." *New England Quarterly*, Vol. 17, no. 2 (June, 1944), pp. 229–54.

Elsey, George McKee, "The First Education of Henry Adams." *New England Quarterly*, Vol. 14, no. 4 (Dec., 1941), pp. 679–84.

Focillon, Henri, "John La Farge." *American Magazine of Art*, Vol. 29 (Jan.–Dec., 1936), pp. 311–19.

Ford, Worthington C., "Brooks Adams," Boston, 1927, from the *Proceedings*, Mass. Historical Soc. (May, 1927).

Glicksberg, Charles I., "Henry Adams and the Civil War." *Americana*, Vol. 33, no. 4 (Oct., 1939), pp. 443–62.

———, "Henry Adams and the Repudiation of Science." Vol. 64 (Jan.–June, 1947), pp. 63–71. *Science Monthly.*

Hale, Edward, "H. H. Richardson and His Work." *New England Magazine,* no. 11 (Dec., 1894), pp. 513–32.

Howe, M. A. De Wolfe, "The Elusive Henry Adams." *Saturday Review,* Vol. 7 (Oct. 18, 1930), pp. 237–39.

Kronenberger, Louis, "The Education of Henry Adams—the 6th of the 'Books That Changed Our Minds.' " *New Republic,* Vol. 98 (March 15, 1939), pp. 155–58.

Macfarland, Henry, "Secretary John Hay." *Review of Reviews,* Vol. 21 (Jan., 1900), pp. 33–41.

Madison, Charles A., "Brooks Adams, Caustic Cassandra." *American Scholar,* Vol. 9 (1940), pp. 214–27.

Mencken, H. L., "An American Bonaparte." *American Mercury.* (Dec., 1924), pp. 444–46.

Moore, John Bassett, "Mr. Hay's Work in Diplomacy." *Review of Reviews,* Vol. 32 (Aug., 1905), pp. 171–76.

Pavolini, P. C., "George Cabot Lodge." *Living Age,* Vol. 277 (May 17, 1913), pp. 400–08.

Review of Henry Adam's *History,* Vols. I and II. *Atlantic Monthly,* Vol. 65 (Feb., 1890), pp. 274–80. Unsigned.

Rhodes, James F., "Edwin Lawrence Godkin." *Atlantic Monthly,* Vol. 101 (Jan.–June, 1908), pp. 320–33.

Simonds, Katharine, "The Tragedy of Mrs. Henry Adams." *New England Quarterly,* Vol. 9 (Dec., 1936), pp. 564–82.

Smith, Garnet, "Henry Adams." *Contemporary Review,* Vol. 141 (May, 1932), pp. 617–24.

Stone, James, "Henry Adams' Philosophy of History." *New England Quarterly,* Vol. 14 (1941), pp. 538–48.

Wagner, Vern, "The Lotus of Henry Adams." *New England Quarterly* (March, 1954), pp. 75–94.

Wellman, Walter, "John Hay: An American Gentleman." *Review of Reviews,* Vol. 32 (Aug., 1905), pp. 166–71.

2. BOOKS

Aaron, Daniel, *Men of Good Hope: A Story of American Progressives.* New York, Oxford University Press, 1951.

Adams, James T., *The Adams Family.* Boston, Little, Brown & Co., 1931.

———. *Henry Adams.* New York, Albert & Charles Boni, Inc., 1933.

Allen, Alexander V. G., *Phillips Brooks, 1835–93.* New York, E. P. Dutton & Co., Inc., 1907.

Anderson, Thornton, *Brooks Adams, Constructive Conservative.* Ithaca, New York, Cornell University Press, 1951.

Barrows, Chester L., *William M. Evarts, Lawyer, Diplomat, Statesman.* Chapel Hill, N.Y., University of North Carolina Press, 1941.

Baym, Max I., *The French Education of Henry Adams.* New York, Columbia University Press, 1951.

Beach, Joseph Warren, "The Education of Henry Adams," in *The Outlook for American Prose* (Chicago, The University of Chicago Press, 1927), pp. 202–14.

Bigelow, John, *The Life of Samuel J. Tilden.* New York, Harper & Bros., 1895. 2 vols.

Blackmur, R. P., *The Expense of Greatness.* New York, Arrow Editions, 1940.

Bradford, Gamaliel, *American Portraits,* 1875–1900. Boston, Houghton Mifflin Co., 1928.

Brooks, Van Wyck, *New England Indian Summer,* 1865–1915. New York, E. P. Dutton & Co., Inc., 1940.

Bruce, William C., *John Randolph of Roanoke.* 2 vols. New York, G. P. Putnam's Sons, 1922.

Cargill, Oscar, "The Medievalism of Henry Adams," in *Essays and Studies in Honor of Carleton Brown* (New York, New York University Press, 1940), pp. 296–329.

Carter, Morris, *Isabella Stewart Gardner and Fenway Court;* 2nd ed., rev. Boston, Houghton Mifflin Co., 1940.

Commager, Henry S., "Henry Adams," in *The Marcus W. Jernegan Essays in American Historiography* (Chicago, The University of Chicago Press, 1937), pp. 191–206.

Cortissoz, Royal, *The Life of Whitelaw Reid.* 2 vols. New York, Charles Scribner's Sons, 1921.

Darrah, William C., *Powell of the Colorado.* Princeton, N.J., Princeton University Press, 1951.

Eckenrode, H. J., *Rutherford B. Hayes: Statesman of Reunion.* New York, Dodd, Mead & Co., 1930.

Farnham, Charles H., *A Life of Francis Parkman.* Boston, Little, Brown & Co., 1905.

Fitch, James M., *American Building: The Forces That Shape It.* Boston, Houghton Mifflin Co., 1948.

Fuess, Claude M., *Carl Schurz, Reformer.* New York, Dodd, Mead & Co., 1932.

New York, The Macmillan Co., 1942.

Bigelow, William Sturgis, *Buddhism and Immortality.* Boston, Houghton Mifflin Co., 1908.

Bory, Jean, *French Cathedrals;* photographs by Martin Hurlimann; descriptive notes by Peter Meyer. Boston, Houghton Mifflin Co., 1951.

Bryce, James, *The American Commonwealth.* Vol. 2. New York, The Macmillan Co., 1914.

Buckle, Henry Thomas, *History of Civilization in England.* Vols. I, II. From the 2nd London ed. New York, D. Appleton & Co., 1897.

Cady, Edwin Harrison, *The Gentleman in America.* Syracuse, N.Y., Syracuse University Press, 1949.

Cargill, Oscar, *Intellectual America.* New York, The Macmillan Co., 1941.

Chapman, John Jay, *Causes and Consequences.* New York, Charles Scribner's Sons, 1899.

——, *Practical Agitation;* rev. ed. New York, Moffat, Yard & Co., 1909.

Commager, Henry Steele, *The American Mind.* New Haven, Conn., Yale University Press, 1950.

Dorfman, Joseph, *Economic Mind in American Civilization;* Vol. 3, 1865–1918. New York, The Viking Press, 1946–49.

Dunne, Peter Finley, *Mr. Dooley at His Best,* ed. Elmer Ellis. New York, Charles Scribner's Sons, 1938.

Evans, Joan, *Art in Mediaeval France,* 987–1498. New York, Oxford University Press, 1948.

George, Henry, *Significant Paragraphs from Progress and Poverty.* New York, Robert Schalkenbach Foundation, 1931.

Gilson, Etienne, *The Philosophy of Thomas Aquinas.* Cambridge, W. Heffer & Sons, Ltd., 1929.

——, *The Spirit of Mediaeval Philosophy.* New York, Charles Scribner's Sons, 1936.

Hawkins, D. J. B., *A Sketch of Mediaeval Philosophy.* New York, Sheed & Ward, 1947.

Hay, John, *The Breadwinners.* New York, Harper & Brothers, 1911.

——, *Castilian Days.* Boston, Houghton Mifflin Co., 1899.

——, *Poems.* Boston, Houghton Mifflin Co., 1899.

Hedges, James B., *Henry Villard and the Railways of the Northwest.* New Haven, Conn., Yale University Press, 1930.

Hewitt, Abram S., *Selected Writings,* ed. Allan Nevins. New York, Columbia University Press, 1937.

Hicks, Granville, *The Great Tradition.* New York, The Macmillan Co., 1935.

Hughes, H. Stuart, *An Essay for Our Time.* New York, Alfred A. Knopf, Inc., 1950.

James, Henry, *The American Scene.* New York, Charles Scribner's Sons, 1946.

——, and Stevenson, R. L. S., *Henry James and Robert Louis Stevenson: A Record of Friendship and Criticism;* ed. Janet Adam Smith. London, Rupert Hart-Davis, 1948.

James, William, *Essays in Radical Empiricism.* New York, Longmans, Green & Co., 1912.

——, *The Philosophy of William James;* selected with an introd. by Horace M. Kallen. N.Y., The Modern Library, n.d.

——, *Pragmatism; Together with Four Related Essays Selected from The Meaning of Truth.* New York, Longmans, Green & Co., 1943.

Josephson, Matthew, *The Politicoes,* 1865–96. New York, Harcourt, Brace & Co., Inc., 1938.

————, *The President-Makers*. New York, Harcourt, Brace & Co., Inc., 1940.

————, *The Robber Barons: The Great American Capitalists, 1861–1901*. New York, Harcourt, Brace & Co., Inc., 1934.

Kazin, Alfred, *On Native Grounds*. New York, Reynal & Hitchcock, 1942.

King, Clarence, *Mountaineering in the Sierra Nevada*. Boston, James R. Osgood & Co., 1872.

————, *Statistics of the Production of the Precious Metals of the United States*. Washington, D.C., Government Printing Office, 1881.

————, *Systematic Geology;* Vol. I of Report of the Geographical Explorations of the Fortieth Parallel. Washington, D.C., Government Printing Office, 1878.

La Farge, John, *Considerations on Painting: Lectures Given in the Year 1893 at the Metropolitan Museum of New York*. New York, The Macmillan Co., 1895.

————, *An Exhibition of the Works of John La Farge*, March 23 to April 26, 1936. New York, The Metropolitan Museum, 1936.

————, *The Higher Life in Art*. New York, The McClure Co., 1908.

————, *One Hundred Masterpieces of Painting*. London, Hodder & Stoughton, 1912.

Larkin, Oliver W., *Art and Life in America*. New York, Rinehart & Co., Inc., 1949, pp. 167–367, Chaps. 14–28.

Lipsky, George A., *John Quincy Adams: His Theory and Ideas*. New York, Thomas Y. Crowell, 1950.

Lodge, George C., *Poems and Dramas of George Cabot Lodge*. 2 vols. Boston, Houghton Mifflin Co., 1911.

Lyell, Charles, *Antiquity of Man*. London, J. M. Dent & Sons, Ltd., 1927.

Male, Emile, *Religious Art from the XIIth to the XVIIIth Century*. New York, Pantheon Books, Inc., 1949.

Malone, Dumas, *Jefferson, the Virginian*. Boston, Little, Brown & Co., 1948.

Maritain, Jacques, *Art and Scholasticism*. New York, Charles Scribner's Sons, 1930.

Mill, John Stuart, *The Positive Philosophy of Auguste Comte*. New York, Henry Holt & Co., Inc., 1873.

Morison, Samuel Eliot, *Three Centuries of Harvard: 1636–1936*. Cambridge, Mass., Harvard University Press, 1937.

Morse, John T., Jr., *Thomas Jefferson*. Boston, Houghton Mifflin Co., 1911.

Mumford, Lewis, *The Golden Day: A Study in American Experience and Culture*. New York, Boni & Liveright, 1926.

Nevins, Allan, *The Gateway to History*. Boston, Mass., D. C. Heath & Co., 1938.

Peirce, Charles S., *Chance, Love and Logic;* ed. with an introd.

379

by Morris R. Cohen. New York, Peter Smith, Publisher, 1949.

Perry, Ralph Barton, *Characteristically American*. New York, Alfred A. Knopf, Inc., 1949.

Pevsner, Nikolaus, *An Outline of European Architecture*. Har-
Planck, Max, *Scientific Autobiography and Other Papers*. New
mondsworth, Middlesex, Penguin Books, 1951.
York, The Philosophical Library, 1949.

——, *Where Is Science Going?* New York, W. W. Norton & Co., Inc., 1932.

Rhodes, James Ford, *The History of the United States from the Compromise of 1850 to the Final Restoration of Home Rule at the South in 1877*. New York, The Macmillan Co., 1904–06 (Vols. 5, 6, 7, only).

——, *History of the United States from Hayes to McKinley: 1877–1896*. New York, The Macmillan Co., 1919.

Russell, Bertrand, *Power: A New Social Analysis*. New York, W. W. Norton & Co., Inc., 1938.

——, *The Scientific Outlook*. New York, W W. Norton & Co., Inc., 1931.

(Ruysbroek, Willem van) *The Journey of William of Rubruck to the Eastern Parts of the World*, 1253–55; ed. by William W. Rockhill. London, Printed for the Hakluyt Society, 1900.

Saint-Simon, Henri, *Selected Writings*, ed. by F. M. H. Markham New York, The Macmillan Co., 1952.

Santayana, George, *Atoms of Thought*, sel. and ed. by Ira D. Cardiff. New York, The Philosophical Library, 1950.

——, *Character and Opinion in the United States; with Reminiscences of William James and Josiah Royce and Academic Life in America*. New York, Charles Scribner's Sons, 1924.

——, *The Genteel Tradition at Bay*. New York, Charles Scribner's Sons, 1931.

——, *The Last Puritan: A Memoir in the Form of a Novel*. New York, Charles Scribner's Sons, 1936.

Schlesinger, Arthur, Jr., *The Vital Center*. Boston, Houghton Mifflin Co., 1949.

Schlesinger, Arthur M., *Paths to the Present*. New York, The Macmillan Co., 1949.

Stickney, Trumbull, *The Poems of Trumbull Stickney*, ed. George Cabot Lodge, William Vaugham Moody, and John Ellerton Lodge. Boston, Houghton Mifflin Co., 1905.

Sullivan, J. W. N., *The Bases of Modern Science*. New York, Doubleday, Doran & Co., Inc., 1929.

Taylor, Henry Osborn, *The Mediaeval Mind*. 2 vols. London, Macmillan & Co., Ltd., 1911.

Tocqueville, Alexis de, *Democracy in America*. 2 vols. New York, Alfred A. Knopf, Inc., 1948.

Townsend, Harvey Gates, *Philosophical Ideas in the United States*. New York, American Book Co., 1934.

Turner, Frederick Jackson, *The Frontier in American History*. New York, Henry Holt & Co., Inc., 1926.

Twain, Mark, and Warner, Charles Dudley, *The Gilded Age*. 2 vols. New York, Harper and Brothers, 1915.

Wilson, Edmund, *The Triple Thinkers*. New York, Oxford University Press, 1948.

Gabriel, Ralph H., on Henry Adams in *The Course of American Democratic Thought*. New York, The Ronald Press Co., 1940.

Garraty, John A., *Henry Cabot Lodge: A Biography*. New York, Alfred A. Knopf, Inc., 1953.

Giedion, Siegfried, *Space, Time and Architecture*. Cambridge, Mass., Harvard University Press, 1944.

Greenslet, Ferris, *The Lowells and Their Seven Worlds*. Boston, Houghton Mifflin Co., 1946.

Hitchcock, Henry Russell, Jr., *The Architecture of H. H. Richardson and His Times*. New York, The Museum of Modern Art, 1936.

Housatonic (pseud.), *A Case of Hereditary Bias, Henry Adams as a Historian, Some Strictures on the 'History of the U.S.'* New York, 1891. (Reprinted from the New York *Tribune*, Sept. 10 and Dec. 15, 1890.)

Howe, M. A. De Wolfe, *Barrett Wendell and His Letters*. Boston, The Atlantic Monthly Press, 1924.

———, ed., *Later Years of the Saturday Club*. Boston, Houghton Mifflin Co., 1927.

———, *Portrait of an Independent: Moorfield Storey*, 1845–1929. Boston, Houghton Mifflin Co., 1932.

———, *A Venture in Remembrance*. Boston, Little, Brown & Co., 1941.

Hume, Robert A., *Runaway Star: An Appreciation of Henry Adams*. Ithaca, N.Y., Cornell University Press, 1951.

James, Henry, *William Wetmore Story and His Friends*. 2 vols. Boston, Houghton Mifflin Co., 1903.

James, Henry, Jr., *Charles W. Eliot*. 2 vols. Boston, Houghton Mifflin Co., 1930.

Jordy, William H., *Henry Adams: Scientific Historian*. New Haven, Conn., Yale University Press, 1952.

Josephson, Matthew, *Portrait of the Artist as American*. New York, Harcourt, Brace and Co., Inc., 1930.

Kimball, Fiske, *American Architecture*. Indianapolis, Ind., The Bobbs-Merrill Co., 1928.

Kraus, Michael, *The Writing of American History*. Norman, Okla., University of Oklahoma Press, 1954.

Mather, Frank Jewett, Jr., *Estimates in Art*. New York, Charles Scribner's Sons, 1916.

Matthiessen, Francis Otto, *Henry James: The Major Phase.* New York, Oxford University Press, 1944.

More, Paul Elmer, *Commemorative Tribute to Henry Adams* (prepared for the American Academy of Arts and Letters, 1920). New York, The Academy, 1922.

———, *A New England Group, and Others.* (Shelburne Essays; 11th series.) Boston, Houghton Mifflin Co., 1921.

Morrison, Hugh, *Louis Sullivan: Prophet of Modern Architecture.* New York, The Museum of Modern Art and W. W. Norton & Co., Inc., 1935.

Mumford, Lewis, *The South in Architecture* (the Dancy Lectures, Alabama College, 1941). New York, Harcourt, Brace & Co., Inc., 1941.

Nevins, Allan, *Abram S. Hewitt; with Some Account of Peter Cooper.* New York, Harper & Brothers, 1935.

———, *Grover Cleveland.* New York, Dodd, Mead & Co., Inc., 1932.

Parrington, Vernon Louis, on Henry Adams, in *Main Currents in American Thought.* 3 vols. in 1 (New York, Harcourt, Brace & Co., Inc., 1927), pp. 212–36.

Paton, Lucy Allen, *Elizabeth Cary Agassiz: A Biography.* Boston, Houghton Mifflin Co., 1919.

Pringle, Henry F., *Theodore Roosevelt: A Biography.* New York, Harcourt, Brace & Co., Inc., 1931.

Rukeyser, Muriel, *Willard Gibbs.* New York, Doubleday & Co., 1942.

Saint-Gaudens, Homer, *The American Artist and His Times.* New York, Dodd, Mead & Co., Inc., 1941.

Samuels, Ernest, *The Young Henry Adams.* Cambridge, Mass., Harvard University Press, 1948.

Schriftgiesser, Karl, *The Gentleman from Massachusetts: Henry Cabot Lodge.* Boston, Little, Brown & Co., 1944.

Schuyler, Montgomery, *American Architecture.* New York, Harper & Bros., 1892.

Spiller, Robert E., "Henry Adams," in *Literary History of the United States* (New York, The Macmillan Co., 1948), Vol. II, Chap. 65.

Stegner, Wallace, *Beyond the 100th Meridian: John Wesley Powell and the Second Opening of the West.* Boston, Houghton Mifflin Co., 1954.

Storey, Moorfield, *Charles Sumner.* Boston, Houghton Mifflin Co., 1900.

Taylor, Bayard, "Diversions of the Echo Club," in Wilson, Edmund, ed., *The Shock of Recognition* (New York, Doubleday & Co., 1943).

Thayer, William Roscoe, *The Life and Letters of John Hay.* 2 vols. Boston, Houghton Mifflin Co., 1915.

Thwing, Charles F., *Guides, Philosophers and Friends.* New York, The Macmillan Co., 1927.

Van Rensselaer, Mariana, *Henry Hobson Richardson and His Works*. Boston, Houghton Mifflin & Co., 1888.

Whipple, Thomas K., *Spokesmen: Modern Writers and American Life*. New York, Appleton-Century-Crofts, Inc., 1928.

Wister, Owen, *Roosevelt: The Story of a Friendship, 1880–1919*. New York, The Macmillan Co., 1930.

B. Material Furnishing a Background in Ideas, Events, Attitudes

1. IN PERIODICALS

Adams, Brooks, "The American Democratic Ideal." *Yale Review*, Vol. 5 (Jan., 1916), pp. 225–33.

——, "The Collapse of Capitalistic Government." *Atlantic Monthly*, Vol. III (April, 1913), pp. 433–43.

——, "A Problem in Civilization." *Atlantic Monthly*, Vol. 106 (July, 1910), pp. 26–32.

Adams, Charles Francis, Jr., "The Government and the Railroad Corporations." *North American Review*, Vol. CXII (Jan., 1871), pp. 31–61.

——, "The Granger Movement." *North American Review*, Vol. CXX (April, 1875), pp. 394–424.

——, "Railroad Inflation." *North American Review*, Vol. CVIII (Jan., 1869), pp. 130–64.

——, "Railway Problems in 1869." *North American Review*, Vol. CX (Jan., 1870), pp. 116–50.

——, "What Mr. Cleveland Stands For." *Forum*, Vol. 13 (March–Aug., 1892), pp. 662–70.

King, Clarence, "Active Glaciers Within the United States." *Atlantic Monthly*, Vol. 27 (March, 1871), pp. 371–77.

——, "The Age of Earth." In Smithsonian Institution *Annual Report*, 1893. Washington, D.C., 1895, Government Printing Office, pp. 335–52.

——, "Artium Magister." *North American Review*, Vol. CXLVII (Oct., 1888), pp. 369–84.

——, "The Biographies of Lincoln." *Century Magazine*, Vol. X (Oct., 1886), pp. 861–69.

——, "The Education of the Future." *Forum*, Vol. 13 (March–Aug., 1892), pp. 20–33.

——, "Fire and Sword in Cuba." *Forum*, Vol. 22 (Sept., 1896), pp. 30–52.

——, "Shall Cuba Be Free?" *Forum*, Vol. 20 (Sept., 1895), pp. 50–65.

(King, Clarence), unsigned, "Style and the Monument." *North American Review*, Vol. CXLI (Nov., 1885), pp. 443–53.

Lodge, George Cabot, "Faith." *Scribner's Magazine*, Vol. 34 (Oct., 1903), p. 480.

——, "The Passage." *Atlantic Monthly*, Vol. 89 (Jan., 1902), pp. 74–75.

——, "Outward." *Scribner's Magazine*, Vol. 30 (Aug., 1901), p. 177.

——, "Vista." *Century Magazine*, Vol. 65 (Dec., 1902), p. 186.

2. BOOKS

Adams, Brooks, *America's Economic Supremacy*. New York, Harper and Brothers, 1947.

——, *The Emancipation of Massachusetts*. Boston, Houghton Mifflin Co., 1886.

——, *The Gold Standard*. Washington, D.C., Robert Beall, Bookseller, 1896.

——, *The Law of Civilization and Decay*. New York, Alfred A. Knopf, Inc., 1943.

——, *The Theory of Social Revolutions*. New York, The Macmillan Co., 1913.

Adams, Charles F., Jr., *A Chapter of Erie*. Boston, Fields, Osgood & Co., 1869.

——, *Railroads: Their Origin and Problems*. New York, G. P. Putnam's Sons, 1878.

Amory, Cleveland, *The Proper Bostonians*. New York, E. P. Dutton & Co., Inc., 1948.

Bagehot, Walter, *Physics and Politics*. New York, Alfred A. Knopf, Inc., 1948.

Beard, Charles and Mary, *A Basic History of the United States*. New York, The New Home Library, 1944.

——, *The Rise of American Civilization*. 2 vols. in 1. Rev.

Winters, Yvor, *In Defense of Reason*. New York, The Swallow Press and William Morrow & Co., 1947.

Woodward, C. Vann, *Origins of the New South, 1877–1913*. Baton Rouge, Louisiana State University Press, 1951.

——, *Reunion and Reaction: The Compromise of 1877 and the End of Reconstruction*. Boston, Little, Brown & Co., 1951.

Wright, Chauncey, *Philosophical Discussions; with a Biographical Sketch of the Author* by Charles E. Norton. New York, Henry Holt & Co., Inc., 1877.

Young, John Z., *Doubt and Certainty in Science*. At the Clarendon Press, Oxford, 1951.

C. Reference Works Consulted

British Authors of the Nineteenth Century, ed. by Stanley J. Kunitz and Howard Haycraft. New York, The H. W. Wilson Co., 1936.

Dictionary of American Biography, under the auspices of the American Council of Learned Societies; ed. Allen Johnson and others. New York, Charles Scribner's Sons, 1928–44.

Dictionary of National Biography, ed. Leslie Stephen and Sidney Lee. New York, The Macmillan Co., 1908.

Encyclopaedia Britannica, 1952 ed. Chicago, University of Chicago.

Modern Eloquence, ed. Thomas B. Reed. New York, Modern Eloquence Corporation, 1923.

INDEX

Index

Abu-Simbel (ruin), Egypt, 113

Acapulco, Mexico, 256

Adams, Abigail (Mrs. John), 140

Adams, Abigail Brooks: character, 19; as parent, 34, 42; distressed by Secession, 50; and husband's appointment to English Court, 56; semi-invalid, 192; accident, 196; dying, 198; mentioned, 17, 22, 72, 197

Adams, Arthur: death at five, 20

Adams, Brooks: defensive of father, 19; as child, 19-20; beliefs and disbeliefs, 23; at Seward's party, 50; in London, 56; with Henry to Scotland, 1863, 66; as law student, 94; on corruption in the U.S., 96; *The Emancipation of Massachusetts,* 193; and the crisis of 1893, 250-251; *The Law of Civilization and Decay,* 251, 257, 260, 273; influence on Henry Adams, 250; *The Gold Standard,* 270; for Bryan, 270; having a success, 290; and Pumpelly, 310-311; study of John Quincy Adams, 339-340; *The Degradation of the Democratic Dogma,* 340; "A Problem in Civilization," 342; *The Theory of Social Revolutions,* 343; mentioned, 72, 197, 199, 255, 276, 315, 338

Adams, Charles Francis: in Quincy, 17; character, 19, 125, 134, 191; represented good society in radicalism, 20; and the Bosto *Whig,* 22; and the Free-Soil, Party, 22; candidate for Vice President, 22; and money, 23; beliefs, 23; heir of John Adams and Peter C. Brooks, 23; visited Washington, D.C., in 1850, 23; moved family in Old House, 24; elected to Congress, 47; settled family in Washington, D.C., 1860, 48; influence as Representative, 48-50; appointed Minister to England, 56; as Minister to England, 57-60, 65, 66, 83; on Harvard Board of Overseers, 92; as Presidential possibility, 103; and the Liberal Republicans, 1872, 104; and the *Alabama* claims negotiations, 104, 112; for Governor of Massachusetts, 129; death, 191

Adams, Charles Francis, Jr.: characterized, 19; and his father, 17, 21, 34; dined at the Lees with Henry, 52; shelved Henry's "The Great Secession Winter of 1860-61," 57; and Henry Adams, 60, 345-346; at war, 63-64; after the Civil War, 70-74; his railroad articles, 84; political practicality, 89; "Chapter of Erie," 88; "Railway Problem in 1869," 88; "The Government and the Railway Corporations," 88, 94; "An Erie Raid," 88; and reform, 96; at Liberal Republican Convention, 1872, 104-105; on the Granger Movement, 122; and

389

the crisis of 1893, 250-251; *Autobiography*, 251; death, 348; mentioned, 71, 75, 182

Adams, Charles Kendall: "American State Universities," 123

Adams, Elizabeth Ogden, 347, 373

ADAMS, HENRY:

Immaturity (1858-1872)

And color, 17; born, Feb. 16, 1838, 17; childhood, 18, 19, 20; admired father, 19; beliefs and disbeliefs, 23; in Washington, D.C., at 12, 24; adolescence, 25; of Harvard, 26, 27, 28, 29; and the house in Boston, 28; friendships at Harvard 28, 29, 30; and Richardson at Harvard, 29; enthusiasms at Harvard, 31; wrote for *Harvard Magazine,* 31; acting career at Harvard, 31; oration on "The Fool's Cap and Bells," 31; Class Orator, 31, 32; impatient with Harvard, 32, to Europe on the *Persia,* 1858, 33; appearance in 1858, 33; insecure in 1858, 34; asserting his oneness, 34; first sight of Europe, 34; painful independence in Berlin, 35, 36; and Boston, 36; and Charles Sumner, 36, 49; two-part sketch about the German Gymnasium, 37; his imagination, 36; his Adams practicality, 36; entered Gymnasium in Berlin, 36; early ideas on education, 38, 39; walking tour of Germany, 40; in Dresden, 40-41, 42; as James's young American in Europe, 41; first look at Italy, 41; rejected Berlin, 41; and the Reichenbach family, 42; ambition to write, 42; correspondent for Boston *Courier,* 43; and Rome, 43; two Sicilian sketches,

44; adventure in Sicily, 44-45; met Garibaldi, 45; frivolous in Paris, 46; voted for Lincoln, 47; secretary to Congressman Adams, 48-49; *Boston Advertiser's* "own correspondent," 48; at Seward's party, 50; and social Washington, D.C., of the secession, 51; dined at the Lees, 52; first acquaintance with Hay, 52-53, 56; debated whether to be soldier or not, 56, 60; as secretary to Minister Adams in London, 56, 58, 59; at twenty-three, 57; sense of guilt, 57, 71, 72; and social London, 66, 59; rebelling against family, 59; articles for N.Y. *Times,* 59, 60; and London workers, 60, 66; in trouble over Manchester article, 61; loneliness, 62; development of mind, 62; first attempt at writing history, 63; his ambitions, complex and private, 64; and science, 65, 69; and his father's power, 66; and his generation, 67; vacation to Scotland, 1863, 68; as London gentleman, 68-69; picnic in Shropshire, 71-72; and history, 71; and geology, 72, 79, 102; and evolution, 72; and the relativity of truth, 72; as family tour conductor, 72; and death of Lincoln, 73; and his brother John, 73; and the political act, 74; and his soldier contemporaries, 74; and his friends, 75; subscribed to *Nation,* 75; and the post-war change, 75; at twenty-eight, 77; deducing America, 78; style, 79-80; return to America, 1868, 80-81; characterized, 74-75; fatalism, 74-75; arrived in Washington, D.C., 1868, 82; opinionated young man, 83; and reform, 84, 96, 98; his journalism, 59, 78,

348-349; recollection of wife, 348; appearance in later years, 348; on Marcus Aurelius, 348; eightieth birthday, 348-349; death, March 27, 1918, 348; living quality, 348

Writings

"The Administration—a Radical Indictment!" 336; "The Anglo-Saxon Courts of Law," 128; "American Finance: 1865-1869," 80; "Bank of England Restrictions of 1797-1821," 79; "British Finance in 1816," 77; *Buddha and Brahma*, 215, 269; *Chapters of Erie*, 103; "Civil Service Reform"—Session II, 87; "Count Edward de Crillon," 265; *Democracy*, 52, 136, 138, 139, 148, 150, 152, 153, 159, 165-168; *Documents Relating to New England Federalism*, 1800-1815, 134, 153; *The Education of Henry Adams*, 283, 308, 312, 314-315, 320, 321-330-331, 336, 345; *Essays in Anglo-Saxon Law*, 128; *Esther*, 125, 152-153, 160, 171, 179, 185; "From Our Own Correspondent," 60; "The Great Secession Winter of 1860-61," 51; "Harvard College, 1786-1787," 104: *Historical Essays*, 128; *History of the United States*, 134-135, 141, 151, 152, 153, 159, 181, 116, 187, 191, 196-199; *passim*, 212, 214, 220-245, 250, 252, 265, 337; "Important from England," 59; "The Independents in the Political Canvass," 131; *John Randolph*, 151, 153, 160, 170-171, 193; "John Smith," 62-63, 78, 79, 95; "The Legal Tender Act," 89; *A Letter to American Teachers of History*, 331, 334, 341; *Life of Albert Gallatin*, 135, 138, 150, 153, 160-164;

Life of George Cabot Lodge, 344; *Mont-Saint-Michel and Chartres*, 283, 292-307, 314, 315, 331; "My Old Room," 32; "New York Gold Conspiracy," 89, 95; *Prayer to the Virgin of Chartres*, 283-285; "Primitive Rights of Women," 128-129; review of Green's *Short History of the English People*, 128; review of Lyell's *Principles of Geology*, 79-80; *The Rule of Phase Applied to History*, 329, 331-334, 338; "Session," I, 86; "Session," III, 89, 95; Tahiti, 210-212, 252; "The Tendency of History," 257-258, 274; "A Visit to Manchester," 60-61

125; and Emily Beale, 137-138; description, 139; new dress at Worth's, 139; and the Paris theater, 139; self characterized, 140; letters characterized, 144; amusements, 142; and Henry James, 145, 149; met Elizabeth Cameron, 145; as Washington hostess, 146; over-sensitive nerves, 147; visited Anne Palmer, 147; on Hay as Stalwart, 148; happy in Washington, D.C., 148; weary of social whirl, 149; on Richardson, 149; and *Esther*, 153; and her father's illness, 156; melancholy, 157; suicide, 157-158; recalled by Henry James, 318; mentioned, 133, 137, 183, 190, 193, 249, 251, 274, 316

Adams, Mary: at Seward's party, 50; in London, 57; mentioned, 65

Adams Monument: Saint-Gaudens and the, 194-197; Hay's description, 213; Spring-Rice on, 316; visited by Henry James; mentioned, 249

Agassiz, Alexander: at Harvard, 30; assistant in his stepmother's school, 30; and the Cambridge museum, 74; *Acalephae*, 74; *Embryology of the Starfish*, 74; and Henry Adam's future, 74; influence on Henry Adams, 125, 127; early career, 126; *Three Cruises of the "Blake,"* 193; voyage to Great Barrier Reef, 269; trip to Fiji Islands, 273; worried about business, 287; and Pumpelly, 310; to Easter Islands, 313; death, 341; mentioned, 141, 149, 266, 343

Agassiz, Elizabeth Cary: and Alexander Agassiz, 126

Agassiz, Louis: at Harvard, 27-28; father of Alexander Agassiz, 30; as teacher to Henry Adams, 31; on the Amazon, 74; his

glacial theories, 79

Agassiz school for girls, 76, 106

Alabama claims negotiations, 112

Alameda, steamer, 201

Alexander: King's servant, 246

Alexandria, Egypt, 112

Amalfi, Italy, 114

Amazon River, 74

America: surveyed in centennial issue (Jan. 1876) of the *North American Review*, 128

American Historical Association: Adams, President of, 257-258

American Historical Review, 37, 265

Ames, James Barr, 205

Amiens, cathedral of, 260-261

Amsterdam, The Netherlands, 111

Amundsen, Roald, 344

Andersen, Hans Christian: *The Snow Queen*, 312

Anderson, Larz: first acquaintance with Henry Adams, 218

Anderson, Nicholas: at Harvard, 29; in Dresden with Henry Adams, 41; after the Civil War, 74; and Richardson, 149; on Marian Adam's death, 158; mentioned, 30, 70, 181

Antiquary: Walter Scott's, 316

Antwerp, Belgium, 111

Anuradhapura, Ceylon, 214

Apia, 201, 203, 204

Apthorp, Robert; advice to Henry Adams, 36

Apthorp family; Henry Adams's companions on walking tour, 40

Aquinas, Thomas, 291, 314

Aristarchi Bey, Grégoire: Turkish Minister in Washington, D.C., 142; good friend of Adamses, 144; original of Jacobi in *Democracy*, 167

Arthur, Chester A.: his world, 160; mentioned, 133, 144

Assisi, Italy, 278

Athens, Greece, 276

Atlantic Monthly, 75, 101, 103

Australia: as seen by Henry Adams, 214; mentioned, 210

Back Bay, Boston, 115, 124
Bad Nauheim, Germany, 319
Baden-Baden, Germany, 112
Bali, 210, 214
Bancroft, George: and the German historians' dinner, 112; mentioned, 158
Bancroft, John: Adams's companion on walking tour, 140
Barings (Company): failure of the, 213
Barstow, Henry H.: American consul in Palermo, 44
Basel, Switzerland, 112
Batabano, Cuba, 246
Bayeux, cathedral of, 261
Bayreuth, Germany, 288
Beacon Hill, Boston, 116
Beale, Emily: and *Democracy*, 137-138, 167; friend of the Adamses, 148
Beales, the: friends of Blaine, 146; mentioned, 141
Beaufort, S.C., 254
Beauvais, cathedral of, 263
Beirut, Lebanon, 276
Berlin, Germany: as strenuous, 43; a starting place, 72; revisited by Adams, 112; mentioned, 90
Beverly Farms, Mass.: and the Adamses' happiness, 115; the Adamses' summer residence 123-124; limitations of, 124; mentioned, 77
Bigelow, Sturgis: in Paris with Adams, 274; characterized, 274-275; in Paris, 279; mentioned, 183
Bingen, Germany, 112
"Black Friday," 88
Blaine, James G.: as possible reformer, 87; in the Hayes-Tilden election, 129-131 *passim;* and the Adamses, 146; mentioned, 144, 160, 192
Blake, William: *Nebuchadnezzar*

of, 111
Blois (château), 263
Bloomingdale Asylum, N.Y.C., 249, 253
Bonn, Germany, 111-112
Boojum: Adams's dog, 143
Boston, Mass.: and Adams's childhood, 18-19; and abolitionism, 12; preferred by Henry Adams to Berlin, 40; the limitations of, 124; mentioned, 24-25, 27-28, 30, 62, 75-76, 82-83, 84, 250, 346-347
Boston & Albany Railway Station, Springfield, Mass.: built by Richardson, 124
Boston Bay, 76
Boston *Herald*: on Marian Adams as hostess, 145
Boston *Whig*: anti-slave paper, 21
Brattle Square Church, Boston: built by Richardson, 124
Brewer, William H.: his geological expeditions, 100
Brindisi, Italy, 112
Bristow, Benjamin H.: presidential candidate, 1876, 129-130
Broadway, N.Y.C., 75
Brookline, Mass., 124
Brooks, Ernest, 246
Brooks, Peter Chardon: and Charles Francis Adams, 22-23; death, 23
Brooks, Phillips: and Henry Adams, 125; preached Richardson's funeral, 181; and Saint-Gaudens, 195; mentioned, 145
Brown, B. Gratz, 105
Brownell, William Crary: on Clarence King, 147
Browning, Elizabeth Barrett, 44
Browning, Robert: the Rome of, 44; and immortality, 70
Bryan, William J.: as symbol, 257; mentioned, 268, 270, 271-272
Buchanan, James: in the White House, 27; behavior before Civil War, 50
Budapest, Hungary, 276

Buddhist thought: influence on Adams Monument, 194
Bull Run, battle of, 60
Burr, Aaron: Adams's study of, 135
Business system: corrupt, 85
Byzantine art: Adams and, 270

Caen, cathedral of, 261
California, 99
California mountain climbs: in King's *Mountaineering*, 101
California mountain people: in King's *Mountaineering*, 101
Calumet and Hecla copper mines: Alexander Agassiz' interest in, 126
Cambridge, England (the University), 69
Cambridge, Mass.: the girls of, 28; mentioned, 74, 76-77, 116
Cameron, Elizabeth: new friend of the Adamses, 145; Adams's correspondence with, 204; "pretty Mrs. Cameron," 250; at St.-Germain-en-Laye, 275-276; Adams sent *Prayer* to, 283; mentioned, 148, 188, 189, 274, 348
Cameron, James Donald: friend of Blaine, 145; to Switzerland with Henry Adams, 250; retirement from Senate, 273; and Adams's Cuban Report, 272; at Fort William, 290; mentioned, 189
Camerons, the: to South Carolina with Adams, 250; mentioned, 186
Canada, 348
Capri, steamer, 34, 44, 46
Cenfuegos, Cuba, 246
Century Club, 309
Century Magazine, 193
Ceylon, 210, 214
Change: after the Civil War, 173
Chanler, Margaret: Adams's acquaintance with, 316; mentioned, 315, 318

Chanler, Winthrop, 278
Charles River, Mass., 30
Chartres: Adams's first sight of, 261, 262; revisited by Adams, 271; mentioned, 338
Chase, Salmon P., 82
Château de Marivault, 347
Chaumont (château), 263
Church, John A.: "Mining School in the United States," 98
Church of the Ascension, N.Y.C., 181
Clarendon St., Boston, 116
Clark, John Forbes, 260
Clemens, Samuel, 103
Cleveland, Grover: Adams disgusted with, 270; mentioned, 133, 144, 192
Cleveland, Ohio: not good for Hay, 137
Colman, George: *The Poor Gentlemen of,* acted in by Henry Adams, 31
Cologne, Germany, 112
Color: and Henry Adams, 17
Colorado, 100-101
Colorado River, 100
Columbian Exposition: and Henry Adams, 250, 253
Como, Lake, 112
Compromise bill of 1850, 25
Compton, Frances Snow: Adams's pseudonym, 152
Congress: corrupt, 85; first modern piece of legislation, 100; mentioned, 48, 78
Conkling, Roscoe: in the Hayes-Tilden election, 129
Conservative Christian Anarchists: Adams's political party, 281; mentioned, 287, 314
Cooper Union, 75, 195
Corbin, Grant's brother-in-law, 88
Cotuit, Mass., 108
Coutances, cathedral of: importance to Adams, 261-263, 269, 280 *passim*
Cowboy: myth of the, 102

397

Cox, J. D.: as reform leader, 96-97; "The Civil Service Reform," 98

Crisis of 1893: in Boston & Nahant, 250; effect on Adams family, 250-251, 265-266; effect on Henry and Brooks Adams, 251-252; mentioned, 249

Crowninshield, Benjamin: at Harvard, 29, 30, 31; in Germany with Henry Adams, 40, 41; mentioned, 70

Cuba: Adams and the Revolution in, 247-248, 270-271; mentioned, 246, 250, 254, 255, 277

Cunliffe, Robert, 70, 198

Custer, George Armstrong, 102

Daisy: Marian Adams's horse, 142-143, 218

Damascus, 276

Dana, Richard Henry: as radical, 20, 22; mentioned, 73

Daniele, Cuban outlaw: protected Adams and King, 247

Darwin, Charles: and Clarence King, 102; coral reef theory, 207; mentioned, 79

Davis, Bancroft, 141

Davis, Jefferson: sworn in as President of Confederacy, 56

Deane, Charles, 72, 77

Deeside, the; Henry Adams's visit to, 250

Demavend, Mt.: climbed by Spring-Rice, 280

Democratic Party of Massachusetts, 84

Denmark, 66

Derby Day, 76

Dessau, Germany: visited by Henry Adams on walking tour, 40

De Tocqueville, Alexis: influence on Henry Adams, 65

District of Columbia: landscape of the, 142

Dos Bocas: description, 246; mentioned, 248, 256

Douglas, Stephen A.: party given by, 51; and his debate with Lincoln, 53

Doyle, Francis, 111

Dresden, Germany: importance for Adams, 42, 72; revisited by Adams, 112

Dwight, T. F., 135, 157, 197, 199, 218

Edinburgh Review, 85, 89

Egypt: visited by Henry and Marian Adams, 112-114 ; revisited by Henry Adams, 275-276; mentioned, 210

Eisenach, Germany: visited by Henry Adams on walking tour, 40

Elbe River: and Henry Adams's adventure with the pretty Russo-Swede, 41

Elder, William: "Aborigines of Nova Scotia," 28

Eleanor of Aquitaine, 309

Eliot, Charles W.: tutor at Harvard, 30; and Henry Adams, 92; his new ways, 104; mentioned, 94, 249

Emancipation Proclamation: influence in London, 66

Emmons, Samuel Franklin, 99

England, 60, 62-63, 68, 78, 86, 89

English Lakes, 138

Equilaz, Don Leopoldo, 140

Estes Park, Colo., 99, 101

Europe: and the mechanical arts, 217; mentioned, 80, 88, 91

Evarts, William M.: welcomed Adams to Washington, D.C., 82; not an independent, 97; attorney in *Alabama* claims negotiations, 112; Secretary of State, 136

Everett, William, 69, 196

Fang-alo, Samoan girl, 205, 208, 213

Fanua, Samoan girl, 205

Fatalism: Adams's early, 80
Fenollosa, Ernest, 183
Fiji Islands, 210
Fish, Hamilton, 82
Fisk, Jim: and Henry Adams, 88, 95
"Five of hearts," 137
Florence, Italy, 73, 112, 114
Floyd, John B.: Buchanan's Secretary of War, 51
Fontainebleau, France, 263
Fortieth Parallel Survey: described, 100
Forum Magazine, 270
Fourth of July, 77
France, Anatole, 217
Francis, St., 309
Franco-Prussian War, 91
Free-Soil party, 22
Fresh Pond: skating on the, 28
Friedrich-Wilhelm Werdersches Gymnasium: Adams at the, 37-39

Gag Rule, 21
Gallatin, Albert: in *Life of*, 160-165; *passim;* in *History*, 220-245
Gallia, ship, 138
Gardner, Isabella Stewart, 193
Garfield, James A.: visit to Old House, 87; shot, 144; his new cabinet, 147; mentioned, 133, 145
Garibaldi, Giuseppe: Adams and, 44
Gaskell, Charles Milnes: Henry's meeting with, 69; and Henry Adams, 69, 89; Adamses' host at Wenlock Abbey, 111; lent house to Adamses, 115; mentioned, 90, 260
Gaskell family: at Wenlock Abbey, 71
Gauguin, Paul: arrival in Tahiti, 210
Georgenthal, Germany: visited by Henry Adams on walking tour, 40

Georgetown: suburb of Washington, D.C., 84
Georgia, 71
Germany: revisited by Adams on honeymoon, 111-112
Gettysburg: battle of, 66
Gibbon, Edward, 87, 197
Gibbs, Willard: and Henry Adams, 332-334
Gilman, Daniel Coit: contribution to contennial issue of *North American Review*, 128
Gladstone, William E., 213
Godkin, Edwin L.: and the *Nation*, 75; friendship with Charles and Henry Adams, 97; at Liberal Republican Convention, 1872, 104; knew secret of *Democracy's* authorship, 137; visited Henry James, 194; mentioned, 135, 158
"Goldbugs," the, 252
Gould, Jay, 88, 95, 213
Granada, Spain, 140
Grand Review of the armies: described by Marian Adams, 77
Grand Teton, the, Wyo., 255
Grant, Ulysses S., 82, 84, 87, 88, 96, 104, 160
Grant regime, 86
Grantism, 129
Gray, William, 190
Greece, 276
Greeley, Horace: nominated for President, 105
Green River, 100
Gryanowski, E.: "Comtism," 122
Gurney, Ellen Hooper: the "exquisite," 107; death, 197; mentioned, 99, 156, 191
Gurney, Ephraim Whitman: Adams's friend, 94; his household, 98; his understanding of Henry Adams, 106-107; death, 191

Hague, James D.: on Clarence King, 147, 289
Hague, the, The Netherlands, 111

Halsted, Murat, 83
Hanna, Mark, 268
Harrington, Seward's secretary, 50
Harrison, Benjamin, 192, 198, 206
Harte, Bret, 103
Harvard (College and University): during Henry Adams's undergraduate years, 27-28; *passim*, 31; transformation under Charles W. Eliot, 92-93; Adams began teaching career at, 93; break in Adams's teaching at, 109; Adams refused honorary degree from, 249; mentioned, 26, 76, 123, 259
Harvard Magazine: Henry Adams's writing for, 31
Harvard Square, 93
Harvard Yard: life under the elms of the, 27-28 *passim*
Havana, Cuba, 246
Hawaii, 202
Hay, Adelbert Stone: to the Yellowstone with Adams, 255; death, 288
Hay, Clara Stone: marriage to John Hay, 136; death, 348; mentioned, 137, 272, 275, 277, 288, 319, 337
Hay, Helen, 271, 276
Hay, John: met Henry Adams, 52; his isolation in Warsaw, Ill., 53; at Brown University, 53; his White House diary, 54; to Washington, D.C., with Lincoln, 54; Secretary of the Legation, Paris, 74; and Henry Adams's future, 75; his verse characterized, 103; with the New York *Tribune*, 102, 128, 144; and Clarence King, 127-128, 253; and the biography of Lincoln, 128, 137, 193, 249; and Amasa Stone, 136, 137; married Clara Stone, 136; Assistant Secretary of State, 136, 144; and Adams and King, 137; and Boojum, 143; for Blaine, 145, 148; on Clarence King, 147; as Republican, 193, 270; to South Carolina with Henry Adams, 256; on Adams in the wilderness, 256; to Europe with Adams, 271; his campaign for McKinley, 271; and McKinley election, 272; Minister to England, 273; arrival in London as Minister, 273; to Egypt, 275; named Secretary of State, 277; pressure of his work, 280, 281; struggle with Senate, 281; illness, 287, 318-319; his son's death, 288-289; shaken by year of deaths, 288; his foreign problems, 309; his public world, 312; visit to Saint-Gaudens, 313; to St. Louis Exposition with Adams, 313; facing death, 319; death, 319; diaries and letters edited by Henry Adams, 337; mentioned, 70, 142, 189, 192, 196, 200, 204, 213, 216, 266, 267, 269, 278, 289, 312, 315, 343
Hayes, Rutherford B.: nominated for President, 130; as President, 133; mentioned, 133, 135, 145, 160
Hayes, Mrs. Rutherford B.: mentioned 145, 147
Hayes-Tilden dispute, 133
Hays, the, 186, 189
Hazen, W. B.: "The Great Middle Region of the U.S.," 122
Heidelberg, Germany, 112
Hemans, H. W.: "Prussia and Germany," 98
Hewitt, Abram S.: helped in formation of U.S. Geological Survey, 136; mentioned, 142
Higginson, Henry Lee, 74, 260
Higginson, Ida Agassiz, 74
Higginson, James J., 40
Hilton Head, S.C., 107
Hoar, Ebenezer, 83
Hoar, Samuel, 83
Hokusai, 185
Holland, Sir Henry, 69

Holmes, John, 110
Holmes, Oliver Wendell, Jr.: and Marian Adams, 77; his review of Kent's *Commentaries on American Law*, 121; mentioned, 206, 317
Holt, Henry: knew secret of *Democracy's* authorship, 138; with the Adamses in Paris, 139-140, 141; and proofs of *Esther*, 152-153; mentioned, 157, 158, 162
Homer: and the American war, 66
Hooper, Edward: his early life, 106; wife's death, 146; and Saint-Gaudens, 195; illness, 280, 287; death, 287; mentioned, 77, 197, 316
Hooper, Ellen Sturgis, 107
Hooper, Louisa Chapin, 347
Hooper, Robert W.: described, 76; illness, 156; death, 157; mentioned, 107
Hooper nieces, 275
Houghton, Richard Monckton-Milnes, Lord, 69, 192
"Housatonic": attack on Henry Adams's *History*, 214
Howard, Catherine L., 107
Howells, William Dean: appointed Consul to Venice, 55; and the *Atlantic Monthly*, 75; and King, 100; *A Foregone Conclusion* reviewed in *North American Review*, 122; his socialism, 194
Howland, George, 309
Hubert, Henri, 344

Iddings, Joseph P., 255
Impressionists, the, 217-228
Independents, the: meeting at Old House, Quincy, 88; their assumptions, 97, 100; their Convention, 1872, 104; New York City meeting, 1876, 130; failed to hold together, 1876, 130-131; mentioned, 96, 98

Iroquois, American naval ship, 44
Isis, Adamses' houseboat, 112, 114
Italy: Adams's first look at, 41; Adamses' honeymoon travels in, 112; mentioned, 77, 90, 114

Jackson, Andrew, 21
James, Alice, 140
James, Henry, Sr., 74
James, Henry: the Rome of his *Roderick Hudson*, 44; and Henry Adams's future, 75; on Marian Adams, 77, 148, 318; description of Ellen Gurney, 107; contribution to *North American Review*, 119; on Ivan Turgenev, 121; on Gautier, 122; and John La Farge, 125; on Marlborough Street, 131; with the Adamses in London, 138, 139; with the Adamses in Paris, 139; *Daisy Miller*, 139; *The Portrait of a Lady*, 139; popularity, 139; and Europe, 140; *The Tragic Muse*, 194; *The Princess Casamassima*, 194; and the Robert Louis Stevensons, 203; on Hay's English reception, 273; *William Wetmore Story and his Friends*, 310; visit to Washington, D.C., 317; *The Wings of the Dove*, 317; *The Ambassadors*, 317; *The Golden Bowl*, 317; on Washington, D.C., 317-318; isolation, 340-341; death, 348; mentioned, 315, 337
James, Robertson, 74
James, Wilkinson, 74
James, William: on the Amazon, 74; after the Civil War, 75; and Marian Adams, 77; hired as Harvard instructor, 92; Henry and Marian Adams, 140; "Rationality, Activity and Faith," 154; exchange with Adams, 341-342; individualism,

401

404

Napoleon I, 220–245 *passim*
Napoleon III (Louis Napoleon), 65, 273
Nation, 75, 135
Negro wage labor, 74
Nelly, Samoan girl, 205
Nevada, 99
New England: sympathetic to abolitionists, 25; in flux, 25; Adam's college friends belonging to, 28, 29; Henry Adams first departure from, 34; as strenuous, 43; unconscious assumptions of, 76; and Henry Adams, 93-94; mentioned, 17, 83, 92
New England duty, 108
New England pride, 109, 111
New York City, 75, 82, 88, 96
New York *Times,* 59, 62
New York *Tribune,* 102, 105, 144
Newbern, N.C., 65
Newcomb, Simon: "Exact Science in America," 122; contributor to centennial issue of *North American Review,* 128
Newport, R.I., 74, 80
Nice, France, 72
Nicolay, John: in Springfield, 53; and the biography of Lincoln, 128, 193, 249; mentioned, 137
Nikko, Japan: Adams and La Farge in, 183, 185
Nordhoff, Charles, 83, 97
Normandy, region of France, 259, 262
North, the, 67, 75, 82
North Africa, 112
North American Review: Adams's "John Smith" published in, 78; as outlet for the Independents, 95; under Adams, 98, 100, 109, 116, 117, 120, 128; mentioned, 85, 86, 87, 89, 97, 104, 193
Northern Pacific Railway: route surveyed by Pumpelly, 144
Norton, Charles Eliot: on Anthony Burns, 25; as editor of *North American Review,* 78;

article on Italy in *North American Review,* 98
Nuremberg, 41, 112

Ohio, 75
Old House, Quincy, 17, 18, 21, 24, 192, 196, 199, 343
Osaka, Japan, 185
Otaota, Samoan girl, 205

Palermo, Sicily: during Garibaldi's occupation, 44-46
Palfrey, John Gorham: as radical, 20; inspired *John Smith,* 62; mentioned, 78
Palgrave, Francis: *The Golden Treasury,* 70; friend of Henry Adams, 70, 78, 111
Palmer, Anne: Marian Adams's visit to, 147
Palmer, Ralph, 70, 111
Panama, 344
Panama Canal, 344
Papara, Tahiti, 209, 211, 221
Papeete, Tahiti, 209
Paris, France, Adams on, 262; Paris mentioned, 65, 70, 74, 114, 140, 210, 217, 255, 259, 263, 276, 311, 347
Park Street Church, Boston, 18
Parker's (the Parker House,) Boston, 28
Parkman, Francis: on the *Siberia,* 110; "The Ancien Regime in Canada, 1663-1763," 121; Adams's praise for, 250; mentioned, 155
Parnell, Charles Stewart, 213
Pascal, Blaise, 287
Peary, Robert Edwin, 344
Pepe, cook at Dos Bocas, 246-247
Perry, Nora, 53
Perry, Thomas Sergeant: and Marian Adams, 77; and the *North American Review,* 95, 119; and John La Farge, 125; mentioned, 317
Persia: Spring-Rice in, 281
Persia, the (ship), 33

Petronius Arbiter, 255
Phillips, William Hallett: to the Yellowstone with Adams, 255; for Cuba, 270; death, 275; mentioned, 198, 250
Place de l'Etoile, 268, 308
Plymouth, Mass., 17
Pocahontas, 55, 62, 63
Poe, Edgar Allan, 53
Politics: as a religion, 23
Pomare, King of Tahiti, 209
Portland Place, London, 68, 69
Possum, Adams's dog, 143, 218
Potomac River, 84
Powell, John Wesley: on the Green and Colorado rivers, 100; formation of U.S. Geological Survey, 136
Pragmatism, 342
Priestley, Joseph: H. H. Richardson's grandfather, 30
Prince, Henry Adams's horse, 142, 156, 218
Proclamation of Neutrality, England's, 57
Providence, R.I., 53
Pumpelly, Raphael: influence on Henry Adams, 126; description, 127; *Across America and Asia*, 127; in the Montana country, 144; to Central Asia, 310-311; second expedition to Asia, 313; mentioned, 149

Quarterly, the, 89
Quincy, Mass.: and summer, 17; description, 18; Henry Adams's leavetaking of, 34; mentioned, 74, 87, 250

Ramsden, F. William: British Consul at Santiago, Cuba, 246-248
Rarotonga, 210
Ravenna, Italy, 271
Raymond, Henry J.: of the New York *Times*, 48; published Henry Adams's London articles, 59

Red Sea, 210
Reichenbach, Augusta: threat to Henry Adams's susceptibilities, 42
Reichenbach, Heinrich: Henry Adams's Dresden host, 42
Reichenbach, Theodor: Henry Adams's Dresden friend, 42
Reid, Whitlaw: editor of the New York *Tribune*, 102; promoted Greeley for President, 105; mentioned, 144
Republican party: post-war fanaticism of, 73; and the reformers, 97; mentioned, 336
Richardson, Henry Hobson: his grandfather, Joseph Priestly, 30; at Harvard, 30; in Paris, 46, 70; first work in the United States, 75; and Henry Adams's future, 75, and the Brattle Square Church, 124; and the Springfield, Mass., railway station, 124; and Trinity Church, 124-125; influence on Henry Adams, 126; building railway stations, 144; on vacation with Phillips Brooks, 145; the Nicholas Anderson house, 145, 149; the Hay-Adams house, 150, 186, 190-191; death, 181; Marshall Field Warehouse, 193; and Saint-Gaudens, 195; Tati Salmon, like, 208; mentioned, 76, 141, 156, 190, 195, 253, 280, 290, 343
Richmond, Va.: fall of, 73
Rock Creek, 88
Rock Creek Cemetery, 157, 194, 249
Rockhill, William W.: Adams's travels in Greece with, 276
Rodin, Auguste: Adams's visit to, 263
Rome, Italy, 114
Roosevelt, Edith, 188
Roosevelt, Theodore: and Spring-Rice, 188; Civil Service Commissioner, 198; reviewed *Law*

Webster, Daniel, 20, 22

Weed, Thurlow: on Hay, 74

Weimar, Germany: visited by Henry Adams on walking tour, 40

Wells, David A.: Johnson's Special Commissioner of Revenue, 83; as reform leader, 96, 120; as contributor to *North American Review,* 121; mentioned, 85, 87

Wendell, Barrett, 341

Wenlock Abbey: its importance for Henry Adams, 71, 72; Henry and Marian Adams at, 110-111; mentioned, 79, 90

Westminster Review, 89, 95

Wharton, Edith, 337

Whigs, anti-slave, 22

Whiskey Ring scandal, 130

White, Henry, 315, 337

White, Horace, 96

White House, the: the Adams's call at, 145; mentioned, 88, 315

Whitman, Sarah Helen, 53

Whitman, Walt, 75

Whitney, J.D.: his geological explorations, 100; "Geographical and Geological Surveys," 123

Whitney, Mt., climbed by Clar-

ence King, 100; mentioned, 248

Wilson, Charles L.: Secretary of London Legation, 57, 59

Wilson, Woodrow, 349

Wingate, Charles F.: "The Reign of the Ring," 122; on the Tweed Ring, 123

Wittenberg, Germany: visited by Henry Adams on walking tour, 40

World War, First, 75, 344, 349

Wormley's Hotel, Washington, D.C., 141

Wright, Chauncey: essays for the layman in *North American Review,* 98

Wright, Frank Lloyd, 125, 253

Wright brothers, 320

Wyoming: great diamond swindle of, 100

Yale Review, 216

Yellowstone country, Wyo., 255-256

Yokohama, Japan, 182

Yorkshire, 71

Yosemite Park, Calif.: boundaries surveyed by Clarence King, 100

Young, Ernest: "The Anglo-Saxon Family Law," 128